CONTINENTAL STRANGERS

FILM AND CULTURE
John Belton, Editor

FILM AND CULTURE

A series of Columbia University Press
Edited by John Belton

For the list of titles in this series, see page 277.

CONTINENTAL STRANGERS

German Exile Cinema

1933–1951

GERD GEMÜNDEN

COLUMBIA UNIVERSITY PRESS   NEW YORK

Columbia University Press
Publishers Since 1893
New York   Chichester, West Sussex
cup.columbia.edu
Copyright © 2014 Columbia University Press
All rights reserved

The author and Columbia University Press gratefully acknowledge the support of the Dean of Faculty Office at Dartmouth College in the publication of this book.

Library of Congress Cataloging-in-Publication Data
Gemünden, Gerd, 1959–
   Continental strangers : German exile cinema, 1933-1951 / Gerd Gemünden.
     pages cm.— (Film and culture)
   Includes bibliographical references and index.
   ISBN 978-0-231-16678-2 (cloth) — ISBN 978-0-231-16679-9 (pbk.) — ISBN 978-0-231-53652-3 (ebook)
   1. Motion pictures—United States—History—20th century. 2. Motion pictures—United States—Foreign influences. 3. Motion picture producers and directors—Great Britain—Biography. 4. Political refugees—Germany—History—20th century. I. Title.
   PN1993.5.U6G457 2014
   791.43097309'044—dc23
                                                                  2013030080

Cover Design: Jordan Wannemacher
Cover Image: © Deutsche Kinemathek - Museum für Film und Fernsehen

CONTENTS

Acknowledgments vii

INTRODUCTION 1

Part One
PARALLEL MODERNITIES 19

1. A HISTORY OF HORROR 21
2. TALES OF URGENCY AND AUTHENTICITY 48

Part Two
HITLER IN HOLLYWOOD 75

3. PERFORMING RESISTANCE, RESISTING PERFORMANCE 77
4. HISTORY AS PROPAGANDA AND PARABLE 102

Part Three
YOU CAN'T GO HOME AGAIN 129

5. OUT OF THE PAST 131
6. THE FAILURE OF ATONEMENT 160
EPILOGUE 189

Notes 193
Selected Bibliography 229
Index 263

ACKNOWLEDGMENTS

For those writers who are also academics, there are the tenure books and then there are the ten-year books. This one certainly falls into the latter category; in fact, from conception to completion *Continental Strangers* took almost as long as Bertolt Brecht lived in exile, though working on it was a far more pleasurable experience than Brecht's, if we can trust his reports about his misery in Santa Monica, California.

Although writing, by nature, requires solitude and turning one's back on one's surroundings, it wouldn't be possible without exchange, exposure, and debate. This book has benefited tremendously from those who have discussed it with me, who have provided smart, alert audiences for listening, who edited and critiqued it, and who helped me navigate archives. Most important were the friends and colleagues who debated ideas with me and who read and commented on my work. Some did so anonymously, but among those known to me, I appreciate Bruce Duncan's untiring efforts to rid my prose of Teutonic quirks—no small task! Al LaValley read each and every chapter, always pointing me toward new books I ought to read and old films I had overlooked. Noah Isenberg and I swapped respective chapters and commentary on my book on exile and his on Edgar G. Ulmer, as well as productive criticism over the phone and over legendary martinis. Marianne Hirsch and Leo Spitzer, who have long been my role models for combining intellectual brilliance with a commitment to friendship, generously shared their expertise and experience. Johannes von Moltke provided critical interventions at crucial times, and Yuliya Komska read and summarized for me an entire play in Czech. My thinking about the concept of exile cinema was profoundly shaped by Tony Kaes when we first collaborated on a publication on this topic. Dana Polan gave graciously of his time and insight and prevented me—hopefully—from making this an auteurist study. More than anyone else, Rick Rentschler helped me shape this book, following it closely from its beginnings, a 1997 Dartmouth conference on Detlef Sierck / Douglas Sirk, through its many incarnations to its present form. Rick, Dana, and Bruce were also part of a 2012 Manuscript Review at Dartmouth under the auspices of the Leslie Humanities Center, which also included Veronika Fuechtner, Udi Greenberg, and Amy Lawrence, all of whom contributed valuable and extensive feedback. I thank them and the Leslie directors Adrian Randolph and Colleen Boggs for making that review possible—a truly intense and inspiring afternoon and evening of discussion and critique that made this manuscript a better book.

The many colleagues who invited me to present my research, in various stages of its development, also deserve my gratitude. They include Ofer Ashkenazi (Hebrew University, Jerusalem), Karin Bauer (McGill University), Tim Bergfelder (University of Southampton), Mila Ganeva (Miami University), Sabine Hake (University of Texas, Austin), Markus Heide (Humboldt Universität Berlin), Laura Heins (University of Virginia), Noah Isenberg (The New School), Martin Kagel (University of Georgia), Lutz Koepnick (Washington University), Brigitte Mayr and Michael Omasta (Vienna), Fatima Naqvi (Rutgers University), Philipp Stiasny (Freie Universität Berlin), Johannes von Moltke (University of Michigan), and Marc Weiner (Indiana University).

No research committed to archival work would be possible without the guidance and knowledge of archivists. Among the many professionals I relied on, I'd like to thank first and foremost Barbara Hall at the Academy of Motion Picture Arts and Sciences Margaret Herrick Library (I love walking up that Kirk Douglas stairway), and Hans Helmut Prinzler, Werner Sudendorf, Gerrit Thies, and Peter Latta at the Stiftung Deutsche Kinemathek,

Berlin. Similarly helpful were Marje Schuetze-Coburn (Feuchtwanger Memorial Library, USC), Sandra Joy Lee (USC Warner Bros. Archives), Ned Comstock (USC Cinematic Arts Library), and Maya Buchholz and Evelyn Hampicke (Bundesarchiv/Filmarchiv, Berlin), who helped me find my way through a truly Kafkaesque film archive.

At Dartmouth I'd like to thank the generations of students who took my class on exile cinema; they challenged me to think through the issues and to articulate why this topic matters today. I can only hope this book convinces them. If it does, credit must go to my extraordinary student Ruth Welch (Dartmouth '13), who served as my Dartmouth Presidential Scholar in 2011–12. Anthony Helm, at Jones Media Library, provided much-needed assistance with film stills. At Columbia University Press I am indebted to Jennifer Crewe, the associate director, and to John Belton, the Film and Culture series editor, for taking an interest in my work and for their professionalism. The copy editor of this book, Joe Abbott, deserves much praise for his meticulous attention to detail. While the book reflects the contributions of many, its shortcomings are of course entirely my own.

Last but not least, I want to thank my family for all their support, which, among other things, included sitting through many really bad anti-Nazi films. Lou and Sean, you are a great reality check! I dedicate this book to Silvia, who in more senses than one will always be my first reader.

CONTINENTAL STRANGERS

FIGURE 0.1 Peter Lorre as Ugarte in *Casablanca*.

INTRODUCTION

The stranger [is] the man who comes today and stays tomorrow.
—GEORG SIMMEL[1]

To translate is always to transform. It always involves a necessary travesty of any metaphysics of authenticity or origins.
—IAIN CHAMBERS[2]

BEYOND *CASABLANCA*

Early in Warner Bros.' 1942 classic wartime romance *Casablanca*, the small-time crook Ugarte (Peter Lorre) asks the film's hero, Rick Blaine (Humphrey Bogart), what he thinks of him: "You despise me, don't you?" Rick replies, "If I gave you any thought, I probably would." Although Ugarte is of negligible importance to the protagonist, and Peter Lorre's screen time in the film is minimal (he is gunned down shortly thereafter), this role has become one of the most memorable in the actor's long and varied Hollywood career. As the *Hollywood Reporter* noted, "Lorre is in and out of the picture in the first reel, yet the impression he makes is remembered."[3]

Lorre's Ugarte is a shifty individual whose murder of two German couriers carrying exit visas sets the plot in motion. Just before he is shot, he asks Rick to hide them for him ("Just because you despise me, you're the only one I can trust"), and they subsequently become the coveted prize everyone seeks to obtain. A trader in identities, Ugarte is someone who can assign a new name and thus a new life to another person. At the same time, his shiftiness and mobility points to his own dislocation; we never find out where he's from or how he got to Casablanca in the first place.

Lorre's Ugarte is highly evocative of the actor's status as an exile, who had to reinvent himself in the Hollywood studio system after having abandoned a successful career on the screens and stages of Weimar Germany. In this process Lorre and his numerous European colleagues had to become adept at learning essential exilic strategies such as the changing or camouflaging of identity, of impersonation and make-believe, many of which are also on view in *Casablanca*, where they are employed by the numerous other smaller and bigger players struggling to survive. In many of his other Hollywood films Lorre would also play characters whose ethnic or sexual identities are ambiguous, just as his moral standings (is he a good guy or a bad guy—or both?) were often open to question. In Robert Florey's *The Stranger on the Third Floor* (1941), he is simply credited as "the stranger," a figure he also played in many of his American films, underscoring not only the characters' but also often the actor's sense of precariousness, liminality, and nonbelonging.

With refugees willing to sell their souls to get to America to escape the encroaching Nazis, the theme of exile is front and center in *Casablanca*, which has led critic Thomas Elsaesser to describe it as "everyone's favorite émigré film."[4] The film opens with a montage of newsreel and documentary footage that traces the "tortuous, roundabout refugee-trail" of thousands eager to escape an "imprisoned Europe." On this trail the city of Casablanca becomes an important stopover and point of embarkation toward the "freedom of the Americas." As it turns out, all those gathered in the city are also either refugees, exiles, expatriates, foreign invaders, or part of an occupying force, while the natives are consigned to mere backdrop. What gives the film a special flavor is the fact that most characters are played by actors who themselves were foreigners in the United States. Of the credited actors, only Bogart, Dooley Wilson (who plays the pianist Sam), and Joy Page were American-born; all others, including Ingrid Bergman, Conrad Veidt, Paul Henreid, Claude Rains, Sydney Greenstreet, S. Z. Sakall, and Lorre, as well as almost all of the seventy-five minor performers, were expatriates, émigrés, or refugees of some sort or other, as were the director, Michael Curtiz, and the composer of the film score, Max Steiner.[5]

The script of the film was based on an unproduced play by Murray Burnett and Joan Alison and inspired by Burnett's 1938 trip to Vienna, where he was exposed to rampant post-*Anschluss* anti-Semitism. While the Casablanca created by him and Allison, as well as the Warner Bros. recreation, bears little resemblance to the real city of that name, it comes remarkably close to capturing the atmosphere of Marseilles, as it is described in the numerous memoirs and novels of those who passed through that city on their way to Spain, Lisbon, and the United States.[6] Rick's Café, the central locale of the film (and the single locale of the play), is a transitory space where exiles and émigrés make up the staff and the customers, where the French police prefect rubs shoulders with Nazi officers in pursuit of a Czech resistance fighter, and where visas are bought and sold. Rick Blaine is himself an exile of sorts; he is an expatriate who left home to fight for republican and progressive causes in Spain and Northern Africa but whose ideals and beliefs have long since eroded, and who, when asked about his nationality, responds by saying "a drunkard."

Yet despite these references to exile, Elsaesser's remark about the "favorite émigré film" status of *Casablanca* is somewhat ironic. On the one hand, the theme of exile and displacement is rarely treated extensively in Hollywood feature films of the 1940s, making the pool from which to choose rather small. (Among the few other possible contenders are *Hold Back the Dawn* [Mitchel Leisen, 1941, with a script by Billy Wilder] and *So Ends Our Night* [John Cromwell, 1941, based on a novel by Erich Maria Remarque].) What is more, the main focus of the film is not the toils of the stranded refugees in Casablanca but the relationship between Rick Blaine and Ilsa Lund (Ingrid Bergman), his former mistress and wife of the Czech resistance fighter Victor Lazlo (Paul Henreid). The drama revolves around whether the disappointed lover, Blaine, can overcome his pain and pride and help Ilsa and Lazlo escape the Nazis by offering them the exit visas.

Casablanca is a classic conversion story about a selfish and disillusioned man who has a political reawakening and forgoes the love of his life to serve the larger cause of his country and the Allied forces. Advocating personal sacrifice, courage, and the willingness to serve a greater cause, the film's ideology partakes of Hollywood's eagerness to do its share in the war effort by educating the American audience about the necessity to give up a prized individualism for the good of the country. Since the film supports the fight against Nazi Germany, one could argue that it also takes up the plight of those who had been driven by the Nazis to Casablanca, but it does so in ambiguous ways. Rick's conversion from an expatriate into a patriot is not an option available to the "suspicious characters," which is what the voice-over labels the many foreigners in the city at the beginning of the film. In fact, after the first wave of arrests that follow the murder of the German couriers, the "usual suspects" will again be "rounded up" (as Captain Renault's famous line tells us) at film's end, and the cycle of their criminalization will be perpetuated to ensure Rick's getaway from Casablanca. Even though Rick ultimately helps Victor Lazlo escape from Casablanca, it is clear that the fight against Nazism will now be much more his responsibility than Lazlo's. The exiles, the film underscores, are unable to fight fascism themselves, or even to articulate their predicament, as becomes emblematic when Ilsa asks Rick to "think for both of us, for all of us."

The tension in *Casablanca* between simultaneously foregrounding the presence of exiles and debunking their political impact raises interesting questions about how we are to understand the contribution German exile filmmakers made to the American film industry during the 1930s and 1940s. In what follows, I want to outline the historical dimensions of these contributions, their political thrust, as well as the larger theoretical argument that informs this study. As will quickly become clear, *Casablanca* is really only the proverbial tip of an iceberg that even to contemporary observers remained largely invisible and that to this day has been misunderstood and overlooked by historians of film and of culture more generally.

PATTERNS OF MIGRATION: FROM WAVES TO FLOOD TO TRICKLE

Peter Lorre was one of hundreds of German-speaking film professionals who lived and worked in Hollywood during the mid-1920s and after. While some were émigrés who came to better their lot and further their professional careers, most were Jewish refugees who escaped the threat of the Nazi death camps. It is estimated that at some point during the 1930s and 1940s at least eight hundred German-language émigrés and exiles found temporary or extended employment in the Los Angeles film industry.[7] They, in turn, were part of a much larger and culturally very significant colony of German-language artists and intellectuals who found refuge in Los Angeles, leading Ehrhard Bahr, in his aptly titled study *Weimar on the Pacific*, to describe the city as "the most important center of German exile culture during the 1940s."[8]

How can we define exile cinema in terms of production, distribution, aesthetics, and politics? What marked exile cinema's relationship to American (and also German) film history? And who were these German film exiles, and what positions did they assume in the studios? The term *German* is here employed to mean German-language film professionals who had a significant part in the film industry of the Weimar Republic. They include not only German citizens proper but also nationalized Germans such as Fritz Lang (who acquired citizenship in 1924); Austrians such as Billy Wilder, Fred Zinnemann, and G. W. Pabst; and professionals from parts of the former Austro-Hungarian Empire, some of them already refugees from political persecution or anti-Semitism in countries that include Hungary (such as Mihály Kertész, alias Michael Curtiz), the Soviet Union (such as Victor Trivas), or the Ukraine (Anatole Litvak, for example). German exiles are thus "Mitteleuropäer" (central Europeans), who are often bi- or multicultural and bi- or multilingual and may have experienced uprooting prior to their displacement from Nazi Germany, making their exile in Hollywood a stage in a much longer journey.

Exile, too, is a term that requires clarification, since a distinction has to be made between the émigrés who left of their own free will and those who became refugees because of political persecution or racial discrimination. The former group includes Lubitsch and his entourage, F. W. Murnau, William Dieterle, Marlene Dietrich, and many others. Until 1933, travel to Hollywood was not a one-way street but a two-way traffic across the Atlantic, the most prominent example of which is the truly international career of producer Erich Pommer.[9] To compete with the German Ufa studios, American moguls went on frequent "talent raids" to Europe, hiring away highly skilled professionals in order to weaken the only national cinema that could rival Hollywood at the time while bolstering their own rosters.[10] The sheer size of these waves led contemporary American commentators to speak of a German invasion, conjuring images of German military aspirations still fresh in people's minds from World War I propaganda. It is a unique feature of this migration story that its main motor was success, not economic hardship; only those who had proven themselves were invited to come. The German filmmakers' high level of professional training, as well as Weimar cinema's considerable international cachet, became the main reason why, after 1933, German filmmakers proved to be the artists who were by and large most successful in continuing their careers in exile. An important supporter in their efforts was the agent Paul Kohner, who represented many of them, and who nicknamed himself "Amerikohner" to indicate his successful straddling of two cultures.[11]

With the coming of sound, the transatlantic waves began to show clearer professional contours. Acclaimed European actors left Hollywood because their accents made it impossible for them to maintain their star status. Most

FIGURE 0.2 Prominent exiles and émigrés mingle in Hollywood in the 1930s. *Left to right*: G. W. Pabst, Joseph Schildkraut (in white), Fritz Lang, Peter Lorre, Erich von Stroheim.

notable were Conrad Veidt and Emil Jannings, who returned to Germany, the latter permanently, Veidt only until 1933, when he emigrated to England for political reasons, only to return to Hollywood in 1941 (where he would star as Major Heinrich Strasser in *Casablanca*).[12] Important stars of early 1930s German cinema such as the English-born Lilian Harvey and Heinrich George briefly tried their luck in Hollywood sound film, while directors Ludwig Berger and Paul Martin worked in both silent and sound film, but all of them gave up after their plans did not pan out, only to assume major billing under Goebbels. Yet while sound spelled the end of some careers, it was the beginning for others. Warner Bros. hired a number of Germans, including Dieterle, Günter von Fritsch, and Salka and Berthold Viertel to make foreign-language versions of their films.

Once the Nazis came to power, the transcontinental exchange became very restricted until it ceased altogether. After 1933, Jews like Lubitsch, Edgar G. Ulmer, and Fred Zinnemann were not able to return, even if they had wanted to, turning émigrés de facto into exiles; while they may not have experienced persecution and flight, they were now stateless. Others assumed the *position* of an exile. Dietrich, Dieterle, and Veidt resisted advances by the German film industry to lure them back, deciding instead to take a very vocal stand against the Nazi regime, which in turn led to smear campaigns both during and after the war in Germany. The point here is that exile is not just a condition into which one is driven but also a stance that one can assume. Such a stance had many faces, which could include participating in educating an American public about conditions in Nazi Germany and, after Pearl Harbor, in the U.S. war effort, or voicing an implicit or explicit critique of the adopted homeland and its perceived ignorance about, or lack of intervention in, Europe. For yet others the sole aspiration of exile was to stay alive, no matter what artistic or political concessions it involved, making survival itself an act of resistance.

As these remarks about international movement of talent make clear, the German filmmakers' emigration to Hollywood happened in waves, with numbers peaking in the mid-1920s, in 1933, and in 1938. With the Nazis' ascent to power the German film industry swiftly introduced anti-Semitic rules, causing the first large-scale exodus of film personnel, which included Lorre, Robert and Curt Siodmak, Fritz Lang, Billy Wilder, Otto Preminger, and Henry Koster, while a second followed the annexation of Austria and the expansion of the German Reich. Many of the exiles did not come directly to the United States but emigrated first to neighboring countries, particularly Austria, Hungary, France, the Netherlands, and Great Britain. As the rule of Nazi Germany expanded, however, these sanctuaries ceased to provide security and jobs.[13] Each wave was marked by its own set of class distinctions, professional clout, and career opportunities, with earlier arrivals generally faring much better than later ones and younger professionals such as Wilder and Koster having an easier time in adapting to a new language, culture, and working environment than did seasoned veterans like Joe May or Fritz Lang. When Douglas Sirk, Reinhold Schünzel, and Frank Wysbar arrived in the late 1930s with significant screen credit from Nazi feature films in their respective résumés, they were met with outright hostility. While for some German filmmakers employment in Hollywood might always have been the ultimate career goal, Hitler's arrival certainly hastened their departures. Billy Wilder best expressed the difficulty in judging one's own choices. Throughout his career he told interviewers that he would have come to Hollywood, Hitler or no Hitler, only to explain toward the end of his life to filmmaker Cameron Crowe that he had left Germany "because I did not want to be in an oven."[14]

As the above names indicate, exile cinema, like the Hollywood studio system, was dominated by men. The most prominent exiled female filmmakers were actresses, including stars Marlene Dietrich, Luise Rainer, and Hedy Lamarr. But there were also notable exceptions such as screenwriters

Salka Viertel, Gina Kaus, Vicki Baum, and Anna Gmeyner.[15] As the preferred writer and confidante of Greta Garbo, Viertel wielded significant influence at MGM. Even more important for the exile community was Salka's salon. A meeting place in the 1920s for the émigré filmmakers and their new American colleagues, the salon helped to integrate the first wave of refugees after 1933, and then took on a decidedly more political flavor when, beginning in 1936, the Popular Front began to form in Hollywood. An active member in the European Film Fund and in the Hollywood Anti-Nazi League, Viertel also became instrumental in raising political awareness among the larger population of Los Angeles.[16]

With the defeat of Nazi Germany many filmmakers contemplated a return to Europe. The anticommunist witch hunt of the McCarthy era, which recalled the climate of bigotry the exiles had hoped to escape forever, provided an additional incentive to leave the United States. Yet few of the returning emigrants found success in postwar West Germany; most of the Germans who tried to gain a foothold there eventually returned to Hollywood. The truly commercial successes like Preminger, Koster, Wilder, and Zinnemann never really considered returning to Germany. While the migrations of the 1920s were marked by a coming and going, wartime exile was a final station for many.

GAINED IN TRANSLATION

Commentators have predominantly seen the oeuvre of exile artists as being shaped by the experience of losing one's language and culture, the trauma of political persecution, the nostalgia for a time and place forever gone, and the pressure to assimilate in a country they often found socially different and culturally inferior. These sentiments are most poignantly expressed in Theodor W. Adorno's autobiographical reflections on his "damaged life" in Los Angeles, which describe the experience of exile as one of anguish and suffering: "Every intellectual in emigration is, without exception, mutilated and does well to acknowledge it to himself, if he wishes to avoid being cruelly apprised of it behind the tightly-closed doors of his self-esteem. He lives in an environment that must remain incomprehensible to him. . . . He is always astray. . . . His language has been expropriated, and the historical dimension that nourished his knowledge, sapped."[17] This discourse of loss and estrangement also informs the general view of prominent historians such as John Russell Taylor and Anthony Heilbut. Both present the story of the Hollywood exiles with little critical distance to the parameters within which the exiles themselves invariably described their lives. The telling titles of Taylor's and Heilbut's respective works—*Strangers in Paradise* and *Exiled in Paradise*—indicate that the master narrative for understanding European refugees in Hollywood in the 1930s and 1940s is that of an encounter between two utterly different cultures that revolves around biblical notions of expulsion and redemption.[18]

Yet as Edward Said has argued, the efforts to compensate for the loss incurred by exile may also stimulate creativity and challenge one to be inventive, mobile, and resourceful. Being decentered and detached grants the nonnative a critical distance that affords privileged vistas into the host culture; being aware not of one but at least two cultures creates, Said argues, a "plurality of vision" that is truly comparative and contrapuntal in nature.[19] Similarly, Salman Rushdie has argued that processes of cultural transfer are better understood if we focus not only on what impedes such transfer but also on what enables it: "The word 'translation' comes, etymologically, from the Latin for 'bearing across.' Having been borne across the world, we are translated men. It is normally supposed that something always gets lost in translation; I cling, obstinately, to the notion that something can also be gained."[20]

Indeed, displacement and disorientation provide (admittedly forced) opportunities for self-examination and social critique. The films of Lang, Lubitsch, Lorre, and Ulmer are marked by the position of what Anton Kaes has called "the stranger in the house," that is, of the outsider who gains entry yet remains ever cognizant of his or her origins, a somewhat uncanny presence that does and does not belong.[21] Dieterle, Wilder, and Zinnemann may have mastered the idiom and modes of production of the Hollywood studio system, winning a combined ten Academy Awards, but they also retained the critical edge typical of the foreign-born artist. Even after becoming a major screenwriter and director, Wilder would feel the sting of being considered an intruder. After a screening of *Sunset Blvd.* (1950), Louis B. Mayer attacked the director as a foreigner who had bit the hand that fed him, demanding that he "be tarred and feathered and run out of town."[22]

The story of the Hollywood exiles is, of course, part of a much larger narrative. The twentieth century has been called the century of exiles, refugees, and displaced people. According to Said mass migration and dislocation are the most formative experiences of the past one hundred years, occurring both in the form of being uprooted and forcibly moved from one's country or through colonial imposition. As a result of Nazi warfare thirty million people in Europe were driven from their homes, and the "final redistribution of population in Europe alone after the end of the war resulted in the permanent migration of another twenty-five million."[23] Ironically, Hitler's call for a racially homogenous Germany led not only to mass migrations of unprecedented dimensions but also to a hitherto unseen mixing of nations and ethnic populations. This in turn created a vast landscape of international and intranational conflicts and frictions but also of dialogue and exchange, much of which is still with us today. It must be argued—against Adorno—that film is not necessarily an agent of homogenization, even though it often facilitates cultural assimilation. Despite being a mass-produced, serialized commodity, film remains fraught with ambivalence and is thus a medium that can communicate difference. Made by a minority, yet according to large-scale, industrialized modes of production, and for commercial profit, German exile cinema is part of a popular cinema; yet it presents a much more immediate and effective political response to Nazism than the so-called *Exilliteratur*, which was predominantly written in German because it intended to uphold a true, or better, German tradition outside of Nazi Germany for the benefit of a postfascist society.

THE MAJOR AND THE MINOR

How are we to envision the relation of exile cinema to Hollywood cinema? The vast majority of U.S. film critics and historians have seen German exile cinema as part of an American national cinema, worthy of a footnote at most. By and large, they have treated directors such as Lubitsch, Wilder, Zinnemann, and Sirk as an integral part of U.S. film history without paying much attention to national origins or distinctive cultural sensibilities—a strategy that often follows the exiles' own efforts of camouflaging their outsider status and their eagerness for assimilation.[24] Films like *To Be or Not to Be, From Here to Eternity, High Noon, Some Like It Hot*, and *All That Heaven Allows* are classics that belong in the pantheon of the studio era, yet the fact that they were directed by exiles rarely gets noticed. Others, like Dieterle, have attracted little to no critical attention, while a B director like Ulmer is celebrated more for his "cult" status than for his artistic achievement.[25]

Those who have considered exile cinema an entity in itself, such as Jan-Christopher Horak and Helmut G. Asper, have tried to give this large body of work some coherence by defining it along lines that are somewhat problematic. For Horak, only film professionals who left Germany *after* the Nazi takeover are seen as exiles, and exile films are those for which exiles assumed the three key positions of director, writer, and producer, thereby omitting all films made by the large studios under the supervision of American producers. Horak's exile cinema constitutes a small body of work—he cites two hundred films, many of which were made in other countries of exile—that emulates the "other Germany" ("das andere Deutschland") of German exile literature and culture. According to Horak, "German exile cinema was much like exile literature and the exile press, a continuation of the democratic principles of German cultural life, as it had developed before Hitler's rise to power."[26] In so doing, he overlooks that Bertolt Brecht, Thomas Mann, and most key German exile authors continued to write in German for a postfascist society, whereas German exile cinema was an English-language cinema, made by American studios for an American audience. For Horak these films belong neither to the host nation's national cinema nor to the history of German cinema; they stand as "unlucky hybrids" that fall between the cracks of historiography.[27]

Far from calling these films unlucky, *Continental Strangers* argues that exile cinema has to be understood as a cinema of in-between that uses its very status of hybridity to its advantage; the strangers of the title are not just the film professionals, who created them, but the films themselves, which stand in uncanny proximity to mainstream American cinema, because they are both similar and different. An essential part of the Hollywood studio system, exile cinema creates an aesthetic and political uniqueness by drawing on traditions of Weimar cinema, as well as by forming a double or dark mirror of Nazi cinema.[28] It is precisely this in-betweenness that marks exile cinema as one of creativity and ingenuity.[29]

Reworking both American and non-American genre conventions, exile cinema forces us to rethink national cinema in less monolithic, homogeneous, or hegemonic terms. Rather than understanding exile and national cinema as opposites, we should see them within a dialectic that underscores the heterogeneity of national cinema. Not only today, but already in its classic period, U.S. national cinema was itself composed of several cinemas rather than just one dominant cinematic movement, just as Hollywood, by virtue of its hegemony, was already then part of nearly every Western national cinema. As shown above, a close relationship between German and U.S. studio film production has existed since World War I, taking on multiple forms of rivalry, competition, and exchange, thereby firmly establishing Hollywood in the historical imaginary of Weimar and Nazi cinema, and, to a lesser degree, also vice versa. Hollywood was always more international, perhaps even transnational, than its critics assumed.

We also need to bear in mind that the Los Angeles film industry was founded by first- or second-generation Jewish emigrants from Central and Eastern Europe.[30] Adolf Zukor, the founder of Paramount, came from an orthodox Jewish family in Hungary; also from Hungary was William Fox; Louis B. Mayer, head of MGM, was from Russia; and Carl Laemmle of Universal came from southern Germany. Many of them actually had a close relationship to the German language: Fox was part of a German-speaking family, and the moguls Harry Cohn (Columbia) and Marcus Loew (MGM) were the children of German and Austrian immigrants, as were producers Irving Thalberg and Walter Wanger.[31] For the most part, these first- or second-generation immigrants ardently sought to assimilate to the American way of life and to create a film industry that celebrated American history and the virtues and achievements of its society. Yet while this assimilation was predicated on the erasure or denial of their origins, particularly their Jewish origins, its success also facilitated the further incorporation of other nonnative professionals, something from which the German film exiles profited tremendously.

Rather than thinking of German exile cinema as an alternative or countercinema, then, it is more productive to think of it as a cinema that insists on the *political* within a system of production that predominantly—though not exclusively—fosters apolitical, quasi-universal entertainment. In this context Hamid Naficy's influential notion of an "accented cinema" merits consideration. Naficy uses the term to describe how a film's narrative, visual style, form of address, and mode of production and distribution can be read as being shaped by, and thus reflecting, the experience of dislocation of its author or director. Brushing up against dominant modes of filmmaking, the forte of accented films, Naficy explains, is precisely their lack of shine and their imperfection, which endows them with a certain sense of authenticity that "glossy" products mostly lack. For Naficy, accented cinema is a cinema that inherently challenges mainstream or dominant cinema, ascribing to it a political dimension simply because of its very existence. As Lutz Koepnick has shown, Naficy's notion is of very limited use for understanding the contribution that German exile filmmakers made to the Hollywood studios, because it relies on a romantic understanding of authorship and auteurism for which the studio system left little or no room, and because it ultimately essentializes and thus dehistoricizes any notion of political filmmaking.[32] Indeed, one irony of U.S. national cinema is that it disavows migration yet is itself largely the creation of immigrants (just as the country itself is a nation of immigrants). Accents, real or symbolic, have to be erased if one's voice is to be heard, unless that voice is specifically marked as exotic and other. Migration thus figures within the historical unconscious of Hollywood cinema—and it is the achievement of German exile cinema to turn its spotlight on this unconscious.

A different yet related way of thinking about exile cinema's place in the host country is to understand it as a minor cinema, along the lines of a minor literature, which Gilles Deleuze and Félix Guattari employ in their book on Kafka.[33] Bahr has used the term for his understanding of the German exile literature of Los Angeles, arguing that it is deterritorialized, collective, and political much in the same way that the German-speaking community was in turn-of-the-century Prague.[34] I would agree that politicization and collectivization are indeed essential to the community of exile filmmakers. The "diasporados," as Curt Siodmak called them, were very much a group of like-minded central European refugees, predominantly Jews, who, although often in direct professional competition with each other, created an extensive network of organizations. These organizations, such as the European Film Fund, fostered solidarity and became instrumental in securing affidavits for exit visas, providing financial support to the less fortunate, staging large-scale public events, and informing American citizens about political developments in Europe.[35] Exile films were political in that they tried to communicate to an American public the danger of fascism, both as it existed in Nazi Germany and in what they perceived to be a threat to U.S. democracy. Yet unlike the prose of Kafka, these films were not articulated in a minor language and therefore not deterritorialized. It was, as I noted above, an English-language cinema, and the visual language that it employed was essentially the idiom of classical Hollywood in the studio era. This shared idiom was not only the consequence of the necessity to turn a profit but also of the very history of international cinema.

Hollywood studio films have many creators; they do not bear the imprint of the single artist of literature, music, or art. To think of an (exiled) Hollywood director as a subversive auteur à la Naficy who can use the medium as a tool for personal expression is to underestimate institutional pressures and Taylorized modes of production. Yet biographies do matter, as experiences of persecution and hardship (even if by proxy) shape political awareness. While films do not simply reflect individual experiences, as contested collaborations they quite eloquently attest to the efforts and struggles that went into their creation. Archival research lets us uncover the (often heated) negotiations among directors, writers, censors, and producers or studio heads; and by tracking various stages of script development, altered scenes, and imposed endings, we can document (forced) compromises, as well as successful attempts at circumventing internal and external censorship.

This is also why the study of genres or cycles is key to understanding exile cinema. Genres are, of course, first and foremost a commercial priority for the Hollywood studios. They are vital to producers because they create and direct audience expectations, letting producers anticipate the response to their product. Genres also play a key role in marketing certain films and their stars. The ability to work within certain genre conventions is crucial for any Hollywood director. As part of mass media, genre films are agents of homogenization, but they are also saturated with ambivalence and indeterminacy. Because of their formulaic nature, genre films register repetition and deviance with great accuracy, allowing us to see how exile cinema inflected, manipulated, or subverted existing conventions. The exiles worked in virtually all existing Hollywood genres and cycles, including melodramas, musicals, westerns, costume dramas, and even science fiction, but their impact is most strongly felt in the genres, subgenres, or cycles covered in this study, which include horror, the screen biography (or biopic), comedy, the anti-Nazi film, and film noir. Apart from the anti-Nazi film, which was a genuinely new creation forged first to respond to the threat of Nazi Germany and later to bring Hollywood into line with the government's war effort, these genres can all claim a strong ancestry in Weimar cinema. What distinguishes exile cinema is that it brings into contact indigenous and foreign styles, moods, and conventions (including expressionism, the *Kammerspiel*, the street film, and the realist films of the New Objectivity [*neue Sachlichkeit*]) to create genuinely new or hybrid formulas that have recourse to the past in order to articulate their topicality and relevance for the present.

Studies of influence have often neglected the radically different historical circumstances that occasion the use or citation of certain older genres, thereby overlooking how biographical experiences, institutional pressures, and the political moment shape how films are produced, exhibited, and experienced.[36] To recover the high degree of topicality that films now considered classics once displayed, my six case studies of exile films treat them as events that interact and respond to their environment in conscious or unconscious ways. Focusing on the condition of the various films' production, distribution, and reception in the United States (and, in the case of *Der Verlorene*, in Germany), individual chapters analyze how each film positions itself in regard to contemporary *American* political events, social institutions, or artistic developments. None of the films considered here is the lone result of an individual's exile creativity; rather, they are all constituted objects arising out of concrete circumstances and serving particular functions that involve intricate relationships with social institutions (especially the studio system) and filmic styles (both indigenous and imported). As is to be expected of a study that relies on emblematic readings, selecting individual films means not considering others. The works of Robert Siodmak, Otto Preminger, Max Ophüls, and Douglas Sirk, for example, would have warranted equal attention, as would have the work of a large number of other film professionals.[37]

READING FOR EXILE

Exile cinema tried to alert an American public to the internal and external threat of fascism and dictatorship. Yet there were profound limitations on what and how political concerns could be communicated to film audiences. Like other professionals in the Hollywood studios of the 1930s and 1940s, the exiles were part of a system characterized by a centralized control of production, distribution, and exhibition; by a division and hierarchy of labor; and by a standardized system of mass production in the service of addressing the taste cultures of a mass public. Beyond the rule of the market, and the prediction of producers of what an audience would or would not accept, the Production Code put very real limits on what could be said and shown. Its regulations affected not only the realm of sexuality, morals, religion, and the law but also the policies toward foreign countries. As the chapters on Lubitsch and Dieterle show, exile cinema struggled particularly with America's—and Hollywood's—anti-Semitism, which resulted in strict forms of self-censorship that made it virtually impossible for filmmakers to create films that brought attention to the plight of European Jews, let alone point to forms of American bigotry.

Given these circumstances, what does authorship mean when one is in exile, a condition often marked by a loss of authority and authorial control, including control over the narrative of one's life and the means of professional creativity? If we want to account for the contribution of Hitler refugees to other national cinemas, we cannot limit our focus solely to certain niches in which some individuals were able to articulate their sense of displacement and despair. We need to think of the political in much broader terms than merely the thematic or ideological content of a given film. As Thomas Elsaesser has argued, the illusionary dimension of filmmaking needs to be considered political in itself: "The extent and kind of involvement the émigrés had with the political realities of their time were . . . refracted via the politics of make-believe, so that the stylization of film noir, the double-entendres or sight gags of sophisticated comedy, and the 'imitations of life' of melodrama might turn out to be just as politically engaged as the anti-Nazi film."[38]

In this larger definition of the political, essential exilic strategies such as the shifting and camouflaging of identity, masquerade, impersonation, travesty, cross-dressing, cultural mimicry, and passing come into view as well, devices that are prominent in the comedies of Wilder and Lubitsch and their dark, only seemingly sarcastic, sense of humor. Similarly, the mise-en-abyme of a Fritz Lang film and its implied play with illusion also challenges viewers to reflect on the possible conditions of representation. Exile cinema relies heavily on allegory, because "historically, we can note that allegory seems regularly to surface in critical or polemical atmospheres, when for political or metaphysical reasons there is something that cannot be said."[39] Reading for exile therefore involves uncovering not only the way in which the exilic dimension becomes articulated but also the ways in which such an uncovering remains an impossible task. (One literal example of this impossibility is the simple fact that many of the exiled filmmakers had to work without screen credit and thus remained invisible, most [in]famously cinematographer Eugen Schüfftan, who was not allowed to join the guild of cinematographers.)[40]

◊ ◊ ◊

The following chapters are devoted to individual films and offer typological readings that trace the historical axis of exile cinema while spanning a cross section of important directors, writers, and genres. These case studies propose emblematic interpretations that illustrate through close readings larger historical and theoretical claims. The first segment, "Parallel Modernities," focuses on *The Black Cat* (Ulmer, 1934) and *The Life of Emile Zola* (Dieterle, 1937) and analyzes how these films grafted the experience of the crisis-ridden Weimar Republic onto the United States of the mid-1930s, when the Great Depression led isolationist-minded Americans to ignore the threat of European fascism and even to consider a totalitarian form of government.[41] Drawing an explicit parallel between a past terror and an impending one, *The Black Cat* used the horror film to conjure up the threat of coming warfare, while *The Life of Emile Zola* couched its antifascist agenda in the popular genre of the biopic and showcased the relevance of the lessons of nineteenth-century French anti-Semitism and bigotry for twentieth-century democracies.

The U.S. entry into combat obliged Hollywood to participate in the war effort. The second segment, "Hitler in Hollywood," explores how exiles contributed their firsthand knowledge of history and politics. At last the exiles' support of their new homeland fully aligned with their goal of fighting Nazism. Actors and actresses encountered the rare opportunity when their accents became desirable, even if, ironically, Jews on occasion had to play SS commanders. But Hitler's declaration of war also put the German colony under intense political scrutiny and duress. While they were not rounded up into concentration camps like the Japanese, German passport holders were submitted to a nightly curfew, which led *Aufbau* columnist Hans Kafka to speak of a "Curfewstendamm" in Los Angeles (a pun on Berlin's prime commercial promenade, the Kurfürstendamm).[42] The tension of being under surveillance by the same country whose ideology was mobilized to fight fascism in Europe marks the early 1940s exile films in contradictory and complex ways.

The new cycle of the anti-Nazi film was syncretic; it drew on spy films, thrillers, gangster films, and other action- and suspense-driven formulas. Lubitsch's outrageously funny *To Be or Not to Be* (1942) is an anomaly, because its main generic motor is comedy, which many viewers considered incompatible with the straightforward, earnest ideology of combatting Nazis. Yet Lubitsch's use of comedy empowered viewers by debunking Nazism's penchant for performativity. In a darker, accusatory move, the film also implicated Hollywood itself in the murder of the European Jewry at the hands of the Nazis. The chapter on Lang and Brecht's *Hangmen Also Die* (1943) considers one of the many artistic responses to the assassination of Reinhard Heydrich and the brutal retaliation by the Germans, analyzing the creative yet contradictory use of modernist techniques in the service of government propaganda. Both films combined daring modernist visual style and narratives with the demand to deliver politically effective propaganda.

The last segment of the book, "You Can't Go Home Again," focuses on the postwar period in the United States and Germany. Fred Zinnemann's little-known film noir *Act of Violence* (1949) revolves around the trauma of World War II (and thus harks back to *The Black Cat*) while pointing to the kinds of betrayals that will mark Hollywood during the Red Scare. In particular it raises fundamental doubts about the self, reality, home, and traditions. The chapter on Peter Lorre's *Der Verlorene / The Lost One* (1951) chronicles the challenge of reemigration to Germany. Lorre's experience proved representative for the majority of exiles and émigrés who, like him, tried unsuccessfully to return to a culture that no longer existed and a country that had no room for the returnees. The two chapters demonstrate that both postwar America and postwar Germany provided radically different living and working environments that exiled many German-language filmmakers anew.

◇ ◇ ◇

PARALLEL MODERNITIES

One
A HISTORY OF HORROR

> *For an exile habits of life, expression or activity in the new environment inevitably occur against the memory of these things in another environment. Thus the new and the old environments are vivid, actual, occurring together contrapuntally.*
> —EDWARD SAID[1]

> *[My father was] a European intellectual who had based most of his thinking on the great minds of the German language, only to find that it led to a stupid monster of an Austrian painter named Hitler. For the rest of his life he tried to understand how civilization could end up in barbarism.*
> —ARIANNÉ ULMER CIPES[2]

THE CULTURAL MOMENT OF 1934

Nine months after Hitler's rise to power, in early 1934, the impact of the new regime in Germany began to be felt in the German-speaking film community in Hollywood. In December of 1933 veteran Joe May had arrived, often considered the inventor of the "monumental film" (grand-scale historical melodramas, sometimes consisting of several parts) and boasting an oeuvre of more than seventy films as director. He was soon followed by Billy Wilder, a budding Ufa screenwriter who had just completed his first directorial assignment in France. Their two very divergent Hollywood careers, with Wilder winning six Academy Awards and May descending into poverty, would be emblematic of the lessons of exile. Producer Erich Pommer, composers Erich Wolfgang Korngold and Franz Waxman, director Fritz Lang, writer Walter Reisch, and actors Peter Lorre and Curt Bois would all come later that year. The Weimar diaspora they would find there consisted, by and large, of eminent film professionals who had arrived during the previous decade and had weathered the waxing and waning demand for European film personnel, which had dramatically decreased with the advent of sound.

The recent arrivals provided the German Hollywood colony with eyewitness accounts of the atrocities in Berlin and elsewhere, the burning of the Reichstag, the daily harassment by the *Sturmabteilung* (SA) and other thugs, Goebbels's infamous Kaiserhof speech in which he outlined the alignment of the film industry along racial ("völkisch ")" concerns, the concomitant erasure of Jewish names from film credits, and the beginning exodus of other film professionals that included the likes of Max Ophüls, Robert and Curt Siodmak, Erik Charell, Kurt Bernhardt, Robert Wiene, Wilhelm Thiele, Henry Koster, Joe Pasternak, Arnold Pressburger, Seymour Nebenzal, Victor Trivas, Felix Jackson, Albert Bassermann, Fritz Kortner, Alexander Granach, Elisabeth Bergner, Conrad Veidt, Felix Bressart, Franz Planer, Eugen Schüfftan, Curt Courant, Rudolph Maté, Hanns Eisler, theater impresario Max Reinhardt, and playwright Bertolt Brecht, all of whom would eventually end up in Los Angeles.[3] Unlike the first wave of emigration of the mid-1920s, when American producers went on talent hunts in the Ufa studios, many of the new arrivals—traumatized by the experience of being a refugee but relieved to have gotten out alive—would accept the flimsiest of contracts. In the coming years the line between those who had come to America for career reasons and those who escaped political or racial persecution would begin to blur.

Also in 1934 Dorothy Thompson would become the first American correspondent to be expelled from Nazi Germany, largely because of her book *I Saw Hitler* (1932), an account of her interview with the dictator-to-come in 1931 that had warned American readers of the imminent threat of his political takeover. Often considered the most influential journalist of her time, Thompson did much through her depiction of the struggling artist turned politician to create awareness of the threat he posed to world peace.[4] Her predictions would prove correct: in June of 1934 SA leader Ernst Roehm was assassinated by Hitler's troops to consolidate the power of the National Socialist German Workers Party (NSDAP); in July Austrian chancellor Engelbert Dollfuss was killed by Nazi agents, because Austria was threatening to align itself with Mussolini to stay independent from Germany; in August the death of eighty-six-year-old president Hindenburg allowed Hitler to merge the office of president with the office of chancellor, thereby making him the country's sole leader.[5] Soon after her return to New York City in August, Thompson published a widely discussed article, "Good-by to Germany," in which she characterized the mood and political events in Austria and Germany that had culminated in her expulsion. The American public began to take note of Nazi Germany.

Hollywood, of course, was still a lot farther away from Europe than the East Coast and professionals there tended to be absorbed in their own world. But the liberal and progressive forces in the film industry did pay attention to the gains reactionary forces had made in Germany, Italy, and Spain, and for the Jewish moguls, Hitler's rabid anti-Semitism brought back memories of the pogroms in Central and Eastern Europe that their families had fled only a generation or two earlier. Warner Bros. closed its operations in Germany in July 1934, allegedly because of the murder of a studio representative in Berlin, but Paramount, Fox, and MGM did business there until 1939. Warner Bros. would also become the first studio whose films addressed the threat of National Socialism.[6] Goebbels was well aware of the political influence that the Hollywood studios wielded, and already in 1933 he ordered the German consulates in San Francisco and Los Angeles to monitor the activities of German film professionals, using intimidation tactics to discourage them from participating in projects considered undesirable to the Third Reich; a growing number of Nazi-sympathetic "Auslandsdeutsche" (Americans of German origins) became important tools in boycotting certain films. As these developments make clear, 1934 was a cultural moment of the highest political significance for Hollywood, especially for the émigré community.

One response was that that same year exiles and émigré film professionals began to make more overtly political films, to the degree that this was possible within the confines of the highly regulated studio system and the Production Code. Joe May's *Music in the Air*, produced by Erich Pommer with a script by Billy Wilder and Robert Liebmann and a score by Franz Waxman, was essentially still the same escapist fare seen in the Ufa music films, but G. W. Pabst's *A Modern Hero* outspokenly criticized American capitalism and the figure of the social climber and sought to unmask the myth of the American dream. As Jan-Christopher Horak has argued, the linking of money with human sexuality caused critics to find fault with the film and kept audiences away, making it "hardly surprising that Pabst could not find further employment in Hollywood."[7] In a somewhat different vein, Dieterle's *Fog over Frisco*, a fast-paced gangster drama, presented political content more obligingly. It combined several of the modernist elements that would later contribute to the subversive appeal of film noir. The most original combination of political critique and genre cinema would be provided by Edgar G. Ulmer's venture into horror film.

HOW TO BE CUTTING EDGE WHILE CUTTING CORNERS: ULMER'S MESSY MODERNISM

Ulmer's *The Black Cat* must be seen as one of the earliest and most radical examples to infuse a genre film with a significant political topicality, resulting in one of the most unsettling films in Universal's horror cycle. Unlike Fritz Lang, Bertolt Brecht, Peter Lorre, or Billy Wilder, Edgar G. Ulmer is not commonly thought of as a Hollywood exile, not only because he first arrived in the United States in 1924 but because for much of his career he was in exile *from* Hollywood, carving out a living in New York, New Jersey, and Canada, or in the Poverty Row studios on the fringes of the Los Angeles film industry. Indeed, *The Black Cat* is his *only* film to be produced by one of the big Hollywood studios, despite an oeuvre of almost fifty films as director. But geographical and cultural displacement did occur in his life, albeit long before the advent of Hitler, which was the pivotal experience for most of his peers. Ulmer lost his father during World War I, reducing him to the status of orphan, since his mother was unable to care for him, and he was sent to school in Sweden through the Hoover commission. At age nineteen, the precocious Ulmer traveled to New York as part of Max Reinhardt's troupe to stage *The Miracle* on Broadway, the first of his many transatlantic endeavors. In the mid-1920s he advanced to assistant chief art director at Universal, but after working on F. W. Murnau's *Sunrise* (1927), he returned to Berlin to codirect *Menschen am Sonntag / People on Sunday* (1930), the now famous low-budget film for which he shared credit with Robert and Curt Siodmak, Billy Wilder, Fred Zinnemann, and Eugen Schüfftan. Ulmer then settled in Hollywood again, this time to work at Universal, first as an assistant and then on his own directorial assignments. Throughout his career, which extended into the mid-1960s, Ulmer would remain constantly on the go, moving between the East and the West Coast and later also again between Europe and the United States.[8]

Yet, like Zinnemann, Lubitsch, Salka and Berthold Viertel, and so many other German-speaking Jews who emigrated before 1933, Ulmer considered himself an exile from Nazi Germany and annexed Austria: "If I had stayed I would have wound up in Auschwitz or Dachau," he told Peter Bogdanovich.[9] And Ulmer's daughter Arianné Ulmer Cipes explained, "I think after Hitler [my father] never felt at home again in Europe."[10] The first critic to make a case for Ulmer as a director whose work was profoundly shaped by the experience of exile was Noah Isenberg, who insists that even though Ulmer chose to leave Austria before he was forced to flee, he, like a "true" exile, "maintained a similar state of in-betweenness, between old world and new, Europe and America, high culture and mass culture, throughout his career."[11] On a thematic level the influence of exile can be seen in the many films that foreground characters who are displaced and forever wandering about, most notably of course in Ulmer's most acclaimed film, *Detour* (1945). The existential restlessness of the exile also marks the lives of the two antagonists of *The Black Cat*, Hjalmar Poelzig and Vitus Werdegast (and indeed that of Bela Lugosi himself). In more general terms Ulmer also shared other exiled filmmakers' astute awareness of political events, both in his native Austria and adopted homeland. This awareness frequently inflects his films, even if mostly in circuitous and allegorical ways.[12]

Among Ulmer's films *The Black Cat* stands out for its creative fusing of German and American film traditions and genre conventions, providing a careful balance in which the film's many more trivial or faulty aspects, such as the ellipses in the script, the disappointing secondary cast, and the crude attempts at comic relief, are offset by an innovative use of a classical score, an extraordinary set design, and a casting against type of Boris Karloff and Bela Lugosi. The plot revolves around a deadly conflict between Hjalmar Poelzig (Karloff), a famous Austrian architect, and Dr. Vitus Werdegast (Lugosi), a Hungarian psychiatrist, former friends whom a wartime betrayal has turned into bitter enemies. A young American couple on their honeymoon, the Alisons, are unwittingly drawn into this conflict when the bus on which they are traveling with Werdegast has an accident and Werdegast escorts them to Poelzig's home. A long, drawn-out, and ultimately deadly cat-and-mouse game ensues between the two former friends, which takes on ever more bizarre forms. This includes, among other strange twists, Werdegast's search for his former wife, who after his incarceration became Poelzig's wife but was then killed and embalmed by Poelzig, as Werdegast learns in horror; Poelzig's subsequent marriage to Werdegast's daughter Karen, whom Poelzig also kills when Werdegast intrudes; and the celebration of a Black Mass, where Mrs. Alison is to be sacrificed at the altar. In the end the Alisons narrowly escape from Poelzig's modernist edifice before Werdegast, in a self-destructive gesture, blows everything to smithereens.

Like many Universal horror films of the 1930s, *The Black Cat* hovers on the border of A-level production and B film. Apart from certain directorial choices, this must be attributed to purely monetary concerns. While Universal thought of its horror films as A films that were meant to break into the first-run market (and were associated with significant cost for sets, makeup, costumes, and major stars), Universal A films often resembled

B productions from other studios. They were often afforded fewer setups and fewer takes, and they had to rely on stock footage for locations and minor stars. *The Black Cat*, shot in fifteen days with a budget of $91,125, was a significant scale-back from *Dracula* and *Frankenstein* (which cost $355,000 and $262,000, respectively), because Universal thought that pairing Karloff and Lugosi would by itself attract large audiences. It nevertheless made a $140,000 profit for Universal, proving that the horror cycle was still viable and giving Ulmer his first real recognition as director.[13] Ironically, Ulmer chose to direct the independent low budget western *Thunder over Texas* (1934) as his next project, rather than another Universal production. Soon thereafter his affair with Shirley Castle, the wife of Carl Laemmle Sr.'s nephew Max Alexander, became public, putting an end to any possible employment at Universal and, indeed, at any major Hollywood studio.

Critics, following Ulmer's own account, have agreed that his move away from the big studios involved a conscious strategy to retain a sense of uncompromised artistic freedom. The director famously told Bogdanovich that he "did not want to be ground up in the Hollywood hash machine."[14] While the means at his disposal were much more limited for his Yiddish-language films around New York, for his work at PRC (Producers Releasing Corporation), and for his later European coproductions, artistic control, so the argument goes, remained largely in his hands—provided he stayed within the budget and the films turned a profit. Thus the director retained a "personal" touch and developed an individual style. Building on the "discovery" of Ulmer, the artiste, by French cinephiles such as François Truffaut and Bertrand Tavernier, American critics like John Belton and Andrew Sarris admired how Ulmer turned economic constraint into a virtue and an art, and they celebrated how his ultrapragmatic mise-en-scène of problem solving was the sign of a true auteur. Sarris saw Ulmer as "one of the minor glories of the cinema. Here is a career, more subterranean than most, which is the signature of a genuine artist. . . . That a personal style could emerge from the lowest depths of Poverty Row is a tribute to a director without alibis."[15] Belton is even more emphatic: "Ulmer is clearly an auteur: his films all bear the stamp of a single and consistent narrative personality, but the raw material with which he works—scripts and performers especially—varies tremendously in quality from film to film. His set design, lighting, editing, and camera technique frequently transcend the banality of his scripts and the weakness of his actors' performances."[16] Perhaps the biggest single factor contributing to Ulmer's auteur status is his long interview with the filmmaker and film historian Peter Bogdanovich, a confirmation of the truism that behind every great auteur (Hitchcock, Fuller, Sirk) there stands a great interview. Apart from embellishing on his contributions to the great German films of the 1920s, Ulmer strove to grant his cinematic output a coherence and unity that is all but invisible to the naked eye.

While I do not want to discredit the pioneering work of John Belton, auteurist criticism is contested, and it seems particularly problematic in regard to Ulmer.[17] On the most obvious level, often the quality of Ulmer's films is not argued but simply asserted; one quickly notes that the same quotes, the same tropes, and the same biographical criticism of Belton's original work gets rehearsed again and again, and any careful analysis is quickly abandoned in favor of hagiography. In the end auteurist criticism becomes an unstoppable engine of aesthetic valorization. What is more troubling for our context is that auteurism seems to imply a transcendence of history, an assertion that cannot be upheld for Ulmer. It is particularly problematic to claim *The Black Cat*, an A film made for a major studio, as an auteurist work, precisely because its conception, production, and execution were fraught with controversy and compromise, involving censorship issues, extensive rewriting and reshooting demanded by studio brass, and divergent marketing strategies typical of large-scale studio productions. To call *The Black Cat*, as Bernd Herzogenrath has done, "a personal work of art, an underground avant-garde film," is certainly overstating the case.[18] Instead, it is precisely the negotiation of different national film traditions and their respective genre conventions that caters to, and frustrates, audience expectations, ultimately making this production so rich and rewarding.

Although Ulmer's political concerns find a voice in this film, they were compromised both by what studio executives considered to have commercial potential with contemporary audiences and by what was acceptable to the Hays Office. The concept of auteurism becomes even more questionable under the duress of exile, which for filmmakers meant the loss of a sense of control over their lives and careers. If we want to fathom the exilic dimension of *The Black Cat*, we must instead take a closer look at how Ulmer worked on this Universal horror film both within and against the grain of studio conventions, budget restrictions, and audience expectations.

THE CABINET OF HERR POELZIG: FROM HAUNTED SCREEN TO UNIVERSAL HORROR

In his interview with Bogdanovich Ulmer made references to two German sources that shaped *The Black Cat*: "Junior [Laemmle] gave me free rein to write a horror picture in the style we had started in Europe with *Caligari*," adding that his film "was very much out of my Bauhaus period."[19] The puzzling double reference to two very different and aesthetically even incompatible sources offers an important clue to what Ulmer wanted to achieve with his first film to be produced by a major studio. On the one hand, it can be read as a typical Ulmerian gesture to establish cultural capital.[20] Robert Wiene's 1920 classic of German silent cinema, *The Cabinet of Dr. Caligari*, and the Bauhaus school of architecture and design are among the shorthands for "German culture" that must have held the biggest name recognition in Los Angeles at the time. By invoking them, Ulmer obviously laid claim "to be part" of these traditions. He did so with justification; after all, he began his career as set designer on *The Golem, How He Came into the World* (Paul Wegener, 1920), where he served as an apprentice to Hans Poelzig (the namesake for Hjalmar Poelzig), who, together with Walter Gropius and Mies van der Rohe, was among Germany's great architects.[21] While Poelzig was never part of the Bauhaus, the school he founded in Breslau (with its emphasis on workshops) became a model for the Weimar Bauhaus, and Poelzig's own architectural style stood in close dialogue to the more avant-garde Bauhaus movement. Ulmer's collaboration with Poelzig was a formative experience, as set design would play a prominent role in virtually all of his films, usually with sets that he conceived himself, as in *The Black Cat*. Furthermore, and unlike most other exiles, Ulmer collaborated on many significant expressionist films, particularly those of Murnau. His first German feature, *People on Sunday*, abides as a masterpiece of the New Objectivity, with which the Bauhaus had much in common.

Yet the overall project of *The Black Cat* as captured by the shorthand "Caligari" and "Bauhaus" clearly transcends biographical considerations. It combined two key examples of Weimar culture that, despite their differences, stood for the promise, achievements, and ultimately failure of modernism. Both were heralded as radical new beginnings in literature, the arts, architecture, and design, and both were highly influential within German cinema of the 1920s, often appearing in hybrid form in films such as Fritz Lang's *Metropolis* and *M*. With the National Socialists' rise to power, both movements fell into disrepute, and their main proponents were forced into exile. Recalling them in the American context of 1934 offers a gesture of preservation and commemoration but also an attempt to reanimate their progressive energies at a moment of political crisis.

What is at stake in Ulmer's 1934 horror film—and in German exile cinema in Hollywood in general—has to be understood in light of the parallels experienced by so many émigré and exile filmmakers between the modernity of Weimar Berlin and that of prewar and wartime Los Angeles. The Depression-ridden United States of the early 1930s triggered in the exiles a dubious moment of historical recognition, an uncanny déjà vu of sorts, of the failure of Weimar modernity and democracy, which had also been inaugurated by large-scale unemployment and political radicalization of the left and the right. What they now witnessed in their newly adopted homeland was a replay of the scenarios of political, economic, and social crises of the late Weimar years.[22] In hindsight it must have become clear to Ulmer that particularly the aftermath of World War I, which was never fully acknowledged nor worked through by Germans and Austrians, provided the seeds for the rise of Nazism. The burden of the tremendous war reparations, the humiliation associated with the Versailles Treaty, and the myth of the German army's having been stabbed in the back were cleverly exploited by right-wing groups, ultimately paving the way for the National Socialists.

The specter of the lost war augured the very real possibility of a new and even greater armed conflict. As Ulmer biographer Stefan Grissemann maintains, Ulmer feared the coming of a war, which he believed the United States would lose.[23] The war also looms large in his unfinished and unpublished novel, *Beyond the Boundary* (written in English in 1935), in which Ulmer tells a thinly veiled autobiographical story of George, a boy who grows up in postwar Vienna. Having lost his father in the war, as Ulmer did, George suffers from the misery and poverty of his upbringing and the social stigma of the absent father. The hypocrisy of Austrian propaganda is chastised in no uncertain terms: "The newspapers carried in screaming headlines the accounts of victory. The same newspapers also printed, as inconspicuous [sic] as possible, huge casualty lists. Everybody knew that these casualties were censored and actually presented only a small fraction of the appalling losses. The hysterical patriotism of the people whipped by propaganda to a fever pitch in the first two years of the war had vanished."[24] It is this specter that motivated Ulmer to recast the horror film as a war film.

At the same time, Weimar modernism is recalled as a progressive force to push the envelope of a genre that, while having been surprisingly successful in 1931 and 1932, was beginning to decline in popularity. Ulmer's idiosyncratic infusion of war into the horror genre reflects Weimar cinema's treatment of World War I. Rather than consigning films like *Caligari* and *Nosferatu* to the realms of the supernatural and the fantastic, without any ties to contemporary Germany, Anton Kaes claims that they react to, and work through, the trauma of the lost war. For Kaes the lost war resonates in these films, even if—or better: precisely because—any direct reference to modern warfare is altogether absent: "[*Caligari*'s] historical unconscious—what it does not speak aloud—is the memory of traumatic experience. The film itself serves as a flashback to an event that has hardly passed, inviting the audience to recover the memory, however discomfiting."[25]

It is Kaes's achievement to have mapped the hidden topicality of a body of films that have traditionally been situated along very different lines of German (film) history. While Lotte Eisner praised them for their affinity to the irrational and uncanny dimensions of German romanticism, Siegfried Kracauer read them as a preview of the coming atrocities of the Third Reich. Both accounts were written by German-Jewish exiles after World War II and in the language of their respective host countries, and both are informed by a post-Holocaust perspective that cannot bracket out the knowledge of what came after Weimar.[26] Kaes, in contrast, reads these films within the cultural moment that gave rise to them, reconstructing the powerful and complex resonances and moments of recognition they must have held for contemporary audiences.

For most Americans World War I was a far more distant experience and its consequences far less traumatic than for Europeans. Thus the allusions to the war in *The Black Cat* may by and large have escaped contemporary viewers in the United States. But what surely did not escape them are the daring innovations that Ulmer brought to the horror film to articulate his larger argument about the achievements and failures of modernism.

The critical success of *The Cabinet of Dr. Caligari*; *The Golem, How He Came into the World*; and *Nosferatu* (F. W. Murnau, 1922) caused Hollywood to first take the horror film seriously. Universal fostered the genre, hoping to find a niche in the first-run market, producing thirteen of the roughly thirty horror films made by the eight majors in the 1930s, and hiring substantial European talent for this purpose. Paul Leni, who had directed *Waxworks* (1924), was signed by Carl Laemmle to adapt the Broadway comedy *The Cat and the Canary* (1927), followed by *The Man Who Laughs* (1928), starring Conrad Veidt. Murnau's *Sunrise* for Fox of the same year, for which Ulmer was credited as assistant art director to Rochus Gliese (already a collaborator of Wiene's and Murnau's in Germany), combined motifs from the Weimar street film with the horror narrative of the intrusion of the outsider. These films employed the well-known trademarks of German expressionist cinema such as chiaroscuro lighting, eccentric set design, and garish makeup. The premature deaths of Leni in 1929, horror star Lon Chaney in 1930 (who starred in *The Phantom of the Opera*, on which Ulmer worked as set designer), and Murnau in 1931 brought an end to silent horror, but the stage had been set for the genre's future growth in sound.

In 1931 *Dracula* became the founding film of the horror sound film cycle and Universal's biggest moneymaker of the year. Its cinematographer was Karl Freund, who worked under Tod Browning's direction. Freund went on to film *Murders in the Rue Morgue* (Robert Florey, 1932), before debuting as a director with *The Mummy* that same year; Karl Struss, who had shot *Sunrise*, did the camera work on Rouben Mamoulian's *Dr. Jekyll and Mr. Hyde* (1931). Between 1931 and 1936 the studio released nineteen horror features, cultivating product differentiation (ever new monsters) before turning to sequels (e.g., *The Bride of Frankenstein* [1935]). When stricter enforcement of the Production Code began in 1934, horror films became a privileged target for censorship (*The Black Cat* provides a prime example); as a result, two years later the interest in the genre declined, the A-budget devotion to horror concluded, and the Universal empire toppled.

The majority of films in the cycle enlisted European-born professionals in key positions, most notably, of course, Boris Karloff and Bela Lugosi. The Hungarian-born Lugosi can, in fact, also be seen as a German import of sorts. In 1919 he fled Budapest for Vienna for political reasons. Somewhat improbably, Ulmer claims to have known Lugosi "since the time he was Minister of Culture in the communist government of Bela Kuhn in Hungary."[27] One year later, Lugosi starred in Berlin in Murnau's *Januskopf* ("Janus-Head," a variation of the Jekyll-and-Hyde story), followed by *Die Teufelsanbeter* ("The Devil Worshippers" [Marie-Louise Droop and Muhsin Ertugrul, 1920]), the kind of fare that would become his specialty at Universal.[28] Lugosi's Caligari figure in *Murders in the Rue Morgue* is a particularly telling example of the cut-and-paste technique of some of Universal's horror films. The presence of German émigrés in horror films was higher than in any other American genre until the advent of the anti-Nazi film, and it often paved the way for long-lasting careers.[29]

While personal continuities marked the entirety of the cycle, the stylistic affinities were more pronounced in Universal's silent pictures, as the transition to sound stifled the fluidity of the camera (a trademark of Murnau's films in particular) and the novelty of expressionist design and lighting wore off. The dialogue-heavy *Dracula* and *Frankenstein* betrayed their proximity to the stage adaptations that had popularized Bram Stoker's and Mary Shelley's novels, further enhanced by the fact that Lugosi and others who had acted in Broadway productions also starred in the films. References and allusions to German films such as *Nosferatu* became confined to plot elements and individual ideas and lacked their predecessors' visual elegance and stylistic flamboyance. Not until *The Black Cat* would German expressionism be revisited by Universal in more than just a perfunctory or clichéd manner.

The most striking feature of that film, apart from the pairing of the two horror superstars Karloff and Lugosi, is certainly the set design, which provides an allegorical expression of the legacy of German modernism. Typical for exile filmmaking's plurality of vision, Poelzig's Bauhaus of horror invokes not only the culture of the abandoned homeland but also that of the adopted new home. Critics have cited Frank Lloyd Wright's Ennis House in the Hollywood Hills as a concrete inspiration for Ulmer's set.[30] Built in 1924, and thus still a comparative novelty at the time of *The Black Cat*'s production, Wright's modernist, fortresslike residence was (and still is) an imposing structure, the key building component of which was concrete, which was poured into blocks. Given its imposing look and prominent location, perched high above the Los Angeles freeways, it is perhaps not surprising that the Ennis House has become a popular setting for horror and science fiction films, including *The House on Haunted Hill*, *Blade Runner*, and *The Day of the Locust*. California earthquakes and mudslides of the past decade have made the house uninhabitable and turned it into a modernist ruin that sits vacant. The Ennis House thus stands (at least for now) in the long tradition of the abandoned mansion, a staple of the British gothic novel, which itself is another important source for *The Black Cat*.

In this literary genre, decaying castles, manors, or towers figure prominently, not only as principal locations but also as larger symbols for the clash between the present and the dark secrets of the past. Like Ulmer's critique of rationalism, these novels often conveyed to an increasingly secular and skeptical age that remnants of a pagan and mythical past could not be so easily rejected as contemporaries believed. Horace Walpole's *The Castle of Otranto* (1764), often considered the founding text of the genre, became a major source for Edgar Allan Poe's "The Fall of the House of Usher" (1838), which exercised a far more important influence on Ulmer's film than Poe's story "The Black Cat." Indeed, that story was invoked by Universal for box-office purposes only. Poe's tale of the Usher dynasty and Ulmer's film share a sense of futility and oppressiveness within a closed-in universe from which there is no escape. Just as Poelzig's compound ultimately explodes, the climax of Poe's tale has the titular mansion split and sink into the bog; while no concrete explanation is supplied, there are strong allusions to incest and murder that render this ending inevitable. These allusions find a direct resonance in Ulmer's film, which is deeply disturbing precisely because of its suggestiveness. Unlike other films of the genre, which often feature a particular monster's bestiality, violence here happens offscreen or is alluded to by sounds (when Poelzig kills Karen) or shadows (when Werdegast skins Poelzig alive like a cat, as if to rid himself of his own cat phobia). What is not said in *The Black Cat* is far more unsettling than what is spelled out. Finally, much attention is given in Poe's story to "preserving her [Usher's deceased sister's] corpse," much like the dead female bodies on display in Poelzig's cabinet of necrophilia, and both tales are driven by narratives of the return of the repressed that end in utter annihilation.[31]

What distinguishes the house of Poelzig from the house of Usher and other gothic domiciles is the startling contrast between the ultramodern décor and architecture of the villa and the subterranean torture chambers and dungeons of bygone times, which creates a disturbing spatial and temporal asynchronicity. As Donald Albrecht has observed, the attention to detail in something as ephemeral as a film set is truly extraordinary in Ulmer's

FIGURE 1.1 The Cabinet of Herr Poelzig.

film: "Each of the set's individual rooms exhibits an impressive formal and spatial complexity. The bedrooms, for example, are vertically divided by cantilevered projections supported along one wall by freestanding, wedge-shaped piers. Every room is sparely furnished with chrome tubular chairs polished to a high sheen. Luminous walls and ceilings, light fixtures, sliding doors, and digital clocks are among the electrically driven devices that serve the inhabitants of this elegant Corbusian *machine à habiter*."[32]

Yet despite the open floor plan and clean, angular lines, this is a closed world. The painted backdrops behind the windows emphasize the sensation of being locked in, reiterating a claustrophobia that emanates from the whole film. As in a wartime siege or a trench, there is an all-pervading sense of entrapment and hopelessness, and the Alisons' escape at the last moment has the feeling of a happy ending tagged on to a tale that really should not allow for any survivors.

A formidable iron spiral staircase connects Poelzig's villa to the former fortress on which it is built. Its gun turrets and calculating charts are also the products of a rationalist architecture, this time one of steel and concrete in the service of modern warfare; the cultured, refined side of modernism above, this film suggests, cannot exist without its destructive, death-embracing other below. No creaking doors or cobwebs, the staple of the genre, are found here, only the remnants of clinical and cynical tools of mass destruction. Only the room where Poelzig celebrates his Black Mass and plans to sacrifice Joan Alison is dominated by the kind of expressionist set design on which *Dracula* and *Frankenstein* relied, reinforced by Poelzig's and his followers' theatrical robes and makeup, and an overly dramatic use of light and shadow.

The Black Cat infuses the supernatural elements of classic horror with a dreamlike, nightmarish realism. It seems that not only Joan Alison has gone "mediumistic" (as Werdegast calls it in his faux-psychoanalytic lingo, after he has given her a powerful narcotic), but so have Poelzig and Werdegast themselves. Karloff's and Lugosi's somnambulist movements underscore their respective characters' hypnotic state of mind, yet another of the many allusions to *Caligari*, and throughout the film Poelzig is seen in the black silk nightgowns and pajamas of a waking dead. In the very first shot of him we see him rise from his bed like Nosferatu from his coffin or Cesare summoned by Dr. Caligari, the silhouette of his dark, chiseled body appearing like a statuette against the indirect light of the window behind him, with his lifeless wife horizontally stretched out in front of him—a composition

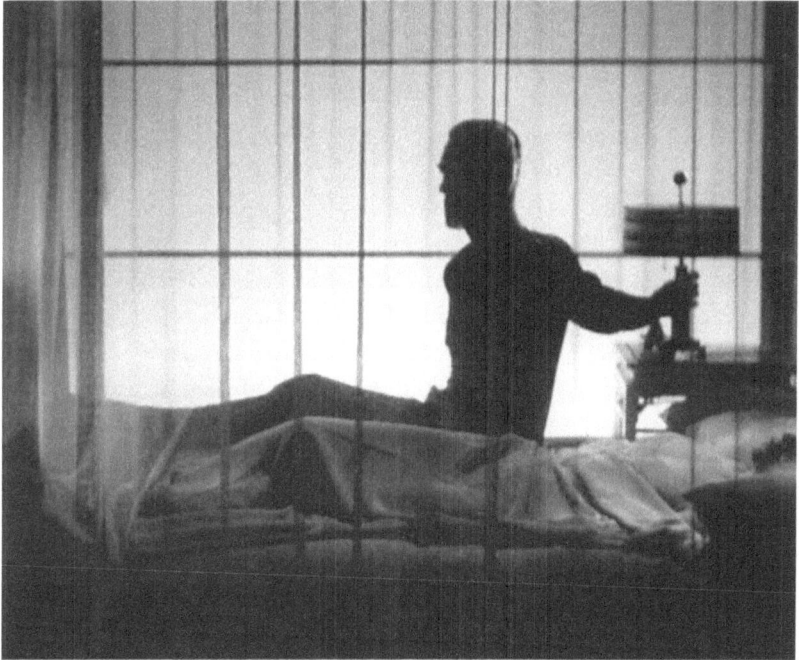

FIGURE 1.2 Poelzig rises from his bed like a vampire from a coffin.

that emphasizes the calculating and inhuman nature of this military traitor turned high priest of rape and murder.

Perhaps the most startling sequence in the film, however, is not one driven by action or dialogue but by the roaming camera of John Mescall, which detaches itself from the characters and inspects the dark underworld of Poelzig's villa. The scene occurs when Poelzig first takes Werdegast underground to where he embalms his victims, including Karen, who was first Vitus's and then Hjalmar's wife. Werdegast pleads, "Why is she like this?" as the camera moves away from a medium close-up of the psychiatrist's face and toward the calculating charts, carefully tip-toeing along the thick concrete walls of Fortress Marmaros, before climbing up the long spiral staircase that connects the two levels. William K. Everson has criticized the film's modernist camera work as "sometimes too tricky for its own good" but concedes that "the striking, pictorial quality of the film creates a decidedly non-Hollywood and non-stereotyped horror film."[33] In this particular scene the camera becomes its own independent player. Separated from the point of view of any character, and thus violating the norms of classic storytelling, Poelzig's words to Werdegast in this one-minute sequence cease to be part of a dialogue and become the voice-over commentary of an omniscient narrator, accompanying the unfettered camera:

> "Come, Vitus. Are we men or are we children? Of what use are all these melodramatic gestures? You say your soul was killed, that you have been dead all those years. And what of me? Did we not both die here in Marmaros fifteen years ago? Are we any less victims of the war than those whose bodies were torn asunder? Are we not both the living dead? And now you come to me playing an avenging angel childishly thirsting for my blood. We understand each other too well. We know too much of life. We shall play a little game, Vitus. A game of death, if you like."

Occurring in the only scene where such a prolonged effect is created, Poelzig's comments about the deathly bond of two undead survivors become the central metaphor for the entire film.

Finally, no discussion of how *The Black Cat*'s negotiation of genre conventions pushed the envelope of the 1930s horror film would be complete without attending to its innovative use of music. Unlike any other Universal film from the cycle, *The Black Cat* has a fully orchestrated score that provides music for fifty-five of the film's sixty-five minutes of running time. It combines an impressive original score by Heinz Roemheld, a thirty-two-year-old Berlin-trained composer, with his arrangement of classical music by Tchaikovsky, Chopin, Schubert, and Liszt. If Ulmer can be trusted (and Roemheld actually confirms this account), the classical score was the director's idea and meant to express the refined taste of Poelzig. As William Rosar has shown in an essay on the scores of Universal's horror movies, what was particularly innovative in this film was not only to have music underlying almost the entirety of the film (including scenes with dialogue), at a time when music was typically confined to the opening and closing credits, but also to associate certain characters with certain passages that serve as leitmotifs.[34] As Rosar notes, the film opens with Liszt's *Hungarian Rhapsody* for the scenes at the Budapest train station. His brooding *Tasso* theme then becomes Werdegast's leitmotif, while Tchaikovsky's *Romeo and Juliet* serves as the Alisons' theme. Poelzig is introduced with a flurry of Liszt's *Sonata in B Minor*, the "Devil Sonata" (as is well-known, Liszt himself had a fascination with Satan), while Brahms's *Sapphic Ode* is Karen's theme.

The film also cleverly switches between diegetic and nondiegetic music, first having a futuristic device that looks like a clock but turns out to be a radio playing Chopin's *Second Piano Prelude*, while later Poelzig himself plays Bach's *Toccata, Adagio and Fugue in C* on the organ. At the Black Mass we hear diegetic music for the last time when the organ is again played, this time by an unidentified guest (played by John Carradine, who would star in *Bluebeard* [1944], Ulmer's second horror film).

The decision to score the film in almost its entirety harks back to silent cinema, but the innovative use of leitmotifs for individual characters also heightens psychological depth and directs the emotions of viewers. Stefan Grissemann has rightly observed that music in Ulmer's films tends to "dictate our feelings a little too much," but in the case of *The Black Cat* that criticism seems overstated.[35] Here the music underscores the trancelike acting of Karloff and Lugosi or the uncanny, self-propelled exploration of the camera discussed earlier, where Poelzig's self-reflexive monologue about the living dead is underscored "by the hymn-like allegretto movement of Beethoven's *Seventh Symphony*."[36] How controversial and daring this use of music was at the time can be seen by the fact that studio head Carl Laemmle Sr. objected more vehemently to it than to any other of the many controversial aspects of the film (including its depiction of violence and critique of religion) and at one point even threatened to bar the film from release.[37] Yet when the film turned out to be Universal's biggest moneymaker of the year, those concerns were quickly forgotten.

To be sure, the film is no well-rounded masterwork of 1930s horror but, rather, an intriguing example of what I call Ulmer's messy modernism—an aesthetics consisting of radical innovations and daring inventions but also marked by strife with studio executives and censorship agencies and what are simply bad choices by the director. What may seem "avant-garde" or elliptical storytelling to some may just be the incoherence of a script that suffered from hasty writing or last-minute cuts and changes. And what are we to make of Poelzig's Latin chant "cum grano salis," which is made up of clichés and meaningless phrases when the occasion calls for something far more serious? Why dress up the bus driver in the very same uniform that Emil Jannings wore as hotel porter in *The Last Laugh*? Interestingly, contemporary critics paid much attention to such distracting details, frequently dwelling more on them than the daring subject matter. Thus the critic for *Film Weekly* wrote, "Boris Karloff and Bela Lugosi piling horror upon horror until it all becomes just silly. Lots of screams, but neither rhyme nor reason" (March 15, 1934), and the *New York Times* called the film "more foolish than horrible" (May 19, 1934). As Gary D. Rhodes has summarized the reception of the film, "the film's use of potentially explosive topics like Satanism had little-to-no effect on audience reaction. . . . Recorded responses simply didn't take its use of topics like Satanism seriously."[38] Yet as I noted earlier, the film was a commercial success that proved that the public did not heed these negative reviews.

THE LIVING DEAD AND THE RETURN OF THE GREAT WAR

In contrast to the American reception of the film, *The Black Cat* proved to be more controversial abroad. Cuts were required in Australia, Japan, Poland, and England, and the film was banned in Italy and Finland, primarily because of its depiction of Satanism and extreme violence. The Austrian censors also took offense at its treatment of religion but ultimately banned it because "one of the main characters is portrayed as an Austrian traitor and criminal."[39] In doing so, they took notice of Ulmer's radical interpretation of World War I in the guise of a horror film, which largely escaped American critics and audiences.

When Edgar G. Ulmer's *The Black Cat* premiered in Hollywood on May 3, 1934, the film was anticipated as the latest installment in Universal's highly successful cycle of horror films. In advertising campaigns and promotional materials much had been made of Universal's first-time pairing of its two biggest draws of the series, Boris Karloff and Bela Lugosi (which Ulmer claims to have been his idea).[40] Teaming up the stars who had embodied Dracula and Frankenstein's monster, as well as numerous only slightly less scary abominations, led audiences to expect a double whammy of fright. But *The Black Cat* proved to be distinctively different. Unlike its famous predecessors, it was not based on nineteenth-century British novels and their highly successful Broadway adaptations but on an original screenplay by Peter Ruric after a story by Ulmer and Ruric (though Ulmer claimed later to have worked on the script as well); the plot, as I have stated, had only the faintest connection to the famous story by Edgar Allan Poe.[41] Furthermore, it was one of the few films in the cycle to have a contemporary setting, even if the location, the Carpathian Mountains, at first evoked the remoteness and otherworldly quality of *Dracula*. But most distinctive was the fact that *The Black Cat* was the only film from the 1930s horror cycle to explicitly foreground the connection between the horror genre and the trauma of World War I. Devoid of the monsters that had appeared in previous Universal films, it focused on the monstrosity of humans under the extreme conditions of modern warfare and its aftermath. The film therefore refrains from the graphic horror associated with some abominable other and instead only hints at acts of terror, the full extent of which must be imagined by the viewer. *The Black Cat* successfully blurred the line between the fantastic and supernatural elements of a horror film and the unsettling, dreamlike, and nightmarish realism of an antiwar film.

While Lugosi's and Karloff's characters in other films of the horror cycle are mostly remembered for their respective costumes, makeup, and scary looks, *The Black Cat* features the two actors in their psychologically most complex roles. The Hungarian psychiatrist Dr. Vitus Werdegast and the Austrian engineer Hjalmar Poelzig are old friends whom a wartime betrayal has turned into archenemies, yet the different neuroses from which they suffer create a mutual bond. Both share the fate that a spiritual death befalls those who physically survive the war, turning them, as Poelzig astutely observes, into the "living dead" who lead zombielike existences. While Werdegast has survived fifteen years of internment as a prisoner of war only because of his desire for revenge, Poelzig has become a devil worshipper and necrophiliac, who embalms his female victims and exhibits them in large glass cases. It is highly significant (and emblematic of the repetition compulsion that Freud diagnosed in shell-shocked war veterans) that both need to return to the site of prior torment to settle their final score. And although the film features an unprecedented array of crimes and abnormalities that include sadism, torture, incest, murder, revenge, Satanism, necrophilia, ailurophobia (the fear of cats), voyeurism, and—in an earlier draft of the screenplay—rape, the master narrative is clearly one of betrayal and reckoning with wartime events.

Always a highly efficient narrator, Ulmer wastes little time introducing the trauma of the bygone Great War as the central motif of terror in *The Black Cat*. The film opens on a bustling Budapest train station where a young American couple on their honeymoon, identified by a close-up of their papers as Mr. and Mrs. Alison, settle into their seats. Their intimate privacy is soon interrupted when another traveler is placed in their compartment. He introduces himself as Dr. Vitus Werdegast, the literal meaning of which—"to become a guest"—is not only an ironic comment on his badly timed intrusion on the honeymooners but also a foreshadowing of the more sinister and consequential intrusion on his wartime friend, Hjalmar Poelzig. Yet Werdegast is not the sinister outsider we may expect him to

FIGURE 1.3 Werdegast relives the trauma of the Great War.

be, given Lugosi's previous roles in horror film, but rather a victim himself, as we soon learn. Having commented to Peter Alison how much Alison's wife, sleeping at his side, resembles his own, when he had to leave to go to war "for Kaiser and country," Werdegast speaks of his past: "Have you ever heard of Kurgaal? It's a prison below Omsk on Lake Baikal. Many men have gone there. Few have returned. I have returned. [Pause.] After fifteen years, *I* have returned."[42] Peter Alison (and with him the viewer) can only imagine what Werdegast must have endured there and what he may hope to find upon his return.

As befits the ominous tale of the intruder, a torrential rainfall greets the travelers in Vishegrad, from where they continue on by bus. As if on cue, the bus driver sounds the theme of the Great War, telling his passengers of the war casualties in the hills they are driving through: "All of this country was one of the greatest battle fields of the war. Ten thousands of men died here. The ravine down there was piled twelve deep with dead and wounded men. The little river below was swollen red, a raging torrent of blood. The high hill yonder, where engineer Poelzig now lives, was the site of Fort Marmaros. He built his home on its very foundation. Marmaros, the greatest graveyard in the world." A close-up of Werdegast, listening with his eyes shut, suggests how the past is being replayed in his mind, the atrocities he lived through coming alive again at the very moment he traverses the battlegrounds again some fifteen years later.

For the first time we see him in the trancelike state that will overcome him during much of the remainder of the film. And the war continues to claim its victims—immediately after the driver has finished his tale about the greatest graveyard in the world, he loses control of his vehicle and dies at the very same place ten thousand soldiers found their deaths before him. The Alisons, Werdegast, and his servant survive without greater harm and in the rain make their way to Poelzig's house, introduced by a painted establishing shot (one of Ulmer's trademark money-saving devices) as a gleaming and unworldly modern fortress atop a hill ringed by the white crosses of the graves of the war dead.[43]

In his interview with Bogdanovich Ulmer explained that the setting and the plot of *The Black Cat* was inspired by an idea of the Prague writer Gustav Meyrinck, who had written the novel on which Wegener's *The Golem*

FIGURE 1.4 A gleaming Bauhaus mansion built on the corpses of the Great War.

was based—incidentally a film on which Ulmer claims to have worked, even though he was only fifteen years old at the time (there is some evidence that he actually did): "Meyrinck at that time was contemplating a play based on Doumont [sic!], which was a French fortress the Germans had shelled to pieces during World War I; there were some survivors who didn't come out for years. And the commander was a strange Euripides figure who went crazy three years later, when he was brought back to Paris, because he had walked on that mountain of bodies."[44]

If one takes a closer look at the real battles surrounding Douaumont, a fortress near Verdun considered impregnable and of utmost significance for the French defensive system, one quickly realizes that reality bred even stranger stories than Meyrinck's. The huge fortress was constructed of steel and concrete, with vaults that could house an entire battalion of infantry, but when the Germans attacked and conquered it on February 25, 1916, it was manned by only fifty-seven soldiers, a fact unknown to the Germans. The French later mounted a counterattack, which would eventually degenerate into the drawn-out trench warfare that was already a feature of the western front; they finally recaptured it on October 24 but only after incurring huge losses. While the Germans held the fortress, they, too, became victims of several bizarre mishaps: "A chain reaction of explosions sets afire containers of flamethrower fuel, and the burning liquid flows down the fort's corridors, reaching a store of 155 mm shells. The resulting mighty explosion blows up or asphyxiates most of the men inside the fort. The survivors, their faces blackened with smoke, fall victim to machine-gun fire from their own comrades, who take them to be French African invaders, as they race out of the fiery interior. The disaster claims 650 lives."[45]

The Black Cat presents a fictional history of World War I drawn from actual events and influenced by Meyrinck's ideas.[46] Although the plot contains no Euripides figure who literally walks on the dead, it does feature two survivor figures who seem to be locked into eternally repeating the experience of war. For the psychiatrist Werdegast it is quite clear that Poelzig, whom Werdegast tracked through North and South America and Spain, is compelled to return to the scene of his prior misdeeds: "You sold Marmaros to the Russians. Scuttled away in the night and left us to die. Is it to be wondered at that you should choose this place to build your house? The masterpiece of construction built upon the masterpiece of destruction. The masterpiece of murder. The murderer of ten thousand men returns to the place of his crime." But Werdegast himself follows the same repetition compulsion, as he can only confront Poelzig at the very place where he was betrayed. As if to underscore the suspension of time, Poelzig shows Werdegast his embalmed wife, Karen, who looks exactly how Werdegast remembers having last seen her eighteen years ago.

The inability to escape a cycle of repetition informs not only the personal history of the two antagonists but also the overall image of history portrayed in the film, as becomes evident in the structure of its main setting. Poelzig's Bauhaus-style edifice is a modernist marvel of chrome and glass, replete with sliding doors, an intercom system, a striking staircase, and an open floor plan. Residing on top of the former fortress's formidable foundations, it stands in complete contrast to its dark bowels, which feature an impenetrable system of corridors and chambers that serve Poelzig's sinister purposes. Here, behind huge steel doors, Poelzig keeps his cabinet of embalmed women in glass cases, next to the gun turrets and calculating charts still intact from the war. Adjacent is the large room where he holds his satanic masses and performs his ritual murders, with the embalming rack nearby, where he kills his second wife and where he will find his own death at the hands of Werdegast. A level lower are the leftover explosives that will blow up the entire structure after Werdegast flips the "red switch," igniting an apocalyptic inferno that, redolent of the battles of the Great War, will claim the lives of the last two surviving soldiers. While ostensibly separated as three independent layers, the antiseptic and sterile modern edifice cannot cover the odor of death and decay that lies beneath; Werdegast repeatedly remarks that he can still "sense death in the air," and even Peter Alison quips that if he were ever in need of someone to build him "a nice, cozy, unpretentious insane asylum, [Poelzig] would be the man for it." Madness pervades the ultrarational functionalism of the glass-and-chrome modernism, because at the very foundation of reason, the film suggests, lies an irrationalism that cannot be repressed. Ulmer's critique of culture is clearly indebted to that of his fellow Austrian, Sigmund Freud: underneath a thin veneer of refined culture lurk sexual deviations and dark religious fanaticism that can hardly be kept in check, ever threatening self-destruction—a self-fulfilling prophecy that leads to the real and all-consuming climactic violence that ends the film.

It is striking that the three levels of Hjalmar Poelzig's edifice symbolize key moments of Austro-German wartime and postwar history: while the deepest one, holding the buried explosives, obviously represents the destructive power of war, interspersed with the graves of its victims, the expressionist chapel where Poelzig celebrates Lucifer calls to mind the expressionist sets of *Caligari*, *Waxworks*, and *Warning Shadows*.

FIGURE 1.5 Poelzig celebrates a Black Mass.

FIGURE 1.6 Glass and chrome dominate the upper level of Poelzig's edifice.

The Bauhaus-style fortress on the top, finally, evokes the cold, detached modernism that emphasized the functionality, transparency, and visual clarity of this new architecture, while also hinting at the New Objectivity, or "neue Sachlichkeit," a movement in the arts and literature meant to leave behind what it perceived to be the extreme subjectivity and irrationalism of expressionism. By showing these layers to be fatefully connected, *The Black Cat* refutes any view of history that promises progress or a certain teleology.

The landscape that surrounds the fortress is also deeply saturated with history, as the previously quoted lines by the bus driver make clear. Ulmer's Carpathians are the location of very real violence, not the otherworldly horror of *Dracula*. The scene of two policemen arguing about whose hometown is more beautiful (one of few scenes meant to provide comic relief) fits in here. Although it pokes fun at the rivalry of local boosters and their provincialism, it also highlights the desire to emphasize the beauty of a country that is otherwise depicted as scarred by war (and thus explains to some degree why the Alisons would choose this location over Niagara Falls for their honeymoon). More important, *The Black Cat* employs a concept of foreignness that differs from that depicted in most horror films of the period. Lugosi and Karloff are still typed as the ethnic others they portrayed in virtually all films in this genre, but the conflict here is *between* those others (with the Alisons thrown in as pawns) and not between an American (or British) citizen and an outside threat. Thus while Karloff's character still denotes the sexual deviance and decadence typically associated with the Old World, Lugosi gets to undo that stereotype by playing his most sympathetic role in a horror film, even if that role was originally conceived by Ulmer to be far more menacing and ambiguous.[47] What is more, Karloff's perversity, no matter how strange and bizarre it may be, is suggested to have stemmed from his wartime experience and not to be an inherent character trait. The Carpathians emerge as the location of past and present conflict, a conflict that is grounded in history, not myth or legend, and this conflict has bearings on outsiders when they happen to be in the wrong place at the wrong time. How saturated with real tragedy this very location would turn out to be would become evident only ten years later, when in 1944 the Germans entered Hungary and built one of the biggest concentration camps in the country in Mateszalka, close to the Jewish district of Marmaros.[48]

The importance of the topicality of World War I for Ulmer becomes more evident if we consider some of the changes between the script and the released film.[49] Originally, Werdegast was to explain his participation in the war by saying, "For God and country," not "For Kaiser and country," as the released film has it, a change that was presumably added to highlight the alliance between the Austro-Hungarian Empire and the German monarchy. The bus driver was far more explicit in listing historical detail, pointing out that the thousands who died here included "Austrians, Hungarians, Russians," thereby pointing to Ulmer's belief that war knows only losers, no winners. And the horror of trench warfare, which is mostly associated with the western front, was emphasized to also have occurred in the East: "That hill over there was taken by the Russians twenty-two times—and retaken by our brave men." The omission of these lines must be attributed not to the Hays Office but to studio executives who felt audiences might get bogged down with historical detail that was of little meaning to them.

Equally revealing are the instances in which Ulmer sought to link the aftermath of World War I with the rise of Nazism. Much more was made in the script of the arrival of the guests to the Black Mass, who were to be greeted by Werdegast while Poelzig readies himself for his duties. The list of names suggests members of a decadent Austrian nobility (with some typical Ulmerian in-jokes thrown in). Among them we find Hauptmann Eichel, Fräulein Krug, Graf Trivers, Count Windischgraetz and his sister, Count Hauptmerde, and Herr Sternberg, most likely a jab at the phony nobility of Josef von Sternberg; the implication is that their loss of prestige and power after the collapse of the empire has made them susceptible to devil worship, much as the disenfranchised German petit bourgeoisie of the late Weimar Republic voted Hitler into power. Most startling in this group are a certain "Herr and Frau Goering," the latter spotting a slight, Hitleresque mustachio on her upper lip that provides a linking of Nazism with androgyny and homosexuality (possibly an allusion to Roehm's widely known homosexuality)—a daring coupling of fascism with sexual deviancy that would not be more fully explored until Visconti and Cavani did so in Italy many decades later.

In light of the significance of the Great War for this particular tale of terror, other World War I films come into focus as significant subtexts. These include Weimar antiwar films such as *Namenlose Helden* (Kurt Bernhardt, 1925), *Westfront 1918* (G. W. Pabst, 1930), *Niemandsland* (Victor Trivas, 1931), *Die andere Seite* (Heinz Paul, 1931), and particularly Paul's documentary *Douaumont* (also 1931), a self-described "reconstruction" of events that mixes documentary footage of the titular bastion with reenactments of wartime events of former soldiers. Premiered at a time when Ulmer was in Berlin, it includes images of white graveside markers that conspicuously resemble the crosses in the foreground of the establishing shot of Poelzig's mansion.⁵⁰ Prominent among American films are King Vidor's *The Big Parade* (1925), MGM's biggest hit of the silent era, and Ernst Lubitsch's *Broken Lullaby* (1932), made for Paramount. Most prominently, however, figures Universal's own 1930 antiwar drama *All Quiet on the Western Front*, directed by Lewis Milestone and based on Erich Maria Remarque's famous novel. A huge critical success, the film won Academy Awards for Best Picture and Best Director for Universal, finally establishing it as a studio to be taken seriously, and marking a significant personal success for Carl Laemmle Jr., who had only recently assumed its leadership. *The Black Cat* can be seen to carry *All Quiet on the Western Front*'s indictment of the futility and absurdity of the war into the postwar period, showing how for those who experienced the horrors of combat the war will never end, while indirectly warning of the threats of a new and possibly even more destructive war.⁵¹ A film with a strong pacifist message, *All Quiet on the Western Front* also implicitly criticized America's strong isolationist position during the first years of the war, hinting that the belated U.S. intervention into the war was responsible for bloodshed that could have been avoided. By alluding to that film's implied criticism of the politics of nonintervention at the very historical moment that Nazi Germany was ascending to the status of European superpower, *The Black Cat* revives the memory of World War I as a warning to Americans not to repeat the mistakes of the past.

The Black Cat works through the trauma of World War I in a way that emulates the strategies Anton Kaes analyzes in Weimar films such as *The Cabinet of Dr. Caligari, Nosferatu, Die Nibelungen* (Fritz Lang, 1924), and *Metropolis* (Fritz Lang, 1926). A displaced work of mourning, Ulmer's film looks back on a period of German and Austrian history as it threatens to repeat itself in a new and different historical, political, and geographical configuration. Some three years later, that threat had become far more concrete, prompting Warner Bros., the most politically outspoken major Hollywood studio at the time, to produce a series of films that couched the threat of Nazism (both from within and from outside) in genres hitherto considered solely for their entertainment value. The biographical dramas, or biopics, directed by William Dieterle can count as the most accomplished examples of Warner Bros.' aspirations.

 Two
TALES OF URGENCY AND AUTHENTICITY

> *Whoever turns biographer commits himself to lies, to concealment, to hypocrisy, to embellishments, and even to dissembling his own lack of understanding, for biographical truth is not to be had, and even if one had it, one could not use it.*
> —SIGMUND FREUD[1]

> *The motif of escape, to which the majority of biographies owe their existence, is eclipsed by the motif of redemption.*
> —SIEGFRIED KRACAUER[2]

THE CRITICAL BIOGRAPHY

In his 1930 essay "The Biography as an Art Form of the New Bourgeoisie," Siegfried Kracauer provides a succinct critique of a genre that enjoyed widespread popularity in Germany and elsewhere during the years following World War I. Kracauer notes a preference among Western European authors to focus on the lives of historical figures such as politicians, diplomats, and military leaders.[3] Kracauer explains this phenomenon to be neither a form of hero worship nor a mere fad or fashion but a reaction to the profound crisis of meaning that has grasped us in the wake of the atrocities of modern warfare. In contrast to the modern novel's attempt to render visible the effects of the loss of a unifying system of reference precisely by taking leave of traditional notions of realism, biographies of historical figures counter the disappearance of a fixed-coordinate grid by relying on the documented work of history. In so doing, Kracauer argues, the genre offers the established bourgeoisie, as the main readership of these books, a form of escapism that distracts it from the precariousness of its own state of existence.[4]

Only three years after this incisive critique, Siegfried Kracauer had to flee Nazi Germany for Paris, where he immediately began researching the life and times of the composer Jacques Offenbach. Kracauer explained his choice of topic with the necessity to reach a wider French as well as international audience through a book with commercial potential. The choice of genre, nevertheless, seemed baffling. How could someone who had taken biographers to task so easily join their ranks? Kracauer's decision to write on Offenbach must be seen as a reaction to his own precarious status as an exiled intellectual. His fall from the position of one of Germany's leading journalists to a geographically and politically uprooted intellectual, indeed, paralleled the experience of volatility that he saw as the genre's attractiveness to the bourgeoisie. Yet Kracauer's interest in Offenbach was not gratuitous or opportunistic. At stake in *Jacques Offenbach* were not disinterested, historicist contemplations that "can no longer find their way back to the present," nor the worship of a singular individual, but instead a "Gesellschaftsbiographie"—a biography of a society that entertains remarkable parallels to the one that drove Kracauer into exile.[5] In his preface he wrote: "In light of the events of today no one will misunderstand that the phantasmagoria of the Second Empire is of particular actuality."[6]

Kracauer was only one of many exiled writers and intellectuals who turned to literary biography (or whose previous work as biographer underwent a significant politicization).[7] Kracauer's self-understanding as a biographer, unlike that of his colleagues, entertained significant parallels to the development that the screen biography, or bio-picture, was undergoing in Hollywood during the second half of the 1930s—parallels that Kracauer himself must have been aware of, since in 1938 he reworked his *Offenbach* into a "Motion picture treatment," which he hoped to sell to the studios with the help of director William Dieterle.[8] At that time William Dieterle was part of a group of film professionals at Warner Bros. (which included producer Henry Blanke, cameraman Tony Gaudio, and stars Paul Muni and Edward G. Robinson) who, under the supervision of studio producer Hal Wallis, were involved in creating a series of films that would revolutionize the genre.[9] The six films made by this team—*The Story of Louis Pasteur* (1935), *The White Angel* (1936, about Florence Nightingale), *The Life of Emile Zola* (1937), *Juarez* (1938, about the Mexican president), *Dr. Ehrlich's Magic Bullet* (1940, about the German scientist), and *A Dispatch from Reuter's* (1940, about the founder of the news agency)—all depicted famous non-American individuals whose life stories highlight significant parallels between the times in which they lived (primarily the second half of the nineteenth century) and contemporary Europe and America.

Warner Bros.' decision to have its biopics highlight scientists, politicians, and artists stands in contrast to a trend in American magazines that Leo Löwenthal examined in his influential study, "Biographies in Popular Magazines." He observed a dramatic decline after World War I in biographies devoted to political leaders, or what he called "idols of production," while interest in "idols of consumption"—organizers of leisure time that include entertainers, athletes, newspaper and radio men, models, and owners of restaurants and resorts—had steadily increased.[10] One finds a stronger emphasis on "the human interest situation," on the private affairs of public figures, and the biographers' strategy to speak about their subjects in undiscriminating superlatives and a cliché-ridden language that leads to a pseudo-individualization of heroes. In light of this trend Warner Bros.' serious screen biographies stand out because of their subject matter, as well as the failure to follow genre conventions that call for a romance or love interest or some plot device that highlights the melodramatic dimensions of the biographee's life. Despite their focus on great individuals, their narratives are sober, restrained, and devoid of sentimentality, using music and other devices to heighten emotions very sparingly, thereby acquiring an almost documentary dimension.

The six films in the cycle show creative tensions that resemble those of Kracauer's Offenbach biography: on a formal level they negotiate a path between a populist form of representation indebted to nineteenth-century notions of realism and a resistance to the shock of modernism; on the political level they strike a balance between escapist entertainment and a progressive agenda (namely, to articulate the experience of exile and win support for the fight against Nazi Germany); and on the historiographical level they face the challenge of constructing parallels, or points of recognition, between a representation of the past and the lifeworld of its target audience without bending historical facts.

The driving creative force behind the Warner Bros. biopics was William Dieterle. A stage actor who had trained under Max Reinhardt, Dieterle had supporting roles in many Weimar films, including *Hintertreppe / Backstairs* (Leopold Jessner and Paul Leni, 1921), *Das Wachsfigurenkabinet / Waxworks* (Paul Leni, 1924), and *Faust* (F. W. Murnau, 1926). Like Lubitsch, Murnau, and E. A. Dupont, Dieterle came to Hollywood to further his career, not for political reasons. There is evidence, however, that there were other incentives to accept an offer by Warner Bros. in the summer of 1930, namely, to escape financial obligations that had arisen after his short and unsuccessful stint as a theater owner and a co-owner (with his wife, Charlotte) of the production company, Charha-Gesellschaft.¹¹ Dieterle was a central figure in the exile and émigré community in Los Angeles and instrumental in organizing support efforts and providing exiles with affidavits.¹²

As a director Dieterle was eager to create films that brought a largely isolationist-minded American public closer to the threatening events on the Continent. Hired by Jack Warner in 1930 to direct German-language versions of their international features, Dieterle, like many other émigrés, developed into a fierce opponent of Nazi Germany and resisted lucrative offers to lure him back. Dieterle's ambition was to provide serious entertainment with high production values and meaningful stories. He sought to rise above the many B pictures he had been assigned to direct, a career move he pursued by hitching his fortunes to those of actor Paul Muni, with whom he had worked on *Dr. Socrates* (1935), a gangster tale about a country doctor. A major star at Warner Bros. after the success of *I Am a Fugitive from a Chain Gang* (1932) and *Black Fury* (1935), and with unprecedented approval about the scripts he was offered, Muni rightly perceived Dieterle's biopics as an opportunity for the stage-trained acting he excelled in. Equally important for the success of the cycle was the fact that the director's political views coincided with Warner Bros.' farsighted commitment to oppose Nazi Germany, making it the only Hollywood studio at the time to have withdrawn its films from the German market. Finally, Dieterle's promise of providing "European sophistication" resounded with the studio's aspirations to improve its public image, which at that point rested largely on its highly popular but lowbrow gangster movies and its musicals.¹³ Indeed, Dieterle's collaboration with Max Reinhardt on *A Midsummer Night's Dream* (1935) had been a first attempt by Warner Bros. to raise its cultural status.

The success of Dieterle's 1935 Pasteur film paved the way for what two years later would become the studio's biggest critical and box-office success of the decade—*The Life of Emile Zola*. Often considered the first anti-Nazi film to come out of the Hollywood studios, the film infuses the biopic with a political topicality rarely seen before in this genre. Its dramatic retelling of the famous French writer's courageous efforts to rehabilitate Captain Dreyfus, the innocent victim of France's greatest judicial scandal, is both a gripping piece of entertainment and a political parable, rousing its audience to feel pity and fear for its obstinate and admirable protagonist, formidably played by Muni. While the experience of injustice and oppression resounded with a Depression-ridden audience,¹⁴ it also offered lessons about civic duties and democratic principles at a time when Nazism was preparing to expand its power beyond Germany and, indeed, Europe.¹⁵

Most important, it reminded viewers about the achievements of their young democracy while admonishing them not to take these for granted—a case also made by Thomas Mann in his lecture, "The Coming Victory of Democracy," with which he toured the country in 1938.[16]

The film offered Dieterle an opportunity to translate onto the screen his widespread political and humanitarian efforts on behalf of the European refugees; it also allowed him a chance to reflect the very culture from which he and his fellow refugees had been expelled, the theater and intellectual culture of Weimar Germany. Premiering in New York on August 11, 1937, *The Life of Emile Zola* became an outstanding success with both critics and audiences.[17] It was nominated for ten Academy Awards and won three, giving Warner Bros. the prestige it had sought for many years.[18] Firmly establishing Dieterle as an A-list director (after many years of a seesaw career), the film highlights the achievements of numerous Central European émigrés and exiles, including Joseph Schildkraut, who won an Academy Award for Best Supporting Actor, Vladimir Sokoloff (an erstwhile émigré from Moscow who had spent ten years as an actor in Berlin and Vienna), and scriptwriters Heinz Herald and Geza Herzceg, who won the award for Best Screenplay.[19] It also came under attack, however, for taking too many liberties with historical facts and for evading the issue of Dreyfus's Jewishness.[20]

Despite its critical success and its historical significance for Warner Bros., *The Life of Emile Zola* and the other films in the cycle have received little critical attention.[21] One often-cited reason is the view that they don't need it, because they are self-evident, transparent pieces of entertainment and propaganda. Yet the "transparency" of these films is the effect created by the visual and narrative components of the genre, which were modeled to perfection in Dieterle's and Muni's collaboration. Their realism, in other words, is the product of careful aesthetic choices, which, as it turns out, are not without ambiguity and contradiction. As we will see, the film's claim to authenticity is both supported and undermined by its topicality and message-driven dimension—a friction, I would argue, that makes it exemplary for exilic filmmaking.

"THE TRUTH IS ON THE MARCH": TALES OF AUTHENTICITY

As a genre, the biopic can look back at a venerable tradition, both in Hollywood and in Germany. Weimar cinema includes the Fridericus Rex cycle, which focuses on different aspects of the life of the famous Prussian King, Ernst Lubitsch's *Madame Dubarry* (1919, remade by Dieterle as *Madame Du Barry* for Warner Bros. in 1934), and *Anna Boleyn* (1920), as well as *Danton* (1920) and *Peter der Grosse* (1921, both by Dimitri Buchowetzki), *Waterloo* (Karl Grune, 1929), and *Dreyfus* (Richard Oswald, 1930). The so-called genius film became a favorite form of the biopic during Nazi cinema, often starring Emil Jannings or Heinrich George. In Hollywood the life of famous historical figures, politicians, scientists, artists, and all forms of entertainers had been movie material from the very beginnings of the film industry, becoming particularly important with the advent of sound. As George F. Custen states in his authoritative study of the genre, between 1927 and 1960 the major studios produced almost three hundred biopics.[22] Among exile directors, Dieterle is the only one to excel in this genre, yet many others dabbled in it, mostly producing films that cannot rival their other achievements. These include *Devotion* (Curtis Bernhardt, 1946, on the Brontë sisters), *The Song of Scheherazade* (Walter Reisch, 1947, on the Russian composer Rimsky-Korsakov), *The Court-Martial of Billy Mitchell* (Otto Preminger, 1955, on the American general), *The Spirit of St. Louis* (Billy Wilder, 1957, on Charles Lindbergh), and *A Man for All Seasons* (Fred Zinnemann, 1966, on the philosopher Thomas More). Salka Viertel provided the screenplay for *Queen Christina* (1933) and, uncredited, the story for *Madame Curie* (1943).

The calling card of the bio-picture has always been its claim to realism and authenticity, its ambition to present history "as it really happened." As Custen states, every biopic needs to convince viewers that "every effort had been expended to bring them true history in the guise of spectacle, as well as suggesting that the research for each film was, for the first time, bringing to the screen a true portrait, or at least a singularly true version of the accurate characterization of a person."[23] These efforts reached new and unprecedented dimensions in the Warner Bros. cycle under Dieterle's direction, with meticulous attention paid to sets, costumes, décor, and makeup of the star.

Truly impressive historical research went into preparation for writing and filming, which was subsequently also used in promotion materials. Large compendiums, called bibles, were assembled by the studio's research department, which contained detailed narrative and pictorial information that was used for every aspect of production, assuring a unified look of the period and the biographee.[24] There was also meticulous documentation of the life of every historical person used in the film, often accompanied by

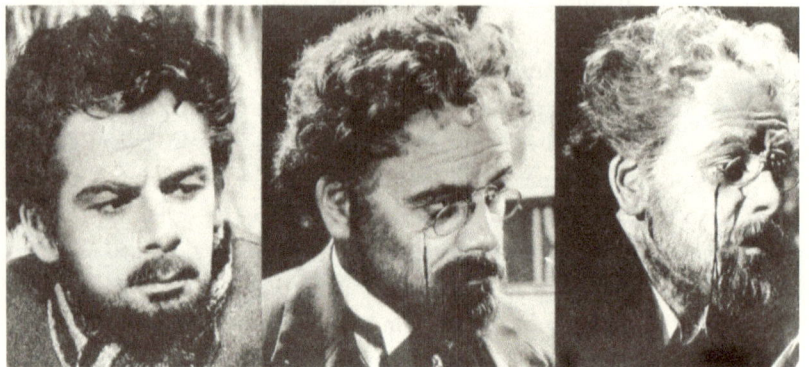

FIGURE 2.1 Makeup ages Muni to indicates three important stages of Zola's life.

signed release forms from living persons indicating their approval of the film. In the case of *Zola* this included an approval by Dreyfus's son Pierre, who—also on behalf of his mother, Lucie, Alfred's widow—consented to the film. So thoroughly established a claim to historical truth about the biographee and the authentic feel for the period provided the leeway the film would need for its fictionalization of Zola's life.

While the film's title suggests a narrative that will cover the entire life span of a famous writer, its actual focus is the Dreyfus affair (and producers at Warner Bros. thought of it as their Dreyfus film, not their Zola film). Following genre conventions, the film opens with a young Emile Zola, who with his friend Paul Cézanne (the quintessential biopic sidekick who highlights the strengths and flaws of the protagonist) is a young starving artist in the Quartier Latin in Paris. The film goes on to efficiently chronicle Zola's trajectory from literary breakthrough and rise to fame (made possible by a chance encounter with a prostitute who provides Zola with the material for first his novel, *Nana*) to self-complacency, as he becomes one of the bourgeois he had earlier criticized, which leads to a break with Cézanne. After this thirty-minute exposition a new plotline promising suspense and intrigue is introduced: secret documents are taken from the French military command and delivered to the German Embassy in Paris. A close-up of Count Esterhazy's doorplate cues viewers to the identity of the perpetrator and focuses our attention on the question of whether or not he will be found out. In quick succession the military command, who need a scapegoat, wrongly single out Alfred Dreyfus for his Jewish origins. While we watch Dreyfus being framed, arrested, sentenced, and deported, a self-satisfied Zola haggles over the freshness of lobsters at Les Halles market. It is not until Mme Dreyfus personally intervenes on her husband's behalf that the writer resolves to take up the fight for the innocent man. His open letter to the president of France, "I Accuse," creates a public outcry and provokes a mock lynching of Zola. Zola is sued for libel, tried, and sentenced to one year in prison. Following the advice of his friends, he flees to England. One year later, new political leadership in France finally brings about new developments in the Dreyfus case. The real traitor, Count Esterhazy, is forced to flee to England, and Dreyfus is finally freed. On the eve of Dreyfus's reinstatement Zola dies of asphyxiation at his desk. Anatole France delivers the eulogy in the Pantheon, calling the writer "a moment in the conscience of man."

The story of Dreyfus was well known to the American public as it had been recounted in numerous obituaries following his death in 1935. This allowed the filmmakers to focus on Zola's intervention in the case rather than the case proper, taking some noticeable liberties with historical facts. One such liberty is making *Nana* his breakthrough novel, while in reality it was an achievement of a later part of his career; another is having Zola's death occur on the eve of Dreyfus's reinstatement for heightened dramatic effect, while Zola in fact died several years earlier. The film also omits that in 1899 Dreyfus was granted a presidential pardon on the condition that he not seek a revision of his verdict, which disappointed many of his supporters; the actual reinstatement in the army did not take place until 1906.

In virtually all biopics the tension between fiction and historical truth was established at the very beginning, often through the use of a title card. The opening for *Dr. Ehrlich's Magic Bullet*, for example, explains the quest of the protagonist—"to fight the scourges of mankind"—and then goes on to state, "This is the story of his devotion to that ideal." At first sight the title card of *The Life of Emile Zola* seems to be no exception. It reads: "This production has its basis in history. The historical basis, however, has been fictionized [sic] for the purposes of this picture and the names of many characters, many characters themselves, the story, incidents and institutions, are fictitious. With the exception of known historical characters, whose actual names are herein used, no identification with actual persons, living or dead, is intended or should be inferred."

What is striking about this title card is that the film that follows includes not a single character among the main or supporting cast who is actually *not* based on a historical figure. This misleading disclaimer, which suggests more fictionalization than actually took place, must be seen as part of the studio's efforts to diffuse any potential legal battles resulting from the film's touchy subject matter. Yet it also points to the larger political issues at stake, which were clearly meant to transcend the narrative presented on the screen.

The tension between the film's claim to authenticity and the politicization of the fiction is particularly on view in a key scene. About halfway through the film the famous writer is visited by Mme Dreyfus, the wife of Captain Alfred Dreyfus, who presents the writer with new evidence about the corruption of military leaders in the hope of eliciting Zola's support to clear her husband's name. Zola, however, is unwilling to help her; the sentiment of the French public is overwhelmingly against Dreyfus, he explains, and any form of protest would be meaningless and, indeed, dangerous. His own days of "fighting, turmoil, and strife" are over, the latter sentiment brought across vividly at the beginning of the scene when, having received a letter from the French Academy promising his induction, he comments to his wife: "Now, my dear, there is nothing more to desire." But of course there is desire left in Zola. At the end of the scene, after a distraught Mme Dreyfus has left, we watch Zola tear apart the letter from the academy and examine the papers she has left behind. Zola is ready to fight again. Inserted between these two shots of Zola reading very different documents is one of him glancing at the self-portrait of his friend Paul Cézanne, leaving no doubt why the writer suddenly changed his mind. By remembering the parting words of the painter that he, Zola, has become successful, rich, and fat, the writer is roused from his bourgeois slumber and contentment, an acknowledgment confirmed by a wink of the eye toward the canvas of the longtime companion.

Mme Dreyfus's visit fulfills several important dramatic functions in the film. It combines the two narrative strands that have developed separately during the last thirty minutes of screen time, namely Zola's growing complacency, indicated by his accumulation of objects and his penchant for good food, as well as the simultaneous developments in the Dreyfus case, which climax with Dreyfus's imprisonment on Devil's Island. For heightened dramatic effect each scene depicting the captain's misery is contrasted with one of Zola's self-absorbedness and disinterest. With Mme Dreyfus's visit to Zola, the life of Zola and the life of Dreyfus become inextricably bound.

Yet the scene of Zola's meeting with Mme Dreyfus is not only of significance for the internal logic of the screenplay. Showcasing how the writer resolves to forgo the comfort of his bourgeois home and to risk life and limb for a greater cause also provides viewers with a conversion story that invites admiration and emulation. After Pearl Harbor and the U.S. entry into the war, the political conversion story would become a standard plot structure—most famously in *Casablanca*—but in 1937 this was still daring. If until now the focus has been on Zola the writer, the film now shifts to his role as public figure and orator. It is precisely at this point that Cézanne's function as Zola's moral compass and catalyst for change becomes improbable. For even though the painter is repeatedly portrayed as a defender of truth—first in the opening sequence that shows the two starving bohemians arguing about art in a drafty Paris attic, and then again when Cézanne decides to move to the Provence region so as not to be corrupted by the riches of city life—his commitment to truth remains very much a commitment to *truth in art*. Indeed, Cézanne is never shown as the daring public troublemaker and eloquent "mole" that the young Zola considers himself to be. Zola's conversion cannot be fully explained by the narrative itself; it must be seen in the larger political appeal the film intended. Clearly, Zola's turn from complacent bourgeois, who rubs his stomach and smokes his pipe, into a fierce and feared orator is foremost a response to events that were taking place offscreen at the time, making the film a warning call about the rise of Nazism in Germany and the imminent threat it posed for the rest of Europe and the United States.

It is this scene, then, that embodies perhaps better than any other the fundamental contradiction that informs the bio-picture—that the genre's claim to a higher truth can only be achieved by relying on fiction and that authenticity needs to be staged to be recognized as such. The pretrial encounter between Zola and Mme Dreyfus depicted here never took place; indeed, there is no evidence that they ever met or that she was instrumental in the efforts to clear her husband's name (within the family, this responsibility fell to Dreyfus's brother Mathieu, who has a tiny role in the film). Zola was never invited to join the Académie française, much as he may have hoped. Finally, the Paul Cézanne of history was not interested in political or social reform and would turn out to be an anti-Dreyfusard. But the scene *rings* true because of its careful placement as a turning point in the story, because the melodramatic plea of the suffering wife reignites Zola's fire, and because of the sense of realism created through the sets of Zola's home, its furnishings and décor, the costumes of the characters, and so forth.

The creative tension between authenticity and its staging also pervades the casting decision of the biographee. As Custen states, part of the biopic's appeal is to watch the life of a famous person presented on the screen by another famous person, the film star, thereby providing a double articulation of fame. There is, as Jean-Louis Comolli puts it, always a "body too much" in historical features—the body of the real historical figure, whom audiences know, and who may have already been subject to fictionalized portrayals, and the body of the actor who not only has to resemble the famous person but also must disappear into that portrayal in order to be believable as the fictionalization of his or her life.[25] Paul Muni's goal was to completely submerge himself into the historical figures he played. His portrayals of Pasteur, Zola, and Juarez did not offer variations of himself but rather their complete characterization.

This disappearance of the actor into his character was aided, of course, by the fact that none of these subjects meant much, if anything, to American audiences at the time. But Muni's achievement is also the result of his detailed preparation for the role and of his acting style, which he developed on the Yiddish stage in New York, where he learned to become totally absorbed in a role, meticulously emulating gestures, facial expressions, and personal tics of the biographee.[26]

Muni's range becomes particularly apparent when he plays off against Gale Sondergaard's Lucie Dreyfus. Her limited facial expressions and bodily

FIGURE 2.2A–C Paul Muni disappears into Benito Juarez, Louis Pasteur, and Emile Zola.

posture, often showing her head tilted to one side, and predominantly captured in soft-focus medium close-ups, express suffering and powerlessness vis-à-vis Muni's virility, wit, and agitation. Muni's acting style also comes into relief when compared to the Dr. Ehrlich or Julius Reuter of Edward G. Robinson; a far more versatile actor than Muni, Robinson maintains a distance from the role he embodies, carefully avoiding the kind of overacting of which Dieterle sometimes accused Muni.[27]

While Muni's goal was to achieve complete congruity between actor and role, from the perspective of the studio the goal was not quite so. Biopics were considered star vehicles and carefully constructed around the lead actor or actress (apart from Muni and Robinson, the Dieterle biopics also featured Bette Davis and Kay Francis). This thinking is evident in Ernst Lubitsch's reaction to writers Heinz Herald and Geza Herzceg. When they first approached him with their idea for a Zola film, the Paramount director replied, "I don't have an actor that can play this role, Blanke has Muni."[28] Producers were aware that audiences came to see the star, not a Zola or a Pasteur, about whom they knew next to nothing. Thus Hal Wallis gave clear instructions about Muni's makeup, so as to avoid complete obliteration of the actor. It is more important, Wallis wrote, "to retain the impression for the audience that Paul Muni is playing the part than . . . to reproduce Zola exactly and so disguise Muni as to lose the Muni personality."²⁹ The studio's investment in the bio-picture was precisely to cash in on "the body too much," to explore the play between historical figure and its embodiment by a more famous actor, ultimately augmenting the fame of the studio's property, its star. What is remarkable about the Dieterle films starring Muni is that although people came to see Muni, not Zola, Pasteur, or Juarez, they remembered the role, not the star. By *making* Zola real to his audiences, Muni became Zola.³⁰

The film's claim to realism also rests on its close affinity to the historical Émile Zola's investment in naturalism. With its emphasis on ordinary protagonists, historic detail, social milieu, and political commitment, much of Zola's own oeuvre corresponds to Warner Bros.' screen realism. As Leo Braudy has shown, this compatibility explains why Zola's novels and stories have been repeatedly adapted by Hollywood.³¹ The film's working title, "The Truth Is on the March," is not only the one Zola gave his collected interventions in the Dreyfus affair (published as *La vérité en marche* in 1901), but it captures *in nuce* Zola's vision of his own art (the slogan survives in the film on a poster adorned by a torch similar to the one held by the Statue of Liberty). Zola's penchant for mixing panoramic overviews with detailed descriptions corresponds to the biopic's narrative convention of contrasting efficient elliptical storytelling (when, for example, Zola's rapid rise to fame is visualized by an endless flow of book covers) with the precise study in character and situations described in the conversion scene. Equally important are Zola's mass scenes, which are a staple of most biopics (as they are of many Dieterle films, where they also reflect the influence of Max Reinhardt's stage).³² Zola's reliance on omniscient narrators provides the kind of invisible storytelling that marks classic Hollywood narratives, camera work, and editing; indeed, Hollywood would not begin to acknowledge the shock of modernism, with its emphasis on subjectivity, perspective, the lack of narrative closure, convoluted plotlines, and moral ambiguity until the advent of film noir, more than four decades after nineteenth-century realism and naturalism had run its course.³³

"HITLER + MUSSOLINI = NAPOLEON": TALES OF URGENCY

Dieterle biopics display an astonishing coherence regarding style, sets, feeling for the historical period, and, of course, narrative conventions. They all revolve around a non-American protagonist, always an extraordinary individual who overcomes obstacles through courage and determination, be it the disbelief or hostility of colleagues and peers; the hypocrisy of society; or, in more subdued tones, the bias against gender, race, or ethnicity. In the process the protagonist becomes a figure to be emulated in the search for truth, justice, and equality, at once larger than life and remarkably ordinary and mundane. The films are all set in the second half of the nineteenth century and invite comparison with the period of the American Civil War, also a critical juncture in history. Lincoln is repeatedly a direct or indirect point of reference because, these films imply, the protagonists depicted here were equally important for the future development of their respective nations as the famous American president was for his. The connection to Lincoln and the American Civil War is most strongly articulated in *Juarez*, which shows the embattled Mexican president as a close friend and ally of Lincoln, and in *A Dispatch from Reuter's*, where Paul Reuter saves his reputation by being the first to report the assassination of the president. However, the experience of war and its repercussions more generally are also fundamental to the plot of *The White Angel*, which chronicles Florence Nightingale's experience with wounded soldiers, and, of course, to that of *Zola*.[34]

As I noted earlier, all films in the cycle drew attention to the potential impact of current political events in Europe on the United States. As the series progressed, these allusions would become ever more explicit. While *Pasteur*, the first in the series, confines itself to creating sympathy for the noble cause of a selfless, upright foreign scientist, by the time *Juarez* is completed, references to Nazi Germany are hardly disguised at all. As screenwriter Wolfgang Reinhardt, the son of Max Reinhardt, explained to producer Henry Blanke, "every child needs to understand that Napoleon with his intervention in Mexico is none other than Hitler plus Mussolini with their adventure in Spain."[35] This is an overt allusion to the bombing of the Spanish town of Guernica by the German Legion Condor on April 26, 1937, which occurred during the shooting of the film. *The Life of Emile Zola* incorporates many unambiguous references to Nazi Germany, most of them coming on the heels of the conversion scene. Once Zola has published his famous "I Accuse," we see the burning of Zola's books, then of his and Dreyfus's effigy, and a scene in which Zola narrowly escapes a lynch mob. On the evening of his accidental death Zola shares with his wife (and the viewers) what will be his last admonition: "Thousands of children sleeping peacefully tonight under the roofs of Paris, Berlin, London, all the world. Doomed to die horribly on some titanic battlefield, unless it can be prevented—and it must be prevented!"

FIGURE 2.3A–B Obvious allusions to the American Statue of Liberty and Nazi book burnings.

In keeping with their message-driven narratives, Dieterle's biopics revolve around issues of communication; they are all about getting the word out—be it about the existence of bacteria or infectious diseases and their treatment, about unsanitary conditions in army hospitals, or about judicial scandals. Means of mass communication such as the newspaper and the wire, or posters plastered on the walls of public spaces, figure prominently in all of them; the Reuters film offers the most celebratory treatment of the democratic, egalitarian, and unambiguously positive effects of modern mass media. Dieterle's protagonists all speak the truth, and they speak it clearly. Doubling the efforts articulated on the level of the narrative, the biopics *themselves* spread information about protagonists who are successful at doing the same. Invariably, these films include a scene in which the great man (or woman), after being shunned by the establishment or the public at large, is vindicated in a public forum, often the occasion for an extended speech or monologue directly addressed to viewers. The Zola film is no exception, but the time and space it allows its protagonist by far exceeds that of the others—indeed, the nearly six-minute monologue that Paul Muni delivers at Zola's trial constituted the longest uninterrupted speech any actor had ever delivered to date on an American screen. Muni's monologue from the trial scene, as well as his reading of the entire "I Accuse" article, were even sold as audio recordings on gramophone records.

While the trial of Emile Zola was a historical reality and needed to be part of the film, it afforded Dieterle the opportunity to explore the natural affinity between the position of the jury at the trial and the audience in the movie theater. The trial scene thus allowed him to appeal to the audience's sense of justice by providing people with the illusion that they had the power to decide, that they were, in fact, "viewers with a job to do."[36] This position also heightened the outrage about the judge's conduct, as well as the verdict that found Zola guilty and Dreyfus's suffering unchanged.[37] Having been lured into a participatory role, viewers could not help but feel indignant and convinced of the need for retribution.

As Thomas Elsaesser has suggested, the inclusion of the impassioned speech (be it delivered in a trial situation, to a crowd, or to a group of journalists) should be seen as indicative of how Hollywood in the mid-1930s began to assume the position of mouthpiece of the nation. "Dieterle's films appear to typify a system of address inflected by the cinema's changing role as a forum of public debate within the context of fulfilling a specific ideological task: making good on Hollywood's claim to speak with a voice representing the whole nation thanks to its ability to create an imaginary consensus audience."[38] For this task Dieterle's non-American subjects proved especially suitable—they transcend issues of creed, class, or regionalism that would hamper any American figure and thus appear as impartial advocates of humanity at large.[39]

It is tempting to interpret the biopics' narratives as self-representations of Dieterle as the bourgeois artist struggling with the studio system. Both narratives emphasize how the hero struggles to retain his vision, invention, or humanitarian ideal against the social forces that threaten to appropriate it. Émile Zola, the public intellectual who draws attention to grievances and takes a stand for truth and justice, mirrors Dieterle's perception of himself defending his artistic freedom inside the studio system and in the fight against Nazi Germany.[40] Dieterle's friend Bertolt Brecht surely saw Dieterle's cycle as an allegory of the director's struggles in the studios. Just as each of the protagonists has to demonstrate courage and resolve to overcome obstacles, so the films themselves "constitute a brave act by Dieterle. Each of them is the result of never-ending struggles with the companies who made them and whose employee the director was."[41] Saverio Giovacchini has expanded that reading to include not only Dieterle and the exile community but also the New York intellectuals who were drawn to Hollywood in the 1930s: "Rather than a person's biography, these films [the biopics] resembled a collective hagiography of the Hollywood progressive."[42] But as Elsaesser has argued, this reading relies too much on anecdotal evidence; many of the virtues that these films celebrate stand in direct opposition to the division of labor on which the studio system was built. The great individuals depicted in these films "work either in isolation (writer, politician in exile) or under conditions of artisanal production (inventors, doctors, scientist) rather than as parts of a corporate hierarchized enterprise such as the studio system."[43] One might add that the altruistic and egalitarian credo of a Reuter, Ehrlich, or Pasteur represents the very opposite of the film industry's profit ethos.

Rather than allegories about the professionals who made them, the biopics are contested collaborations; they do not simply reflect individual experiences, nor do they bear the imprint of a single creator. But they are often eloquent about the struggles and efforts that went into their creation. One key concern of these struggles in *Zola* was the question, How Jewish is Dreyfus?

"I WONDER HOW HE EVER BECAME A MEMBER OF THE GENERAL STAFF": THE JEWISHNESS OF CAPTAIN DREYFUS

The Life of Emile Zola has often been discussed during the last two decades in the context of Hollywood's representation of the Jew prior to and during World War II. Repeatedly, commentators have taken the film to task for being too timid in its portrayal of anti-Semitism. In *Hollywood's Image of the Jew* Lester Friedman writes, "Warner Brothers produced a universally-acclaimed film about the famous Dreyfus case that failed to emphasize why he was singled out, how he could be so unjustly accused, and why people were so willing to believe him guilty."[44] Similarly, Colin Shindler argues that the film "renounces the right to make an effective statement on current anti-Semitism in Nazi Germany."[45] Warner Bros., claims Patricia Erens, altogether evaded the anti-Semitic sentiments that motivated the case.[46]

The representation of Jews in the 1930s and 1940s by Hollywood was shaped by contradictory positions within the studios, the Production Code Administration (PCA), and progressive forces within the industry. By and large, the studios avoided overt references to Jewish identity or to any particular ethnic identity, highlighting instead the universal aspects of individual identity. Even those Warner Bros. biopics that feature famous Jewish protagonists, such as *Disraeli* (1929) and *The House of Rothschild* (1934), provide narratives of assimilation that promote universal values. (George Arliss, the star of these films, relied on lots of makeup to convey important interior transformations, which Muni copied.) This is clearly also the strategy of the Zola film. The complete absence of the word *Jew* in the film was without question conspicuous. In his memoir Dieterle reports the difficulty of making the Zola film in a way that assumed a position against "Hitlers Rassenwahn" (Hitler's racist mania) while being careful not to offend the many American Nazi sympathizers who might have boycotted the film.[47] The so-called German American Bund, founded in 1936, was particularly active in Los Angeles, creating a miniature Third Reich, with youth organizations for boys and girls, managing a bookstore that specialized in anti-Semitic literature, and hosting a "German Day" at the Hindenburg park to celebrate "Deutschtum." Part of the compromise Dieterle agreed on with the studio was that the word *Jew* could only be used three times.[48] As the documents in the Warner Bros. Archives at USC show, the complete removal of the word from the final script was sanctioned by Jack Warner himself. This was in part a concession to the pressure exerted by Joseph Breen, head

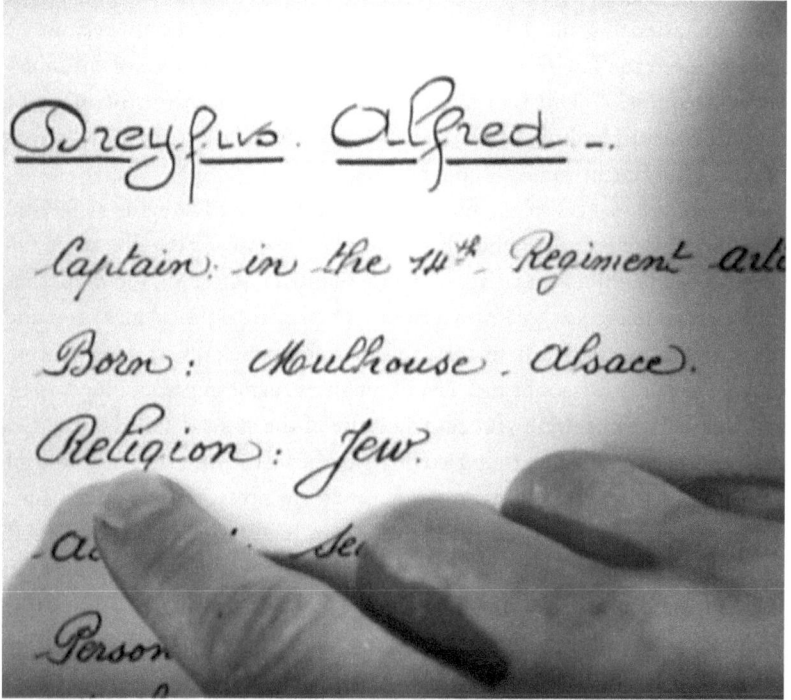

FIGURE 2.4 The finger on the ledger—the only brief reference to Dreyfus's Jewishness.

of the Production Code Administration, to remove all overt signs of Dreyfus's Jewishness; it was also in accordance with the studio's reluctance to present the battle against Hitler as primarily a Jewish affair, a sentiment that was widely shared by other Hollywood moguls before Germany's invasion of Poland.[49] In its stead a shot was inserted showing the ledger of the military personnel with Dreyfus's name and "Religion: Jew," while one of the commander's voices is heard commenting: "I wonder how he ever became a member of the general staff." It remains unclear who decided to include this shot, which is not part of the script, and whether Joseph Breen's office knew of it.

Members of the exile community also thought it wrong to overemphasize the Jewish suffering under Hitler, even if for different reasons. Two years into the war, Klaus Mann wrote: "Nothing could be more fallacious than to present the Nazi ordeal as an unpleasant experience exclusively for the Jews. Hitler's heinous anti-Semitism has already played too predominant a part in our propaganda. I have always considered it a dangerous mistake to overemphasize this one particular angle. Hitler is evil, not only because he has outlawed the Jewish race: he persecuted the Jews because of his inherent wickedness."[50] This sentiment is also found in the works of many of the more overtly political exile writers—Jewish and non-Jewish—such as Brecht, Lion Feuchtwanger, and Anna Seghers.

Clearly, the makers of the film did not want to mark Dreyfus as Jewish. The question remains whether this had to be the case for the film to be understood as an intervention against anti-Semitism. After all, the numerous thinly veiled references to Nazi Germany's repressive political measures and mass hysteria were clearly understood as such by the public, as contemporary reviews readily confirm.[51] The filmmakers furthermore assumed a certain knowledge of the Dreyfus case, because of the many detailed obituaries that had been published only two years earlier. Studying the reception of various Jewish-themed films in the mainstream press, the American Jewish press, and statements issued by American Jewish organizations, Felicia Herman has shown that contemporary audiences by and large commended *Zola* for its courage and timeliness, and Jewish organizations and Jewish audiences, in particular, agreed that "the film struck just the right note of protest, asserting its anti-antisemitism subtly and skillfully."[52]

Jewishness also enters by virtue of the fact that Jews (and emigrants) played versions of their own lives. As Jews, Muni and Schildkraut were banned from the German screen, as was Vladimir Sokoloff, who portrayed Cézanne, which made the fact that they were cast in a major Hollywood production a triumph over adversity. While it is true that Muni never got to play a Jewish role in Hollywood, contemporary audiences were aware that he was of Jewish origin, since he first became famous at the New York Yiddish Theater.[53] Schildkraut, too, was primarily known from the stage; on Broadway he excelled in roles that gained him the moniker "European Valentino," suggesting a foreignness that built on Schildkraut's many representations of Europeans in supporting roles.[54]

In downplaying the Jewish aspect, Warner Bros. simply followed the main sources of the screenplay. In his widely read book *Zola and His Time* (1928), for which he would receive screen credit only after threatening a lawsuit, Matthew Josephson claimed that at an early stage of the struggle, the Dreyfus Affair "ceased to be only a Jewish question and became a more or less bloodless civil war between two implacable forces in French life."[55] Much of the literature on Dreyfus from this period agrees that while the initial scapegoating of Dreyfus is a clear act of anti-Semitism, the reluctance on the part of the military and the government to admit wrongdoing was fueled as much by chauvinism and exaggerated nationalism that came in the week of France's defeat by Germany in 1871, making the case of Dreyfus a symbol for widespread French political and social problems.

A similar interpretation informs German representations of the Dreyfus case from the late 1920s. During this period, before Hitler actually claimed governance over the country, the fight against National Socialism first began. In a climate of extreme political polarization and volatility German writers and artists interpreted the Dreyfus case as an object lesson about what can happen if reactionary forces win the day, and they turned it into the subject matter of a play, a source book, and a film, all of which received widespread public attention that the German professionals involved in the Warner Bros. film had experienced firsthand in Berlin. For the making of *The Life of Emile Zola*, these sources were reexamined and became a major influence for the screenplay.

Certainly the most important of these sources was the play *Die Affäre Dreyfus*, by Hans José Rehfisch and Wilhelm Herzog, which premiered in Berlin in June 1930. The play, like Dieterle's film, gives ample room to the trial against Zola but situates the conflict between loyalty, truth, and honor within the military elite. While it makes open references to Dreyfus's Jewishness (both authors were also Jewish and had to flee Germany after Hitler's rise to power), it is treated less with reference to ethnicity or religion than through its association with money, blaming greed, rather than race, as the prejudice on which anti-Semitism thrives. This is in line with the play's strong emphasis on class issues and its depiction of the military establishment as an aristocratic elite out of touch with the democratic principles of a modern society. Zola, who is given much less room than in Dieterle's film, comes across here as a revolutionary rather than the humanist that Dieterle paints.

Like Dieterle's film, the play uses events in France to showcase what the authors perceived as the strongest political threats in contemporary Germany: the increasing disunity in the working class, the rise of militarism, the disregard for human rights, and the possibility of a military coup. In this regard the play proved as timely and prophetic as Dieterle's warnings about Nazi Germany some seven years later. In the film Dieterle even pays subtle homage to the by then largely forgotten work by including a shot of the painting of the crucified Jesus adorning the courtroom, which in *Die Affäre Dreyfus* is accompanied by the line "Dear Gentlemen, haven't you heard of a sanctioned miscarriage of justice which for nearly two thousand years has been the disgrace of mankind?"[56]

Only two months after the premiere of Rehfisch and Herzog's play, Richard Oswald's film *Dreyfus* was released.[57] It starred Fritz Kortner as Dreyfus, Albert Bassermann as Oberst Picquard, Oskar Homolka as Major Walsin-Estherhazy, and Heinrich George as Zola; while the latter would expand his Weimar fame under Goebbels, all others soon had to emigrate and would eventually end up in Los Angeles. The film relied on new evidence in the case presented in Bruno Weil's widely read book *Der Prozess des Hauptmanns Dreyfus* (also 1930, and published in France the same year), which illuminated the role of the German military attaché in the affair.[58] Calling his film a "reportage," Oswald's work chronicles the events in the case as a suspense story observed by an invisible third party. Like the play, the film makes it clear that Dreyfus is Jewish; nonetheless, his persecution is seen as part of a larger assault on civil rights, of which ethnic minorities were not the sole targets. Particular emphasis is paid to street violence, primarily caused by a mob of patriotic but ignorant youths whose aggression comes across as confused rather than malicious. Oswald's Zola is a fatherly figure who takes it upon himself to redirect these lost souls. In one scene he confronts a mob with the words "Come to your senses, you young people!"[59] This gesture is indicative of how the fight over youth became central in the struggle between ideologies of the left and the right. Heinrich George's portly Zola, played with a theatricality similar to Muni's but more aligned with the working class than the bourgeoisie, is emblematic of the film's plea that public figures of courage and moral integrity need to come forward and serve as role models for political action. An early sound film, *Dreyfus* indulges in the opportunity to let characters speak, but because of the technical limitations of the new technology, the film looks stagey and lacks the fluidity and visual elegance that had characterized the late Weimar silent film.

Dieterle's *Zola* borrows several important plot elements and editing devices from Oswald's popular film, including Mme Dreyfus's visit with the writer (here accompanied by her brother-in-law Matthieu) and frequent crosscutting between Paris and Devil's Island. In *Dreyfus* we also find the shot of the painting of Jesus in the courtroom, through which Oswald, like Dieterle after him, acknowledges the significance of Rehfisch and Herzog's play.[60] When Dieterle's Zola alludes to the infamous legend of stabbing the military in the back, the so-called Dolchstoßlegende, which was created by the German military to blame communist and progressive forces for the defeat in World War I and was subsequently exploited by the Nazis, we witness an overt attempt to appropriate Zola for the Weimar left as a figure who fights the impending fascist takeover.[61]

LIFE AFTER ZOLA

William Dieterle's cycle of screen biographies was intended to infuse a popular genre with a topical urgency to both educate and entertain viewers. In this endeavor Dieterle drew on the theater and cinema of the Weimar Republic, which makes sense, given the period's widespread politicization of art.[62] Contemporary American critics enthusiastically applauded the new look of the genre and praised Warner Bros. In doing so, they contradicted Joseph Breen's concerns, expressed in a personal note to Jack Warner, that scenes such as the burnings of books or the mock lynching of Zola and Dreyfus "may leave your picture open to the accusation that it is propaganda and, as such, unworthy of serious notice."[63] Precisely those scenes caused the public to take notice.

Outside of the United States, people also took notice. Jack Warner states in his autobiography that Dieterle approached him with the news that "Mussolini wants you [i.e., Warner] to make a picture on the life of Michelangelo."[64] Nothing came of the idea, but Joseph Goebbels, always a keen observer of the American film industry, began promoting Nazi Germany's version of the biopic, the so-called genius film, which flourished in the early 1940s. Following Warner Bros.' recipe of using historical role models for contemporary object lessons, these films focus on artists, musicians, scientists, and great politicians (almost all of them German) whose achievements and struggles are shown to be part of the Third Reich's greatness. Yet while these films have been read as projections of the *Führer* cult, they also foreground failure, disappointment, humiliation, strained relations to authority, and a constant undermining of established power, as Eric Rentschler has observed. Any antiauthoritarian or incendiary potential is always channeled against illegitimate powers, making acts of rebellion part of a larger cause that justifies such behavior.[65]

Hans Steinhoff's *Robert Koch, der Bekämpfer des Todes* (1939) is a case in point. Incorporating many of the genre conventions established by Dieterle, the film highlights the German country doctor's struggle against the medical establishment, much like the *Pasteur* film, even including repeated positive allusions to the French scientist. Like Dieterle, Steinhoff sends a clear message that scientific success requires strong moral conviction, belief in oneself, and self-reliance. By emphasizing that ignorant bureaucracy rather than racial prejudice governs the Berlin establishment, the film provides a strong ideological corrective to *Dr. Ehrlich's Magic Bullet* (then in production, with exile Albert Bassermann in the role of Koch), which would call German anti-Semitism by its name. When we become witness to Koch's final triumph, we understand not only that he is a rebel with a cause but also that the virtues he extols—most importantly, the willingness to sacrifice one's (family) life for the greater good—will be of utmost importance for Germany's future political ambitions.[66]

While the German film industry was eager to copy Dieterle's genre formula, he was no longer welcome in the Reich, as he learned shortly after the premiere of *Zola*.[67] Closer to home, Dieterle's overtly liberal politics also began to have serious consequences, leading to a gray-listing that ultimately led him to return to Germany. The paradox of Dieterle's Americanization, which sets him apart from many exile directors, is that he was always a faithful devotee and defender of the Hollywood studio system, with its hierarchical and specialized mode of production, and that the self-conscious stylization into a "European director" did not occur until he had completed an American apprenticeship.[68] Then, suddenly, much was made of the fact that Dieterle wore white gloves on the set—giving him the same aristocratic look that Fritz Lang's monocle and Billy Wilder's riding crop would accomplish—when in fact the habit was a conscious reminder of his humble beginnings when, as Weimar director, he also had to move the sets around. Dieterle is also exceptional insofar as he is the only Hollywood filmmaker whose reputation is built exclusively on the screen biography, gaining him the moniker "the Plutarch of Hollywood" and suggesting an affinity to the literary émigrés and exiles that few other film professionals shared (with important exceptions being Fritz Lang's collaboration with Brecht and his friendship with Adorno, and Kracauer's connection to cinematographer Eugen Schüfftan).[69] Not just in his biopics but in his work as a whole, Dieterle had to rely on good scripts. His rather conventional direction ably adopted materials for the screen but rarely granted them the visual brilliance of a Lang or Lubitsch. When he was belatedly recognized in his native Germany, it was above all for his ethics and his humanity.[70] While Jean-Luc Godard immortalized Fritz Lang in *Le mépris* (1963), a biopic on William Dieterle remains a most unlikely prospect.

POSTSCRIPT

When Siegfried Kracauer first published his study of Jacques Offenbach, his longtime companions Theodor W. Adorno and Walter Benjamin severely criticized the book. In their correspondence Benjamin expressed his dismay regarding Kracauer's shift of perspective regarding the genre of biography, while Adorno took Kracauer to task for what he perceived as crass commercialism: "It is so completely bad that it may easily become a bestseller."[71] Adorno, who would later live in the same American city as Dieterle, never commented on the biopic cycle, but it is safe to assume that his criticism of Dieterle's films would have been even harsher than that of Kracauer's volume. For Adorno and Max Horkheimer, Adorno's longtime friend and coauthor of *The Dialectics of Enlightenment*, political resistance was inextricably tied to aesthetic resistance, favoring a form of modernism that insisted on the separation of art and reality. Art for them was the negation of the negativity of reality—a negation through which the work of art preserved its autonomy and claim to truth. Adorno and Horkheimer saw the culture industry as a form of mass deceit that threatens this autonomy by forging a false reconciliation between art and reality. Nevertheless, in 1948 Horkheimer wrote to Fritz Lang to propose a film project. His idea was a biopic on the English lawyer, author, and statesman Thomas More (eventually made by Fred Zinnemann as *A Man for All Seasons* but without any connection to Horkheimer). We do not know if Dieterle was part of that sales pitch. If he was, he may well have had the last laugh about the lessons of exile.[72]

Part Two

◇ ◇ ◇

HITLER IN HOLLYWOOD

Three
PERFORMING RESISTANCE, RESISTING PERFORMANCE

> Whoever looks Hitlers [Hitlern] in the face must be reminded of Charlie Chaplin.
> —RUDOLF ARNHEIM[1]

FIGHTING NAZISM BEFORE PEARL HARBOR

William Dieterle's biopics demonstrate (and one could also add his anti-Franco film *Blockade* [1938]) that by the late 1930s Hollywood's exile and émigré community had begun to wage a battle against fascism in Germany and elsewhere in Europe through feature films that were unambiguous about their political implications but nevertheless reached large audiences, an accomplishment that many veteran Hollywood producers had long believed to be impossible (and in some cases undesirable). In this effort the exiles were supported by the determination and courage of Warner Bros., as well as a significant number of liberal and left-wing film professionals who had settled in Los Angeles during the 1930s, many of them accomplished writers, journalists, and intellectuals who had relocated there from New York.[2] High-profile filmmakers and intellectuals, among them Fritz Lang, had formed the Hollywood Anti-Nazi League in 1936, at the instigation of Prince Hubertus zu Loewenstein, the exiled leader of the German Center Party; Willi Münzenberg, a Swiss-German communist; and his American representative, Otto Katz.[3] An important part of the larger Popular Front movement, which was committed to defend American democracy against fascist aggression and to press the Roosevelt administration into taking the Nazi threat seriously, the League intended to draw on the star power of Hollywood celebrities and the instrumental role of film to mobilize public opinion. The League's long list of sponsors read like a who's who of Hollywood, including moguls like Carl Laemmle and Dore Schary, stars like Eddie Cantor and Gale Sondergaard (of *Zola* fame), and of course the majority of exiled film professionals. Alongside the stars, who represented a broad spectrum of political persuasions, an army of volunteers was busy organizing public lectures, sending around petitions, or taking out adds in newspapers; one memorable event at the Los Angeles Shrine Auditorium drew an audience of ten thousand.[4] Lubitsch left the League in 1938 (as did producer Walter Wanger), fearing that it was being infiltrated by communists. The 1939 Hitler-Stalin pact effectively ended the activities of the League.[5] Many of its most vocal members would later become victims of blacklisting, including Donald Ogden Stewart, Melvyn Douglas, Hy Kraft, and Herbert Biberman.

A related institution was the European Film Fund, which was established to facilitate the emigration of exiled writers and filmmakers, and their subsequent financial support in the United States. The organization was managed by Paul Kohner, the most important agent for exile filmmakers, who at a gathering at Salka Viertel's house convinced Ernst Lubitsch to head the organization. While Charlotte Dieterle and Lisl Frank did most of the behind-the-scenes work, Kohner was able to persuade studio heads such as Louis B. Mayer and Harry Warner to supply exiled writers with one-year contracts that secured their immigration visas and provided minimal funds for survival after their arrival. Of the many authors who garnered employment this way (e.g., Heinrich Mann, Alfred Döblin, Alfred Polgar, Walter Mehring, and Leonard Frank), only Hans Lustig managed to find more permanent work in the studios. The majority resented that their writing was routinely ignored by the higher-ups, yet their paychecks depended on their daily presence on the studio lot. Nevertheless, the European Film Fund was a highly successful institution that outlasted World War II.[6]

The news from Europe confirmed that there were concrete reasons for these measures. In March of 1938 Nazi Germany executed the so-called *Anschluss* of Austria (which led Warner Bros. to shut down its operations in Vienna), and Madrid surrendered to Franco; in April Mussolini attacked Albania; in September Czechoslovakia ceded the so-called Sudetenland to Germany in an effort to appease Hitler, only to be invaded the following March. Contested by the League, a November 1938 visit by filmmaker Leni

Riefenstahl to the United States galvanized Hollywood filmmakers into public boycotts and protests. During Riefenstahl's stay, the Nazis staged the *Reichskristallnacht*, a large-scale pogrom against the German Jews in which synagogues were burnt and Jewish-owned shops were vandalized. Less than a year later, on September 1, 1939, the Nazis invaded Poland, thus causing the onset of World War II. Only four days later, FDR promised that the United States would remain neutral. Ten days after FDR's proclamation, the Hays Office followed suit and banned all production of anti-Nazi films. Until the attack on Pearl Harbor in 1941, American isolationism would remain the official policy of the administration, an approach strongly supported by large parts of the population, as well as the Hollywood studios.

Given these severe restrictions by forces outside the film industry, which only augmented the Production Code's stipulation that "the history, institutions, prominent people and citizenry of other nations shall be represented fairly," it is remarkable that a handful of films that were explicit about the threat emanating from fascist countries reached U.S. theaters at all.[7] Chief among them was the Warner Bros. film *Confessions of a Nazi Spy*, directed by the Russian-German exile Anatole Litvak and cowritten by John Wexley (who would go on to collaborate with Brecht on the script of Fritz Lang's *Hangmen Also Die*). Released in April of 1939, and thus several months before the Hays Office directive cited above, the film was an explicit attack on Nazi Germany, showcasing how a Nazi spy ring operating in New York was preparing an all-out attack on the United States. By dramatizing how the Nazi menace infiltrated the homeland, the film forcefully connected U.S. everyday life with events in faraway Europe. Based on a true story by FBI agent Leon G. Turrou, first serialized in the *New York Post* in 1939 and subsequently turned into a best seller, the film allowed Warner Bros. to cash in on the considerable controversy Turrou's book had caused and provoked a serious (and calculated) outrage from the German government.[8] As in the many anti-Nazi films produced after Pearl Harbor, exile and émigré actors were able to secure jobs in both leading and supporting roles and as numerous extras, even though many of them chose not to have their real names appear in the credits in order to protect relatives in Germany from possible retaliation.

Yet even more than in Dieterle's *Zola*, the question of Jewish victimhood was downplayed in Litvak's film, and the actions of the Bund were portrayed as targeted against political rather than racial or ethnic entities. As files in the Warner Bros. Archives at USC demonstrate, John Wexley's revisions of the script deleted overt references to anti-Semitism, a strategy that was in keeping with studio policies, though not with the intentions of star Edward G. Robinson, who vehemently objected. Wexley's alterations also reflect the opinion of a majority of exiles, who at this time thought of Hitler's racial hatred as the by-product, rather than the driving force, of his imperial aspirations. It was Charlie Chaplin's *The Great Dictator* (United Artists, 1941) that would provide the first explicit reference to the fate of the Jews under Hitler. More daring still, the film did so in the form of a comedy, changing the point of attack from an ideology critique that came from the outside to one that sought to undermine Nazism from within. Chaplin's risqué use of humor made it an important precursor to Ernst Lubitsch's even more daring *To Be or Not to Be*. It was precisely both films' dark and outrageous use of laughter that generated much controversy at the time.

Chaplin's film premiered in October of 1940, a time when isolationist sentiments remained strong so that the film "could be laughed at with disinterested appreciation."[9] This policy ended with the attack on Pearl Harbor on December 7, 1941, and Hitler's subsequent declaration of war against the United States. Pearl Harbor occurred about midway through the production of *To Be or Not to Be*, the principal photography of which began on November 6, 1941, and wrapped on December 23. While the U.S. entry into the war did not occasion any substantial changes to the script (indeed, it confirmed the filmmaker's prophetic depiction of Nazi aggression), it had a negative influence on the film's reception, for the American public seemed unwilling to laugh about a political threat it suddenly needed to take seriously.

To Be or Not to Be pursues a double strategy. On the one hand, it is quite explicit about America's—and in particular the film industry's—role in the destruction of the European Jews and therefore takes its viewers to task for what Lubitsch perceives to be sins of omission. Yet paired with this self-critique, which also entails a profound skepticism about Hollywood's willingness to tackle taboo subjects and participate in any enlightening or emancipating political process, the film also advocates self-empowerment. By debunking the performative dimension of Nazism, it provides viewers with a blueprint to undo Nazi might.

EXILE AND PERFORMATIVITY

The case of Ernst Lubitsch is particularly interesting for the discussion of exile filmmaking. Lubitsch left Germany in 1922, the first of many high-profile film directors, producers, cinematographers, and stars lured by the opportunities of a Hollywood career long before the advent of fascism. Yet as for many other German Jews, Hitler's rise to power made a return to Germany impossible. Because of the ways in which he had flaunted his Jewishness in his early films, Lubitsch was despised by Hitler and stripped of his German citizenship in 1935. In Berlin train stations a poster of Lubitsch could be seen with the caption, "The Archetypal Jew"; he (like Peter Lorre) was specifically targeted in Fritz Hippler's 1940 hate film *Der ewige Jude / The Eternal Jew*.[10] If Hitler considered Lubitsch to be un-German, for Americans in 1922, when anti-German sentiments were still flying high, Lubitsch was too German, and he was asked to camouflage his Germanness, which he refused to do.[11] Yet thereafter Lubitsch ceased to be closely associated with his home country.[12] The most European and un-Teutonic of German émigrés, and the most "closely attuned to a Hollywood style and mentality, even before he set foot in the United States,"[13] his forte became sexual comedies that took place in "Lubitschland"—a highly stylized version of Paris, Vienna, "Sylvania," or some other Balkan monarchy that sometimes needed to be located on the map with a magnifying glass. Lubitsch, like Max Ophüls, became an expert for revisiting times and places that for Americans connoted "The Old World" but had little to do with his native Berlin. The creation of such simulacra became a trademark for many exiles whose success depended specifically on their ability to provide representations of Europe that were in synch with the contemporary American imagination, while at the same time bestowing these representations with the stamp of being "made by an exile."[14]

This logic of staged authenticity, of meeting the demand for the "real thing" while shaping it according to the tastes of the time and place in which it is to be consumed, lies at the heart of exile cinema. *To Be or Not to Be* essentializes exile cinema; it centers on the performance of reality and all that attends such a performance: mimicry and masquerade, cultural camouflage, mistaken identity, impersonation, travesty, cross-dressing, and ethnic drag. While the film is ostensibly about a temporal crisis—a world unhinged by the Nazi invasion of Poland—its mode of address is shaped by a spatial crisis. The challenge for the Hollywood exiles was to communicate to the people of the United States the dimensions of the crisis in central Europe; but what is more, *To Be or Not to Be* also conveyed how the reality of that crisis was shaped, and misshapen, by Hollywood's politics of representation.

HITLER IN WARSAW

The first shots of *To Be or Not to Be* fix, in rapid succession, on the names above shops, which a voice-over reads: "Lubinski, Kubinski, Lominiski, Lozanski & Poznanski," commenting, "We are in Warsaw, the capital of Poland. It's August 1939. Europe is still at peace. At the moment life in Warsaw is going on as normally as ever." The initial disorientation catalyzed by four close-ups of foreign names is quickly overcome by an omniscient narrator, who provides the viewer with a concrete sense of time and place, thereby initiating a pattern of confusion and resolution—or seeming resolution—that will prevail throughout the film. Indeed, the peacefulness is immediately disrupted as the camera shows us the stunned faces of Poles while the narrator exclaims in a staccato voice:

> But suddenly something seems to have happened. Are those Poles seeing a ghost? Why does this car suddenly stop? Everybody seems to be staring in one direction. People seem to be frightened, even terrified, some flabbergasted. Can it be true? It must be true, no doubt! The man with the little mustache—Adolf Hitler! Adolf Hitler in Warsaw when the two countries are still at peace? And all by himself? He seems strangely unconcerned by all the excitement he is causing. Is he by any chance interested in Mr. Maslowski's delicatessen? That's impossible—he's a vegetarian! And yet—he doesn't always stick to his diet. Sometimes he swallows whole countries. Does he want to eat up Poland too?

The hyperbole in the voice of the narrator, the exaggeration in the face of the Polish bystanders, and the humorous comment about Hitler's appetite mark the film as a comedy, as does the reference to Hitler as the man with the little mustache, an obvious allusion to Chaplin. By the time the narrator raises his voice again and asks, "Anyhow—how did he get here? What happened?" we feel that the question is more about how Hitler got into the film than into Poland. The film will reveal that these two questions are indeed closely related. The opening scene ends with the narrator once more proclaiming to resolve a mystery by providing information: "Well, it all started in the general headquarters of the Gestapo in Berlin . . . "

The following scene provides an explanation of "Hitler's" presence in Poland, but again by first fooling the viewer. In the Gestapo headquarters, officers are interrogating a Hitler Youth about his father's criticism of Hitler. Only when Hitler (Tom Dugan) enters the scene and answers the "Heil

FIGURE 3.1 The very first shot of Lubitsch's film shows the name Lubiński.

Hitler" salutes of his many subordinates by responding "Heil myself!" does theater director Dobosh (Charles Halton) intervene. We realize that we are, in fact, on the stage of the Teatr Polski, where a troupe of actors is rehearsing the play *Gestapo*. The first five minutes of the film thus efficiently establish the tension between illusion and reality that will be explored in ever more dazzling and complex ways throughout the film. Time and again the viewer will be caught off guard by events that look staged and phony but are indeed real and by what appears real or normal but is in fact staged.

The plot of *To Be or Not to Be*, after a screenplay by Edwin Justus Mayer and an original story by Ernst Lubitsch and Melchior Lengyel, features a continual reversal of roles, costumes, and situations that force its protagonist, Joseph Tura (Jack Benny), to impersonate in quick succession numerous characters. As François Truffaut famously quipped, "An hour later, or even if you've just seen it for the sixth time, I defy you to tell me the plot of *To Be or Not to Be*. It's absolutely impossible."[15] Be that as it may, a rudimentary plot summary goes as follows: soon after the scene of the rehearsal (discussed above), the Germans invade Poland and all theaters are closed. A few months later, in England, Professor Siletsky (Stanley Ridges), a double agent for the Nazis, coaxes the exiled Polish flyers in the RAF into sending messages through him to relatives in Poland, hoping to eliminate the Polish underground. Lt. Sobinski (Robert Stack) becomes suspicious of Siletsky when Siletsky fails to recognize the recipient of his message (which reads "To Be or Not to Be"), the famous Polish actress Maria Tura (Carole Lombard). Sobinski parachutes into Poland to warn the Polish underground. When Maria is summoned by Professor Siletsky to receive her message, she overhears him making arrangements to deliver his information to Colonel Ehrhardt (Sig Ruman), a Nazi officer. Immediately, Joseph Tura, in his garb from *Gestapo*, poses as Ehrhardt and meets Siletsky to intercept the information. The ruse seems successful, but when Tura becomes overly jealous about the message to his wife, Siletsky gets suspicious and escapes into the theater, where he is shot onstage. Now Tura has to play Siletsky for his meeting with Ehrhardt. After the Nazis discover the body of Siletsky, Tura/Siletsky is called in again for questioning. Tura has just convinced Ehrhardt that the real professor was a fake when the theater group, in Nazi garb, arrives to show that Tura/Siletsky is an impersonator after all, and they take him into custody. When the real Hitler arrives in Warsaw, the troupe sees its chance to escape Poland. While Hitler attends the opera, they stage an incident in which a phony Hitler (played by Bronski) and his entourage leave the opera in outrage, only to board the real Hitler's plane to escape to England.

As this summary shows, viewers will not only be confused by the narrative's many surprising turns but will also come out of the film skeptical about the possibility of distinguishing between the staged and the authentic.[16] In no small measure the sense of disorientation is also the result of Rudolph Maté's cinematography. Throughout the film his camera will juxtapose and superimpose spaces that connote radical differences—for example, safety vs. danger; intimacy and privacy vs. public and publicity; sites of theatrical performance vs. sites of the performance of the real. Such spatial discontinuity underscores the sense of historical crisis that propels the story. The camera thus captures that what is at stake is not just times out of joint—as Hamlet will tell us—but also space out of joint.

In a film titled after the most famous line from Shakespeare's most famous play, we should not be surprised to see the playwright's belief that the whole world is a stage put to the test. The film introduces us to a world where the stakes to perform one's part right have never been higher. When Hitler appears, the curtains—in this case the blinds of the delicatessen—will go down for someone. As stated, one of the film's central aesthetic strategies is a confusion and collusion of performance and reality. This strategy arises partly from the fact that the players in the theater group constantly seem to be onstage, ever willing to put on a performance even at the most inappropriate and dangerous moment. This behavior is most blatant in Joseph Tura, who appears in the roles of Hamlet, a German officer in the play *Gestapo*, Colonel Ehrhardt when trying to outsmart Siletsky, Siletsky in a confrontation with Ehrhardt, and once again as a Nazi officer when fooling the Germans so that he might escape to England. Even when not in costume, he is constantly posing, assuming dramatic stances, and exaggerating, yet his and the other actors' great difficulty to separate their onstage and offstage persona repeatedly threatens the credibility of their performance, most notably when Tura's vanity and jealousy reveal his true identity to the real Siletsky.

Most critics have agreed that the film celebrates masquerade and impersonation as powerful strategies for defying the Nazis; conducted in the right context, a theatrical performance has the power to decide over life and death, over being or not being. Seen in this light, the film offers a strong endorsement of humanism and individual courage that is often found in wartime Hollywood features. Yet this upbeat aspect is only the more obvious strategy in which *To Be or Not to Be* shows performance and politics to be linked. To that end the film accentuates the concrete historical conditions under which such performativity needs to be considered, thereby not only enacting but also raising the Shakespearean notion of the world as a stage to a higher power. *To Be or Not to Be* discloses the political implications not only of a theater that, under duress, has to become worldly, as well as the performativity of its occupying force. This involves highlighting the specific role performativity had in Nazi Germany, while also alerting viewers to the kind of performances that could *not* be represented on the screen in wartime Hollywood.

As the German exiles knew well, the might of Nazi dictatorship rested on its ability for making power visible. The Nazi Party's many forms of self-representation included a variety of performances and spectacles, from military parades, torchlight marches, and large-scale political rallies to the use of radio and film as mass media. The Nazis infused the everyday with a sense of the extraordinary and the exciting. Fantasy production was particularly important to the mission of Joseph Goebbels's Ministry of Propaganda and Enlightenment, a ministry of illusion rather than a ministry of fear (as Fritz Lang would imply in his anti-Nazi film of that title from 1944). Goebbels insisted that it was the responsibility of the film industry not only to capture the splendors of Nazi rule onscreen but to stage them according

FIGURE 3.2A–B Chaplin's Hynkel imitates Hitler's oratory poses as photographed by Heinrich Hoffmann.

to the laws of cinematography. "Hitler's regime," Eric Rentschler has stated, "can be seen as a sustained cinematic event."[17] What was important to Goebbels, as he explained to the thousands of soldiers called away from the front to star as extras in the monumental *Kolberg* (1945), was how it all looked on film. The Nuremberg rallies, performed by the masses for the masses, became awe-inspiring only through the mass-medialization of Leni Riefenstahl's ingenious cinematography and editing. Contrary to Riefenstahl's postwar claims that she merely pointed her camera at that which was in front of her, the 1934 rallies are a prime example of a spectacle organized and executed for and through film. The now famous composition from *Triumph of the Will* that shows Hitler from the back with the Germans looking up to him is quoted by Lubitsch in the opera scene, the only shot of the real Hitler in *To Be or Not to Be*.[18] The quote indicates that Lubitsch, like many exiles, was very familiar with Nazi propaganda; more important, the shot suggests that when you want to show the real Hitler, you have to do it the way he has been immortalized by Riefenstahl's film.

Adolf Hitler himself is, of course, the central figure of Nazi performance, not only in a symbolic sense in that all spectacles culminate by visually endorsing and enhancing the power and the glory of the Führer, and confirming the illusion of Nazism's omnipresence and pervasiveness. Before coming to power, Hitler had taken acting lessons, and he always carefully rehearsed poses for his speeches.[19] *The Great Dictator*, a feature meant to ridicule Hitler's demonic rhetorical skills, was in fact inspired by Chaplin's having seen Heinrich Hoffmann's photographs of Hitler striking oratory poses.

Quipping that Hitler had stolen his mustache, Chaplin felt authorized to parody somebody who he claimed had parodied his figure of the little tramp.[20] His Adenoid Hynkel was thus a copy of someone who had copied him, leading to a peculiar conversion of the two people who at the time commanded the highest name recognition in the world. As the opening sequence of *To Be or Not to Be* indicates, Lubitsch's comedy immediately exploits the double entendre of "the man with the little mustache," and throughout the film false beards will be used as significant props for a dramatic fusion of comedy and political tyranny.

In a world where everybody is a potential ham, the most successful performance appears so real that it goes unquestioned. According to this logic, the ultimate ham, the one who puts on the greatest act, is Hitler. However, only someone who has not entered the symbolic realm of Nazism will remain able to distinguish between the real Hitler and his impersonators—the Polish girl who asks for Bronski's autograph, and Dobosh, who feels that Bronski does not look like the Hitler in the portrait, even though that portrait was taken of Bronski in Hitler costume. Those who have been taught to obey the Führer by respecting his representations (his portrait, the Hitler salute, etc.) relinquish the ability to question the authenticity of representations.

The Nazi's penchant for pomp and spectacle includes a showmanship that resembles that of the actors. When the Nazis first invade Warsaw, the theaters are closed because, as one actor comments, "the Nazis themselves are putting on the show, only a much bigger one." Like Joseph Tura, Colonel Ehrhardt is eager to hear about his fame and repeatedly inquires, "So, they call me 'Concentration Camp Ehrhardt'?" Yet unlike the Polish professionals, these "actors" have no sense of their role playing; for them the insignia of Nazism, its uniforms, and the ubiquitous Hitler salute are not props but the embodiment of power, a confusion that is easily exploited by the professional Polish actors. Whenever an actor gets into serious trouble, a simple Hitler salute will trigger a Pavlovian response by the Nazis, and Bronski-as-Hitler can even command some Nazi pilots to eject from a plane without parachutes.

In a very concrete historical sense Lubitsch's film can be read as an ironic response to the so-called Gleiwitz incident, the charade that started World War II. On August 31, 1939, members of Hitler's SS, pretending to be Poles, "invaded" the small Silesian town of Gleiwitz, attacked the municipality, and captured the small radio station to broadcast an inflammatory anti-German message in Polish. To make the charade more convincing, a group of condemned criminals from the Sachsenhausen concentration camp, dressed in Polish uniforms, were given lethal injections, shot, and left behind as "casualties." The dead bodies were presented to reporters the next day, giving Hitler a fig leaf of respectability for invading Poland. Reinhard Heydrich, known for his penchant for high drama and quirky details, masterminded the operation. In his speech to the Reichstag the next day, Hitler stressed that his "love of peace" and "infinite patience" were now at an end: "As of 5:45 a.m. we are returning fire." Though the true nature of this incident was hardly known in the United States, it is likely that Lubitsch found out about it from Richard Ordynski. A Polish stage and film producer and journalist, Ordynski had witnessed the fall of Warsaw and supplied Lubitsch with detailed information about the theater life in the city during the occupation by the Wehrmacht and the subsequent moving in of the Gestapo.[21]

Lubitsch's version of the *teatrum mundi* encompasses not only the performances of the Teatr Polski that undermines the power of the Nazis in Poland; more importantly, it also demonstrates that Nazism in general relies on performance to exert its powers. This does not mean that we should understand Nazism as a role that people simply put on to express or disguise an interior self. It does not exist as an essentialist entity prior to its modes of reenactment. Rather, it means that the reality of Nazism is performative: it is real only to the extent that it is performed. It is the genius stroke of Lubitsch's film that this simple truth is brought to light only by the performance of the theater group.

THE ABSENT JEW

To Be or Not to Be insists on the performative dimension of reality. It also draws our attention to those realities that remain unperformed, revealing the political mechanisms that govern the construction of accepted representations. What is most striking in a film about the Nazi invasion of Poland

and the subsequent rule of the Gestapo is its failure to address the fate of the Eastern European Jews. Or, to be more precise, what is absent in Lubitsch's film is the word *Jew*. The film's political significance lies precisely in the ways in which this absence comes to be represented *as* an absence in the film. The film not only makes visible the (self-)censorship that dictated film production in wartime Hollywood; it explicitly draws attention to the real disappearance of the Jews in Europe. In this regard *To Be or Not To Be* marks a decisive move beyond *The Life of Emile Zola* and *Confessions of a Nazi Spy*. In both, the representation of the Jew fell victim to censorship by the studio heads and the Hays Office; Lubitsch's film, in contrast, renders visible the mechanisms that produce invisibility.

Here a short historical digression is in order. During the 1920s, Hollywood produced a plethora of films dealing with Jews, ghetto life, czarist oppression, and Jews in rural areas in Europe. After 1933 this ceased to be the case.[22] America's policy of noninterventionism caused a reinterpretation of the Production Code in which the Code's call for a fair representation of the "citizenry of other nations" led to an almost complete abstinence of critical judgment.[23] The Hollywood moguls, almost all of them first- or second-generation Jews from central Europe eager to assimilate, readily complied with a policy that forbade representing the fight against Hitler as primarily a Jewish concern.[24] As Lutz Koepnick has shown, this self-censorship did not change until the 1940s: "It took not only the beginning erosion of studio control and the influx of innovative talent around 1939, but also the outbreak of World War II in Europe and the final closing down of the important German export market in 1940 to convince Hollywood studio bosses to reinterpret the code and make European fascism an explicit theme in American narrative film."[25] When *To Be or Not to Be* was released, in March 1942, Jewish characters, with the important exception of Chaplin's barber in *The Great Dictator*, were a decided rarity in Hollywood films.

The film's only clearly marked Jewish character is Greenberg (Felix Bressart), introduced as such when he accuses a fellow actor of being a ham by saying, "What you are I wouldn't eat!"[26] That same scene also establishes Greenberg's main adversary, Adolf Hitler. Even though on a narrative level Greenberg comes to the defense of his friend Bronski—who, dressed up as Hitler, has just been reprimanded by Dobosh for the ad-lib "Heil Myself!"—on a visual level the film dramatizes the *conflict* between Hitler and the European Jew. As Joel Rosenberg has pointed out, Greenberg is seen sticking his "gloriously semitic nose . . . in Hitler's ear, causing Bronski's Hitler to awaken, turn his face towards Greenberg's, and lean back in a sort

FIGURE 3.3 Greenberg can smell Hitler in Bronski.

of goose-faced amazement."[27] Greenberg's insistence that he can "smell" Hitler in Bronski underscores in an ironic way the significance of his nose as both a weapon to detect fascism and a confirmation of the Nazi doctrine that physiognomy is a marker of race.

While Greenberg proudly asserts his Jewishness, many of the other members of the cast can be seen as assimilated Jews trying to camouflage their origins. This is particularly true for Joseph Tura, whose name recalls the Torah but who is not explicitly coded as Jewish in the film. Played by American radio star and comedian Jack Benny, the former Benny Kubelski, whose subtle Jewish humor was well known to contemporary viewers, the joke is that "we" know that Tura/Benny is Jewish but the Nazis do not.[28] Greenberg, in contrast, is played by the exile Felix Bressart, a German Jew from East Prussia whose successful career in Weimar comedies and parodies of the military was cut short with the Nazis, and whose modest profile in American films does not instill his character with the offscreen fame of a Jack Benny.[29] Though Greenberg is a proud Polish patriot, his unassimilated status renders him more vulnerable than other members of the cast. It is no

FIGURE 3.4 Greenberg is conspicuously absent from the rescued Teatr Polski troupe.

accident that he is not among those who manage to escape to safety at the end of the film. We see him last when he is escorted away from the theater, where he had caused a commotion and thus made possible the getaway of his friends, and the film deliberately leaves his whereabouts unresolved, thus instilling in the happy ending a disturbing undertone.

The disappearance of the European Jews, as enacted by Greenberg, is inextricably bound to the practices of Hollywood censorship and self-censorship. Greenberg is the only character to defy Hitler *as* Jew and *because* he is a Jew, and it is only logical that the film culminates in a confrontation between Greenberg-as-Shylock and Bronski-as-Hitler. Describing Shylock as proof that Shakespeare "thought of me" when he wrote *The Merchant of Venice*, Greenberg recites the famous Rialto speech three times in the film, each time dramatically shifting its meaning. In the first instance, we see Greenberg and Bronski backstage in Viking dress waiting for their cue in the troupe's performance of *Hamlet*. Greenberg recites the Shylock speech only to lament that all he ever gets to do "is carry a spear." This sequence is introduced by a poster announcing *Hamlet*. Greenberg's second recital, in contrast, is preceded by signs proclaiming "Verboten" and "Death Penalty," which indicate the fall of Warsaw and set a tone of threat and defeat. Only the lines "If you prick us, do we not bleed? If you tickle us, do we not laugh? If you poison us, do we not die?" are heard now, underscoring the victimization of the entire Polish people. Yet the melodrama is infused with a subtly comic tone—when Greenberg ponders "if we will ever carry a spear again," the camera pulls back from a medium close-up to reveal that he and Bronski are leaning not on spears but on snow shovels in the wintry Warsaw. This image is again indicative of Lubitsch's linking of performativity in the film to real-life occasions. Snow shoveling was a form of forced labor for Polish Jews, yet the remark about carrying a spear again also refers to both a hope for the return of the status quo—namely, peacetime Warsaw with its theaters open again—and the rise of the Polish resistance, which, as the voice-over immediately following this sequence informs us, is indeed spreading hope throughout the Polish population.

The last quotation of the Rialto scene provides a sharp contrast to the comic tone of the first instance and the tragic tone of the second. Now Greenberg indeed plays a Jew who confronts Hitler. When asked what he wants from the Führer, he responds, "What does he want from us? Why? Why? Why? Aren't we human? Do we not have eyes . . . ?" Greenberg's questions remain unanswered, just as many Jews were never able to confront Hitler directly about the reasons for their fate. Greenberg finally plays the Shylock he always wanted to play and concludes his monologue with the line he had held back in the earlier instances: "And if you wrong us, shall we not revenge?" Significantly, *revenge* will be Greenberg's last word in the film, and its delivery is accompanied by Bressart's first full close-up of the film, thus emphasizing a refusal of victimhood. Furthermore, this line is *not* included in the script and must be seen as a direct response to the changed political situation after the attack on Pearl Harbor.

It is important, furthermore, to note Lubitsch's alterations to Shakespeare's play, which reads as follows: "I am a Jew. Hath not a Jew eyes? Hath not a Jew hands, organs, dimensions, senses, affections, passions; fed with the same food, hurt with the same weapons, subject to the same diseases, healed by the same means, warmed and cooled by the same winter and summer, as a Christian is? If you prick us, do we not bleed? If you tickle us, do we not laugh? If you poison us, do we not die? And if you wrong us, shall we not revenge?"[30]

Greenberg's speech has been purged of all references to religion and ethnicity. It leaves out the opening sentence "I am a Jew," then throughout

FIGURE 3.5A–C The three Rialto scenes.

replaces the word *Jew* with *I* or *We*, and finally omits the comparison "as a Christian." Even for an audience familiar with Shakespeare's play, these alterations may have been too subtle to be noticed—none of the critics writing in our time have noticed them—yet the Jewishness of the Shylock figure was blatant enough to come across as highlighting a censoring of "the one who cannot be named," thus drawing attention to the ways in which Hollywood increasingly forced Jews to camouflage their ethnic and religious identity in the 1930s.[31]

Greenberg also most clearly represents the voice of the director, a claim that is justified given the fact that the film was directed and independently produced by Lubitsch and United Artists (cofounded in 1919 by Chaplin) and based on Lubitsch's original idea.[32] Indeed, the very first word of the film, *Lubinski*, as well as the obvious reference to Lubitsch's earlier film, *The Shop Around the Corner*, which is also set in Eastern Europe, makes an auteurist association more than obvious. What is more, the similarities between Greenberg/Bressart and Lubitsch are far-reaching. They include

the fact that Lubitsch began his career as a bit-player in Max Reinhardt's theater, who like Greenberg dreamed of playing the big part; Lubitsch's fervent belief in comedy (Greenberg reminds us five times in the film of the value to score "a terrific laugh"); and even the feeling of being an outsider.

Though a native Berliner, Lubitsch, like Bressart, was considered an "Ostjude" (Eastern Jew), because his parents had emigrated from Russia and took residence in the Scheunenviertel, the Jewish part of Berlin. For the highly assimilated Western Jews these new arrivals threatened to undo their successful assimilation and integration into the German middle class, and they did everything to keep the immigrants from the East at bay. Many of Lubitsch's early films display the stereotypes of the (Eastern) Jew that the Western Jews were so adamantly refuting. Several of them take place in the garment trade, in which his father worked, and feature young Jews from the shtetl who strive hard to make it in the metropolis of Berlin. Like Bressart's Greenberg, Lubitsch's various Sally figures (always played by himself) proudly assert their Jewishness through humor, chutzpah, and a mixture of rudeness and crudeness.[33] Lotte Eisner's reviews of Lubitsch's early comedies deride them as "Jewish slapstick"—a verdict that attests not only to the completely different cultural sensibilities between "Ostjuden" and "Westjuden" like herself but also carries overtones of feeling threatened that one's own successful assimilation to German bourgeois culture may be undone by the influx of Jewish immigrants from the East.

Yet the main similarity I want to consider here is less one of biography than of positionality, of assuming a certain cultural identity at a moment of crisis. Just as Greenberg is one of very few explicitly Jewish characters to reach the screens of Hollywood after 1933, *To Be or Not to Be* is the first and only of Lubitsch's American films in which, after a score of escapist sexual comedies and light fare, Lubitsch assumes the position of an exiled central European Jew who interrogates the American public about *their* role in the impending Holocaust.[34] Not since his early silent films had Jews appeared explicitly as characters in his films, nor had he made—apart from the World War I drama *The Man I Killed* (a.k.a. *Broken Lullaby*, 1931)—a film that addressed the consequences of modern warfare.[35] In that respect Bressart's Greenberg, who fervently believes that a "laugh is nothing to be sneezed at," yet is never seen laughing himself in the entire film, becomes a melancholic and touching embodiment of the many schlemiels Lubitsch himself had created at the beginning of his career.

A central concern of the film is with various forms of censorship that link the institutions of representation with the representations of institutions, thereby turning the film into an allegory of Hollywood filmmaking. The Teatr Polski is barred from performing the play *Gestapo* by the Polish authorities so as not to offend Nazi Germany (but to no avail, for Hitler nevertheless invades Poland), while Greenberg is barred from playing Shylock, though the film leaves it unclear whether this is for lack of talent or because *The Merchant of Venice* is a play that for whatever reasons cannot be performed at the moment. (This form of censorship stands in contrast to Joseph Tura, whose lack of talent does not prevent him from fulfilling his dream of playing Hamlet in the land of Shakespeare). Similarly, of course, Hollywood filmmakers refrained from portraying the fight against Hitler as a cause that involves Jews both as primary victims and as active in the resistance to Hitler.[36] Yet the film portrays not only the mechanisms of censorship but also their creative circumvention: the Poles *do* get to use their costumes and lines from the play *Gestapo* to outwit the Nazis, even turning the Nazis into unknowing participants when Colonel Ehrhardt inadvertently quotes from the play by telling the joke about a cheese being named after Hitler; and Greenberg *does* get to play the revenging Jew, even though his audience, Hitler's escort, fails to recognize who is in front of them. While the actors first acquiesce to the demands of the Polish censors, and then lament that there are "no censors to stop the kind of show the Nazis are putting on," they *do* finally learn how to circumvent both forms of censorship.

THE END(S) OF COMIC RELIEF

To Be or Not to Be pursues a double strategy. It unmasks the performativity of Nazi might, empowering (at least in theory) contemporary viewers in the fight against Nazi Germany, which after the attack on Pearl Harbor and Hitler's declaration of war had suddenly become a political reality. In doing so, Lubitsch also refutes the reductive image of the German Nazi as a demonic, one-dimensional, and essentially ontological evil that informed the vast majority of anti-Nazi films that Hollywood would produce between 1939 and 1945.[37] On another level *To Be or Not to Be* interrogates and educates the American audience about Hollywood's censorship laws, thereby suggesting the industry's complicity in, or at least complacency about, the Holocaust of the European Jews.

When the film was first released on March 6, 1942, however, neither of these aspects played a role in its hostile critical reception. Instead, it was attacked for its perceived callous and tasteless portrayal of the suffering of the Polish people at the hands of the Germans. As Thomas Doherty has put it, "What the Nazis did to Poland, wartime critics did to Lubitsch."[38] Lubitsch was taken to task primarily for commingling generic conventions that were perceived to be incompatible. Critics bemoaned that the film was an "incongruous mixture,"[39] "a disastrous attempt to reconcile two irreconcilable moods,"[40] and a "shocking confusion of realism and romance."[41] "Mr. Lubitsch," quipped Bosley Crowther, "is a Nero, fiddling while Rome burns."[42]

In a detailed discussion of the humor at stake in Ehrhardt's line "What he [Joseph Tura] did to Shakespeare, we are now doing to Poland" (according to Lubitsch's close friend and longtime collaborator Walter Reisch "the chief source of the negative reaction"),[43] Stephen Tifft has argued that part of the uneasiness critics had with this line was its implied union between the moral standards of the Nazis and a bourgeois American audience. The film was disturbing to contemporary audiences, Tifft claims, because it revealed their own latent kinship to the Nazis, whom they despised and feared. Laughing *with* the Nazis at the expense of a Polish actor marks the point where "comedy starts to scatter its aggression and to disseminate germinal political meanings unexpectedly."[44]

Indeed, this dissemination of meaning creates a form of humor that spares neither its creator nor its audience, yet one needs, in fact, to expand this focus on the unsettling ambiguities in the film to understand its reception history. It is precisely the film's modern or even postmodern dimension—its unorthodox generic mixing, its play with "Schein" and "Sein," or appearance and reality, its mode of dazzling representation, and its simultaneous debunking and affirmation of political propaganda—that not only caused its relative box-office failure when it was first released but has also allowed the film to recoup this loss by amassing a symbolic capital in contemporary discussions about the possibility of comic representations of the Holocaust.

In one of several replies to his critics Lubitsch explained the unorthodox nature of his strategy of representation: "I was tired of two established, recognized recipes, drama with comedy relief and comedy with dramatic relief. I made up my mind to make a picture with no attempt to relieve anybody from anything at any time."[45] The film mixes comedy and drama in rather unprecedented ways, signaling the transition from 1930s screwball comedy, the genre of the past, to wartime melodrama, the genre of the present. It also combines an undoing of Nazi propaganda with a straightforward advocating of the heroic plight of the Polish people.[46] As in many wartime productions, audience identification is engineered in such ways that we recognize in the characters facing the Nazi threat our own morals, and we are easily persuaded to cheer on their fight. Yet unlike in the combat films that would follow Pearl Harbor, here it is not only the political forces (the Polish resistance or the Polish flyers in the RAF) that show ingenuity in fighting the Nazis. Rather, it is first and foremost the Teatr Polski and their satire on Nazism, the banned play *Gestapo*, which they get to perform after all, if under completely unexpected circumstances, that proves most devastating to the Nazi cause. Plotting in their secret headquarters underneath the theater, the troupe becomes a literal underground force and the main reason for the resurgent resistance movement, a causal relationship further emphasized by letting the "defeat" of Hitler at the opera be followed by the explosion of a utility plant.

In what can be seen as another twist in the film's daring (post)modern narrative, the efforts of the Teatr Polski are aided significantly by the Polish underground and the Polish army in exile, particularly Lieutenant Sobinski (Robert Stack). He is smart enough to unmask Professor Siletsky as a spy, to evade the German army when he parachutes into Poland (a scene that commands significant screen time), to shoot the Professor in the theater, after Tura's overacting led him to flee the scene, and to fly the escaped theater troupe to England. When the actors witness the explosion of the railway station while escaping to the airport, they are struck with admiration, and for once they are turned into spectators in someone else's even bigger show.

Pivotal to these mixed modes of representation is, of course, Shakespeare, whose work is both a contested symbol for the location of culture and a model for divergent aesthetic strategies. We will recall that Lubitsch's acting career began in the famous Shakespeare productions of Max Reinhardt; in Lubitsch's own films Shakespeare's combination of the popular and high drama would serve as a recurrent model.[47] In *To Be or Not to Be*, Shakespeare stands not only for the very essence of English culture and tradition but also for broadly shared humanistic concerns. The land of Shakespeare is home to the exiled Polish flyers and thus the location from which the Polish struggle for freedom will be fought, just as England's significance was to remain the last Western European democracy to withstand Nazi invasion. The very first shot of the film shows London's Big Ben, the logo for Alexander Korda's production firm and an important location for the film to unfold within. Unlike the phony studio sets of Warsaw that we will see soon after, this is a "real" location and no voice-over is needed to identify it.

But, ironically, Shakespeare does not only stand for Western culture and the fight against Nazism. Just as the British would exempt Beethoven from German barbarity, the Nazis seem to consider Shakespeare one of their own. Ehrhardt has seen a prewar performance of *Hamlet* and is cultured enough to recognize Tura's butchering of the play. In *Mein Kampf* Adolf Hitler even cited Hamlet's famous line to articulate the necessity of warfare: "When the nations of this planet fight for existence—when the question of destiny, 'to be or not to be,' cries out for a solution—then all the considerations of humanitarianisms or aesthetics crumble into nothingness."[48] As a widely accepted symbol for culture and humanism, Shakespeare becomes a contested property for Poles, British, and Nazis. In the end, of course, the film reclaims Shakespeare for its Western viewers by privileging Greenberg's humanistic interpretation of the Shylock figure over Hitler's, who merely saw in it a confirmation and endorsement of his own anti-Semitism. And yet the film also indicts its viewers by using *The Merchant of Venice* as an example of productive controversy that in 1942 had no equal on Hollywood's screens.[49]

Lubitsch's politically daring aesthetic strategies become most evident when compared to two other contemporaneous attempts at comic portrayal of Nazism and the plight of the Jews, Chaplin's *The Great Dictator* and Leo McCarey's *Once upon a Honeymoon* (1942). Unlike *To Be or Not to Be*, both films drew a clear line between vice and virtue and were therefore easier for critics to like. Chaplin's double role as Adenoid Hynkel and the Jewish barber neatly separates two political realms and does not challenge the film's audience into conflicted identifications. For its most urgent political message, Chaplin felt it necessary to directly address the audience at the end of the film, thereby taking leave not only of the realm of comedy but even of fiction—the very form of "relief" Lubitsch did not want to afford his viewers—a departure that for Rudolf Arnheim in a 1940 review signaled the failure of the film.[50] While Chaplin commented well after the war that "had I known the actual horrors of the German concentration camps, I could not have made *The Great Dictator*; I could not have made fun of the homicidal insanity of the Nazis,"[51] Lubitsch worked in full awareness of the persecution of the Jews in Eastern Europe (even though he could not assume his audience to possess, let alone accept, that knowledge). His commitment to comedy as the most effective mode of addressing and representing this crisis has thus to be considered even more daring.

If Chaplin's film was an important source for Lubitsch's work, McCarey's *Once upon a Honeymoon* followed in the footsteps of *To Be or*

Not to Be, even to the point of recycling the very same establishing shot of Warsaw that opens Lubitsch's film. The film demonstrates how one year of war had dramatically changed Hollywood's interpretation of the Production Code. Here Ginger Rogers plays a former American burlesque star who passes herself off as an English aristocrat in order to marry an Austrian aristocrat, but then gets educated by an American journalist (Cary Grant) about her husband's secret activities in the service of the Nazis. In the course of the film Rogers helps a Jewish woman escape deportation, gets holed up in a concentration camp over night, and finally faces the danger of forced sterilization.

While *Once upon a Honeymoon* and *The Great Dictator* were popular successes, over time their reputations have withered. McCarey's film was daring in detailing the threats of Nazism, but its clumsy narrative and its wavering between political drama and comedy makes it hard to watch today. Chaplin's film has fared even worse in post-Holocaust criticism. As Adorno remarked in a radio address in 1962, "*The Great Dictator* loses its satirical force and becomes offensive in the scene in which a Jewish girl hits one storm trooper after another on the head with a pan without being torn to pieces. Political reality is sold short for the sake of political commitment; that decreases the political impact as well."[52]

Lubitsch's film has had a rather different reception history, evolving from a much-attacked tasteless farce into a postmodern holocaust comedy avant la lettre. As Thomas Elsaesser has argued, the achievement of Lubitsch (and other exiles) consisted in denying the audience a moral ground that lies outside of representation, an outside of the text that, as the poststructuralist critics have taught us, would provide us with a comforting but illusory omniscient view on reality: "It was precisely the clash of illusionary realms [*Scheinwelten*] which enabled emigrants like Lubitsch and Lang to develop a moral point-of-view."[53]

With *To Be or Not to Be*, the erstwhile émigré Ernst Lubitsch becomes an exile, creating an anti-Nazi comedy that not only debunks the power of Nazism but also alerts U.S. audiences to Hollywood's role in the struggle against Hitler. As a call for intervention, the much-celebrated "Lubitsch touch," that refined visual strategy for circumventing Puritan morals and the Production Code, is made to serve a far more overt political purpose precisely at the moment when Lubitsch realized the importance of being Ernst.

Four
HISTORY AS PROPAGANDA AND PARABLE

With every announcement of a victory [Siegesrapport] by Hitler, my significance as a writer decreases.
—BERTOLT BRECHT[1]

If I am anything, I am an anti-Fascist.
—FRITZ LANG[2]

THE ASSASSINATION OF THE REICHSPROTECTOR

On May 27, 1942, Reinhard Heydrich, the Reichsprotector of Bohemia and Moravia, as the Nazis called the governing body of occupied Czechoslovakia, was ambushed and mortally wounded when a bomb was thrown into his open car as he drove through the streets of Prague. He succumbed to his injuries on June 4. The Nazis retaliated in the most brutal fashion, arresting some thirteen thousand people, many of whom were deported to camps or killed, and murdering the entire male adult population of Lidice, a village near Prague, which was suspected of having harbored some of the assassins. Heydrich's excessive force and brutality against the Czech population had already earned him the nickname "the Hangman," and news of his injury and eventual demise elated the suffering Czechs, even if they could not express it openly. Yet the retaliatory measures, which included deporting most of the women and children of Lidice to concentration camps and burning and leveling every building of the town, made many question whether the killing of the Hangman was the most effective way of undermining Nazi power, especially since his successor immediately continued Heydrich's hard-line approach.

In the United States and elsewhere, the Czech act of resistance, as well as the subsequent Nazi atrocities, drew an immediate and impassioned response. In the exile community in Hollywood, Thomas Mann spoke on behalf of many when he told listeners in his June broadcast of *Deutsche Hörer!* that Heydrich's death "was the most natural death... a bloodhound like him could die."[3] Even more immediate was Bertolt Brecht's reaction, who noted only one day after the attempt on Heydrich's life in his diary, "Thinking with [Fritz] lang on the beach about a hostage film (on occasion of Heydrich's execution in Prague)."[4] As we know, this hostage film would eventually become *Hangmen Also Die*, Brecht and Lang's only collaboration in Hollywood and one of the few American films for which Brecht would receive screen credit. Produced by Arnold Pressburger, with a score by Hanns Eisler and starring Hans von Twardowski as Heydrich, as well as Alexander Granach, Reinhold Schünzel, and Tonio Selwart in prominent roles, it was an exemplary exile production and one of the most powerful anti-Nazi films that this short-lived genre produced. Heydrich would also figure prominently in Douglas Sirk's *Hitler's Madman*, while a hostage crisis scenario is explored in Frank Tuttle's *Hostages* (both 1943). Both films are further proof of how significant the U.S. film industry considered events in Czechoslovakia to be.

Heydrich himself was certainly Hollywood material. A tall, blond, and blue-eyed man and father of four children, Heydrich embodied the "Aryan" ideal. He was highly educated, with a passion for music, but at the same time unscrupulous and calculating. Thus he fit every stereotype of the Nazi *Übermensch*. Often rumored to be designated Hitler's successor, Heydrich had been put in charge of Bohemia and Moravia in September of 1941, and he vowed to force the occupied Czechs into submission. As the mastermind behind the Roehm putsch, he had gained the Führer's confidence by having his men uncover "false evidence" that SA leader Roehm was planning to overthrow Hitler, a strategy of playacting that Heydrich also used in the so-called Gleiwitz incident (described in the previous chapter). He further orchestrated the Wannsee Conference, which ratified the blueprint for the Holocaust of the European Jews. Even though Lang and Brecht would give the Reichsprotector only a small role at the opening of *Hangmen Also Die*, Hans von Twardowski's interpretation of the Heydrich figure as an effeminate, sadistic ruler who exploits the fears of his underlings reverberates throughout the film.

Few artists can claim to have responded as quickly as Brecht and Lang to Heydrich's assassination, but the retaliatory massacre at Lidice would quickly give rise not only to widespread public outrage and international acts of solidarity with the Czech people but to commemorate the victims in prose, drama, and poetry. In fact, events in Czechoslovakia provided a rare instance in which exile writers and intellectuals, exile filmmakers, American politicians, and large segments of the population shared similar ideological and political goals, allowing the exiles for once to become a part of a larger, national and international alliance against Nazi Germany. While the Nazi erasure of Lidice was meant to be a manifestation of their power and an act of intimidation that would prevent future acts of resistance (much like the bombing of the Spanish town of Guernica in 1937), the excessive cruelty had the opposite effect. In July of 1942 the suburb of Stern Park Gardens, Illinois, changed its name to Lidice, an example followed by towns in Mexico, Peru, Venezuela, Palestine, Cuba, Brazil, Panama, and Great Britain. Numerous writers strove to commemorate the village and the suffering of its population, foremost among them Edna St. Vincent Millay, whose prose poem, "The Murder of Lidice" invokes the pastoral setting of the village. Its opening lines are quoted at the film's beginning. Various literary collections gave voice to similar outrage and solidarity, including *Lidice Lives Forever* (1942), *The Story of Two People* (1942, published by the Czech National Council of America), and *Lidice* (1944), a tribute by members of the PEN committee.

Notable among examples of exile literature is Gustav Holm's novel *This Was Lidice*, which chronicles the lives of various fictitious characters in Lidice from just prior to the German occupation to the total annihilation of the town. Written in the months following the Nazi raid, Holm's tale betrays an urgency to keep the spirit of the Czechs and other oppressed people alive so that the victims' deaths would not have been utterly meaningless. Holm's mantra is "Nedame se" (never surrender), which is introduced early in the novel and also forms its closing statement—a phrase that also repeatedly occurs in *Hangmen Also Die*, suggesting that Holm, Lang, and Brecht (as well as most other members of the exile community) had recourse to the same limited sources to understand the details surrounding Heydrich's death and the Czech resistance. In fact, all of them had to rely on their imagination to fill in the rest. Thus, both Lang's film and Holm's novel prominently foreground the Czech underground's strategies for sabotage, which include pamphlets that teach how to render guns and bombs ineffective, and give voice to the population's disdain for certain quisling figures.

Furthermore, Holm's novel features a young female protagonist who sacrifices her life and that of her adopted children to shield the assassins, just as Professor Novotny becomes a martyr figure in Lang's film. Just how limited any access to the historical truth was at the time becomes evident by the fact that Holm (and later Sirk) believed that the inhabitants of Lidice had indeed sheltered the assassins. This was later revealed to be a lie spread by the Nazis so that they might save face, a disclosure that *Hangmen* intuitively anticipated. It shows the Nazis covering up the fact that Czaka, whom they executed after the Czechs had skillfully framed him, was in fact not Heydrich's assassin.[5]

Holm's novel is only one of several literary adaptations that were published soon after the massacre of Lidice. Another is the 1943 novel *You Can't Do That to Svoboda*, by John Pen, an alias for Hans Székely, a Hungarian-born screenwriter with important film credits both in Weimar Germany and Hollywood. There is the 1942 play *Slepcova píšetalka aneb Lidice* (The blind man's whistle, or Lidice) by the librettist Adolf Hoffmeister, which revolves around a blind seer who ironically turns out to be the only one who can provide testimony about the crimes at Lidice. Two additional novels set during the Nazi occupation were in progress when Heydrich was killed. Stefan Heym's *Hostages* focuses on the lives of five Czechs who are taken hostage after a Nazi officer mysteriously disappears in a bar. Written in (somewhat faulty) English by the young exile author, the potboiler was rushed into publication by the publisher, who, given the subject's topicality, correctly assumed he had a bestseller on his hands. Although it was not published until December 1942 and thus was an unlikely source for Brecht and Lang, the affinities between Heym's novel and *Hangmen Also Die* are considerable. As the title suggests, the plot revolves around a hostage scenario, which, like Lang's film, includes internal dissent and ends with the hostages' execution, even after the Nazis find out that their officer took his own life. The novel also prominently portrays the work of the underground and a quisling figure much like Czaka. Heydrich makes a very late entry in the story as he orders his ineffective underling, Commissioner Reinhardt, to the eastern front. The parting words of Reinhardt to Heydrich are of particular significance: "I have failed and concede my failure. I am going to a horrible death. But I tell you, Your Excellency, that my successors, and even you yourself, must fail in the same way, and that you will meet a more violent end than I."[6] When the novel was published, Heydrich's death had become a historical truth, making the statement a strong propagandistic tool that implied that Heydrich's successor, too, would face a similar fate.

Of all these novels Heym's was by far the most popular and talked about. But the most accomplished author to work on this material was Heinrich Mann, Thomas's impoverished older brother. His novel *Lidice* (1943) was published in Mexico by the exile press El Libro Libre and mostly ignored by the American public, but the exile community reacted with some bewilderment. Mann's is a somewhat grotesque and satiric tale that includes, among other plot twists, a Czech who pretends to be Heydrich and uncovers a plot against him by his own SS guards, only to become a fugitive while the real Heydrich, based on the tales circulated by his impostor, is believed to have become too powerful and is therefore killed by his own men. The novel was initially titled "Der Protektor," but the events at Lidice caused Mann to change the title. In light of the real massacre his over-the-top fiction seemed in bad taste.[7]

Yet Mann's novel was an anomaly. Most literary reactions to the massacre in Lidice were published in its immediate aftermath and emphasized the suffering of the victims in an attempt to mobilize public opinion against Nazi terror. This is certainly also true for *Hangmen Also Die*, *Hitler's Madman*, and *Hostages*. Released the year following Heydrich's assassination, all three films were less concerned with commemorating the victims than with using the Czech resistance as a cause around which to rally the support of the American population. All three films erroneously believed the assassin to have come from within the Czech underground; the fact that they were actually parachuted into the country from England at the orders of the government in exile was not known publicly until after the war.

Both *Hitler's Madman* and *Hostages* were made on significantly smaller budgets than Lang's film and characterized by a far more conventional style, relying heavily on romance, charismatic underground leaders, melodramatic engineering of identification, and an upbeat ending. *Hitler's Madman*, Douglas Sirk's first American feature, was produced by Seymour Nebenzal, written by Emil Ludwig and Albrecht Joseph, with the uncredited Edgar Ulmer serving as set designer and second unit director; it starred numerous exile actors in small roles, including Hans von Twardowski, Ludwig Stoessel, Wolfgang Zilzer, Johanna Hofer, and Lisa Valetti. Initially called *Hitler's Hangman*, the film had to be renamed when reshooting delayed its premiere until after the release of Lang's *Hangmen Also Die*. The producers nevertheless kept the opening and closing image of the film, a hangman's noose over which the credits roll. Heydrich is indeed the central figure of Sirk's film. Not only a hangman but also a madman, this anti-intellectual and antireligious Nazi is the incarnation of evil, and throughout the film he serves as a contrast to the God-fearing villagers of Lidice—a ruthless killer

FIGURE 4.1 Sirk's Heydrich as the proverbial blond monster.

and anti-God who imposes his presence on a peaceful community. In the hour of his death Heydrich is cut down to size. Courage abandons him as he relates to Gestapo head Heinrich Himmler that the war is lost and that Hitler's and Himmler's hour of death is close, too. Sirk's Heydrich is played by John Carradine, who, according to the director, had the same agitated voice as the real Heydrich, whom he once met at an Ufa event in Berlin.[8] In contrast to Lang, Sirk believed that casting a native speaker of English who resembled Heydrich would create a more pressing sense of immediacy and hence a greater sense of necessity to act. As a consequence, in *Hitler's Madman* the threat of Nazism is weakened once Heydrich has been killed (even though the mass murder of the population of Lidice takes place after his death), whereas in *Hangmen Also Die*, no matter how many Nazis are killed (Heydrich, Inspector Gruber), the threat continues as an impenetrable bureaucracy creates new murderers busy at work at their desks.

Even more than in *Hitler's Madman*, in *Hostages* the antifascist message competes with a love story, as scriptwriter Lester Cole—later to become one of the Hollywood Ten—was forced by the studio to seriously dilute the political nature of Heym's novel. (Heym subsequently distanced himself from the film.) The film features strong performances by Oskar Homolka as the quisling Pressinger (the same actor Brecht had hoped to cast as a quisling figure in his film) and Reinhold Schünzel as a self-serving Nazi officer. The conversion story of Milada (Luise Rainer) is also very gripping: the daughter of Pressinger, she is initially apolitical but is awakened by the courage of the resistance, ultimately siding with the underground against her father, who is executed.

Among the three films, Lang and Brecht's is generally considered the most ambitious. Focusing on the tensions that arise within the Czech population when the Nazis begin to search for the assassin, *Hangmen Also Die* combines blatant elements of propaganda and Brechtian didacticism with a suspense-driven narrative that successfully envelops viewers. Based on Lang's idea, the story follows Dr. Svoboda (Brian Donlevy), Heydrich's assassin, as he seeks cover with the Novotny family while the Nazis take hostages among the Czechs, hoping to coerce them into betraying the murderer hiding among them. When the family patriarch, Professor Novotny (Walter Brennan), is taken hostage, his daughter Masha (Anna Lee) wavers between saving her father by giving up Svoboda or shielding the assassin, as her father and her civic duty demand. Hot on the heels of Svoboda is Gestapo Inspector Gruber (Alexander Granach), who is killed in a showdown with Svoboda and his allies. In what is clearly a sign of both Brecht's and Lang's fascination with masses, the film puts a significant emphasis on the Czech population, repeatedly showing us cross sections of a society that act as one when circumstances demand. A small crowd, for example, prevents Masha from talking to the Gestapo, while a group collaborates, in an intricate subplot, in framing the quisling Czaka as the assassin. At the film's end the Czech population can savor an important victory in the fight against Nazism, a fight that is only about to begin, as the closing title, "Not the End," makes amply clear.

BRECHT AND LANG REVISITED

A highly celebrated film, *Hangmen Also Die* marked a highpoint in the exile community's struggle against Nazi Germany. Critics, however, have largely ignored the film proper, focusing almost exclusively on Brecht and Lang's contested collaboration, primarily, one can suspect, because the anti-Nazi film as a genre has attracted so little scholarly interest.[9] The difficulties between the two men stemmed from their different approaches to the function of film and propaganda in the fight against Nazi Germany, differences that are by and large symptomatic of the rift between exile filmmakers and writers and intellectuals. The tension that marked Lang and Brecht's collaboration ultimately resulted in a film that is better for its internal contradictions, its varying representational strategies, and its layered aesthetic registers. To reassess that creative tension, it is important to first revisit the much-written-about collaboration between the playwright and the filmmaker, stressing the points of convergence where previous commentators (including Brecht himself) have mostly seen dichotomies.

As has been well documented, the differences between Brecht and Lang arose over a number of issues, some professional and some personal. These differences have been given greater attention than the positive results of their collaboration, partially because Brecht's posthumously published *Arbeitsjournal* details with acerbic wit his misgivings about the film's production rather than any sense of achievement—misgivings that he might have never voiced openly at the time, since Lang (and others) professed disbelief when they came to light. Both Lang and Brecht had a different understanding of what it meant to be a member of the American exile community circa 1942. Lang had come to the United States in 1934, after a short stopover in France, in the hope of continuing his highly successful Weimar career. (A visit to New York in 1924 had already convinced him that the future of filmmaking lay in this country.) In his first American film, *Fury* (1936), Lang demonstrated a commitment to a critique of social injustice in the United States, an injustice to which he had been sensitized because of his experience of fascism in Germany. As Anton Kaes has argued, the film reflects Lang's intervention into American politics from the position of an outsider who cares about his adopted homeland. The film operates with a "double-edged critique from the vantage point that compares and judges the new against the old, the unknown against the known, the indigenous against the foreign."[10] Lang sought to alert an ignorant and isolationist American public that racism, xenophobia, and prejudice could easily engender a fascist state. Knowledge of Nazi terror also informed Lang's growing anxiety about the influence of the Bund and other fascist organizations in the United States. Writing to Otto Katz in 1937, he stated, "The Nazi movement is now growing terrible not only here [in LA] but in all America. Big camps are being formed and, although many Senators have protested against it, it seems that the American legislation cannot do anything against this in a legal way."[11] When Lang became an American citizen in December of 1939, he called it "the proudest day of his life"—surely a display of a newly found patriotism but also a sigh of relief at having escaped Hitler's clutches.[12] By the time the United States entered the war, Lang clearly saw himself as an assimilated and naturalized immigrant who fought Nazi Germany *as* an American.

Bertolt Brecht, in contrast, did not consider himself an exile or emigrant but rather a refugee, and he continued to write in German for his desk drawer. Even after eight years of flight from Hitler, Brecht still thought of exile as a transitory state and was biding his time until it was safe to return to Germany, where he hoped to participate in rebuilding a democratic society. Poignantly summarizing the difference between himself, the "Flüchtling" (refugee), and the immigrant Lang, who defended the American way of life, Brecht claimed, "[Lang] sees a special life style where i see only high capitalism."[13]

Unlike Fritz Lang, William Dieterle, Ernst Lubitsch, or Billy Wilder (all of whom had become citizens by 1939), Brecht did not consider Los Angeles an obvious choice of place to continue a successful career but rather the last stop in a migration that had begun in Denmark in 1933, and that had led him across Scandinavia and the Soviet Union, before arriving in San Pedro in July 1941. Brecht had favored Los Angeles over the theater capital New York as his American domicile at the urging of his friend Lion Feuchtwanger, who lured him with the prospect of selling his talents to the U.S. film industry. Despite his misgivings about Hollywood, which he couched in the famous verses of his "Hollywood Elegies," about the market where lies are sold and where the stench of greed and misery suffocates the City of Angels, Brecht continuously wrote scripts, outlines, and treatments throughout his six-year stay (more than fifty in all), which he hoped to sell to the film industry.[14] Apart from Feuchtwanger, his collaborators included Salka Viertel and Charles Laughton, and he wrote one screenplay specifically for Peter Lorre. Yet apart from *Hangmen Also Die*, none of them ever made it onto the screen.[15] Most Brecht scholars have considered these scripts and film stories insignificant and much inferior to the plays and poems written during his fifteen years of exile. In this verdict they followed Brecht himself, who repeatedly called them bread-and-butter jobs that he pursued while scolding the industry for which they were written.

Yet Brecht's aversion to Hollywood has been exaggerated, both by himself and by critics who have followed his lead. When Brecht began writing scripts for Hollywood, he did not change careers but rather returned to his beginnings, which lay as much with film as with theater.[16] Moreover, the

German film industry of the late 1920s and early 1930s, particularly Ufa after Alfred Hugenberg's takeover, did not differ significantly from 1930s Hollywood in ideology, output, product differentiation, star system, and institutional hierarchies.[17] Brecht's writings about his failed lawsuit in the wake of G. W. Pabst's adaptation of his *Threepenny Opera* perceptively describe the German film industry's capitalist engine, which also drove Hollywood, if in even more cut-throat terms. In the German film industry of the 1930s there was still room for a counter-cinema like Slatan Dudow and Brecht's *Kuhle Wampe* (1932), but that was merely the exception that proved the rule.

Brecht's experience with the contradictions of the pre-Nazi German film industry prepared him well for what was expected of him in Hollywood, even if he always resisted catering to those expectations. Consider this anecdote from Salka Viertel's memoir, *The Kindness of Strangers*, in which she recalls working with Brecht on "Silent Witness," a wartime story that was never produced:

> Brecht drove up one morning in his battered Ford and said that it was utterly ridiculous to have financial worries, when he and I could put our brains together and invent a saleable film story . . . 'because what the producers want is an original but familiar, unusual but popular, moralistic but sexy, true but improbable, tender but violent, slick but highbrow masterpiece. . . .' Brecht bit into his cigar and assured me that we could write our story in such a way that they would not notice what a highbrow masterpiece it was.[18]

It is clear from Viertel's description that Brecht understood the contradictions and hypocrisy of the studio system quite well and that with the aid of Viertel, a successful screenwriter for Greta Garbo, he hoped to break into the studio system. Brecht's strategy was to get into the belly of the beast without being chewed up in the process, to conform to Hollywood conventions without compromising his artistic integrity. Surely he knew what he was getting himself into when he agreed to work with Lang. More than money was on his mind when he agreed to cowrite a script about the Heydrich assassination in Prague, for the didactic and propagandistic elements of the anti-Nazi film were in keeping with Brecht's long-standing interest in breaking down the barriers between art and politics.

Unlike writers such as Heinrich Mann, Alfred Polgar, Leonard Frank, Walter Mehring, or Alfred Döblin, Brecht did *not* come to the United States with a pro forma studio contract that helped him secure entry papers but rather through the help of friends such as Feuchtwanger, Dieterle, and Lang. Brecht was not forced to waste time and energy in some scriptwriter's office but chose to write for the studios as a lucrative, if highly unreliable, way of supporting his family and himself. Despite his invectives against Hollywood, during his six years in Santa Monica Brecht derived most of his income as an independent screenwriter; for *Hangmen Also Die* he would collect the proud sum of $10,000.

Lang's and Brecht's collaboration was marked from the beginning as much by shared commitment as by creative dissent. After reading about the attempt on Heydrich's life in the *Los Angeles Times*, they immediately agreed that the focus of their story should not be on the actual assassination plot but the reaction of the Czech population under Nazi duress. In a matter of weeks they completed a forty-page outline, "437!! Ein Geiselfilm" (437!! A hostage film), which contained the fully developed plot. A considerably longer version of the outline, a ninety-five-page English-language treatment titled "No Surrender," which Hans Viertel translated, provided even more plot detail; its substance was almost entirely incorporated into the final film, except for the treatment's overtly happy ending. These two documents, which have only been recently discovered and published, prove not only beyond doubt that John Wexley, an additional writer hired by Lang and Pressburger to help Brecht with his flawed English, contributed few original ideas but also that Lang and Brecht had early on agreed on major plotlines, characters, settings, and themes.[19] In light of this consensus the subsequent dissonances diminished in importance.[20]

These dissonances included, as we know, certain approaches to mass scenes. Brecht's interest was to highlight the resistance of the Czechs as a collective rather than focusing on a single (heroic) individual (which Lang preferred, since it was the standard Hollywood formula), while also allowing for contradictions and unsympathetic traits among the Czechs. In a scene later cut by Lang, Brecht depicted the hostages as showing signs of anti-Semitism only minutes prior to their own execution. This scene, claimed Brecht, conveyed the startling and contradictory impact of totalitarianism on the population. Lang, however, felt that this complexity would be lost on most American viewers, who were not accustomed to mixed messages; indeed, he feared that it might undercut the film's propagandistic force. Lang was also aware that a film that emphasized the collective over the individual could renew suspicions that he was a communist, a criticism he had confronted a few years earlier. Yet Lang, too, was fascinated by mass scenes. His representations of lynch mobs in *Metropolis*, *M*, and *Fury* recur in *Hangmen*, significantly with a positive twist on mass agitation. Consider, for example, the scene in the movie theater, when the moviegoers break into spontaneous applause after news of the shooting of the Hangman makes its round.

Lang and Brecht also had different perceptions about the film's intended audience. The American population had virtually no knowledge of the nature of fascism, claimed Lang; the film must therefore facilitate an understanding of the terror spread by Nazism, even if that meant endorsing certain stereotypes and simplifying characters and historical facts, concessions that Brecht sharply criticized: "The American film has hardly progressed beyond the state of situational comedy and tragedy. The average lover, the average bad guy, the average hero, the average master mind is moved across certain situations."[21] Instead, Brecht hoped to make a film that could also be used in postwar reeducation efforts, a resolve that was of no interest to Lang, who had no plans for returning to Europe.

Serious differences arose over other issues, only some of which actually affected the film. One of them was salary. Brecht repeatedly asked Lang to intervene on his behalf with Pressburger for raises, which the producer considered blackmail and ultimately led him to side against Brecht in the Screenwriters' Guild credit arbitration. Casting decisions were another bone of contention. Brecht was banking on roles for exile actors in non-Nazi roles, lobbying on behalf of Oskar Homolka for the role of Czaka and for a small role for his wife, Helene Weigel, but Lang insisted that all Czechs should be played by native English speakers in order to strengthen identification with the citizens of Prague. This personal snub apparently hurt Brecht more than most other points of contention and may account for the derisory tone he adopted vis-à-vis Lang in his *Arbeitsjournal*. Yet it is also clear that in Hollywood, as in the pre-Nazi German film industry, casting decisions lay firmly with the director or producer, never with the writer. For that reason Brecht's hopes to have a say in the matter were unrealistic and unwarranted. To be sure, Lang, too, was profoundly unhappy with Anna Lee in the role of Masha Novotny, who was chosen for the role by Pressburger, attesting to the power of the producer even in an independent production, on which Lang, after all, served as coproducer.

The final straw for Brecht was certainly Lang's cutting of the lengthy script with the help of yet another writer (after Pressburger moved up production by several weeks), in a procedure that corresponded to industry practice and not personal whim. This led to some of Brecht's strongest accusations against Lang.[22] Lang, for his part, chose a conciliatory approach.

Long after Brecht's death, he said, "I personally think that it will not be possible to write the very truth without calling Brecht untruthful and I ask myself if the whole thing is really so important to besmirch the memory of a fine and great writer, who was maybe carried away by his emotions."[23]

TALES OF CONVICTIONS AND CONVERSIONS

While *To Be or Not to Be* was begun before Pearl Harbor, and premiered when the American population still needed to be convinced that isolationism and pacifism were no longer the right policy toward the Axis powers, *Hangmen Also Die* was released in the spring of 1943, at which time the war no longer required justification. But even though the Nazi war machinery had been stopped at Stalingrad earlier that year, there were still few wins to report for the Americans. To support the war effort, Hollywood films sought to send out clear political messages and to convey confidence that the enemy could be overcome. The black humor and mixed messages of Lubitsch's film, despite its unambiguous endorsement of the Polish underground, would have been considered far too daring and risqué by the newly created Office of War Information (OWI). Its guidelines for film professionals stipulated that films should address themselves in straightforward ways to specific concerns: Will the film help win the war? Does it contribute something new to our understanding of the world conflict? Does the picture tell the truth, or will the young people of today have reason to say they were misled by propaganda? Will it be a purely escapist film that harms our war efforts by creating false pictures?[24]

As a result of the unprecedented alignment of the Hollywood film studios with the U.S. war effort, between 1939 and 1946 about 180 feature-length anti-Nazi films were made that shared a political agenda, representational strategies, and stereotypical characters. As Jan-Christopher Horak defines this cycle, these are films that are meant to unmask the antidemocratic aspects of fascism and the negative consequences for those who endure life under a fascist regime while contrasting them with the humanistic freedom of American democracy.[25] At the same time, these films were conceived to make a profit and entertain a mainstream audience. Hence, anti-Nazi films frequently used genre conventions familiar from crime fiction and the spy thriller, but there were also anti-Nazi screwball comedies such as *Once upon a Honeymoon* (Leo McCarey, 1942), parodies like *Nazty Nuisance*

(Glen Tryon, 1943), and animated films by the Disney studio.²⁶ These were supplemented by documentaries, most notably Frank Capra's seven-part series *Why We Fight* (1942–45), to which Anatole Litvak contributed *The Battle of Russia* (1943).

Often, these films offered little but well-trodden genre pictures with gratuitously added propagandistic undertones. In the Humphrey Bogart vehicle *All Through the Night* (Vincent Sherman, 1941) a mobster becomes political when his favorite baker is killed by a fifth columnist, while in William Thiele's *Tarzan Triumphs* (1943), the ape-man battles the Nazis, turning the lord of the jungle from an erstwhile isolationist into a ferocious enemy of the Third Reich—after Boy, his companion, is kidnapped, he vows: "Now Tarzan make war on Hitler!" This diversity of genre conventions, audience address, and political commitment makes it difficult to see the anti-Nazi film as a proper genre (as Horak does) and instead suggests considering it as a cycle or series (similar to arguments about film noir). Nevertheless, as Sabine Hake has argued, the unique alignment of politics and entertainment "introduced the stereotypical characters, narrative structures, and identificatory patterns that would henceforth dominate the filmic representations of screen Nazis" with long-lasting repercussions not just in the American film industry but also Europe and beyond.²⁷

Fritz Lang's own tetralogy of anti-Nazi films is a case in point about the diversity of the films in this cycle. His first foray in this vein, *Man Hunt* (1941), about a Hitler assassination gone wrong, is a suspense-driven thriller in which a British captain has to battle the fifth column in the United Kingdom. Soon after *Hangmen Also Die*, Lang directed *Ministry of Fear* (1944, after a novel by Graham Greene), yet again an England-set film about the fifth column, but here a realistic portrayal of Nazism becomes secondary to weaving a spy yarn that features a microfilm hidden in a cake, a mysterious private detective, and a love interest that concludes in a romantic happy ending. Lang's postwar *Cloak and Dagger* (1946) stars an American scientist turned secret agent who must realize that the Nazis most likely have engineered an atom bomb.²⁸

While many films in the cycle were successful at the box office, their political merit was subject to dispute. Lowell Mellet, speaking for the OWI in November 1942, complained: "We get a stream of pictures that had no more relation to reality than the newspaper comic strips, pictures that were calculated to confirm our naïve notion that all Germans are either super spies, masters of scientific warfare or Hitler blockheads, that all Japanese are buck-toothed saboteurs in horn-rimmed glasses, and that any American war correspondent, given the aid of a good looking blonde, is able to handle the entire situation."[29] Commenting on anti-Nazi films such as *Man Hunt*, *Escape*, *Underground*, and Charlie Chaplin's *The Great Dictator*, Klaus Mann was equally cynical about what he perceived as the ineffectiveness of Hollywood's war efforts: "Hollywood clings, sterile and cowardly, to its all-familiar patterns and devices. They venture on the most appalling topic of human history with the shabby tricks of the Wild West and gangster thrillers. Don't they feel that a new idiom is needed to communicate those tremendous experiences?"[30]

Apart from a reluctance to engage with fascism in a more detailed and realistic manner, the vast majority of anti-Nazi films were indeed marred by overtly patriotic messages, repetition of certain plot devices, and highly stereotyped characters. Even some of the artistically more ambitious or realistic contributions—such as *Arise, My Love* (Mitchell Leisen, after a script by Billy Wilder and Charles Brackett, 1940), *The Mortal Storm* (Frank Borzage, 1940), *The Cross of Lorraine* (Tay Garnett, 1943), and *Watch on the Rhine* (Herman Shumlin, 1943, after the play by Lillian Hellman)—could not quite do without them. But as propagandistic tools these films were very effective indeed, as most contemporary reviews attest.

The rising significance of the series coincided with the arrival of a large (and final) wave of refugees from Europe. Exiles were now asked to contribute their firsthand knowledge of history and politics, while German-language actors and actresses found that their accents had actually become desirable, even if, ironically, Jews now had often to play SS commanders.[31] As Horak has shown, the anti-Nazi film was the series in which exiles proved economically most successful; they participated as producers, directors, writers, or actors in about one-third of the films he considers to fall under that rubric. Among the films directed or written by exiles we *do* find less-stereotyped characterizations, surprising plotlines, and remarkable individual performances. Some of the more noteworthy films include *Fly-by-Night* (Robert Siodmak, 1942), *Nazi Agent* (Jules Dassin, 1942), *Five Graves to Cairo* (Billy Wilder, 1943), *Margin for Error* (Otto Preminger, 1943), *Tonight We Raid Calais* (John Brahm, 1943), *The Strange Death of Adolf Hitler* (James P. Hogan, 1943), and *None Shall Escape* (André de Toth, 1944). German novelists now saw their works adapted for the screen, among them Erich Maria Remarque in *So Ends Our Night* (John Cromwell, 1941), Anna Seghers in *The Seventh Cross* (Fred Zinnemann, 1944), Vicki Baum in *Hotel Berlin* (Peter Godfrey, 1945), and Stefan Heym in *Hostages*. Nonetheless, the Office of War Information's support of the U.S. war effort, combined with the studio system's need for economic success, ultimately granted exile (and nonexile) film professionals few creative liberties in their representations of the fight against Hitler.

These demands certainly had their impact on *Hangmen Also Die*. Even though it was an independent production, the film operates squarely within the ideological parameters that define the anti-Nazi film; given Washington's unprecedented intervention into the film industry it could not have been otherwise. Brecht and Lang's idiosyncratic synergies nevertheless gave rise to an important film. On an ideological level it highlighted the significance of collective thought and action, diminishing America's prized individualism. Enemy characters were handled more ambiguously than in most other films of the series, and Lang's modernist mise-en-scène challenged studio conventions. Important also was Hanns Eisler's idiosyncratic music, which retained political messages that were curtailed in the script. As Sally Bick has argued, his "covert musical statements . . . allowed Eisler a secretive and personal way to resist the commercial values he loathed in Hollywood's motion picture industry."[32] Among these, Bick lists Eisler's refusal of linking any musical theme to specific dramatic concepts, thereby circumventing Hollywood's use of a leitmotif; his use of twelve-tone serial passages; his allusions to little-known passages from classic Czech composers such as Smetana; and his quoting of the *Kominternlied* (the communist anthem "L'internationale") at the end of the film. Yet as Bick also points out, some of these references must have been too subtle for audiences, and even Lang missed the reference to the *Kominternlied*.

Like *To Be or Not to Be*, *Hangmen Also Die* is set in a central European country that suffers under Nazi occupation and in which the underground movement plays a central role. Both films rely heavily on viewer identification with the occupied citizens, portraying them sharing the same values, cultural traditions, religious beliefs, and history as people in the United States, a nation of immigrants to which central Europeans have significantly contributed. Lang considered it crucial that the Czechs speak accent-free English to underscore these symmetries. Professor Novotny's admonishment to his students not to "let yourself be snowed under at Valley Forge," a reference to George Washington's winter retreat after heavy losses in battle, clearly was meant to align U.S. history and democracy with the Czech plight for self-governance.

Similarly, the film's emphasis on a family, a plot device found in many films in this series, allows us to experience the Nazi threat in an immediate way, while also casting the family as *pars pro toto* of society. As the occupiers augment pressure on the Novotnys, each family member assumes a specific task. While the patriarch, as hostage, becomes a martyr (significantly, at the film's conclusion we do not know whether he survives), the daughter is forbidden to save him by betraying the assassin and even has to jeopardize her engagement by simulating adultery, and the young son is imposed upon to keep the spirit of the resistance—and possibly that of his father's memory—alive.[33] Only if all three fulfill their responsibilities, the film suggests, will the Czech people as a whole have a chance to persevere.

Yet while viewers' sympathies are firmly anchored in this family, as well as with the heroic Svoboda and Dedic, the larger-than-life leader of the underground, these allegiances are balanced by a repeated emphasis on groups and masses. While Svoboda demonstrates courage, the underground and even the entire Czech people must come to his rescue, and it is ultimately their solidarity that the film celebrates. It was important, Brecht noted, "that the underground makes mistakes which the people correct."[34] The power of the collective is underscored in a series of scenes that are carefully interwoven with those parts of the narrative that focus on individuals—the scene in which a group gathers to prevent Masha from going to the

FIGURE 4.2 The hostages, one of several important collectives in the film.

Gestapo (a group of which she will later become a part); in the elaborate framing of Czaka, which requires the careful coordination and courageous participation of people from all walks of life; and in the scenes with the hostages, who represent a cross section of a society in which class distinctions do not matter.

A collective produces the message-driven poem "No Surrender," which, set to music by Eisler using the melody of the communist "International" song, is recited at the end of the film. As Eisler and Adorno commented in *Composing for the Films*, "at the end, there is a *long shot* of the city of Prague, as though to show the real hero of the picture, the Czech people."[35] To be precise, there are actually two shots of the Prague castle, which echo three similar shots of the same location that open the film. Whereas the opening shots are preceded by a title card that informs viewers about the activities of the Hangman, thereby framing the castle as the seat of the hated occupiers, the closing shots, which are accompanied by Eisler's dynamic marching music, hold the promise that the Czechs will reclaim the castle.[36]

The fascination with the masses should be seen as a point of conversion and not dissent between Brecht and Lang. Brecht was intrigued by the fact that the activities of the Czech underground mirror those of the German oppressors: "Terror is being enforced because the Czech workers are sabotaging production for Hitler's war in the East. Thus German terror is depicted in the same anonymous terms as the Czech assassination of Heydrich."[37] But *Hangmen Also Die* also sustains a Langian fascination with the masses and the mob redolent of his earlier films. Mirrored networks of the police and the criminals, which are at the core of *M*, reoccur here. In Comolli and Géré's assessment, "the victims are much like the executioners. Machine against machine."[38] Prague is as much a city in a state of emergency as Berlin was in *M*, creating similar states of paranoia in the cities' respective citizenry; the hunt for the murderer in their midst, replete with surveillance devices (and the knowledge of how to defeat them), informers, and dragnet operations are likewise similar plot devices.

If the depiction of the masses and the emphasis on collective spirit runs counter to most stories of wartime heroism, the ideological line between good and bad, us and them, is also considerably more blurred in this film than in most others in the cycle. We should recall that for propaganda to work, it is not enough to articulate what we are fighting for and why; equally important is an effective portrayal of the enemy. This means that the successful anti-Nazi film must explain the threat to democracy and freedom as absolutely serious, a threat that cannot be ignored or underestimated;

FIGURE 4.3 The staging of the new hierarchy at Hradschin Castle.

but once the enemy has been taken seriously as an adversary, it is equally important that he be cut down to size so that he appears surmountable.

The creative tension between insurmountable evil and its inherent weakness is clearly articulated in the impressive opening sequence of *Hangmen Also Die*. Inside the Prague castle a group of Czech industrial and military leaders anxiously await the arrival of the Reichsprotector. When Heydrich enters, the power relations of the occupation are quickly revealed, as the Czech collaborators are intimidated and humiliated through Heydrich's militaristic posture and openly sadistic behavior. In one scene the German monster literally stares down an eye-patch-wearing, decorated Czech officer as the officer picks up a whip, which Heydrich intentionally drops to humiliate him (despite such bootlicking, the officer will later become one of the hostages). Heydrich addresses his audience (and viewers) exclusively in German, underscoring his sense of cultural superiority, a (Brechtian) distanciation that forbids any empathy or comprehension. As Comolli and Géré have put it, Heydrich's "first and only appearance weighs heavily. The character is designed by the fiction to contrive within a single scene, to convene and concentrate in his person, through his body, his face, his attitude the signs of a radical negativity, everything necessary to make him instantly and eternally hateful to the spectator. This body, this voice, these eyes bear death, castration, abnormality, sexual ambiguity. No hint of amiability; quite the contrary, in fact, something equivocal, venomous, petty even in his extremes of cruelty."[39]

Yet no matter how intimidating Heydrich's looks and demeanor might be, his powers also have limits. Pamphlets urging workers to slow down have been found in the Skoda factory and indicate chinks in his armor. The humoristic, even Disney-esque cartoons of a resting turtle humorously undermine Heydrich's military prowess. (The pamphlets will resurface in Czaka's apartment, where they have been planted to incriminate him, suggesting a deadly power that has outlasted the Hangman's.) Ultimately, the people who have authored, distributed, and followed the message of these pamphlets will also bring down the Hangman; while the assassination is the deed of one, the assassin's ultimate escape is made possible by the effort of many.

The strength of the Heydrich figure is further compromised by the mixed coding of his gender identity. There is a decidedly effeminate dimension to the performance of Hans von Twardowski (an openly gay actor in Weimar Germany). The pants seem a nudge too tight, he swivels the whip a bit too carelessly, his Hitler salute is limp-wristed, and lipstick accents his malicious smile.

Lang and Brecht here suggest a link between Nazism and "abnormal" sexuality that was often found in American films of the period, emphasized also in Tonio Selwart's role as Gestapo chief Haas. In an interview with Peter Bogdanovich, Lang explained, "With the one who has a pimple [Haas], I wanted to show that the depraved Nazi official a) has syphilis, b) doesn't give a damn what he's doing in the presence of this woman because he is probably a homosexual."[40] Von Twardowski's Heydrich comes into relief when we compare this role with the Nazis he usually played—mostly tall, stalwart, heal-clicking German officers that leave little room for ideological or sexual ambiguity, as he does in *Casablanca*, *Confessions of a Nazi Spy*, *Once upon a Honeymoon*, and *Background to Danger*. Other exile actors were also typecast in more narrow ways. Conrad Veidt often played the cultured, aristocratic swine, while Erich von Stroheim got to replay his "Hun" roles from World War I propaganda films such as *The Heart of Humanity* (Allen Hollubar, 1918). Rudolf Anders and Reinhold Schünzel repeatedly mimed the uniformed desk assassin, as Schünzel does here in the pedantic and sadistic petty bourgeois Inspector Ritter; and Sig Ruman provided

FIGURE 4.4 Prussian sadism and homosexuality accent the Hangman's affect.

comic relief as the bumbling, law-abiding officer, most memorably as "Concentration Camp Ehrhardt" in *To Be or Not to Be*. (Remarkable is the case of Martin Kosleck, who, by virtue of his uncanny similarity to the German minister of propaganda, got to play Goebbels in no less than five different films.) With the possible exception of Peter Lorre's Sergeant Berger in *The Cross of Lorraine* (Tay Garnett, 1943), none of these Hollywood exile Nazis conveys the same sexual ambiguities as von Twardowski's Heydrich.[41]

Alexander Granach's Inspector Gruber is certainly a Langian figure, but he is also Brechtian. Repeatedly singled out by contemporary reviewers for his bravura performance, Granach's Gruber breaks the mold of stiff, impersonal, by-the-book Nazi inspectors. He wears civilian clothes (including a bowler hat), neglects to do the Hitler salute, drinks beer, keeps company with prostitutes, and works outside the hierarchy of Heydrich/Haas/Ritter. Gruber is a close cousin to the Inspector Lohmann of *M* and *The Testament of Dr. Mabuse*—independent, down-to-earth, and working class. He is not easily fooled by his foes, and he has a wily wit and an astute power of observation. Brecht must have appreciated the class contradictions this character embodies in that his adversaries, the doctors and professors of the Czech resistance, are all upper middle class. Gruber is almost too sympathetic a character, for Americans love to root for the "little guy," which he is in both stature and status. Gruber provides ironic and unsettling twists to the genre's demands of providing clear guidelines with whom to sympathize.

The reworking of one of the genre's most common plot devices, the conversion story, offers an equally intriguing twist. Used most frequently in films just prior to and after the U.S. entry into the war, this formula shows an apolitical bystander undergo a serious political awakening in order to join a greater cause and become willing to make sacrifices. Take, for example, James Stewart as a family friend of a harassed professor in *The Mortal Storm*, or Humphrey Bogart as a cynical and disillusioned bar owner in *Casablanca*, as sports-fanatic mobster in *All Through the Night*, or as world-weary fishing-boat captain in *To Have and Have Not* (Howard Hawks, 1944). The conversions that occur in *Hangmen Also Die* are of a related but ultimately different sort. Masha Novotny has to learn that the victory of the resistance is more important than the safety of her father, while her fiancé, Jan Horak, who believes himself betrayed by her, must realize that she is really protecting Svoboda. A mass conversion also takes place; the Czech people, who first deny shelter to the fugitive assassin on the run, learn to work as one to save him from the clutches of the Gestapo, a scenario that is much harder to convey to an audience, since it cannot be portrayed through individual psychology.[42] Again the film complicates the strict binary opposition between good and bad that structures most anti-Nazi films, and it does so by virtue of two failed convictions. Czaka is elaborately framed and executed for a crime he did not commit (though as a traitor to his people he is certainly worthy of punishment), and Svoboda is *not* convicted for his crime, as the Nazis agree to close the book on the case, even after they realize that they have executed the wrong man. The film ascribes a higher moral ground to the fight of the resistance; they are, the film suggests, above the law. In what is certainly a testament to the film's commitment to the war effort, the Hays Office literally let Svoboda get away with murder.[43]

Previous commentators have considered Langian mise-en-scène and Brechtian distanciation to be diametrically opposed, and many critics have devoted much of their time to establishing "who did what?" Such questioning might have its merits if we were to follow a purely auteurist approach, but it belies the cooperative nature of film production, as well as the many points of convergence between Lang and Brecht. Rather than viewing the two approaches as antitheses, scholars like Gilles Deleuze and

Thomas Elsaesser have suggested a synthesis in which a Brechtian emphasis on antirealism is sublated (*aufgehoben*) in a Hegelian sense in Langian mise-en-scène: it has disappeared as an opposition; it has been elevated to a higher level; and it has been preserved. In *Cinema 2* Deleuze argues that Lang translates Brecht's theatrical notion of antirealism into a cinema of illusionism that does not simply question realism by opposing it to its opposite; rather, *Hangmen Also Die* questions the possibility of representation per se: "Appearances betray themselves, not because they would give way to a more profound truth, but simply because they reveal themselves as non-true."[44] If Brecht demands that the theater audience find its own solutions for the contradictions presented onstage, Lang unsettles filmgoers by portraying the relativity of appearances. *Hangmen Also Die* constantly misleads viewers through characters with false names and fake identities, or through a deliberately confusing mise-en-scène. Consider, for example, the opening sequence that concludes with Heydrich getting into his car to perform executions at the Skoda factory. In the next shot we see a car parked in the left part of the frame that appears to be Heydrich's, since his car left the previous frame exiting to the right. Only later do we find out that this is the getaway car for Heydrich's assassin, and that in an ironic twist the execution Heydrich has talked about turned out to be his own. The film abounds with such examples that call into question the viewers' ability to properly assess the events unfolding on the screen, a representational strategy that Thomas Elsaesser has labeled the transition from anti-illusionism to hyperrealism: "For Brecht, from the point of view of the producer, the cinema was at best a socially more convenient support for documenting the staging of theatrical performances, and at worst (seen from the point of view of its realist potential) a technically very defective apparatus of distanciation because it permitted no division between play-text and performance-text. For Lang, on the other hand, images constitute a reality in themselves, and any critique of reality situates itself at the level of the image: thus the search for truth can only be the play of the different mises-en-scène of falsehood."[45]

Lang's intentionally misleading representation insists on fake identities and false appearances, examples of which include Svoboda's giving away his profession when he dresses a wound too expertly; when wine is spilled intentionally to cover dripping blood; when a false kiss is imprinted too neatly on the cheek; or when a speech is scripted to mislead the Nazis. *Hangmen Also Die* reiterates in a different register the performativity that also informs Lubitsch's *To Be or Not to Be*. Just as in that film the Polish resistance dons the uniform of the enemy in order to undermine its power, in

Hangmen Also Die the framing of the quisling Czaka requires coordinated role playing on the part of the Czech population, a ruse that the Nazis ultimately will have to sanction as the truth.

FROM ANTI-NAZISM TO PREMATURE ANTIFASCISM

When *Hangmen Also Die* was released in April of 1943, it received many enthusiastic reviews. Unlike the dark humor of *To Be or Not to Be*, which critics considered in poor taste, given the dire circumstances in Nazi-occupied countries, Lang's rousing indictment of Nazi brutality and his celebration of Czech courage resonated well in wartime America. Joy Davidman observed that the film "may well be America's finest comment on the war."[46] The success was supported by Lang's self-fashioning as erstwhile antifascist and foe of Goebbels, which played a significant role in its marketing. "From the fierce passion of a man driven from his homeland," Alton Cook wrote in the *New York World Telegram*, "Fritz Lang has drawn a monument of venom and hatred for the Nazi conquerors of Czechoslovakia. Audiences will emerge from [the] theater at once more shaken and more stirred than by any other picture the war has produced."[47] Cook's mention of Lang's refugee status was no accident. It was around this time that Lang began to describe himself in interviews as a fierce Hitler opponent from the beginning. Repeatedly, he told the story of how Goebbels had offered him the job of heading the Nazi film industry and how he had fled Berlin in a cold sweat that same evening, unable to withdraw any money from his bank accounts, a tale we now know Lang significantly altered for heightened dramatic effect.[48] To augment this image, and to provide added publicity for the premiere of *Hangmen Also Die*, Lang's *The Testament of Dr. Mabuse*, his last German film, which was banned by the Nazis, had its U.S. premiere in March of 1943. It was released with a new prologue in which Lang explained that the film "was made as an allegory to show Hitler's processes of terrorism. Slogans and doctrines of the Third Reich have been put in the mouths of criminals in the film."[49] While it might certainly be understandable why Lang was eager to cast himself as an anti-Nazi avant la lettre, this interpretation of the *Mabuse* film remains highly implausible, not least because scriptwriter Thea von Harbou strongly sympathized with the Nazi party.[50]

Regardless of Lang's self-stylization, *Hangmen Also Die* is one of the most acclaimed films in the anti-Nazi series. Despite the strict political, ideological, and generic confines imposed on film in the service of the war effort, it is a modernist text that already points to the thematic, stylistic, and moral ambiguities of film noir. Yet about one year after its release there were signs that these films had run their cycle. With victory in Europe in sight after the landing in Normandy, audiences got weary of upbeat war stories, and the studios were understandably reticent to produce films that no one wanted to see.

As overt politics slowly disappeared from Hollywood films, the aftermath of the fight against fascism would be very political indeed. In 1946 the House Un-American Activities Committee (HUAC), which had been founded in 1934 and had gained real momentum in 1938 under the leadership of Martin Dies, was reactivated to investigate communist infiltration among private citizens, as well as public institutions. Widely believed to be a haven for liberals and "pinkos," Hollywood came under scrutiny, especially filmmakers who had voiced opposition to Hitler before Nazi Germany's declaration of war, a phenomenon now labeled premature antifascism. In Joseph Kanon's murder mystery *Stardust*, which is set among the Hollywood émigrés, Brecht dissects the contradictory implications of this term: "'Premature antifascism,' Brecht said, rolling out the phrase slowly, savoring it. 'What can it mean? There must have been a time when it was good to be a fascist. Then not. It's a trick, finding the right moment. You can be against the fascists, but not too soon. Then you're—well, what exactly?'"[51] Needless to say, neither the Brecht of Kanon's novel nor the real Brecht were ever able to fully comprehend the meaning of this contradictory term.

The HUAC hearings led to extensive black- and gray-listing of Hollywood filmmakers, effectively ending many careers and driving directors, writers, and actors into exile in Europe, Mexico, and elsewhere, while several of the Hollywood Ten spent significant time in jail for alleged contempt. Since the majority of exile filmmakers had been outspoken opponents of Nazi Germany, many of them faced similar threats. Of the people working on *Hangmen Also Die*, Lang escaped being called in front of the committee through backpedaling and maneuvering, yet between 1952 and 1954 he went without work for about fourteen months. Lang's biographer, Patrick McGilligan, claims the director's subsequent accounts exaggerate the threat hanging over him, which seems probable given Lang's inflation of his anti-Nazism avant la lettre in 1943. There is no doubt, nonetheless, that his career suffered. Lang himself never hid his pride about having created several anti-Nazi films, even though he would come to doubt their effectiveness. Thus, even after the war, Lang maintained that "many realities of the struggle against Fascism were not realized by a majority of Americans."[52]

Brecht and Eisler, in contrast, were not so lucky. Both had come under the surveillance of the FBI already several years earlier—as had the majority of exile writers, including Lion Feuchtwanger, Alfred Döblin, Franz Werfel, Berthold and Salka Viertel, and the entire Mann family—and were therefore obvious targets.[53] Hanns Eisler had to endure a rather humiliating hearing in front of HUAC in September of 1947. His brother Gerhart, a prominent communist leader who had repeatedly given false statements to U.S. immigration officials and used false names, was taken into custody and deported. Hanns Eisler, too, was forced to go back to Europe in the spring of 1948. The brothers had been denounced by their sister Ruth, a former communist who was now fighting Stalinism wherever she perceived it.

Brecht, too, was called in front of HUAC in October 1947, famously becoming the "eleventh" of the Hollywood Ten. Unlike his colleagues, who refused to answer the questions about membership in a Communist Party by citing the First Amendment, Brecht did cooperate with the committee to some extent and (faithfully) denied any such membership. He left the United States for Paris the following day. Brecht's play *Galileo*, which he rewrote during his stay in Hollywood with Charles Laughton, forcefully describes the power of the inquisition, a thinly veiled reference to the HUAC hearings.[54] John Wexley, Brecht's collaborator on *Hangmen Also Die*, saw his career come to a sudden end when he was brought before the House Un-American Activities Committee. He was named as a communist after working on the film *Cornered* (1945) and blacklisted in Hollywood.

Most of the other key figures discussed in this study were also affected in some way or other. Lubitsch, of course, was already dead by 1947; he had always been very careful not to participate in organizations and refugee networks that were reputed to support, or be infiltrated by, communists. Lorre was of interest to the authorities because of his drug habit more than because of his political activities. Upon his return to Germany, however, he did have a political awakening of sorts. Dieterle provided a different case. His 1938 film *Blockade*, which today counts as one of the first interventions into the Spanish Civil War on the American screen and which was made for Walter Wanger, an independent producer, immediately drew the attention of HUAC chairman Martin Dies. In the fall of 1940 the FBI began surveillance of Dieterle and his wife, following a tip-off that he was a secret agent for Nazi Germany. Even though this suspicion was quickly dispelled, he remained under observation until 1957 owing to his political commitment in the fight against Nazi Germany and his support for numerous leftist and communist artists.[55] After the war these activities, and particularly *Blockade*, were cited as examples of premature antifascism, leading to Dieterle's gray-listing in the 1950s, which ultimately forced him to resettle in West Germany when he could no longer find employment in Hollywood.

Edgar G. Ulmer had experienced a different kind of blacklisting in the mid-1930s, when Universal boss Laemmle made him persona non grata in Hollywood after he had eloped with the wife of Laemmle's nephew. Working on the fringes of Hollywood, he avoided the limelight that was cast on the directors and producers of big-budget anti-Nazi films. Nevertheless, he, like Lang, frequently claimed to have been intimidated and harassed by undercover agents. In a 1996 conversation with filmmaker Michael Henry Wilson, Ulmer's wife, Shirley, described how a couple of G-men had paid them a visit soon after the release of *Ruthless* in 1948:

> I remember two FBI agents knocked on our door one evening and came in as we were getting ready to go to Europe, and they asked me to leave the room and talked to Edgar at length. Afterward, when they left, they gave him a sealed envelope, which I saw him put in his pocket. When I questioned him afterward, he said, "now that was [one] of the most difficult moments of my life. They wanted me to squeal on friends. They gave me this envelope, which had a special address on it, and I was not to lose this, but was to send it to them with names of anybody that I found suspicious living abroad while I was there." He took the envelope and tore it in half.[56]

Yet there is no record that Ulmer was under observation in the FBI's extensive files, recently made available to the public through the Freedom of Information Act, nor is there any other concrete evidence of his political engagement.

The experience of the Red Scare shook many exiles' faith in the democratic foundations of the United States, a country they had eagerly made their home during the 1930s. Many of them considered a permanent return to Germany, because they no longer felt at home in their adopted country. Yet as shown in the following chapter, instead of just fleeing the United States, and effectively becoming exiles for a second time, some filmmakers instead chose to confront these issues head-on through their work. One of the most prominent figures to do so was Fred Zinnemann.

YOU CAN'T GO HOME AGAIN

OUT OF THE PAST

> *Immigrants ... have much in common with returning soldiers. Veterans and aliens alike must adjust to an environment they interpret in the light of their vision.*
> —SIEGFRIED KRACAUER[1]

> *The house is past.*
> —THEODOR W. ADORNO[2]

> *The killer with the limp is coming your way.*
> —MGM PROMOTIONAL MATERIAL[3]

The critical and commercial success of Fritz Lang and Bertolt Brecht's *Hangmen Also Die* can be attributed to several factors, but the most important may well be that it was the right film at the right time, boosting morale and empowering viewers by showing that Nazi Germany was vulnerable when the political reality of European warfare offered little to support such optimism. By the end of 1943, however, the immense military efforts of the Allies began to have a visible impact, making it possible at long last to envision an end to the war. As a consequence, Congress gutted the domestic operations of the Office of War Information (OWI), signaling to Hollywood that the film industry's role in supporting the war effort had come to an end. The studios welcomed this change as it gave them the opportunity to tell different stories. As *Variety* had reported in July of 1943, box-office revenue for war stories full of gung-ho patriotism had declined by 40 percent.[4] Instead of promoting films that emphasized unity and commitment, the studios now developed projects that offered a more critical look at the United States. One important type of story to gain prominence in the mid-1940s was the crime melodrama, later to be dubbed *film noir* by French critics.

To be sure, *film noir* is a term that has always meant different things to different people. There has been considerable debate over whether it is a genre, a style, a cycle or series, or merely a general mood that pervades certain films. Distinctions are sometimes hard to make, and borders blur. The nightmarish scenes in the prison cells of Gestapo headquarters of *Hangmen Also Die* evoke an expressionism that points both back to Lang's early Weimar films and forward to his later noirs. Warner Bros.' *Casablanca* features a jaded, cynical protagonist who runs a nightclub replete with illegal gambling, corrupt police officers, con artists, and various gangsters, all of which would become stock characters of noir. Rick Blaine's nighttime encounters with Ilsa Lund are cast in the atmospheric lighting favored by noir cinematographers such as John Alton. Yet what sets the film apart from the doom-ridden and fatalistic tales of noir is Rick Blaine's conversion into a selfless team player willing to sacrifice his love and to put his life on the line for a greater cause.

No matter how contested the term as well as its implied canon may be, film noir is today widely accepted as the body of films that most successfully conveys the complex and contradictory political, social, and psychological dimensions of postwar America. A long line of critics, from Raymond Borde and Etienne Chaumeton, through Sylvia Harvey, Dana Polan, and Frank Krutnik, have read noir as minutely registering the effects of World War II, and Paul Schrader has argued in his influential "Notes on Noir," that "post-war disillusionment" is one of four key determinants of film noir.[5] In the 1946 essay "Hollywood's Terror Films," which discusses, among others, Alfred Hitchcock's *Shadow of a Doubt*, Robert Siodmak's *The Spiral Staircase*, and Billy Wilder's *Lost Weekend*, Siegfried Kracauer similarly argued that contemporary films were symptomatic of a postwar American-style decadence. Even though Kracauer did not use the French term, his discussion of the films' themes of violence, sadism, morbidity, and psychological destruction and their shadowy mise-en-scène identified the traits his French contemporaries considered fundamental for the noir series.

There has been considerable debate regarding the European antecedents of noir, which include the visual style of German expressionism and the tropes of the Weimar *Straßenfilm* (street film) that introduced urban realism, moral decay, and sexual temptation in the figure of the femme fatale (most memorably by Lya De Putti, Louise Brooks, and Marlene Dietrich). This is a debate that does not need to be rehearsed here again.[6] What is beyond debate is that exile filmmakers made fundamental contributions to noir.[7] For the exiles, noir's cultural pessimism matched their own feelings of alienation, loss, and displacement. The noir protagonist's disillusionment, cynicism, and sense of being overpowered by fate resonated with the lessons of exile experienced by the refugees from Hitler. The general postwar malaise that has been credited as the source for noir's bleak outlook, furthermore, coincided with the exiles' own post-1945 disappointment stemming from the unfulfilled promises of the New Deal era and the general failure of liberalism (in which they had a vested interest, given the fact that it had provided them with a refuge from fascism). While the percentage of exile filmmakers working in film noir is smaller than in the anti-Nazi film or the horror film, the noir cycle is still arguably the body of films to which exile filmmakers contributed the most artistically. Directors such as Lang, Siodmak, Ulmer, Wilder, and Preminger left an indelible mark on noir, while many lesser-known directors, including Anatole Litvak, Rudolph Maté, John Brahm, Gustav Machaty, W. Lee Wilder, Gerd Oswald, Kurt Neumann, Gunter von Fritsch, and Wilhelm Thiele, often made their best films in this style. Equally important is the contribution of émigré cameramen such as Maté, Alton, Franz Planer, and Eugen Schüfftan; art directors like Hans Dreier; writers such as Victor Trivas; and composers including Max Steiner, Franz Waxman, Miklós Rózsa, Dimitri Tiomkin, and Bronislaw Kaper. It is also notable that directors mostly associated with other genres, including Douglas Sirk, Michael Curtiz, Curtis Bernhardt, William Dieterle, William Wyler, and Max Ophüls, have important noirs to their credit. In this last rubric also belongs Fred Zinnemann, whose *Act of Violence* is an overlooked film that like few others captures the predicament of postwar America. Often considered an anomaly in his works, *Act of Violence* forms part of his overall concern with the multiple legacies of World War II and the location of exile cinema in Hollywood.

THE MAN WITH THE LIMP

The stunning opening sequence of Fred Zinnemann's 1949 thriller *Act of Violence* packs a highly condensed repertoire of visual and narrative tropes now considered iconic in American film noir. A trench-coat-wearing man with a snap-brim hat limps through the wet streets of nighttime New York, his stature dwarfed by the towering silhouette of the Manhattan skyline. Lurching across a deserted avenue, he lashes a rolled-up newspaper against his injured leg like a jockey whipping a foundering horse, until he reaches

FIGURE 5.1 The menacing look of Joe Parkson (Robert Ryan).

his apartment building. A low-angle shot follows him stumbling upstairs, where he switches on the light and hurriedly searches a dresser for a gun buried under some clothes. A close-up of the Colt, brought nearer to the face for careful inspection and the loading of a clip, gives us our first look at a determined-looking man, while Bronislaw Kaper's score flares up and the title of the film flashes across the screen.[8] In less than a minute of screen time *Act of Violence* establishes the mood of impending violence and doom as quickly and efficiently as no other film noir.

As we later learn, the man's name is Joe Parkson (Robert Ryan), and he is setting out on a cross-country mission that will transport him from a rainy, forbidding East Coast metropolis to the bucolic, sunny Southern California town of Santa Lisa. During the several-day Greyhound passage, he never sleeps or averts his forward stare to look out the window. The arrival of the bus, signaled by Kaper's jarring score giving way to a diegetic patriotic tune, coincides with a Memorial Day parade, and the impatient Parkson is made to stop at a crosswalk while the musicians march by. The scene provides the first of the film's many ironic comments on the aftermath of World War II, for Parkson is an ex-GI, as we later find out, who finds himself not only excluded from the commemorations but, as is explicitly shown, at cross-purposes with the marching veterans. He finally manages to cross the road by inserting himself in the small space behind the departing musicians in uniform and before the arriving veterans in civilian clothing—a space of in-between and nonbelonging that marks his own outsider position.

Checking in at a hotel for an open-ended stay, Parkson quickly dismisses the bellhop who brings his luggage, grabs a phone book, and circles the name of Frank Enley. We cut to a close-up of Enley (Van Heflin), his small son on his shoulders and his young wife, Edith (Janet Leigh), at his side, as he listens to the dedication ceremony of a housing project. Identified as a "fellow veteran" and former captain, contractor Enley is congratulated for his leading role in the project and is called onto the stage, where he receives the warm applause of the community, while his admiring wife and son look on.

The memorable opening of *Act of Violence* firmly establishes the op-positions that define the antagonistic relationship of Parkson and Enley before the film sets out to complicate, and indeed undo, the neat binaries. Parkson, a lonely, disabled, and vengeful fringe dweller, is introduced as a classic noir character whose sinister intentions can only be guessed. Enley,

FIGURE 5.2 No room for the veteran in the Memorial Day parade.

in contrast, appears to be the model for postwar American recovery and progress, a wholesome family man and highly regarded community member basking in the glow of his professional and private achievements and the warm California sunshine. As is later revealed, it was precisely the newspaper write-up of Enley's professional success that set Parkson on Enley's trail after years of searching and that now leads to the intrusion of Parkson's life on Enley's.

Remarkably, the sequence conveys the dichotomy between Parkson and Enley through purely nonverbal means. The film literally lunges into action by having Kaper's soundtrack already being heard over MGM's famous lion's roar—a highly unorthodox opening, particularly for this studio—while the title *Act of Violence* flashes over the unfolding action rather than bringing it to a halt. Similarly unusual, and also at the service of keeping up a brisk pace, is the omission of any credits, which are withheld until the closing of the film (in what was, in fact, one of the first films to do so), thereby also augmenting the anonymity of the Robert Ryan character. When Joe Parkson first comes into view, it is in a long shot, his dragging leg providing an audible clue that makes up for the almost complete lack of dialogue of the first minutes. Robert Surtees's camera then captures Parkson from behind and below as he climbs the stairs, and from an extreme low angle as he inspects the gun. Dimly lit by low-key lighting and crammed into the claustrophobic space of his small apartment, Parkson is effectively rendered an anonymous, unbalanced, and uprooted character. The contrast to Enley could not be greater. His identity established by the circling of his name in the phone book, Enley is first shown in close-up, outdoors, and with high-key lighting, the camera slowly pulling back to first include his son and his wife in the frame before the surrounding fellow citizens come into view—a careful contextualization that firmly places him within the community of family and town and informs us about his professional standing, including his distinguished service in the army.

As set up by this conflict- and suspense-building opening, the plot of *Act of Violence* consists largely of Parkson's pursuit of, and confrontation with, Enley, following a trajectory during which Parkson intrudes ever closer into Enley's life without ever facing him directly, until there is a quick brush between them at the film's halfway point, before a prolonged spatial separation of the two antagonists erupts in a final showdown. In well-measured pieces Robert L. Richard's screenplay, based on a story by Collier Young, reveals why Parkson is bent on destruction and what secret lies behind Enley's facade of wholesomeness. When Enley leaves for a fishing trip to the mountains soon after the dedication ceremony, Parkson finds out his whereabouts

FIGURE 5.3 The successful paterfamilias basking in his accomplishments.

from unsuspecting Edith, but Enley escapes. Upon learning about his pursuer, Enley rushes back home and holes up in his house, without providing reasons to his alarmed wife. In the middle of the night Enley sneaks away to a builders' convention in Los Angeles, leaving Parkson yet again to find the vulnerable Edith home alone the next morning. This time the gun-wielding Parkson informs her that her husband was a "stool pigeon" for the Nazis. A worried Edith races after her husband to Los Angeles and finally catches up with him at the conference hotel, where on a fire escape stairway he confesses to her the events that took place in a Nazi prisoner of war camp. Learning about his soldiers' plans to escape, he tells her, he informed the Nazis so as to prevent bloodshed, but the Germans broke their promise, and all were tortured and killed except for Parkson, who narrowly escaped death. The second half of the film has a guilt-ridden and greatly disturbed Enley descend into the bowels of Los Angeles's Bunker Hill area, where an aged hooker (Mary Astor) takes pity on him but unwittingly delivers him into the hands of a "lawyer," who in turn introduces him to the hired killer Johnny. Only when Johnny is about to shoot Parkson can Enley get a hold of himself, and in the final showdown he averts the killing by taking the bullet meant for Parkson.

While the film opens with setting up the stark differences between Enley and Parkson, it becomes slowly apparent that more unites than separates the two characters. Neil Sinyard has pointed out that "as the film develops, it becomes clear that Parkson represents not evil as such but the dark side of Enley which must be brought to light."[9] It should be added that the two men not only share a dark side but that that dark side gets contextualized very carefully as the consequence of *shared* traumatic war experiences. While Enley first appears a winner and Parkson a loser, neither can outrun his wartime experience, be it repression and disavowal or physical and psychological maiming. Both men experience a fundamental crisis that calls into question their respective notions of home and sense of belonging, their masculinity and their ability to relate to women, and their overall place in society. While postwar America is bent on moving forward and aligning itself along ideological lines quite different from the fight against Nazism, the traumatized veterans remain stuck within a completely different temporality. As both Parkson and Enley come to realize, the past keeps intruding onto the present, compelling them to endlessly revisit events to which others are denied access and therefore cannot comprehend.

NATIVE AND NONNATIVE ALIENS

As the epigraph by Siegfried Kracauer indicates, there exist important parallels between the experience of veterans and immigrants. Just as the exile is forced to bridge the fundamental rift between host culture and native culture, the returning soldier confronts a radically changed political and social reality that often proves beyond recognition. The environment to which they both must adjust, Kracauer implies, challenges their respective "visions," which have been formed by traditions that no longer seem to hold. Yet while the exile leaves home in full, if dreaded, anticipation of an encounter with the unknown, the returning veteran is caught off guard by a strangeness he did not anticipate and cannot account for. The cruel irony of the veteran is that his sense of belonging is denied, despite the fact—maybe even because of the fact—that the very service he rendered his nation was meant to preserve his home. The experience abroad, which introduces a plurality of vision similar to that of the exile, is one reason why "home" has acquired a new meaning; another is that in the soldier's absence things have not remained the same either. He is not the same man who left, and he does not return to the same place. Home feels strange, and he feels a stranger in his own house—an experience that also informs the return of the exile to his homeland (as we will see in the next chapter).

Yet to what degree can we even call the cinema of Fred Zinnemann a cinema of exile? To the extent that personal biographies matter in the construction of the exilic, Zinnemann seems a far-fetched example. A native of Vienna, Zinnemann received his training completely outside the German film industry, studying cinematography (with his close friend Gunter von Fritsch) in 1927 in Paris before leaving for the United States in 1929, where he served a three-year apprenticeship in the MGM short-subject departments before signing a long-term contract. His only German film experience includes serving (uncredited) as assistant to director Robert Land on *Ich küsse ihre Hand, Madame* (1928, starring Marlene Dietrich) and to cameraman Eugen Schüfftan on *Menschen am Sonntag / People on Sunday* (1930), his only responsibility being, in his own words, "to carry the camera around and to stay out of trouble."[10] Of Jewish descent, Zinnemann could not return to his native Vienna after the 1938 annexation, but unlike Dieterle, Lang, or Lubitsch, Zinnemann did not undergo a political awakening until his postwar return to Europe.[11]

Trained almost entirely by MGM, Zinnemann was a staunch defender of the classic studio system, including its oft-derided moguls, whose penchant for showmanship he appreciated. Nevertheless, he was considered a maverick who had problems accepting hierarchical structures. He was fired from his first Hollywood job as an extra on *All Quiet on the Western Front* (Lewis Milestone, 1930) after speaking back to an assistant, and in 1947 he was the first director to be suspended by MGM after turning down directing assignments on three consecutive projects, because he felt the scripts were inferior. After fulfilling his MGM contract with *Act of Violence*, Zinnemann would never again sign with a major studio, opting instead to pursue semi-independent productions both in the United States and Europe, and residing in England for the last thirty years of his life.

In contrast to his post-1948 films, *Act of Violence* is very much an MGM film (even if it pushed the studio's envelope on certain levels) and one that Zinnemann considered the conclusion of his apprenticeship in the studio system, rather than a deviation from, or a challenge to, the norms of studio filmmaking, as is sometimes claimed about noir.[12] Yet it was an unlikely film for MGM, a studio that was mostly associated with glossy musicals and escapist fare with high production values; the studio's most famous foray into noir, the polished James M. Cain adaptation *The Postman Always Rings*

Twice (Tay Garnett, 1946), is a far cry from the dark and fatalistic *Double Indemnity* (Billy Wilder), Paramount's 1944 film that broke the decade-long PCA ban on bringing Cain to the screen. Certainly, *Act of Violence* would not have been produced if Dore Schary had not replaced Louis B. Mayer as head of production and eventually president of MGM.[13] Reacting to the larger postwar crisis of the studio system, and opposing Mayer's penchant for splashy entertainment, Schary favored films that conveyed moral concerns, such as *Crossfire* (Edward Dmytryk, 1947), which he had produced for RKO and which earned Robert Ryan an Academy Award nomination for Best Supporting Actor. Ryan's role in this film as an anti-Semitic killer was the foil against which his Parkson in *Act of Violence* reveals his more tragic dimension, not least because the trailer introduced Ryan as "the menacing star of *Crossfire*," thereby setting up audiences to expect an all-out evil killer only to slowly reveal the traumatized victim underneath.[14]

Although Zinnemann left MGM because he cherished his independence, he never thought of himself as an auteur—at least not to the degree that Ulmer or Lang did—but more as a director willing to assign responsibility and independence to those on his team. He derided auteurism as a critical concept, but he also felt deeply hurt when auteurist critics dismissed his films, calling his style flat and impersonal, and his stories too linear, humorless, and overdetermined. In his influential book *The American Cinema* Andrew Sarris grouped him under the unflattering rubric "Less Than Meets the Eye" and concluded, "At its best, his direction is inoffensive, at its worst, it's downright dull."[15]

It is certainly true that thematic concerns provide a greater unity in Zinnemann's oeuvre than formal flair. His most important films all focus on different forms of outsiders and on individuals who face a crisis of conscience or personal integrity, which is of course also true for the existential conflict of *Act of Violence*. Like Frank Enley, at the decisive moment Zinnemann's protagonists usually find themselves completely alone and having to rely on their own moral compass, most famously shown in Marshall Will Kane in *High Noon* (1952). Stylistically, Zinnemann certainly was a less flashy and more sober and self-effacing director than Wilder or Lang and far less of a self-promoter. Since his films are less self-reflexive and opulent than those of peers such as Vincente Minnelli, Nicholas Ray, and Anthony Mann, they have often gone unnoticed. Reluctant to relinquish control over his films, Zinnemann, with twenty-one features to his credit, completed a body of work significantly smaller than that of most directors who can look back on a fifty-year career. And while Zinnemann can claim to have gotten excellent performances out of major stars—including Audrey Hepburn, Gary Cooper, Vanessa Redgrave, Jane Fonda, Frank Sinatra, and Robert Mitchum, and for casting Montgomery Clift in his first released film role while also giving Marlon Brando and Meryl Streep their first screen appearances—the films they made with him are rarely the best in their career. All this has contributed to the fact that scholarly attention to Zinnemann has been scant, even though he was a much-decorated artist, winning a total of four Academy Awards (making him arguably the most recognized exile director after Billy Wilder).[16]

While Zinnemann's early training and career at MGM hardly provided him with the multiplicity of vision and sense of liminality that is central to exile cinema, his immediate postwar experience abroad marked a caesura that proved formative for his subsequent films. If directors such as John Ford, John Huston, Frank Capra, Anatole Litvak, and George Stevens, who had served in the army, could not return to making escapist films, a similar case can be made for the civilian Zinnemann, whose stay in Europe in 1947–48 and soon thereafter in Palestine brought him into closer proximity to the experience of the soldiers on active duty and profoundly changed his attitude toward filmmaking in America. Being in Europe after the war, he commented in a 1994 interview, "opened my eyes. In Hollywood, people were still dedicated to the happy ending, to illusion and to the caricature of life. [In Europe] it was the era of neorealism, people like Rossellini and DeSica [sic]. When I came back to Hollywood, I felt I wasn't quite the same as I had been when I left, while generally people continued to do fake stories with fake endings."[17] For the rest of his career Zinnemann's films would explore the tension between the Old World and the New, and late in life he concluded, "My work is a symbiosis of Europe and America."[18]

The exilic dimension of Fred Zinnemann's cinema manifests itself most consistently through its representation of the experience of fascism in Europe and World War II, providing the subject matter of his strongest films. His first MGM A-level film, *The Seventh Cross* (1944, based on Anna Seghers's well-known novel and starring Spencer Tracy),[19] tells of the escape of seven prisoners from a Nazi concentration camp and was made at the very time his parents, unbeknownst to Zinnemann, were murdered in the real camps in Europe.[20] Shot entirely in the studio, the film can be lauded for its differentiated representation of Germans at a time when anti-Nazi ideology left little room for distinctions between good and bad Germans, but the film suffers from MGM's polished look and well-fed cast, who made for improbable camp survivors.[21] The realist *The Search* (1948), in contrast, inaugurated a radically different form of filmmaking that also marks *Act of Violence*, *The Men* (1950) and *Teresa* (1951), which together constitute Zinnemann's ambitious war tetralogy. The subject matter of these films, in turn, already points forward to such later works as *From Here to Eternity* (1953, about the attack on Pearl Harbor), *A Hatful of Rain* (1957, about a drug-addicted veteran of the Korean War), *Behold a Pale Horse* (1964, about an exile from Franco's Spain), and *Julia* (1977, about playwright Lillian Hellman's relationship with a childhood friend who goes underground to fight the Nazis).[22]

Among Zinnemann's films the war tetralogy stands out for its thematic and aesthetic unity. On the level of subject matter all four films explore the fight against Nazi Germany and the aftermath of the war yet always from a different angle, thus providing a multifaceted portrait of the experience of American soldiers in various European theaters of war and in postwar American society. Focusing on the fate of displaced children in postwar Germany, *The Search* tells the story of an American GI (Montgomery Clift) who befriends a homeless young Czech boy separated from his mother in the turmoil of the war. The encounter is presented through the perspective of the young American soldier and thus for the benefit of an American audience who, according to Zinnemann, needed to be educated about the situation in Europe.[23] *The Men* revolves around the paraplegic veteran Ken (played by Marlon Brando), who struggles to adjust to his physical disability. Taking Joe Parkson's limp to the extreme, the film explores Ken's frustrations and impatience as he is forced to adapt to a radically different life, particularly in his relation to his wife. In the end the future of Ken's marriage remains as doubtful as Parkson's relationship with his girlfriend, Ann. *Teresa*, too, focuses on the strains of marriage, namely between an American soldier on tour in Italy and his Italian bride, whom he brings home to New York—a contrasting portrait of a bicultural relationship during times of war and peace in both Europe and America.

Stylistically, the four films share a commitment to realism that stands in stark contrast to the aesthetics of prewar and wartime Hollywood studio productions and that at times transcends the highly symbolic realism of many noirs. Zinnemann here draws on his apprenticeship with documentary filmmaker Robert Flaherty, according to Zinnemann the most lasting influence of his career, as well as on contemporaneous Italian neorealism, while also harking back to his Mexican film *Redes / The Wave* (1934), on which he had collaborated with photographer Paul Strand in Veracruz.[24] Although *The Search* is not free of sentimentality, particularly in its flashbacks to prewar Prague and in its patronizing voice-over (added without Zinnemann's consent), its casting of child actors, its focus on the experience of children, and its use of real locations, including the rubble of bombed-out German cities, clearly referenced the postwar films by Rossellini, Visconti, and De Sica, then still largely unknown to mainstream American audiences.[25] One of the film's main locations is a Displaced Persons Camp, whose faded Nazi insignia provides an ironic comment on who is responsible for the suffering of the traumatized children it now harbors—a very similar location, indeed, to the one of the deadly confrontation of Peter Lorre's *Der Verlorene / The Lost One* (Germany, 1951). With its Italian setting and partially Italian cast, *Teresa* also invokes neorealism, particularly *Paisan* (Rossellini, 1946). In a 1949 review, Kracauer called *The Search* "a fascinating blend of American and European mentality. There are still vestiges of artificial emotions and Hollywood rhetoric in it, but they all disappear among a mass of scenes which, shot on location, render real distress with real understanding."[26]

Act of Violence shares with *The Search*, *The Men*, and *Teresa* the urgency of telling a wartime story that those who did not live through it will not be able to comprehend. *The Search* and *Act of Violence* are further united by a focus on the camps (also central to *The Seventh Cross*), even if in the noir Enley's experiences as prisoner of war are conveyed only indirectly, namely through his confession to Edith and through a flashback during which he replays in his mind the voices of the interrogating German officers as he runs through the Hill Street tunnel in downtown LA—a haunting moment that forces him to visualize the torturous death of his comrades in the escape tunnel, just as Edith (and the viewer) is forced to imagine what her husband experienced. Significantly, the claustrophobic passage through the street tunnel culminates in Enley's aborted suicide attempt, underscoring the fundamental difference between experiencing and imagining trauma that is central for the film—while his comrades died for real, Enley can only attempt to share their fate.[27]

Focusing on locations that render impossible prewar notions of comfort, security, and belonging, all four films pose the question, What is home? Interestingly, the town of Santa Lisa, where Enley resides—a quintessential American small town that stands for wholesomeness, order, and safety, particularly in MGM films—provides a strong contrast to the DP camp of *The Search*, the recovery ward of *The Men*, and *Teresa*'s cramped New York apartment in which a culturally displaced Teresa is further ostracized by her husband's overbearing mother. The latter three are all locations that signal various states of displacement, itinerancy, and nonbelonging. Yet as the story of *Act of Violence* unravels, it becomes clear that these same experiences have also invaded small-town America. As a consequence, Santa Lisa (a fictional stand-in for Santa Monica, where Zinnemann resided at the time) becomes a place that is not immune to the malice, deceit, and violence that film noir usually stages in urban centers.

THE STRANGER IN THE HOUSE

In his study *Dark Borders: Film Noir and American Citizenship* Jonathan Auerbach has linked film noir's feelings of displacement, dispossession, and doubt to the emergence of the Cold War and the Red Scare. In postwar America circa 1947, when the Cold War redefined the rights and responsibilities of citizenship, Auerbach argues, Freud's concept of the uncanny actually began to function identically to the then-circulating term *un-American*. Reading the noir cycle against the foil of the anticommunist measures taken by the House Un-American Activities Committee (HUAC), Auerbach focuses on how negotiations of anxieties of belonging and not-belonging possess a topicality that has often eluded more abstractly philosophical analyses. As he states, the existential alienation of noir "needs to be more precisely grounded in specific historical and cultural fears about enemy aliens lurking within."[28]

Critics have often read *Act of Violence* as a story of personal crisis and redemption. In this they followed the director, who stated, "An idea that has meant a lot to me is Robert Louis Stevenson's: 'A man's character is his destiny.' It is the theme of some of my most successful films."[29] Yet the story of Enley and Parkson is not only one of personal destiny but also one of the postwar America Auerbach describes. *Act of Violence* can be singled out as a film whose powerful critique of home and sense of belonging is enacted at the cross-section of postwar trauma and of a nation—and film industry—in the grasp of anticommunist witch hunts and the Red Scare.

This topicality is most poignantly established in the film's depiction of the home and of urban and suburban geography. Enley's psychological crisis and his concomitant precarious sense of home and belonging, which also entails his relation to his wife, and his masculine identity, is most powerfully conveyed through the changing representations of his house, which deteriorates from a bright and spacious family home into a claustrophobic and volatile space increasingly under siege. In the scene immediately following the dedication of the housing project, which has established him as a respected home builder and admired husband, everything signals a happy family life, as husband and wife are engaged in playful banter. About to set out on an overnight fishing trip, Enley digs through a closet searching for gear, while Edith mocks his inability to find items in plain view by jabbing, "You've lost your glamour, Major." Frank gets back at her by tossing her his army jacket, which she had surreptitiously snuck into the car. With hindsight, it will become clear that the refusal of the jacket, a reminder of wartime events, as well as Edith's apparently insignificant remark (neither of which was included in the penultimate draft of the screenplay) are subtle forebodings that Frank is not the man Edith thought he was.[30]

The contrast to the second, much longer sequence in the house could not be stronger. Now aware that he is being pursued, an anxious Enley returns home early from his fishing trip and immediately begins drawing the blinds and pulling down the shades, thereby echoing the mandatory blackouts the Los Angeles area experienced only a few years earlier and effectively conveying that the war is not over—it has hit home, after all. Storing gear in the same dark closet that he rummaged in earlier, Enley is literally blinded like a deer caught in the headlights of a car when Edith suddenly turns on a naked light bulb, a visual metaphor that underscores that what has been hidden must be brought to light. Low-key lighting, low-angle photography, and Kaper's disturbing score turn the spaces previously shown as comfortable and comforting into a narrow, confining, and threatening enclave. Enley's home has literally become *unheimlich* in Freud's sense, a place that is homely and familiar but that at the same time harbors something hidden or concealed, now pushing to come to the surface. Prying explanations from a reluctant Frank, Edith finally gets her husband to put a name to the menace lurking behind their front door, and he shows her a picture of himself and Joe Parkson during happier days in the army—the stranger outside is not a stranger at all, nor is he outside.

If the mood in this second scene is one of fear, coupled with Enley's evasive maneuvers, Edith and Frank's final scene in the house is informed by hypocrisy and lies. Returning beat up and filthy from his descent into skid row, where he has hired a killer to take care of Parkson, Frank is caught by Edith as he returns to the house, framed in the doorway like the gun-wielding Parkson was earlier, the two men's identities now blending into one—Frank has become the stranger in the house. A bath and a clean suit and shirt cannot mask his dirty secret. He tells his wife, "It's all over," an outright lie as the viewer knows and as she suspects. But Edith has given up

FIGURE 5.4 Enley reenacts Parkson's illicit entry, rendering him a stranger in his own house.

asking for explanations, and husband and wife pull themselves together to enact a scene of happy domesticity (she is mending some clothes, and he busies himself with the newspaper) that can barely cover up their mistrust and anxieties, while the ticking of the clock, signaling the impending showdown, heightens the suspense (a device used to perfection in *High Noon*). Coaxing his wife into checking up on the sleeping son upstairs, Enley again sneaks away into the night, never to return home.

Notably, Frank's confession to Edith, his single moment of honesty and sincerity, is not rendered at home but in the bleak stairway of the convention hotel—a space of in-between and nonbelonging that recalls Parkson's intrusion into the Memorial Day parade earlier. (In Young's draft this confession takes place in Enley's house; archival materials link the change to Zinnemann's touring of downtown locations.)[31] As Sinyard has observed, in the films of Zinnemann the staircase is frequently used as a dramatically charged location where characters make life-changing decisions (most prominently so in *The Seventh Cross* and *Teresa*).[32] Coming at the exact halfway mark, this turning point is staged as the film's most overtly expressionist scene, replete with ominous shadows, angled photography, and the two characters moving in and out of well-lit and dark places. As Enley confesses his treason, he clutches the bars of the railing, thus invoking the iron bars of the prisoner camp (later echoed by the bars of Georgie's cot that block Enley's parting view of his son), an image that belies the Fire Escape sign's promise of a getaway above Enley's shoulders.

From the same hotel Enley will flee from Parkson into the bowels of the city, running down a never-ending string of stairways until he reaches the part of town populated by its lowliest inhabitants—drunks, prostitutes, and criminals of all varieties—a fitting surrounding for Enley's psychological breakdown and subsequent low point of moral behavior. It is here that the past finally catches up with him, the ugly truth that had been kept at bay in neat Santa Lisa erupting into his face. It is here that in a drunken stupor he arranges for Parkson's elimination, confirming the "lawyer's" verdict that a man who killed once will do it again. And it is here that he tells the tired hooker Pat that he has no home to return to—Parkson's sudden intrusion has forever destroyed his facade of rootedness and safety.

FIGURE 5.5 No exit after all: Enley's confession on the staircase.

A frequent setting of Hollywood films of the 1940s and 1950s, the downtown area around Bunker Hill is a noir location of almost mythical proportions and in many ways the precise opposite, and nemesis, of the Santa Lisa–like suburbia into which so many Angelinos of Enley's creed, class, and ethnicity would escape after the end of the war.[33] In response to pent-up housing demands, caused by a stalling housing development and the recruitment of a workforce from rural areas to the big cities, widespread suburban development took place after the war. Special loans allowed GIs to purchase new homes, especially of the cookie-cutter, inexpensive housing tract variety that Enley's company builds (while he himself resides in a freestanding family home with a garden that Parkson sarcastically describes as "real nice").[34]

The Bunker Hill area, in contrast, was a part of Los Angeles where 98 percent of the homes had been built before 1920, and nothing new was built there after 1930.[35] It became one of "the earliest post–World War II urban redevelopment projects mandated by the 1945 California Community Redevelopment Act and the establishment of the Los Angeles California Redevelopment Agency (CRA) in 1948," but nothing much came of it. "By 1966 the CRA had acquired title to nearly all of Bunker Hill. It was bulldozed out of existence by the end of the decade."[36] It is no accident that home builder and homemaker Enley faces his existential crisis in the Los Angeles location most strongly defined by its opposition to, or neglect of, urban redevelopment, and that this moral breakdown follows the largely satirical representation of the postwar elite of home builders at the Blake hotel, a bunch of drunken, rowdy, and hypocritical men who even hit on Edith.[37] As Ed Dimendberg has astutely observed, it is not only the war that reasserts itself with Parkson's sudden appearance but also the metropolis itself, making postwar urban (re-)development "a latent content of the film."[38]

As the Bunker Hill sequence shows, *Act of Violence* insists on being a topical film with a larger agenda of social criticism, very much in line with Schary's plans for revamping MGM and Zinnemann's directorial ambition, but it also trades quite heavily in the mythological and highly symbolic connotations that Bunker Hill acquired during the 1940s, particularly in the work of Raymond Chandler. Consider how this now classic passage from Chandler's novel *The High Window* (1943) sets the tone for *Act of Violence*:

> Bunker Hill is old town, lost town, shabby town, crook town. Once, very long ago, it was the choice residential district of the city, and there are still standing a few of the jigsaw Gothic mansions with wide porches and walls

covered with round-end shingles and full corner bay windows with spindle turrets. They are all rooming houses now, their parquetry floors scratched and worn through the once glossy finish and the wide sweeping staircases are dark with time and with cheap varnish laid on over generations of dirt. In the tall rooms haggard landladies bicker with shifty tenants. On the wide cool front porches, reaching their cracked shoes into the sun and staring at nothing, sit old men with faces like lost battles. . . .

Out of the apartment houses come women who should be young but have faces like stale beer; men with pulled-down hats and quick eyes that look the street over behind the cupped hand that shields the match flame; worn intellectuals with cigarette coughs and no money in the bank; fly cops with granite faces and unwavering eyes; cokies and coke peddlers; people who look like nothing in particular and know it, and once in a while even men that actually go to work. But they come out early, when the wide cracked sidewalks are empty and still have dew on them."[39]

It is easy to recognize Pat among the women with faces like stale beer; she is a femme fatale who has little femme and no fatality left about her (Mary Astor playing wonderfully against the very type she helped establish in John Huston's *The Maltese Falcon* only eight years earlier), just as the "Johnnys," the "lawyers," and the various bartenders of *Act of Violence* are stock characters out of hard-boiled fiction.

The symbolically charged Bunker Hill is the place where Enley's retreat from light into dark reaches its climax and where he realizes his own state of homelessness, the final approximation of his life and that of the itinerant Parkson. To augment Enley's existential crisis, the editing deliberately jumbles the spatial layout of Bunker Hill, creating a disorienting geography that mimics Enley's increasing mental disturbance but that belies the area's neat layout, thus further enhancing Chandler's willful stylization.[40] Despite its use of real locations and readily recognizable downtown landmarks such as Clay Street and the Angel Flight funicular, *Act of Violence* creates exteriors and interiors that are both "real" and deeply symbolic, an effect further augmented through careful lighting and camera placement, as cinematographer Robert Surtees described.[41]

While there are scenes where Surtees worked entirely without recourse to the studio and without any processing shots, such as the tunnel sequence and Enley's breakdown at a chain-link fence, which acquire a certain verité style, in most cases locations and their spatial relations to each other are reconfigured or dressed up (such as the Glendale train station—also

FIGURE 5.6A–C Angel Flight as the emblematic Bunker Hill location in *Act of Violence*, *Criss Cross* (Robert Siodmak, 1949), and *Kiss Me Deadly* (Robert Aldrich, 1955).

used in *Double Indemnity*—which becomes the Santa Lisa train station). As a result, the film creates a "tension between . . . palpable realist and expressionist impulses," which Patrick Keating has described as fundamental for film noir.[42]

While the film insists that Frank Enley's existential crisis, which leads to the destruction of his home and his family, is the result of his wartime betrayal, it also becomes clear that postwar society has failed veterans like him and Parkson. As I noted earlier, the film entails repeated ironic comments on the disrespectful treatment of the disabled veteran (such as Parkson's exclusion from the Memorial Day parade), as well as an overall indictment of society's unequal distribution of rewards for service rendered during the war. Consider the hired killer Johnny, who boasts that he escaped the war unharmed thanks to a cushy desk job in the army, a clear indication that cowardice and opportunism remain undetected. A particularly strong indictment of postwar America is voiced by Parkson himself, who, in lines cut from the final film, explains to his girlfriend Ann: "You don't care [what

Enley did]—that's the trouble. That's the trouble with the whole world. People don't care, people forget. And as long as guys like Adams [as Enley was called in earlier drafts] can get away with it and come home and be heroes and big-shots, as long as men can lie and betray and kill and not pay for it—it'll all happen again. All over again. From the little things to the big things. From a sell-out to war."[43]

Parkson is largely left to his own devices to cope with his trauma, as his prolonged stays in recovery wards seem to have had no effect on him. With its ideology of progress and moving forward, postwar America also provides an easy cover for Enley's hypocrisy. What is more, the systems of justice and of law enforcement seem ineffective, thereby giving rise both to Parkson's vigilantism and Enley's cover-up of wartime events. The police are not an institution that can deal effectively with Parkson (all they do is send him away when he stalks Enley's home at night, only to have him return the next morning), nor does Enley trust them with dealing with the stalker (though mostly for fear of what his son will think of him when he grows up). In an earlier version of the script Edith even goes to the police to seek protection for her husband but is not taken seriously and is turned away. This vacuum of jurisdiction and law enforcement is filled by the "lawyer" Enley meets in a downtown bar, an impostor who holds forth about how money can buy the justice withheld by society. While Enley's sacrifice at the end of the film may indeed provide an act of expiation that absolves his personal guilt, as the director has stated, it is the larger social and political forces, which first thrust men into war and then fail to facilitate their readjustment to peacetime society, that ultimately stand accused.

While Zinnemann and other European émigrés were busy in the film studios making motion pictures that scrutinized traditional notions of home, in nearby West Hollywood Theodor W. Adorno was penning *Minima Moralia*, his autobiographical reflections on his exile in California. Film historians may best remember Adorno for his aggressive indictment of the Hollywood studio system, or what he called the culture industry, but privately he entertained close contacts with exile filmmakers such as Lang and Salka Viertel, whose courageous criticism of fascism he admired, even if he doubted the ability of commercial filmmaking to communicate political opposition. As *Minima Moralia* shows, for Adorno, too, the experience of exile led to radically interrogating traditional notions of belonging. Not only did he rail against the kind of postwar track homes Enley develops, which he called "factory sites that have strayed into the consumption sphere, devoid of all relation to the occupant," but he also believed that the experience of exile had ended the era of the house itself.⁴⁴ Searching for "the most miniscule degree of morality in the face of unprecedented historical mass suffering," as Nico Israel has put it, Adorno developed a larger moral argument about the impossibility of home and being at home, which he offered up with biting irony: "It is part of morality not to be at home in one's home."⁴⁵

It remains ambiguous whether Enley's confession to Pat that he has no home is just an expression of his exasperation or whether he, following Adorno, consciously renounces his home, because he realizes he has forfeited any right to one. According to Zinnemann the latter is more probable as the director saw the film ending with an act of moral redemption: "The avenger . . . sets out to even the score. In the end, the hunted man . . . expiates his cowardice by giving up his own life."⁴⁶ Yet whether such expiation is indeed possible remains an open question. Will Georgie, Enley's young son, really remember his father as a hero, only because he gave his life so as not to betray his comrade again? We also note that when Parkson walks away from the scene of Enley's death, Ann is at his side, but the two neither embrace nor hold hands, indicating that their future is more than uncertain, and that Enley's death will most likely be of no relevance to Parkson's future life.

◊ ◊ ◊

Act of Violence premiered on December 21, 1948. While the film could not repeat the critical success of *The Search*, it garnered mostly favorable reviews. *New Pictures* praised that the film, "a realistic, tight-knit study in fear, hatred and revenge, is a well-made movie melodrama. Director Fred (*The Search*) Zinnemann . . . gets as much power out of his lens as if it were a fire-hose nozzle."⁴⁷ *Variety* equally singled out Zinnemann's direction, which "craftily builds the mood of tension that features the plot's manhunt," while the *New Yorker* featured a more critical review but also attested that "as directed by Fred Zinnemann, [the film] has feverish moments."⁴⁸ Writing in the *New York Times*, Bosley Crowther noted in an otherwise mixed review that the film "consistently gives evidence of smart direction by Fred Zinnemann."⁴⁹ The strongest endorsement came from the *Monthly Film Bulletin*, which stated, "Van Heflin . . . and Robert Ryan . . . brilliantly characterize the complex human emotions of an avenger and his victim in this unusually moving drama. . . . Strong characterization, fine direction, and good photography combine to put this film high among its kind."⁵⁰ Nevertheless, the film did not acquire longer staying power and did not become part of the film noir canon that began to be formed in the 1970s.

One reason for this is certainly that Zinnemann was never considered an auteur and hence was bypassed in the critical discourse that linked noir to auteurism.⁵¹ Another is that *Act of Violence* is a transitional noir. It lacks important elements of "classic" noirs like the femme fatale, the private eye, and voice-over flashback narration, while also adding scenic daytime settings and a focus on suburban family life, all but absent in most noirs. The inevitability of fate—so strong in Ulmer's *Detour*, Siodmak's *The Killers*, and Jacques Tourneur's *Out of the Past*—is here secondary to personal responsibility and bad judgment. While its realism is saturated with the urban symbolism of classic noir, particularly its downtown sequence, *Act of Violence* introduces an overtly social critique that transcends the more timeless, immanent realm of noir. It is also transitional in that it moves away from the realm of World War II and toward the crises of Cold War America.

THE UNCANNY HOMELAND

In his 1948 essay "Those Movies with a Message" Siegfried Kracauer discusses a number of immediate American postwar films, including *Boomerang* (Elia Kazan, 1947), *Crossfire* (Edward Dmytryk, 1947), *Gentleman's Agreement* (Elia Kazan, 1947), *The Best Years of Our Lives* (William Wyler, 1946), and *It's a Wonderful Life* (Frank Capra, 1946), which all aim to confront "the hopes of the war years with the reality of the postwar."⁵² The majority of these films, Kracauer observes, prominently figure ex-GIs

> in a state of complete bewilderment. . . . Characters of this kind have rarely been seen before on the screen. Visionless, at the mercy of any wind, benumbed even in their love-making, they drift about in a daze bordering on stupor. One is reminded of the Innocents—the characters created by Chaplin, Buster Keaton, and Harry Langdon in their slapstick comedies—who, favored by miraculous luck, always succeeded in outwitting hostile objects and evil Goliaths at the very last moment. It is as if those Innocents had been dragged out of their enchanted universe to face the world as it actually is—a world not in the least responsive to their candid dreams and hopes. The guise

of the discharged soldier assures us that they are now average individuals, stunned by the shock of readjustment.[53]

Whereas films about World War I veterans stressed physical maiming, these films focus on psychological damage and problems of readjustment to country, society, and family. Yet if Kracauer diagnosed in them a pervading sense of general apathy and inertia that stands in stark contrast to certain progressive films of the prewar era (and to the ideology-driven anti-Nazi films of the war years, one might add), most postwar noirs are far more radical both on the level of visuals and of narrative techniques, as well as in the stories that they tell. As Richard Maltby suggests, "these movies are about maladjustment, but more than that, they are themselves maladjusted texts . . . representing the failure of readjustment where Hollywood's musicals, comedies and romances of the period represented its own return to normality and, indeed, its proselytizing for the re-establishment of the ideology of pure and harmless entertainment in a conformist society."[54]

Indeed, it is conspicuous how many noirs feature World War II veterans as seriously troubled protagonists. The heroes and antiheroes of these films are by and large dysfunctional, and their thinking and behavior are determined by hatred, vengefulness, misogyny, and latent violence, making them metaphors for the social estrangement and psychological and political confusion of the immediate postwar years. A cursory look at some of them will bring into relief the similarities and, more important, the differences with Frank Enley and Joe Parkson.

The various problems of the veteran are front and center in Paramount's *The Blue Dahlia* (1946), directed by George Stevens after Raymond Chandler's first original screenplay, which tells the story of three discharged navy buddies returning home. Lt. Commander Johnny Morrison, played by real-life veteran Alan Ladd, becomes a suspect in the murder of his unfaithful wife, while viewers are led to believe that his buddy Buzz Wanchek (William Bendix), who sustained a head injury during combat and now has a steel plate near his brain, is the culprit. Buzz suffers from shell shock, occasional amnesia, and a "short fuse" that can translate into sudden outbursts of violence. Chandler originally scripted Buzz to be the murderer but had to change the ending when the navy objected. The cynical writer Dixon Steele (Humphrey Bogart), in Nicholas Ray's *In a Lonely Place* (1950), is another veteran who becomes a murder suspect and a man whose irrational behavior and explosive temper, particularly toward women, is clearly linked to the war.

Most postwar noirs are careful to couch veterans' acts of aggression within a larger context of trauma and physical and psychological injury, making these men both perpetrators and victims who elicit our compassion as much as our fear. Their penchant to stand up for the "right" cause frequently leads them to get victimized. In *The Strange Love of Martha Ivers* (Lewis Milestone, 1946), Van Heflin plays a recently demobilized GI who gets caught in a triangle between the manipulative and domineering titular protagonist (played by Barbara Stanwyck) and her morally corrupt husband (played by Kirk Douglas), who sets his thugs on Van Heflin. Captain Rip Murdock (yet again Humphrey Bogart) in *Dead Reckoning* (John Cromwell, 1947) is another vet repeatedly beaten as he tries to find the murderer of an air force buddy, all the while being deceived by a nightclub singer. And in Edward Dmytryk's *Cornered* (1945) yet another ex-soldier, in this case a Canadian flyer recently released from a German POW camp, seeks the people responsible for the death of his bride. In all three films the figure of the veteran displays the moral righteousness and ready aggression of a Sam Spade or Philip Marlowe, but always inflected with the existential loneliness that is also the trademark of Hammett's and Chandler's private eyes.

A related form of suffering is experienced by those veterans who return from service to find out that their wives have been untruthful—a plot device found in *The Blue Dahlia, Desire Me* (George Cukor and Mervyn LeRoy, 1947), *The Unfaithful* (Vincent Sherman, 1947), and *The Best Years of Our Lives*—and that contrasts opposing views of loyalty and sacrifice. This form of betrayal is doubly hurtful for the veteran, as the reason for his service, namely to protect home and family from foreign intruders, is rendered irrelevant and erroneous. Most noirs tell this story exclusively from the perspective of the cuckolded male and make no attempt to represent the domestic struggles that may have led women to abandon their husbands.

A particular frequent infliction suffered by the postwar noir hero is amnesia, which is often related to an incident during the war. He is forced to answer the question, "Who am I?" by assembling clues that allow him to reconstruct his former identity. Notable examples include *Spellbound* (Alfred Hitchcock, 1945), *Somewhere in the Night* (Joseph Mankiewicz, 1946), *High Wall* (Curtis Bernhardt, 1947), *The Crooked Way* (Robert Florey, 1949), and again *The Blue Dahlia*. As John Belton has argued, the most existential of all noir heroes is the amnesiac, a figure that becomes emblematic for the entire United States as these veterans' "identity crises mirrored those of a nation as a whole."[55]

If we compare this panorama of noir protagonists to *Act of Violence*, we notice that Zinnemann's film strips away many of the layers found in the noirs of the immediate postwar period, 1945 to 1947. Most notably missing is the sexually promiscuous, domineering, manipulative, or simply independent woman of many of the above films, an indication that by 1948 the male anxieties that had created the femme fatale had subsided. While the war years had given women the opportunity to enter the workforce and serve as heads of households, thereby challenging traditional family hierarchies, by the end of the decade the status ante quo had by and large been reestablished. The image of the woman bent on killing her mate or destroying the family is replaced in *Act of Violence* by two wholesome women seeking to be homemakers. Even the tired streetwalker Pat hopes to gain some money by sheltering Enley in her apartment rather than through offering sex.

In contrast to films such as *Dead Reckoning*, *Double Indemnity*, or *Scarlet Street* (Fritz Lang, 1945), in all of which a femme fatale determines the fate of the male protagonist, *Act of Violence* shows the crisis of gender relations to be caused by the two men's respective unwillingness or inability to communicate with their partners about their experiences in the war, an inability that ultimately destroys one family and (most likely) prevents another one from forming. Enley first tells Edith that he hasn't talked to her about the war because she wouldn't understand and states in their last scene together, "It isn't that I don't want to talk about it. I just don't know how." When Parkson's girlfriend, Ann, urges him for the sake of their love not to pursue Enley, Parkson replies, "Maybe I don't love you enough." For Ann war is an infectious disease; for those who come into contact with it, even by proxy, there is no remedy. "They [Enley and Parkson] are both sick with it [i.e., the war]," she tells Edith, but ultimately so are the women.[56] Where many earlier noirs featured poisonous spider women, here wholesome women get infected by men, who themselves have been contaminated by the war.

The latent violence of Joe Parkson comes closest to the irrational aggression that characterizes many of the male characters described above. As I noted earlier, by drawing on Robert Ryan's recent success in *Crossfire*, which takes place exclusively between former GIs, the promotional materials (including the one-liner that serves as an epigraph of this chapter) created the expectation of Ryan's playing another hate-filled bigot, which the film then undercuts. While the film begins with a focus on Parkson, its real topic is the transformation of Enley, who undergoes radical changes (while

Parkson remains the same character, wearing the same hat and rumpled coat throughout the film). Enley's active repression of what happened during the war can be seen as a reverse form of amnesia, with Parkson reestablishing the bridges to the past that Enley seeks to burn. While many of the above heroes are suspects in murders they did not commit and must spend their energy proving their innocence, Enley conversely seeks to cover up a dirty truth that can no longer be hidden.

For contemporary viewers Enley's identity crisis, if that is the right term for his act of coming to terms with who he really is, arguably resonated less with what happened in Germany circa 1944 than with events that shaped the United States in 1947 and 1948. Particularly Enley's confession to his wife, "Do I have to spell it out for you? Do I have to draw you a picture? I was an informer!" must be understood as a reference to the 1947 HUAC hearings, as several critics have pointed out.[57] In the end Enley's act of cowardice and betrayal, of making deals with those with whom deals cannot be made, is not just a metaphor for the trauma of war but also for the transformation of the entire homeland, which in the wake of the Cold War and the Red Scare was redefining notions of belonging and nonbelonging, of being American and "un-American." Particularly those members of the Hollywood community who were at the forefront of fighting Nazi Germany, which includes the majority of exiles and émigrés, were the first to come up for scrutiny.

For Zinnemann and his fellow Europeans the communist witch hunts provided an uncanny moment of déjà vu of persecution and exclusion that Germany and Austria had experienced in the 1930s. *Act of Violence* implies that a man can be seduced or coerced into betraying others not only in a POW camp in Nazi Germany but also in democratic postwar America. Zinnemann's own experiences with resisting the purges in Hollywood are certainly important in this context. When in 1950 the right-wing director Cecil B. DeMille tried to have Joseph Mankiewicz deposed as the president of Screen Directors Guild, Zinnemann was one of twenty-five signatories calling for a meeting to openly discuss this move, which then led to DeMille's defeat.[58] As Kenneth L. Geist pointed out in his critical autobiography of Mankiewicz, émigrés who signed the petition against DeMille included not only Zinnemann but also Fritz Lang, Walter Reisch, and Billy Wilder.[59] Zinnemann told critic Neil Sinyard that the evening of the meeting was "one of the most extraordinary of my life, a night in which people were really compelled to stick their necks out for what they believed in."[60] There is no hard evidence that Zinnemann himself was ever blacklisted, but several of his close collaborators were, most notably the writer Carl Foreman, who wrote *The Men*, *High Noon*, and (uncredited) *A Hatful of Rain*. *High Noon*, of course, has often been read as an allegory of the cowardice and betrayal that ruled Hollywood in the late 1940s and early 1950s. John Belton summarizes this reading: "Because he was ultimately blacklisted, Carl Foreman's script for the critically acclaimed box-office success *High Noon* (1952) emerges as an obvious example of resistance within the industry to outside investigators such as HUAC. The film's hero, ironically played by a real-life friendly witness, Gary Cooper, is threatened by a gang of cutthroats (HUAC) who are on their way to town (Hollywood). The sheriff-hero is unable to find allies to help him in the (Hollywood) community. He nonetheless confronts and defeats them, waging a battle alone that the townspeople ought to have fought with him."[61]

As an aside it can be added that at the time Zinnemann was making *High Noon*, Lillian Hellman, the subject of his later film *Julia*, was defying HUAC.[62] In a 1996 *Cineaste* interview Zinnemann was careful not to pass facile judgment on alleged traitors. When he was asked, "How did you regard people who named names, such as Elia Kazan and Clifford Odets?" the director responded by saying, "It is hard for me to say, given that I was not in the same situation. I hope I would not have done it, you know, and I hated it."[63]

Six months before the release of *Act of Violence*, in June of 1948, the Soviets blocked railway and road access to West Berlin, prompting the Allies' Berlin Air Lift that officially inaugurated the Cold War. Two years later, the United States entered the Korean War (a veteran of that war is the subject of Zinnemann's *A Hatful of Rain*) to initiate a series of armed encounters with the Soviet Union fought by proxy on and over the terrain of third parties and satellite states. While ostensibly about the trauma of World War II, *Act of Violence* points to the shifting ideological lineup of postwar America. Occupied Germany suddenly became an important ally that had to be built up politically and economically to serve as a bulwark toward the East. While in the United States those who had fought Nazi Germany "prematurely," that is, before it became official U.S. policy to do so, became politically suspect, American denazification in Germany became secondary to strengthening the new ally. The rubble noir *Der Verlorene / The Lost One* (1951), directed by Zinnemann's fellow exile Peter Lorre, can be seen as a film that rewrites *Act of Violence* from a postwar German perspective.

Six
THE FAILURE OF ATONEMENT

It is my contention that through an analysis of the German films deep psychological dispositions predominant in Germany from 1918 to 1933 can be exposed . . . which will have to be reckoned with in the post-Hitler era.
—SIEGFRIED KRACAUER[1]

Where did it begin, if, indeed, it is over? Where did it start? There is certainly no end without a beginning.
—PETER LORRE[2]

THE WAR IS NEVER OVER

Fred Zinnemann's postwar noir *Act of Violence* underscores the impossibility of "going home again" after having seen combat, of seamlessly picking up from where one had left off. The story of Frank Enley and Joe Parkson shows that the war continues on the home front, with equally deadly consequences. It affects not only those who fought in the theaters of combat but also the families to which they return. While the film concludes with a sense of expiation, any real reconciliation comes at a heavy price, as Enley dies and Parkson's future seems uncertain.

To exiled filmmakers the question of homecoming presented itself somewhat differently. Although many of them had been active in the American war effort, only a few had actually served. Fewer still had experienced the violence of war that haunts Enley and Parkson. Instead of dealing with the posttraumatic stress of combat and the prison camp, the exiles, traumatized in their own right when they first had to flee Europe, pondered the question of whether to return to the very country that had chased them out more than a decade earlier. What should they do, now that the war was over? Would a return to Germany heal the wounds, or would it instead deepen the pain? Where did they actually belong, now that the majority of them had become naturalized citizens of a country that had fought Nazi Germany? Billy Wilder spoke for many when he expressed his indecision: "We wondered where we should go now that the war was over. None of us—I mean the émigrés—really knew where we stood. Should we go home? Where was home?"[3]

Yet Billy Wilder and Fred Zinnemann did return to Germany to make films there again. Both did so under contract with American studios, telling American audiences stories about postwar Germany shaped by the perspective of the emigrant returning to his homeland. For both Wilder and Zinnemann the stay in Germany was planned to be of limited duration, in Wilder's case following a prolonged assignment in the service of OMGUS (Office of Military Government, United States). In contrast to Wilder and Zinnemann many other exiles tried to gain a permanent foothold in the German industry, with varying results. In the end, at most a handful of them were able to have a postwar German career that was comparable to their work in Hollywood or the film industry of Weimar Germany. The history of the reemigration of filmmakers is by and large a history of misunderstandings, missed opportunities, and failures.

A special chapter in this history is the case of Peter Lorre and his film *Der Verlorene* (*The Lost One*) from 1951. Apart from Josef von Baky's *Der Ruf* (*The Last Illusion*, 1949), with a script by, and starring, Fritz Kortner, it is the only film made by a reemigrant that explicitly deals with the experience of attempting to return to Germany, addressing questions of guilt and responsibility; of accountability and justice; feelings of belonging and nonbelonging; and hopes and perspectives for the future. Yet whereas Kortner's film advocates a humanist message of optimism and reconciliation (in spite of the protagonist's experience of enduring resentments and virulent anti-Semitism), Lorre's tale offers no such glimmers of hope, insisting instead on the irreparable rift between those who became guilty during the Third Reich and those who did not. If we contrast Lorre's and Kortner's films with two films about reemigration made by German directors who did not emigrate, *Zwischen gestern und morgen* (Harald Braun, 1947) and *Die Söhne des Herrn Gaspary* (Rolf Meyer, 1949), the differences in perspective between those who stayed and those who went into exile becomes very obvious. In both of these films the reemigrant emerges as the figure whose suffering clearly does not match that of the Germans inside the Third

Reich, no matter the circumstances of his expulsion, and who, directly or indirectly, is to be blamed for the misfortunes of those who stayed behind.

No facile scapegoating of the "Emigrant" was possible for Lorre. Instead, *Der Verlorene* held a mirror to Germans so that they might assume responsibility for the crimes of the past. A modest critical success, *Der Verlorene* was shunned by audiences and quickly disappeared from theaters. The enormous gap between Lorre's artistic ambitions and the expectations of German filmgoers circa 1951 is emblematic of the strained relations and impeded communication between those who had left Germany and those who stayed behind.

◊ ◊ ◊

On February 16, 1952, Peter Lorre boarded a plane in Frankfurt to return to the United States, carrying with him only a few personal items and a purloined print of his most recent film.[4] Lorre had come to Germany in the fall of 1950 to write, direct, and star in this production, escaping financial troubles in Hollywood while hoping to revitalize a stalled American career in the country that had first made him an international star. Yet the mixed reception of the film and its dismal box-office returns cut short his aspirations, and a disillusioned Lorre bade a hasty farewell. His first departure from Germany nearly twenty years earlier had been a forced flight, which he shared with many German-speaking Jewish film professionals; back then, he had famously quipped, "Germany is too small for two murderers like Hitler and me." His second departure was free of such dramatic symbols of defiance, albeit traumatic in its own right.

Even though Lorre had made several other popular features before leaving Germany, Fritz Lang's *M* (1931) was the film with which most German postwar audiences still associated him, as did the Nazis, who included a clip of Lorre pleading for his life in the kangaroo court in their hate film *Der ewige Jude* (*The Eternal Jew*, Fritz Hippler, 1940). In his effort to reconnect with German audiences, Lorre would build on the image that Lang had created for him some twenty years earlier. Fragmented by a series of flashbacks, *Der Verlorene* tells the story of a Hamburg scientist named Dr. Rothe (Lorre), whose research is significant for the Nazi war effort. When he learns from his assistant Hoesch (Karl John), an undercover Gestapo agent, that his fiancée, Inge Hermann (Renate Mannhart), has not only leaked his results to the enemy but that Hoesch has seduced her to uncover the betrayal,

Rothe snaps and murders Inge. Since the Nazis still need Rothe, Hoesch and his superior, Colonel Winkler (Helmut Rudolph), cover up his crime, making it impossible for Rothe to atone for his deed. A seriously unbalanced Rothe begins to stalk prostitutes and war widows. Eventually, he commits another murder, but his crimes remain undetected and unpunished. When an Allied war raid destroys Rothe's apartment building, he uses the opportunity to stage his own death. After the war Rothe and Hoesch, now both under assumed names, meet up by accident in a Displaced Persons camp near Hamburg, where Rothe works as a doctor. During a long night of drinking, Rothe and Hoesch take turns recounting their war crimes, with Hoesch wishing to sweep everything under the rug and Rothe insisting that forgetting is not possible. At dawn Rothe shoots Hoesch and steps into the path of an oncoming train, finally imposing the judgment that had been withheld during the Third Reich.

It might seem ironic that Lorre, who repeatedly lamented that Lang's film had typecast him for life as a sex murderer and deranged man, would recreate that role in the one film he wrote and directed.[5] In a 1951 interview Lorre explained that reviving the role of the serial killer was necessary to underscore the continuity between the Weimar Republic and the Third Reich: "The Germany of 1930 and the Germany under Hitler and during the Second World War is one and the same; there is a seamless transition from one to the other. Without the murderer ('Totmacher') of Düsseldorf [that is, Peter Kürten, the model for Lorre's character in *M*], the killer of Hamburg would not be thinkable."[6] Yet *Der Verlorene* goes further, implying in no uncertain terms that the continuities between the early 1930s and the mid-1940s also extend into the postwar period. The part of the film set in 1943–44 remarkably resembles the postwar era: there is a scarcity of food (Frau Hermann, Rothe's landlady, has to embark on lengthy acquisition trips, and there are repeated references to ersatz coffee) and of apartments (after Inge's death her room is occupied by someone sent by the housing department), all signs of hardship that also dominate life in the ruins after the war. There are no obvious signs of Nazism, few people in uniform, and virtually no portraits of the Führer, no Hitler salutes, etc. These Nazi symbols would become staples of most postwar depictions of the Third Reich, intended to underscore a fundamental distance from the past that Lorre's film refuses to accept. Whereas many postwar narratives depicted a clean break, a "Stunde Null" (zero hour) that provided a blank slate for new beginnings, *Der Verlorene* emphasizes that little has changed. Its key antagonists, Rothe and Hoesch, continue to occupy the positions that they held during the war; democratic institutions such as law enforcement and jurisdiction, blatantly ineffective during the Third Reich, are still absent in 1947. The only way for Rothe to achieve justice is to take matters into his own hands.

A GRAYER SHADE OF NOIR

The provocation of *Der Verlorene*, and its untimeliness, lies in its insistence on the historic continuities and parallels connecting the 1930s, the 1940s, and the postwar period in the face of the then-dominant desire to "vergeben, vergessen, verdrängen" (forgive, forget, repress).[7] As Harun Farocki states, "There is hardly another film that has foreshadowed fascism as exactly as *M*, and hardly another that has traced the remnants of fascism as exactly as *Der Verlorene*."[8] But Lorre does more than just revive *M* or downplay specific cues from the Hitler period to raise issues of continuing guilt. He creatively (and critically) reprises generic conventions, narrative patterns, and visual strategies to render his grimly pessimistic and fatalistic view of German history. By drawing on the visual and narrative repertoire of American film noir and 1930s horror films, *Der Verlorene* highlights how the Nazi politics of expulsion and murder become reconfigured after 1945 in spatial and temporal modes of displacement and repression. Yet he takes these conventions further; while the closed and fatalistic world of noir still allows for some sense of atonement (often provided in extensive flashback confessions), *Der Verlorene* is radically uncompromising and forbids any reconciliation or alleviation of guilt, showing instead how any opposition to Nazism—and that of the exiles in particular—has been silenced for a second time. In doing so, *Der Verlorene* provides an eloquent and uncompromising account of the impossibility of reemigration.

The tropes of spatial and temporal displacement that mark Lorre's role in the film reflect his biography, making the film a metacinematic and highly self-reflexive comment on Lorre's German and American star persona, a taking stock of his career precisely as he faced a professional crossroads. The "Lost One" of the film's title is clearly not only Dr. Rothe, who is both spiritually lost and has gone missing (after staging his own death), but also Peter Lorre himself—"der VerLorrene"—who has been absent for almost twenty years. A product of the many intersections of German American film history, the film speaks to the historical reasons that made the cross-fertilizations of two national cinemas possible, namely the forced exile (and now potential reemigration) of Lorre and so many other German-language film professionals.

The opening sequence emphatically introduces the visual and narrative trajectory of the entire film. The credits roll over a brick wall. A similar wall also served as a backdrop for the beginning of Fritz Lang's *Hangmen Also Die* and links Lorre's film to Hollywood's exile cinema. Both films share the same producer, Arnold Pressburger (who predominantly worked with exiles and émigrés in the United States, including Douglas Sirk, Josef von Sternberg, and René Clair), and pursue a political agenda of anti-Nazism.[9] If *Hangmen Also Die* meant to rouse American audiences into action against the Third Reich, *Der Verlorene* interrogates the remnants of that regime amid the rubble of postwar Germany. Whereas Lang mobilized the narrative conventions of the propaganda film to channel viewer identification, Lorre remains closer to the stylistic and generic conventions of film noir, which are meant to invoke the trauma of irrecoverable loss and to convey the impossibility of living in the present. While Lang's film speaks with one voice, Lorre's multilayered and convoluted narrative borders on the incoherent, perhaps befitting his vision of the political conundrum of postwar Germany. If Lang's brick wall concealed the hiding places of the Czech underground that was secretly scheming against the foreign rulers, Lorre's references anguish, claustrophobia, and no exit, none at all.

Der Verlorene begins with a low-angle shot of a horse-drawn cart at a railroad crossing; a train rushes through the frame from left to right, enveloping everything in steam. As the barriers open, a man emerges from the mist and crosses the tracks, his dark coat silhouetted against a gray winter sky. On both sides he is framed by tall, black telephone poles that dwarf him. With the collar of his winter coat turned up, his hands buried in his pockets, and a cigarette dangling from his lip, he resembles the prototypical noir loner.

He enters a compound, is fleetingly greeted by a Polish woman, and then welcomed by a camp worker who informs him about the surprise arrival of yet another load of refugees. The man is called Dr. Neumeister, but, as we later learn, his real name is Dr. Rothe. While he is quickly established as a caring and highly respected physician, we also sense a more reserved and anguished nature underneath. Before he sees his first patient, Rothe downs a shot of liquor. When his coworker offers to find him an assistant, he retorts, "I prefer to be alone." This desire for solitude and anonymity is disrupted when a new assistant, a certain Nowak, presents himself.

FIGURE 6.1 Dr. Karl Rothe, the existential loner of film noir.

The fateful encounter between Rothe and Hoesch (Nowak's real name) sets the plot in motion and provides the film's central conflict. Significantly, it is staged as an oral rather than a visual recognition, foreshadowing the importance of the voice (and the voice-over) for *Der Verlorene*. Working at the doctor's side but outside his field of vision, Hoesch reveals to Rothe in a low voice, "Keep calm, Doctor. Yes, that Nowak, that's me. Unfortunately, it couldn't be avoided." The true extent of the recognition of that voice is silently played out in a medium close-up of Lorre's face; all we see are the eyebrows twitching, the heavy lids getting heavier still, and the look of sadness and despair changing into horror. Panicked, Rothe flees to the train line, and in a suicidal gesture that anticipates the conclusion of the film steps onto the tracks. But the train has already passed, the suicide will have to be postponed. Instead, Rothe returns to the barracks. There ensues what will become an all-night conversation between Hoesch and Rothe that slowly reveals why their chance encounter will prove to be fateful and why, regardless of what their respective aliases suggest, neither one of them has become a new person.

The opening sequence skillfully introduces the various layers that compose *Der Verlorene*. Dominated by stylistic conventions of noir, evident in

FIGURE 6.2 As in *M*, the voice of the murderer is heard before he is seen.

the angled photography and the chiaroscuro lighting of Lorre's many close-ups, the film quickly establishes Rothe as a prototypically torn and traumatized male protagonist. When Rothe's face first emerges from the steam of the train, it references one of noir's central plot devices, the return of a presumably dead or missing person. (This hunch is confirmed when we later learn that Rothe had actually faked his death.) On another level this shot quite literally lets German moviegoers see a face again that had been "lost" since it first etched itself into their minds some twenty years earlier. Yet it is the film's flashback voice-over narration that most clearly establishes the connection to noir. While introducing subjectivity and perspective, this narrative structure contributes to the film's strong sense of fatalism. As the story unfolds backward, the ending is clearly in sight, and as in most noirs so, too, in *Der Verlorene*, it is lethal.

The film is staged as a late-night dialogue in the canteen of the Displaced Persons camp, a reckoning between two men who have tried to escape their past only to realize that it has caught up with them. While Hoesch offers Rothe a pact of mutual silence, Rothe insists on revisiting their shared history. What ensues is a *mutual* reconstruction of the past during which Rothe and Hoesch take turns recounting their *shared* experiences, a dialogue of complementing and competing voices (with Hoesch eventually emerging as an unreliable narrator who first lies about Colonel Winkler's death). Hoesch and Rothe alternately confirm and contradict each other's recollections. Significantly, Hoesch sleeps through substantial parts of Rothe's flashback narration (for example, the entire sequence of the second murder), implying that he does not care to listen to Rothe's regurgitation of things past—a defense mechanism, the film suggests, with which contemporary viewers might sympathize.

This shared retelling is a significant variation of what Maureen Turim has called the confessional flashback, which is "characterized by the protagonist's retrospective examination of the ways he was introduced to his current criminality."[10] According to Turim, in this form of voice-over a man, usually facing imminent death (e.g., the male protagonists of *Double Indemnity* [Billy Wilder, 1944] or *The Postman Always Rings Twice* [Tay Garnett, 1946]), retells his descent into crime in order to gain absolution. In the case of *Der Verlorene*, only Rothe believes in any need for atonement, while Hoesch, an unchanged man, insists that a break with the past and a fresh beginning are possible. Both Wilder's Walter Neff and Garnett's Frank Chambers seek to place the blame on the femmes fatales who ensnared them in a web of violence. Hoesch and Rothe differ in their judgment of Inge Hermann, the closest equivalent in *Der Verlorene* to a manipulative, oversexed woman. While Hoesch and Winkler are glad to be rid of a woman they consider unworthy and who would have had to be taken care of sooner or later, Rothe is seriously unbalanced by Inge's murder and its withheld punishment.

The voice-over flashback, according to Turim, emphasizes the intricate connection between history and memory, with memory assuming multiple and contradictory functions of protecting or strengthening an individual while also haunting or forcing him or her into compulsive repetitions. In most stories where this narrative device is employed (and *Der Verlorene* is no exception), the protagonist faces the return of the repressed: the secrets of the past need to be stated or discovered. This return is often triggered by happenstance, such as Hoesch's sudden appearance at the very camp where Rothe works. In the logic of noir nothing occurs by chance; everything is determined, a belief Rothe firmly embraces as he repeatedly ridicules Hoesch's attempts to see their encounter as "zufällig" (coincidental). This determinism makes noir a close cousin to Greek tragedy, in which destiny is a trap from which the tragic hero cannot escape; as we know from *Oedipus*, the desire to cheat fate is what, in an ironic twist, makes destiny come true in the first place.

Although Hoesch does believe in happenstance, he firmly subscribes to an absolution from individual responsibility, replacing the Greek notion of fate with "die Zeiten" (the times), implying that a certain historical configuration simply made certain moral values and forms of behavior a necessity. Hoesch conveniently forgets that he and the party he served were major contributors to the course history actually took after 1933. Rothe initially assumes a similar position regarding the larger forces that govern our behavior. Trying to convey to Hoesch the senselessness of Inge's murder, he states, "I absolutely cannot explain what happened," denying any intentionality on his part. (Ironically, Hoesch clearly considers this an evasive move on Rothe's part but, nevertheless, responds with a sympathetic nod, as if to imply that he knows all about denying individual responsibility for murder.) This disavowal of authorship is even more prominent in the novelization of *Der Verlorene*.[11] Here Rothe explains, "I didn't murder her because I wanted to. . . . An unknown It, a strange, second person living within me strangled her."[12] This passage clearly resonates with one of Lorre's key inspirations for the film, Guy de Maupassant's short horror story "Le Horla" (1887). In this tale a certain Monsieur believes himself to be possessed by an evil spirit he thinks has latched on to him from a Brazilian ship he sees passing by in the distance. When repeated attempts to rid himself of his tormentor fail, the protagonist commits suicide. It remains up to the reader to figure out whether the evil spirit actually ever existed or was but a figment of the protagonist's imagination.[13]

Yet any attempt to reduce Inge's murder to the doings of some evil spirit clearly overlooks not only Rothe's intentionality but also Hoesch's active role in the crime. Not only is Hoesch responsible for Inge's act of infidelity; he also actively encourages Rothe to rid himself of her. As Rothe explains to Hoesch after the first flashback, "she [Inge] wanted reconciliation. I think she would have succeeded. But then something happened. The phone rang. And suddenly it was as if you were suddenly standing in the middle of the room." Even though Hoesch's voice on the phone is never heard onscreen, the fact that he calls (twice actually, since Inge hangs up on him the first time) causes a dramatic change. In close-up we witness Rothe's face go somber; his lids become heavier still, until his eyes are completely closed; and his fingers begin to wander over the furniture as if they were independent agents (thereby referencing such classic Lorre horror films as *Mad Love* [Karl Freund, 1935] and *The Beast with Five Fingers* [Robert Florey, 1946], in both of which hands take on a murderous life of their own).[14] As ominous music strikes up, identified in the script as the "Horla motif," the fingers first caress Inge's hair and cheek, but when they approach her throat their violent intentions suddenly become clear.[15] Abruptly, Rothe stands up and his dark back blackens the screen, thus obscuring his murder of Inge. As Jennifer Kapczynski succinctly observes, it appears that, modifying "Le Horla," the spirit that takes hold of Rothe has an identity after all—it is Hoesch who "inhabits" Rothe during the murder.[16]

If this assessment of Inge's murder seems to put the blame on Hoesch, some four years later Rothe knows that both he and Hoesch are equally guilty. The Nazis may have given Rothe the motive to kill Inge, and they may have protected him from deserved punishment, but the act of murder was his. Now, in 1947, Rothe and Hoesch are the lone survivors of this particular incident of Nazi-induced violence, and Rothe's repeated remarks to Hoesch about the finality of their situation make it clear what the outcome of their "chance" encounter will have to be. Twice the camera shows Rothe secretly pocketing a gun while talking to Hoesch. "We're at the end. We are here," Rothe mumbles. "We're the last ones. No one comes after us." When a baffled Hoesch asks him to explain himself more clearly, Rothe shows him the gun.

One of the key premises of *Der Verlorene* is the presence of the past. Lorre's peculiar use of the flashback forcefully underscores this. The frequent cuts, ten in all, between events in Hamburg 1943–44 and the camp in 1947 break up the narrative into twenty-one segments and vividly demonstrate how the past encroaches on the present. As Kapczynski comments, this technique exemplifies that "the past cannot be neatly cordoned off but repeatedly reasserts itself as it perforates the present moment."[17] In one of the rare positive German reviews of *Der Verlorene*, Enno Patalas noted that "the flashbacks are no short-cuts for the development of the drama (*dramaturgischer Notbehelf*), but the breaking up of repressed time."[18] This insistence on the interconnectedness of past and present supplants the fatalism of noir with a historical dimension that does insist on the agency and hence political accountability of human subjects.

Accordingly, the aesthetics of noir, while still dominant, particularly in the frame narrative, are played off against other important genre conventions. For the events set in the past, the main modes of representation are those of the horror film, as shown in Inge's murder or in Rothe's experiment with animals in his lab. Yet Rothe is less a mad scientist à la Dr. Gogol of *Mad Love* (a figure itself modeled on Lorre's role as the bald, hunchbacked cocaine smuggler and morphine addict in *Der weiße Dämon* [Kurt Gerron, 1932]) than a vampire-like creature. Undead several times over (he should have been executed for Inge's murder but is spared, only to commit more crimes, and he should have died in the bombing of his apartment, the survival of which allows him to stage his own death), he is a nocturnal being who chain-smokes but never eats and whose malice is invisible to those around him. Fascinated by blood, he shares the modern-day vampire's melancholy and weariness of life. As in Ulmer's *The Black Cat*, horror in *Der Verlorene* clearly connotes not some unnamed larger evil but a violence connected to a specific agency and historical contingency.

These elements of horror are contrasted with the stifling, *Kammerspiel*-like world of domesticity of the Herrmann family, whose dark and gloomy atmosphere provokes Inge's revolt against the controlling parenting of her mother (which Rothe calls "gräßliche Fürsorge" [ghastly caretaking]). Only the conspiracy subplot in Winkler's villa feels oddly out of place in the noir world of doom and despair—this late and somewhat unmotivated addition to the film, which was not included in the script and was somewhat modified in the novelization, is replete with car chases and shootouts that anticipate the popular German cinema of the later 1950s. Laconically labeled by Rothe a "Detektivroman," this is a realm where a password is needed to gain entrance to a decadent underworld in which the German aristocracy (including a Colonel Winkler who suddenly seems to have switched sides) plans to overthrow Hitler. One could defend the inclusion of this episode, which ridicules anti-Nazi resistance, by arguing that it is quite daring in breaking with the usual postwar convention of depicting attempts on Hitler's life as acts of heroism, yet overall it did much to exasperate the credulity of contemporary reviewers.

Lorre sought a new sense of realism, closer to the factuality of a newsreel, something the press kit labeled "Lorrealismus." Its ambition, the press materials explained, "is to achieve the most intense approximation to the reality in which the filmgoer lives, and not just copying its surface."[19] An opening title underscores this claim: "This film is not a work of fiction." This insistence on historical truth ties *Der Verlorene* both to Hollywood's postwar social problem films and contemporary Italian neorealism, to which Lorre's neologism also alludes. The cinematography typical of that movement, characterized by natural light and real locations, certainly informs the high-contrast outdoor photography of Czech cinematographer Václav Vích, particularly the train tracks and the Displaced Persons camp, settings that are both "real" but also highly symbolic. While a key location of such noirs as *Double Indemnity*, *Human Desire* (Fritz Lang, 1954), and *Act of Violence*, the tracks allude to the deportation of the European Jews, which especially German viewers will have been quick to realize. The very fact that the camp is so near to the tracks is telling in itself. Having them appear at both the opening and the ending of the frame narrative, furthermore, gives the film a circular structure. Promising mobility, the tracks actually lead nowhere but to death. It is thus no accident that the first scene of the flashback shows Rothe riding the Hamburg "Hochbahn," the same overcrowded commuter train in which he will later commit his second murder.

Rothe's place of work and hiding is equally overdetermined. The DP camp harbors refugees, so-called *Vertriebene* or *Umsiedler*, from the East, just like the real camp south of Hamburg where the film was shot. Rothe (and Lorre) shares the refugees' status of itinerancy and liminality, their existence on the margins of society. (The script, in fact, makes more of Rothe's relation to the young Polish woman, suggesting a like-mindedness between two outsiders.) The location's somber past as a prison camp during the Third Reich, which is signaled by its watchtowers and barbed wire, serves as a reminder of the fate that the enemies of the state would have faced a few years earlier—most likely the same people who now find shelter in the camp (including Jews like Lorre).

Finally, Rothe's/Lorre's displacement also entertains strong ties to the story line and aesthetics of such neorealist classics as *Germany Year Zero* (Roberto Rossellini, 1948) and *Stromboli* (Rossellini, 1950), as well as Fred Zinnemann's neorealist-influenced *The Search*. Like *Der Verlorene*, all three films use locations as both realistic and highly symbolic sites for their respective protagonists' physical and psychological disorientation, as well as their fatalistic outlook on life. *The Search* provides an important model for Lorre's balancing act between the closed fatalistic world of noir and a postwar realism committed to foregrounding its historical and political topicality.

THE MURDERERS ARE STILL AMONG US

In the 1945 film *Hotel Berlin* (Peter Godfrey) Peter Lorre has a small role as the German scientist Johannes Koenig, who, together with ordinary Germans and a wide array of Nazis, spies, refugees, and various members of the underground movement, experiences the 1945 Allied bombing raids in a luxurious Berlin hotel. Based on Vicki Baum's novel *Hotel Berlin* (1943), a loose sequel to her 1929 best seller *Menschen im Hotel* (*Grand Hotel*), the film packs the usual ingredients of the anti-Nazi film but heightens the drama by making the hotel the film's single location, where the competing forces inadvertently rub shoulders (thereby recalling Rick's café in *Casablanca*). In one of very few films in which he was allowed to play a German, and the only film in which he played a *good* German, Lorre's character represents the political stakes of the film. Early on, a slovenly and unkempt Koenig declares during an air raid, "We [i.e., the Germans] are getting no more than we deserve," only to add, "Maybe you believe there are good Germans left? Ha, ha—a good German!" True to the conversion narrative, Koenig's disillusionment with his fellow countrymen and his fatalistic outlook on the nature of the German people gives way to a change of mind at the end. When, deep in the bowels of some ruins, the German underground prepares leaflets with a radio address by President Roosevelt about the fate of postwar Germany, Koenig, as the sole academic in the group, gets to proofread the message by reading it aloud, simultaneously conveying it to the viewers while also undergoing a change of heart himself:

> I should be false to the very foundations of my religious and political convictions if I should ever relinquish the hope and even the faith that in all peoples, without exceptions, there lives some instinct for truth and some passion for peace, buried as it may be in the German case under a brutal regime. We bring no charge against the German race as such for we cannot believe that

God has eternally condemned any race of humanity.... There is going to be stern punishment for all those in Germany directly responsible for this agony of mankind. We do not traffic in human slavery, but it will be necessary for them to earn their way back into the fellowship of peace-loving and law-abiding nations.

Roosevelt's promise of withholding any wholesale accusation of the German people—the hotly debated notion of *Kollektivschuld*—as well as the prospect of allowing Germans to redeem themselves, provides a glimmer of hope for Koenig and his fellow "good" Germans. What they deserve, Koenig now realizes, are not only the bombs dropping down on them but also an opportunity to prove that not *all* Germans are culprits and that they will be able to learn from past crimes and move forward, no matter what the magnitude of their countrymen's crimes or their own complicity in them.

Lorre's role in the film was written by leftist scriptwriter Alvah Bessie, who later became one of the Hollywood Ten. It is hard to determine, and ultimately a moot point, whether Lorre's own convictions at the time matched those of Johannes Koenig, but the film's conciliatory message certainly spoke for many in the exile community who hoped that Germany's imminent surrender would not come at the price of a wholesale condemnation of the German people. With the production and release of *Der Verlorene*, however, it becomes clear that the views of Dr. Koenig and Dr. Rothe (incidentally both scientists whose experiments with animals are of keen interest to a Nazi regime facing military defeat) about German guilt and responsibility and the promise of atonement differ significantly. The six years that separate 1945 and 1951 also profoundly changed how (German) audiences would look at scientists active during the Third Reich.

With the Holocaust in plain view by 1951, any scientist in Nazi employ had become for contemporary viewers "a figure of moral ambiguity," and we are invited to speculate whether Rothe might not be a close cousin to the notorious Dr. Mengele.[20] When we see Rothe enter his lab for the first time, his offscreen voice comments on his professional situation: "I wasn't doing badly at all." He is immediately seconded by Hoesch: "Yes, you lived quite comfortably all around." A quintessentially apolitical person, Rothe is surprised to learn that his research is of strategic importance, revealing a political naiveté that only the privileged could afford. Only after the Nazis cover up his crime does Rothe begin to comprehend the magnitude of their power and their ruthlessness; only then does Rothe realize that he has become one of the many murderers whose actions are sanctioned by those in power: "I had become a part of these, our times. Its casual notions of the worthiness or the unworthiness of a human life protected me. Of course, this illness of the times ("Zeitkrankheit") was no virus which one could easily put under a microscope and observe and photograph." It is precisely at this point that Rothe's flashback narrative takes on a more analytic perspective, thereby bringing it into closer proximity with Fritz Lang's *M*.

Lorre emphasized the parallels to *M* because he wanted to build on his German star persona and, above all, because he claimed that Lang's film and his film shared a political dimension.[21] While contemporary reviewers lamented that Lorre had relied too heavily on *M*, *Der Verlorene*, and Lorre's role in it, is neither an imitation nor a remake of Lang's film. Rather it compares and contrasts particular historical moments preceding, during, and following the Third Reich in order to historicize German fascism just as its legacies were disappearing in the contemporary discourse of normalization.[22]

More than just studies of two deviant characters, both films portray murders against the background of a city in a state of exception. While Lang depicts the animation of a paranoid populace that recalls a mobilization for war, Lorre shows the tear in the social fabric in a city suffering from constant air raids, hunger, economic hardship, and total surveillance.[23] *M* is populated by the true victims and losers of World War I, an army of mutilated veterans, beggars, and lumpen, unwelcome by those who stayed on the home front and bypassed by the modest recovery of the mid-1920s. A mere rung on the ladder above them, the volatile petit bourgeois, hit hardest by the economic and social fallout of Black Tuesday, is shown to have become the fertile breeding ground for paranoia and, the film implies, political demagoguery. While the mass hysteria that ensues is purportedly the effect of one dangerous individual, the powerful portrayal of the susceptibility of the masses points to the larger political volatility of Berlin, and Germany, circa 1931. Here, as in the Hamburg of 1943–44, law enforcement, a quintessential pillar of modern society, is blatantly inefficient or altogether absent.

In this climate the child murderer Hans Beckert is but the product of a much larger and profound social, economic, and political crisis. Like Rothe, he suffers from a "Zeitkrankheit," the true scope of which not only escapes him but also those who hunt him down. Beckert and Rothe share the status of the victim-perpetrator who befuddles the jurisdiction that is in charge of them. *M* famously leaves it up to the viewer to pass judgment on a truly complex case, while *Der Verlorene* advocates self-justice in view of the moral deterioration of both wartime and postwar society.

To be sure, Rothe and Beckert embody very different traits. As Tim Bergfelder has commented, "whereas Beckert was manic and hyperactive, Rothe is passive and depressive, where Beckert was hysterical and nervously agitated, Rothe is melancholy and lethargic, where Beckert was a social misfit, Rothe is an existential one, and while Beckert was infantile and unreflective, Rothe exudes the resignation and disappointments of middle age and is painfully aware of himself and his immediate environment."[24] But they are surely not altogether different. Rothe is a Beckert-figure augmented by the experience of the tyranny of the Third Reich and the Holocaust. Like Beckert, he first claims that "an other" committed his crimes but ultimately comes to recognize his own complicity and responsibility. In a society capable of such horrendous acts of violence, the film implies, there are no innocent bystanders.

Both films draw on a similar visual repertoire to convey feelings of fear, paranoia, and surveillance, featuring frequent shots of narrow staircases, impenetrable shadows, and mirrors. In both films offscreen sounds and voices create anxiety and disorientation; *Der Verlorene* repeatedly displays signs of "Feind hört mit" (the enemy is listening) that recall *M*'s elaborate surveillance systems.[25] If Beckert's off-key whistling alerts us to his pathological instincts, the nondiegetic Horla motif cues audiences to Rothe's somber and menacing mood. In their influential history of film Ulrich Gregor and Enno Patalas noted how Lorre's film "ties in with the postwar expressionism of early sound film," extending the parallels even beyond *M*.[26]

The relationship between the parallel modernities of *M* and *Der Verlorene* is established most succinctly in the scenes in which Beckert and Rothe examine themselves in the mirror. In what amounts to the viewer's first frontal view of the child murderer, Lang shows us Beckert grimacing in front of a mirror while the voice-over of a graphologist, assigned to establish a psychological profile of the suspect, explains to us that "the writing as a whole displays elusive yet unmistakable signs of madness." Significantly, Beckert is given no voice in this scene but is constructed as the object of a (pseudo)scientific discourse that links handwriting to a certain pathology, an objectification that will pervade the film until, in the climax of the kangaroo court, Beckert is given a chance to speak on his own behalf. Rothe's first examination of himself in the mirror occurs *before* the first murder has taken place. In this scene Rothe inadvertently smears blood from a test animal over his cheeks and forehead, giving his disfigured face a highly premonitory and threatening look, while we hear first Hoesch's and then Winkler's voice urging Rothe "to put an end to it," that is, to kill Inge.

FIGURE 6.3 Beckert distorts his face in front of the mirror.

FIGURE 6.4 Rothe recognizes his face as that of a future murderer.

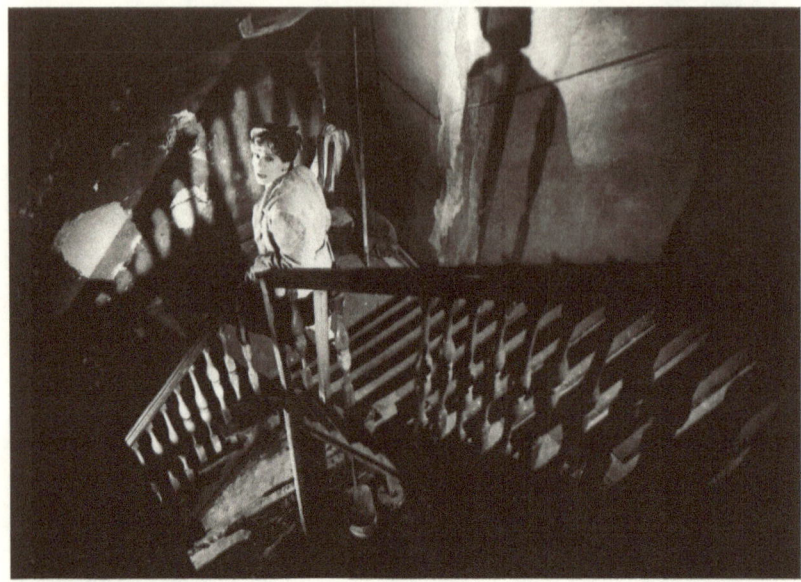

FIGURE 6.5 The spiral staircase not as trap but escape route.

Both mirror scenes connote a duplicitous or schizophrenic subjectivity, augmented by the fact that in both the voice(s) do not belong to the face that is shown, but the shot of Rothe marking himself clearly implies a culpability that Lang's film carefully avoids.[27]

The allusions to *M* are even more pronounced in *Der Verlorene*'s second murder scene, a sequence that takes up a substantial amount of screen time and, like no other, evokes the full social and psychological impact of the permanent state of emergency of wartime Germany. The scene is preceded by two near-murders: When Rothe's new roommate, the naive young teacher Ursula, gets comfy with him in his room late at night, Rothe barely averts his impulses and flees the apartment, hooking up with a prostitute (Gisela Trowe) after losing himself in the seedy parts of Hamburg (much as Enley does on his descent into the netherworlds of Bunker Hill in *Act of Violence*).[28] As she is about to let him into her apartment, in what would have surely spelled her death warrant, she is saved when suddenly, in the dim light of a match, she recognizes Rothe as a "Totmacher" (literally: deathmaker) and escapes by running down the prototypical noir narrow staircase.

Soon thereafter, Rothe will find his last victim, the affection-starved war widow Helene, in an overcrowded train, similar to the one that opened the film's flashback sequence. Helene's flirtatious overtures entice Rothe to a murder he was intent on avoiding; at one point she proudly shows him a jumping-jack toy she just purchased that clearly resembles the one that fascinated Beckert in a shop window shortly before he spotted his next prey, thus evoking the specter of murder. The impending danger seems to be diverted when an obnoxious drunk appears, who pesters Rothe by repeatedly asking him, "Don't I know you from somewhere?" As Romuald Karmakar has astutely observed, the perceptive power of the drunkard, who seems to sense the imminent threat, parallels that of the blind balloon merchant in *M*, who will identify the child murderer by his voice.[29] In the case of *Der Verlorene* it's the eyes ("diese Augen!") that the inebriated man recognizes (using the very phrase, "Irrtum ausgeschlossen" [no mistake possible], that the balloon seller also used to dispel all doubts), confirming on the narrative level what the image track has repeatedly shown before each (attempted) murder: a dimly lit close-up of Rothe's eyes seemingly evacuated of any sense of humanity or compassion, a blank stare that serves as a projection screen for the victim's worst fears.

An air raid seals Helene's fate. When all the passengers are asked to leave the train after the sirens begin to howl, a stoic Rothe remains aboard, prompting Helene to follow suit. Left alone with him on the abandoned train, she fatalistically comments, "If it's going to get you, it's going to get you anywhere." Again, the screen blackens with a shot of Rothe's back as he closes in on his second victim, the moment of murder ironically accompanied by the air raid sirens' signaling that danger has passed ("Entwarnung")—a powerful symbol of the inefficiency and unreliability of the State's handling of true emergencies. If Lang's film originally carried the subtitle, "A City in Search of a Murderer," no one in Hamburg takes note of the sex murderer in their midst. The atrocities of the Nazis and the suffering of the civilian population under constant bombardment provide a perfect shield for Rothe.

Made thirteen years after the end of World War I and two years before the Nazi takeover, *M* registers both the trauma of the lost war, as Kaes claims, and the impending dictatorship, as Siegfried Kracauer argued in his famous study *From Caligari to Hitler*.[30] In 1951 Lorre certainly viewed *M* through the same postwar prism that informed Kracauer's famous 1947 study. But the direction of *Der Verlorene* looks both backward and forward. While the film insists that the 1940s are of a piece with the early 1930s, postwar German viewers are instructed to understand that the past is not dead—it is not even past. In the very last shot of the film, Rothe steps on the tracks, turns his back to the oncoming train, and looks directly at us, the viewers. Is there any clearer way to imply our responsibility in the act of atonement he is about to make?

AN UNLUCKY HYBRID?

When *Der Verlorene* opened in 1951, Germans were no longer interested in acts of atonement. German chancellor Konrad Adenauer's Act of Clemency, which went into effect that same year, had de facto closed the book on denazification. While the film did receive some positive reviews and was given "Special Mention" at the 1952 Bundesfilmpreis Awards, popular audiences avoided it. The general consensus among film historians has been that its politics arrived at the wrong time and place, articulated by someone who, beyond his lack of directorial expertise, was considered ill-equipped to pass moral judgment. Films by reemigrants were unpopular and even more so was reemigration as an explicit or implicit film topic. The deeper roots for Lorre's misfortunes in Germany, however, are grounded in a series of mutual and profound misunderstandings, which are in themselves indicative of the true dimensions of exile. Lorre sought to create a *hybrid* film, an international film made in both English- and German-language versions, with an international cast and production unit, that would be successful in two different markets and would appeal to different audiences.[31] Lorre's desire to create a *German noir*, a film that would simultaneously straddle both American and German film history, proved untenable. Jan-Christopher Horak's notion of "the unlucky hybrid" may well be too negative a term for describing German exile cinema in Hollywood; nonetheless, the films of German reemigrants can indeed be considered unfortunate.

To be sure, the film's production had been under a bad sign all along. Lead actor Karl John broke his leg in a car accident and stalled production for eight weeks; producer Arnold Pressburger died halfway through filming and had to be replaced by his son Fred, who was far less inclined than his father to tolerate Lorre's idiosyncrasies (one of which was to constantly rewrite the script). The final cut of the film was burned in a studio fire and had to be completely reconstructed. Finally, the official premiere at the Venice Film Festival was cancelled at the last moment when, in a blatant display of postwar German film politics, *Der Verlorene* was replaced by Josef von Baky's *Das doppelte Lottchen* (*Lotte Two Times*, based on Erich Kästner's famous novel), and Lorre's film was shown only in an unsubtitled version out of contest.[32] A successful German premiere took place in Cologne on September 18, 1951, but in less than two weeks the film disappeared from German movie theaters.

In the five years since *The Murderers Are Among Us* (Wolfgang Staudte, 1946), cinematic efforts to face the trauma of the lost war, or to assume any responsibility or implication in Nazi terror and the Holocaust, had by and large given way to a desire to leave the past behind.[33] The "Trümmerfilm" (rubble film), a cycle of postwar German films with considerable artistic and political ambition (of which *Der Verlorene* is often considered a culminating, if much belated, example), had been replaced by escapist fare such as *Grün ist die Heide* (Hans Deppe, 1951) and *Dr. Holl* (Rolf Hansen, 1951, with a script by Thea von Harbou), the latter an early example of the "Ärztefilm" (doctor film) fad that would sweep the Federal Republic in the 1950s and that featured doctors as self-sacrificing, dedicated heroes—a far cry from the brooding, melancholy Dr. Rothe.[34]

Ironically, Hollywood would become Lorre's strongest competitor. With the West German market finally reclaimed, and no real homegrown industry (yet) to contend with, American studios released hundreds of films in German cinemas. As Wolfgang Schivelbusch succinctly put it, "Hollywood's attitude at the end of World War II can be summarized in one sentence: war had been waged to win back the European market."[35] The Americans dressed up this strategy in a rhetoric of reeducation that Germans quickly came to resent. They battled the foreign competitor by reprising old Ufa films; in 1951 there were 174 rereleases.[36] In a market swamped by a curious mixture of the old and the new, the foreign and the domestic, little room remained for Lorre's transnational ambition.

While American films were now again being shown in Germany, the films that had established Lorre's star persona in Hollywood—*Mad Love* (1935), the Mr. Moto series (1937–39), *Stranger on the Third Floor* (1940), *The Maltese Falcon* (1942), *Casablanca* (1942), *The Mask of Dimitrios* (1944), and *Arsenic and Old Lace* (1944)—were still completely unknown there. Since many of these provide the tapestry that create the intertextual depth of *Der Verlorene*, the film remained a largely illegible text for Germans. Any resemblance they noted to Lorre's earlier work was filtered through the influence of Weimar cinema on American horror films and film noir, and of course *M*. If we consider, furthermore, how hostilely Germans reacted to the American noirs, this becomes even clearer. As Lutz Koepnick has shown in his study of the relationship between Nazi and exile cinema, imported noirs like Robert Siodmak's *The Spiral Staircase* (1945) met with a lukewarm reception in Germany, not only because of the general resentment toward the work of exiled filmmakers but also because of a perceived cultural imperialism. Analyzing a particularly negative review of this film by Hans Ulrich Eylau, Koepnick suggests that the film was considered dangerous because it allegedly "rekindle[d] fascism in postfascist Germany" and thus "obstruct[ed] any authentic reformulation of German identity after the Nazis."[37] In a strange twist of Kracauer's thesis about the premonitory power of Weimar cinema, it now became the Hollywood exiles' films that came under scrutiny for harboring authoritarian tendencies.

Recent scholarship on postwar German and European cinema has vindicated the complex patterns of influence and parallel developments in the realm of noir vis-à-vis American postwar cinema, underscoring an international dimension of noir that completely eluded contemporary reviewers and audiences.[38] Yet at the time, Lorre's mixed languages were indeed hard to decipher for the general public and critics alike. Addressing his target audiences in an idiom that they were bound to misunderstand, *Der Verlorene* initiated a dialogue that could not but fail, revealing a communication process at cross purposes with itself. Ultimately, Lorre came to realize that his displacement was more profound than he had imagined.[39]

The negative German reception of *Der Verlorene* vanquished any hopes that the film might be shown in the United States. Having become sensitive to German accusations that the implied continuities between the Third Reich and the Federal Republic (by now the United States' most important ally in Western Europe) had been too strong, Lorre feared a similarly hostile reception stateside, still in the grip of McCarthyism. As he stated in 1962, "I have never and will not ever bring it [*Der Verlorene*] over here. It would probably make money too. But there are times when an actor should know enough not to make money. I don't think the State Department would like me to indict any other country's politics."[40]

There remains, of course, the suspicion that the film was really intended to rekindle his *American* career rather than restart a German one. Whatever truth there may be to this, history quickly foreclosed such speculations. Returning from Germany in 1952, Lorre was never able to reach the height of his early and mid-1940s successes. He ended his career much disillusioned, costarring with Vincent Price in Roger Corman horror films and appearances in endless self-parodies on television. He died, lonely and embittered, of a cerebral hemorrhage in his West Hollywood apartment in 1964, his body finally giving in to years of drug abuse. One of his last interlocutors was Fritz Lang, the author of his erstwhile fame. Los Angeles neighbors for more than thirty years, they never made a film together after *M*.

POSTSCRIPT

The story of Peter Lorre and his film *Der Verlorene* is paradigmatic for the history of reemigration to Germany, particularly to the Western Allied zones and later the Federal Republic of Germany. It is a history of missed opportunities, mutual misunderstandings, and disappointment on both sides. In the sole monograph devoted to postwar reemigration, Marita Krauss notes that the more politically motivated the expulsion from Germany, the greater the likelihood of a return; in contrast, those persecuted for ethnic reasons rarely chose to go back to the country that engineered the Holocaust.[41] Since most exiled filmmakers were Jewish, reemigration among them is particularly low. But Jewish or not, few emigrants were welcomed with open arms; most had to struggle with prejudice, resentment, or outright rejection by those who had stayed behind. For the general population the conclusion of the war meant not only the end of Nazi delusions of grandeur but also misery, hardship, and severe physical and psychological destruction. Those who had stayed felt little sympathy for those who had left—and were disinclined to remember the circumstances of the emigrants' flight from Germany. Perceived as siding with the victors, in whose company they often returned, the reemigrants were met with both envy and mistrust. The Germans cast themselves as victims of the war, alleging that "they" had it easy "over there" and had "no idea" what really went on "here." The fact that film personnel like Dieterle and Dietrich, both gentiles who had emigrated during the Weimar Republic, *chose* to side with the Americans against Nazi Germany rather than returning home in the 1930s—in Dietrich's case even snubbing repeated advances by Goebbels—provided uncomfortable proof that there had been alternatives. Their presence highlighted the fatal consequences of false choices, implying a responsibility that Germans at home were unwilling to accept.

The controversy surrounding Thomas Mann, who became a U.S. citizen in June 1944, and his refusal to return to Germany illuminates particularly well the stakes in the debate about reemigration, and the enormous psychological gap between those who left and those who stayed. A Nobel laureate, Mann was considered the incarnation of legitimate German culture, both by the exile community and by postwar Germans. A key figure of the "other" Germany, the liberal humanist tradition despised by the Nazis and now largely exiled, Mann assumed the position of key arbiter of all things German, a position that took on a decidedly political dimension through his frequent lecture tours and his numerous BBC radio addresses, "Deutsche Hörer," in which he warned Germans of the devilish powers that ruled over them. On the question of German guilt Mann assumed a nuanced position that set him apart from writers like Emil Ludwig, who insisted that there is only *one* German character, which is militaristic, arrogant, and aggressive and that the German nation has incurred a *Kollektivschuld* (collective guilt); and from those like Brecht, who believed in *two* Germanies, arguing that Nazi Germany ought not be confused with the rest of the German people and should therefore not be persecuted wholesale (a controversy that came to a head between Brecht and Mann in August 1943 at the house of Salka Viertel).[42] In January of 1945 Mann described Hitler's rule as a mixture of "dreadful error, half blamable, half fate."[43] Three weeks after the German surrender, in his address at the Library of Congress, "Germany and the Germans," Mann provided a much harsher reckoning with German traditions. With the extent of Nazi atrocities now in plain view, he explained that the German's particular sense of interiority ("Innerlichkeit"), a central marker of German cultural identity at least since romanticism, was responsible for the Germans' susceptibility to political ideologies, including National Socialism. Mann insisted that there are not two Germanies, a good one and a bad one, but only one, "which, through a devilish trick, turned from the best into the most evil."[44]

In light of Mann's ambivalent description of the German "soul" and its responsibility for war crimes, it is not surprising that he must have had serious doubts about a permanent return to his home country. Yet soon after the war, this is what many Germans expected of him. In August 1945 the writer Walter von Molo pleaded with Mann in an open letter to return home in order to guide the Germans in their efforts to rebuild the nation. According to von Molo, it was Mann's duty to comfort the suffering Germans "like a good doctor who not only sees the effects of a disease but also understands its cause."[45] Mann's response to von Molo was brusque. He chided him and the Germans for their ignorance about the hardship of exile, and for the naive and insensitive offer to establish ties again "as if those twelve years had not happened at all." Emphasizing the fundamental difference between those who stayed and those in exile, he stated, "I'm afraid that any understanding between someone who witnessed the witches

Sabbath from the outside and those who danced along and waited on Herr Urian, will be difficult."⁴⁶ Mann went on to reject as worthless any book printed in Germany between 1933 and 1945 because it reeked of "blood and shame," thereby implicitly attacking writers such as Frank Thieß, who claimed that a so-called inner emigration had been an effective way to resist Nazism. Deeply hurt by Mann's remark, Thieß rebuked all those who, like Mann, had witnessed the German tragedy from the "balcony seats" of foreign countries.⁴⁷ Mann would eventually settle in Switzerland and only pay short visits to Germany.

While few individuals, and certainly no filmmaker, commanded the public respect and cultural capital of a Thomas Mann, the majority of film reemigrants faced similar responses.⁴⁸ They were expected to return to the German nation-state, share its burden and responsibility, and actively participate in its rebuilding without claiming privileges or even compensation for their suffering, which would have reaffirmed the guilt of those who stayed. As Krauss argues, the common sentiment was that if anyone was guilty, it was those who had left and not served the nation when it mattered most; if the "Emigranten" wanted to rejoin the nation, any atonement was as much their responsibility as that of those who had stayed behind, leading in effect to "an equation of the guilt of the victims with that of the perpetrators."⁴⁹

Beyond general hostility and resentment, filmmakers also faced challenges specific to the film industry. In contrast to Mann, Brecht, Horkheimer, and Adorno, few filmmakers were actually invited back. When Brecht asked Lorre in 1950 to come to Berlin, his invitation was to join him on the stage of the Berliner Ensemble. Brecht famously put his plea in the form of the poem, "To the Actor P.L. in Exile," telling Lorre: "Listen, we are calling you back. Driven out / You must now return."⁵⁰ As we know, the "Verjagte," as Brecht called him (literally, the one who was chased away), did not accept the invitation; we can only speculate whether he no longer considered the theater his true home, or whether he did not want to settle in the GDR. The actor Curt Bois, in contrast, who appeared with Lorre in *Casablanca*, did accept Brecht's call, and after many years on the postwar stage would find success late in life again on the German screen, most memorably as Homer in *Wings of Desire* (Wim Wenders, 1987). At first there were few jobs. The industry was in shambles, and all new productions were heavily scrutinized by the Allies; later, when more films were produced, filmmakers who had worked during the Third Reich were quickly allowed to resume their careers, since, with the onset of the Cold War, denazification became secondary to shoring up an ally against the communist East.

Among all sectors of artistic production, the film industry boasted the most pronounced continuities between the Third Reich and the Western Allied Zones. For the exiles this meant having to work side by side with filmmakers who had been employed under Goebbels, including Veit Harlan, director of the infamous *Jud Süss*, Wolfgang Liebeneiner, Josef von Baky, Arthur Maria Rabenalt, Harald Braun, Robert A. Stemmle, and Thea von Harbou.[51] Curt Siodmak tells how in 1951, during a brief visit to Europe, he met Gustav Ucicky, an old acquaintance from Ufa days and a prolific director during the Third Reich, who was making movies again in Austria by 1947. When Ucicky saw Siodmak at a producer's office in Zurich, he greeted him in broad Berlin slang, "Wo biste denn jewesen?" (Where've ya been?) to which Siodmak dryly answered, "Not in your ovens."[52]

Exiles encountered other obstacles as well. After more than a decade abroad, most of them were unfamiliar with the taste of contemporary audiences. Several, including Lorre, reacted by attempting to build on their successes of Weimar days, drawing criticism for their anachronism, most emphatically in the case of Lang, whose three postwar German films included a remake of the two-part spectacle *Der Tiger von Eschnapur* and *Das indische Grabmahl*, first directed by Joe May in 1921, as well as a loose sequel to his Mabuse series, *Die 1000 Augen des Dr. Mabuse*. Furthermore, after spending years in the U.S. film industry, with its high professional standards and sophisticated division of labor, adjusting to the modest production facilities of postwar Germany was difficult. It was a cottage industry not only in economic terms but also in its provincial aesthetic ambitions. Returning from the United States in 1946, Erich Pommer observed, "When I saw Germany for the first time since 1943, I couldn't believe it: The taste of the audience had not only remained on the same level, no, it had even regressed."[53]

The majority of the numerous Hollywood exiles and émigrés who attempted to get some sort of foothold in the West German industry after 1945 failed.[54] The extensive list of names includes the likes of Fritz Lang, William Dieterle, and Robert Siodmak, but also B directors such as Edgar G. Ulmer, Max Nosseck, Kurt Neumann, and Hugo Haas. The individual reasons for a return varied among the reemigrants, ranging from professional concerns such as the changed production circumstances in a rapidly transforming U.S. industry (Robert Siodmak) through political reasons (notably the black- and gray-listings of Lang, Dieterle, and possibly Ulmer in the wake of the HUAC hearings), or the desire to participate in the building of a better Germany (Brecht, Kortner) to more personal reasons. In Lorre's case the motivation for leaving Hollywood was a mixture of a faltering career, extreme financial pressure, and the desire to dodge police supervision of his drug habit.

While the majority of filmmakers, like Lorre, left Germany again, or transitioned to the stage, where they had begun, some succeeded by acquiescing to German popular tastes. Robert Siodmak, the most successful among the reemigrants, won critical acclaim, the 1958 "Bundesfilmpreis," and an Oscar nomination for his *Nachts, wenn der Teufel kam* (*The Devil Strikes at Midnight*). Like Lorre's *Der Verlorene*, Siodmak's film depicted a serial killer during the Third Reich, but it was far less daring in its implication of German responsibility and personal guilt. His subsequent works included grossly commercial projects such as the Karl May adaptation, *Der Schut* (Yellow Devil, 1964) and a grandiose sandal epic, *Kampf um Rom* (Battle for Rome, 1968). As Siodmak himself commented on his postwar German films, "I only want to entertain . . . and at any rate, the older generation has given up on itself."[55]

William Dieterle returned to Germany in 1958, because he suffered from blacklisting in Hollywood. Like Billy Wilder and Fritz Lang, Dieterle was a longtime Hollywood A-list filmmaker, credited with almost seventy American films. In Germany he was forced to work mostly in television before returning to the theater, where his career had begun in the 1920s. Somewhat unique in the group of returning émigrés were Billy Wilder, Fred Zinnemann, and Douglas Sirk. All three made movies set in Germany for American studios but considered these experiences merely dry runs for a possible relocation to Europe. They eventually decided to continue their careers in the United States (with Sirk retiring in Switzerland and Zinnemann settling in London).[56] Wilder entered Germany already in the summer of 1945 as a U.S. film officer aiding in the denazification of the German film industry, an assignment that eventually went to Pommer.[57] Lang, still the most famous living German director, made the three German films noted above before returning to Hollywood, for good. Two of the three were produced by Artur Brauner, himself an exile—a native of Łódź, Poland, he had survived the Holocaust by fleeing to the Soviet Union. Brauner would become a key figure for many returning émigrés and for German popular cinema in general.[58]

Not all cases of reemigration were devoid of redemption. Directors whose Hollywood careers had been less stellar than those of Lang, Siodmak, Dieterle, and Lorre often fared better in Germany, as their fall from grace had not been as harsh. A somewhat successful returnee was Frank

Wysbar. Having made a mark in the United States as a television producer, he scored a number of hits with German war films such as *Hunde, wollt ihr ewig leben* (*Stalingrad: Dogs, Do You Want to Live Forever?* 1959) and *Nacht fiel über Gotenhafen* (*Darkness Fell on Gotenhafen*, 1960), achieving a modest triumph that had eluded him in Hollywood. Then there were those like Richard Eichberg and Erik Charell, who spent significant time in Hollywood seriously underemployed but whose considerable wealth allowed them to weather this period without hardship. One of the most popular directors and producers of silent films, Eichberg first acquired Swiss and then American citizenship before returning to Germany in 1949, but he still regularly commuted to New York City, where his family lived. Unable to repeat his prewar success, he nevertheless produced several of Edgar G. Ulmer's European pictures. Charell, the director of one of Ufa's biggest moneymakers, *Der Kongress tanzt / Congress Dances* (1931), also returned in 1949 but was similarly able to find only limited success, for example as author of the screenplay for *Im weissen Rössl* (Willi Forst, 1952), a remake of a popular 1935 film. Actor and director Reinhold Schünzel, the Inspector Ritter of Lang's *Hangmen Also Die*, returned in 1949 and had some success as a stage and screen actor before dying in 1954 at the age of sixty-five.

As these examples illustrate, and many more could be added, the history of reemigration is largely a failed one. Beyond the many émigrés and exiles who attempted a return with little or no success, there are, of course, all those who never even wanted to come back to Germany or Austria. As with reemigration, the reasons differed. Some no longer felt any cultural ties; others could not imagine living in a country that had voted Hitler into power or that had applauded the *Anschluss*. Henry Koster quipped that only those who had no success would leave Hollywood anyhow.[59] The list of those who, like Koster, never seriously entertained the thought of a return is almost as long as that of those who tried reemigration. It includes the likes of directors Curtis Bernhardt, Otto Preminger, Ernst Lubitsch (who died in November of 1947), Billy Wilder, Fred Zinnemann, and Douglas Sirk. During her 1961 tour in Germany Marlene Dietrich was told in no uncertain terms that she was not welcome, prompting the retired star to spend her final years in Paris rather than her native Berlin.[60] If we consider how many of the failed reemigrants eventually made their way back to Hollywood, it becomes very clear that for the vast majority it was indeed a ticket of no return.[61]

EPILOGUE

The end of World War II spelled the end of German exile cinema in Hollywood. The shifting ideological allegiances of the United States and the concomitant rise of the blacklist created a political environment ill-suited for the leftist-liberal bent of exile cinema. The postwar decline of the classical studio system and changing public tastes dramatically altered how films were produced, exhibited, marketed, and consumed, further eroding the political commitment that shaped exile cinema. Certainly, directors such as Fritz Lang, Billy Wilder, Douglas Sirk, and Otto Preminger extended their U.S. careers well into the 1950s and beyond, but the political and industrial parameters under which they did so shifted dramatically.

Within the context of U.S. intellectual and cultural history German exile cinema in Hollywood today usually comes into view as a short-lived, if distinct, period in the classic era of studio production and a substory in the much larger history of artists, scientists, and intellectuals who came to this country as refugees from Nazi Germany and war-torn Europe. As I have noted, in the 1920s, 1930s, and 1940s, Hollywood branded its output as a purely American product (a practice that remains in place largely to this day) and was understood as such by popular viewers and professional critics. As a consequence many films by individual exile directors have entered the pantheon of the classic studio era, but their exilic dimension has rarely been acknowledged and is usually absorbed by a historiography that pays little attention to Hollywood's international workforce, its transnational reach, and the diversity of its audience.[1]

In contrast to the United States, where German exile cinema has hardly been established as a distinct era of film history, there have been significant developments in Germany and Austria during the last decades to rediscover and reclaim the films of Ulmer, Zinnemann, and Preminger, to name only a few. To be sure, the 1950s were an unwelcoming decade for the exiles, as the example of Peter Lorre shows, yet beginning with the 1960s, a new generation of German directors emerged that developed an interest in the German film professionals who had left for the United States in the 1920s and 1930s. In 1958 a young Alexander Kluge apprenticed on the set of Fritz Lang's *Der Tiger von Eschnapur*, the first representative of the so-called New German Cinema to seek such a dialogue. In a 1977 obituary to Lang, Wim Wenders spoke of the director as "the lost, no the missed father," a statement that summarized well not only Wenders's relation to the generation of Lang but also that of his peers.[2] Wenders's *Im Lauf der Zeit / Kings of the Road* (1976) is dedicated to Lang and includes an extended homage to *The Nibelungs*. In his *The State of Things* (1982) Wenders quotes from F. W. Murnau's letters from Tahiti in an attempt to link Murnau's existential homelessness with that of the film's protagonist. Indeed, that film can also be seen as an extended homage to the fringe filmmaking that Wenders admired in Edgar G. Ulmer, as the director explains in Michael Palm's documentary, *Edgar G. Ulmer: The Man Off-Screen* (2004). Werner Herzog, too, claimed Murnau as an ancestor for his cinema, throwing in film historian Lotte Eisner for good measure. Herzog's *Nosferatu, the Vampyre* (1979) is a faithful remake of Murnau's classic, while Herzog's 1974 diary, *Vom Gehen im Eis / On Walking on Ice*, chronicles a winter pilgrimage from Munich to Paris to visit the ailing author. A pilgrimage of sorts was also Rainer Werner Fassbinder's encounter with the retired Douglas Sirk in Switzerland; in his emphatic essay "Imitation of Life" Fassbinder celebrated Sirk as a Hollywood auteur and selected him as the role model for his own future explorations of melodrama.[3] Volker Schlöndorff's six-and-a-half-hour TV documentary *Billy, How Did You Do It?* (1992) introduced Billy Wilder to a mainstream German audience. Hans-Christoph Blumenberg cowrote Robert Siodmak's autobiography with the director, and in his film *Beim nächs-*

ten Kuss knall ich ihn nieder (When he kisses again, I'll shoot him, 1995), Blumenberg celebrated the career of Reinhold Schünzel.

To be sure, these acts of claiming ancestry in a "legitimate" German film history, that is, one that is not tainted by collaborations with the National Socialists or the commercial sellout of the 1950s, are not without blind spots and willful distortions. Fassbinder conveniently overlooked the films Douglas Sirk made for Goebbels when he was still called Detlef Sierck, and Wenders bought into the version of Lang's career that the director fashioned for his interview with Peter Bogdanovich. Nevertheless, the directors of the New German Cinema can be credited with rediscovering a generation of filmmakers that at least in Germany had fallen into oblivion. Contemporary directors have built on this foundation. Tom Tykwer and Dani Levy, for example, cite Ernst Lubitsch as an important role model, while Romuald Karmakar and Christian Petzold (as well as writer Elfriede Jelinek) celebrate the work of Peter Lorre. Karmakar's *Der Totmacher / The Deathmaker* (1995), a portrait of serial killer Fritz Haarmann, owes as much to Lang's *M* as to Peter Lorre's repeated performances of mentally disturbed killers; Levy's *Mein Führer—Die wirklich wahrste Wahrheit über Adolf Hitler / My Führer* (2007) can be read as an extended homage to *To Be or Not to Be*, while Lubitsch's *Trouble in Paradise* inspired Tykwer's *Drei / Three* (2010). Through these and other similarly inspired films German exile cinema has taken up again a permanent residence in Germany.

An important factor in the rehabilitation of exile cinema was the work of the Stiftung Deutsche Kinemathek, Berlin. In the 1970s the Kinemathek began organizing substantial retrospectives of key directors, including William Dieterle, Fred Zinnemann, Billy Wilder, Fritz Lang, F. W. Murnau, G. W. Pabst, Ernst Lubitsch, Otto Preminger, William Wyler, Erich von Stroheim, and Robert and Curt Siodmak.[4] These retrospectives regularly incorporated screenings of restored prints (subsequently made available on DVD) and were often accompanied by lavish, thoroughly researched publications. Another important resource was the Kinemathek's journal *Film/Exil* (1992–2005), which reprinted archival resources from the Paul Kohner File and other important depositories, as well as scholarly articles. Similarly, the Austrian organization and publisher Synema has done much to raise awareness about the forgotten achievements of Austrian film personnel, often in conjunction with the Film Museum Vienna and the Filmarchiv Austria. Through these combined efforts the story of the German-language filmmakers in Hollywood comes into view not only as a loss of talent that was never recuperated but also as a tradition that can be reclaimed for making films that resonate with today's national and international audiences.

The point bears repeating that the predicament of the Hollywood exiles is not (and never was) as insular as it may seem. Indeed, there is much to be learned from it for our present-day society. Exile cinema resonates with, and indeed anticipates, a variety of developments that characterize our current globalization, from the increasing interplay of mass media and mass migration and its role in the creation of diasporic communities, to the overall role of commercialized popular culture in the construction of historical imaginaries. German exile cinema of the 1930s and 1940s thus anticipates—even if on a smaller scale—the transnational and diasporic public spheres of contemporary globalization. As Arjun Appadurai has shown, mass media and mass migration are converging in a world where ever-more moving images meet ever-more deterritorialized viewers, affecting subjectivity and identity formation in which the nation-state, as key arbiter of social change, has become increasingly less significant.[5] Studying exile cinema today forces us to rethink the general role of cinema in constructing modern subjectivities.

His experience in the United States led Theodor W. Adorno to believe that exile also entails lessons in ethics. As I noted in chapter 5, Adorno famously wrote in his LA memoir, *Minima Moralia*, "it is part of morality not to be at home in one's home."[6] Edward Said has expanded this moral imperative into an epistemological advantage: "To follow Adorno is to stand away from 'home' in order to look at it with the exile's detachment.... The exile knows that in a secular and contingent world, homes are always provisional. Borders and barriers, which enclose us within the safety of familiar territory, can also become prisons, and are often defended beyond reason or necessity. Exiles cross borders, break barriers of thought and experience."[7] When Said first wrote this in 1985, he looked back on the twentieth century as the century of exiles and refugees, hoping to glean some redemption from a state of existence that for the vast majority spells economic, social, and psychological hardship. Now, some thirty years later, our present century is confronting us with a human migration of unprecedented proportions, made up of political refugees, economic migrants, victims of human trafficking, and all varieties of undocumented people. The International Organization for Migration estimates the number of international migrants in 2010 at 214 million and projects this number to reach 405 million by 2050. It is obvious that together with climate change, migration is the key political, economic, and ethical challenge to confront us now. Given such projections, we can speculate that the lessons learned and taught by the German exiles in Hollywood will be relevant for some time to come.

NOTES

INTRODUCTION

1. Georg Simmel, "The Stranger" [1908], in *On Individuality and Social Forms*, ed. and trans. Donald N. Levine (Chicago: University of Chicago Press, 1971), 143.
2. Iain Chambers, *Migrancy, Culture, Identity* (London: Routledge, 1994), 4.
3. *Hollywood Reporter*, August 12, 1942, 3.
4. Thomas Elsaesser, "Ethnicity, Authenticity, and Exile: A Counterfeit Trade? German Filmmakers in Hollywood," in *Home, Exile, Homeland: Film, Media, and the Politics of Place*, ed. Hamid Naficy (New York: Routledge, 1999), 100.
5. Michael Curtiz was born Mihály Kertész in Budapest in 1888. An actor-manager, he fled the counterrevolutionary, anti-Semitic Horthy regime in Hungary in 1919 and for several years worked in Austria and Germany. In 1927 he came to Hollywood, where for twenty-seven years he worked for Warner Bros. The German exile supporting actors, bit players, and extras include Lotte Palfi, Trudy Berliner, Curt Bois, Wolfgang Zilzer, Ilka Gruning, and Ludwig Stoessel, as well as Hans von Twardowski, an openly gay actor in Weimar Germany, and Helmut Dantine, leader of the anti-Nazi youth movement in Vienna.
6. See, e.g., Lion Feuchtwanger, *Der Teufel in Frankreich* (Berlin: Aufbau, 1992; first published as *Unholdes Frankreich* in 1942); Hans Sahl, *Das Exil im Exil* (Munich:

DTV, 1994); Varian Fry, *Surrender on Demand* (New York: Random House, 1945); Lisa Fittko, *Mein Weg über die Pyrenäen* (Munich: Knaur, 1985); and Anna Seghers, *Transit*, trans. James Galston (Boston: Little, Brown, 1944).

7. The exact number of exiles in Hollywood is contested. A 1987 exhibit at the Filmmuseum Frankfurt lists the names of 1,532 German-language film professionals who can be considered refugees from Nazi Germany. See *Von Babelsberg nach Hollywood: Filmemigranten aus Nazideutschland* (Frankfurt: Deutsches Filmmuseum, 1987). Counting all affected family members, Helmut G. Asper puts the overall number of film exiles at two thousand, of which some eight hundred ended up in Hollywood. See Helmut G. Asper, "Film," in *Handbuch der deutschsprachigen Emigration, 1933–1945*, ed. Claus-Dieter Krohn et al. (Darmstadt: Primus, 1998), 957–70, here 957 and 964. Jan-Christopher Horak, however, sets their number only at above five hundred. See Jan-Christopher Horak, "Exilfilm, 1933–1945," *Geschichte des deutschen Films*, ed. Wolfgang Jacobsen, Anton Kaes, and Hans Helmut Prinzler (Stuttgart: Metzler, 1993), 108. An impressive list of who those exiles were is compiled by Hans Kafka, "What Our Immigration Did for Hollywood—and Vice Versa," *Aufbau* 10, no. 51 (Dec. 22, 1944): 40–41; repr. in *New German Critique* 89 (2003): 185–89.

8. Ehrhard Bahr, *Weimar on the Pacific: German Exile Culture in Los Angeles and the Crisis of Modernism* (Berkeley: University of California Press, 2007), 18. It is estimated that the overall community of Hitler refugees in Southern California included some ten thousand to fifteen thousand people.

9. See Ursula Hardt, *From Caligari to California: Erich Pommer's Life in the International Film Wars* (Oxford: Berghahn, 1996); and Wolfgang Jacobsen, *Erich Pommer: Ein Produzent macht Filmgeschichte* (Berlin: Argon, 1989).

10. Famous recruits included Ernst Lubitsch, Pola Negri, F. W. Murnau, Emil Jannings, Erich Pommer, Alexander Korda, Ludwig Berger, Camilla Horn, Conrad Veidt, Paul Leni, E. A. Dupont, Lya di Putti, and Marlene Dietrich.

11. See *Ich bin ein unheilbarer Europäer: Briefe aus dem Exil*, ed. Heike Klapdor (Berlin: Aufbau, 2007), 29. Kohner began his American career in a production unit at Universal at the time when Veidt, Dupont, von Stroheim, Paul Leni, and Rudolph and Joseph Schildkraut worked there. The Kohner Files in the Stiftung Deutsche Kinemathek Berlin are one of the most important repositories for the study of German exile cinema.

12. On Veidt see my essay "Allegories of Displacement," in *Destination London: German-Speaking Émigrés and British Cinema, 1925–1950*, ed. Tim Bergfelder and Christian Cargnelli (London: Berghahn, 2008), 142–54. On Jannings see my essay "Emil Jannings: Translating the Star," in *Idols of Modernity: Movie Stars of the 1920s*, ed. Patrice Petro (New Brunswick, NJ: Rutgers University Press, 2010), 182–201; and Frank Noack, *Jannings: Der erste deutsche Weltstar* (Munich: Heyne, 2012).

13. For emigration to France see *Hallo? Berlin? Ici Paris! Deutsch-französische Filmbeziehungen, 1918–1939*, ed. Sibylle M. Sturm and Arthur Wohlgemuth (Munich: Text + Kritik, 1996); and Alastair Phillips, *City of Darkness, City of Light: Émi-*

gré Filmmakers in Paris, 1929–1939 (Amsterdam: Amsterdam University Press, 2004). For the Netherlands see Kathinka Dittrich van Weringh, *Der niederländische Spielfilm der dreissiger Jahre und die deutsche Filmemigration* (Amsterdam: Rodopi, 1987). For Austria see Christian Cargnelli and Michael Omasta, eds., *Aufbruch ins Ungewisse: Österreichische Filmschaffende in der Emigration vor 1945*, 2 vols. (Vienna: Wespennest, 1993); Armin Loacker, ed., *Unerwünschtes Kino: Der deutschsprachige Emigrantenfilm, 1934–1937* (Vienna: Filmarchiv Austria, 2000); and Rudolf Ulrich, *Österreicher in Hollywood* (Vienna: Filmarchiv Austria, 2004). For England see Bergfelder and Cargnelli, *Destination London*; Günter Berghaus, ed., *Theatre and Film in Exile: German Artists in Britain, 1933–1945* (Oxford: Berg, 1989); and Tobias Hochscherf, *The Continental Connection: German-Speaking Émigrés and British Cinema, 1927–1945* (Manchester: Manchester University Press, 2011). See also the essays in *Exilforschung: Film und Fotografie*, vol. 21 (Munich: Text + Kritik, 2003).

14. Cameron Crowe, *Conversations with Wilder* (New York: Knopf, 1999), 19.
15. Despite Salka Viertel's significance for German exile culture, the secondary literature on her is sparse. See Katharina Prager, *"Ich bin nicht gone Hollywood!": Salka Viertel, ein Leben in Theater und Film* (Vienna: Braumüller, 2007); Marion Steiner, *Schauspielerinnen im Exil (1930–1945): Vier exemplarische Lebensläufe—Therese Giese, Lilli Palmer, Salka Viertel, Helene Weigel* (Saarbrücken: Müller, 2008); and Michael Lentz, "Nachwort," in Salka Viertel, *Das unbelehrbare Herz: Erinnerungen an ein Leben mit Künstlern des 20. Jahrhunderts* (Frankfurt am Main: Die andere Bibliothek, 2011), 463–94 (revised German translation of *The Kindness of Strangers*, first published in Germany in 1970).
16. On the history of the European Film Fund see E. Bond Johnson, "Der European Film Fund und die Exilschriftsteller in Hollywood," in *Deutsche Exilliteratur seit 1933, Band 1: Kalifornien, Teil 1*, ed. John M. Spalek and Joseph Strelka (Bern: Francke, 1976), 135–46. On the Anti-Nazi League see Johanna W. Roden, "Die Hollywood Anti-Nazi League, 1936–1940," in *Deutschsprachige Exilliteratur seit 1933, Band 3: USA, Teil 4*, ed. John M. Spalek, Konrad Feilchenfeldt, and Sandra H. Hawrylchak (Zurich: Saur, 2003), 514–31.
17. Theodor W. Adorno, *Minima Moralia: Reflections from Damaged Life*, trans. E. F. N. Jephcott (New York: Verso, 1974), 33.
18. John Russell Taylor, *Strangers in Paradise: The Hollywood Émigrés, 1933–1950* (London: Faber and Faber, 1983); and Anthony Heilbut, *Exiled in Paradise: German Refugee Artists and Intellectuals in America, from the 1930s to the Present* (Boston: Beacon, 1983). Thomas Blubacher's recent study *Paradies in schwerer Zeit: Künstler und Denker im Exil in Pacific Palisades* (Munich: Elisabeth Sandmann, 2011) indicates that this trope continues to be the main paradigm through which to understand exiles in Hollywood.
19. Edward Said, "Reflections on Exile," in *Out There: Marginalization and Contemporary Cultures*, ed. Russell Ferguson et al. (Cambridge, MA: MIT Press, 1990), 366.
20. Salman Rushdie, *Imaginary Homelands: Essays and Criticism, 1981–1991* (New York: Penguin, 1991), 17.

21. Anton Kaes, "A Stranger in the House: Fritz Lang's *Fury* and the Cinema of Exile," *New German Critique* 89 (2003): 33–58.
22. Quoted in Otto Friedrich, *City of Nets: A Portrait of Hollywood in the 1940s* (Berkeley: University of California Press, 1986), 421.
23. Angelika Bammer, "Introduction," in *Displacements: Cultural Identities in Question*, ed. Angelika Bammer (Bloomington: Indiana University Press, 1994) xi–xx; here xi.
24. Even though in recent years a number of studies devoted to directors like Wilder, Zinnemann, and Lang have appeared, the exilic dimension of their oeuvre has been largely overlooked. See Crowe, *Conversations with Wilder*; Ed Sikov, *On Sunset Boulevard: The Life and Times of Billy Wilder* (New York: Hyperion, 1998); Tom Gunning, *The Films of Fritz Lang: Allegories of Vision and Modernity* (London: BFI, 2000); Patrick McGilligan, *Fritz Lang: The Nature of the Beast* (New York: St. Martin's, 1997); Arthur Nolletti, ed., *The Films of Fred Zinnemann: Critical Perspectives* (Albany: State University of New York Press, 1999); Neil Sinyard, *Fred Zinnemann: Films of Character and Conscience* (Jefferson, NC: McFarland, 2003); and Gabriel Miller, ed., *Fred Zinnemann: Interviews* (Jackson: University Press of Mississippi, 2005).
25. On Dieterle see Horst O. Hermanni, *William Dieterle: Vom Arbeiterbauernsohn zum Hollywood-Regisseur* (London: World of Books, 1992); Walter Kaul, *William Dieterle: Von Deutschland nach Hollywood* (Berlin: Filmfestspiele Berlin, 1973); Marta Mierendorff, *William Dieterle: Der Plutarch von Hollywood* (Berlin: Henschel, 1993). On Ulmer see Charles Tatum, ed., *Edgar G. Ulmer: Le bandit démasqué* (Paris: Yellow Now, 2002); Stefan Grissemann, *Mann im Schatten: Der Filmemacher Edgar G. Ulmer* (Vienna: Paul Zsolnay, 2004); Noah Isenberg, *Detour* (London: BFI, 2008); Gary D. Rhodes, ed., *Edgar G. Ulmer: Detour on Poverty Row* (Lanham, MD: Lexington Books, 2008); Bernd Herzogenrath, ed., *Edgar G. Ulmer: Essays on the King of the B's* (Jefferson, NC: McFarland, 2009); and Bernd Herzogenrath, ed., *The Films of Edgar G. Ulmer* (Lanham, MD: Scarecrow, 2009). See also Noah Isenberg's critical biography *Edgar G. Ulmer: A Filmmaker at the Margins* (Berkeley: University of California Press, 2014).
26. Jan-Christopher Horak, "German Exile Cinema, 1933–1950," *Film History* 8 (1996): 373–89, here 375.
27. See Jan-Christopher Horak, "Exilfilm, 1933–1945," 1. In the introduction to his compilation of exile materials, "*Etwas besseres als den Tod . . .*": *Filmexil in Hollywood* (Marburg: Schüren, 2002), Asper cites Horak's definition with approval, but in his entry "Film" in the *Handbuch der deutschsprachigen Emigration* he defines exile films more broadly as those in which at least *two* out of three key positions (production, script, direction) have been filled by exiles and which either have a thematic concern for the present or imply a continuation of a Weimar career (960). A pathbreaking document for the history of German exile film is Günter Peter Straschek's impressive five-part documentary *Filmemigration aus Nazi-Deutschland* (1975, 285 minutes).
28. See Lutz Koepnick, *The Dark Mirror: German Cinema Between Hitler and Hollywood* (Berkeley: University of California Press, 2002).

29. Writing on recent German-Turkish literature, Leslie Adelson has criticized the notion of betweenness since it implies that Turks in Germany are suspended on a bridge as if in a no-man's-land. The trope, she argues, "functions literally like a reservation designed to contain, restrain and impede new knowledge, not enable it." While I agree with Adelson's critique as here employed, it needs to be stressed that the context for German exile cinema is quite different. Whereas Turks in Germany may suffer a de facto lack of integration, exile filmmakers were often co-opted into the American studio system, and their imported cultural sensibilities were obliterated or rendered invisible. Stressing their in-betweenness is thus a strategy to highlight multiple cultural and ethnic affiliations where previous commentators saw only one. See Leslie Adelson, "Against Between: A Manifesto," in *Zafer Şenocak*, ed. Tom Cheesman and Karin E. Yeşilada (Cardiff: University of Wales Press, 2003), 131.
30. See Neal Gabler, *An Empire of Their Own: How the Jews Invented Hollywood* (New York: Doubleday, 1989); J. Hoberman and Jeffrey Shandler, *Entertaining America: Jews, Movies, and Broadcasting* (Princeton, NJ: Princeton University Press, 2003); Werner Hanak-Lettner, ed., *Bigger Than Life: 100 Years of Hollywood—A Jewish Experience* (Vienna: Jewish Museum Vienna, 2011); and Steven Carr, *Hollywood and Anti-Semitism: A Cultural History up to World War II* (Cambridge: Cambridge University Press, 2001).
31. See Peter Krämer, "Hollywood in Germany? Germany in Hollywood," in *The German Cinema Book*, ed. Tim Bergfelder, Erica Carter, and Deniz Göktürk (London: BFI, 2002), 227–37, here 229.
32. Lutz Koepnick, "*Mad Love*: Re-membering Berlin in Hollywood Exile," in *Caught by Politics: Hitler Exiles and American Visual Culture*, ed. Sabine Eckmann and Lutz Koepnick (New York: Palgrave, 2007), 195–222; here 195–97.
33. Gilles Deleuze and Félix Guattari, *Kafka: Toward a Minor Literature*, trans. Dana Polan (Minneapolis: University of Minnesota Press, 1986).
34. Bahr, *Weimar on the Pacific*, 19.
35. See Curt Siodmak, *Wolf Man's Maker: Memoir of a Hollywood Writer* (Lanham, MD: Scarecrow, 2001), 303.
36. A prominent example of the influence model is Barbara Steinbauer-Grötsch, *Die lange Nacht der Schatten: Film Noir und Filmexil* (Berlin: Bertz, 1997).
37. For a survey of the critical literature see the bibliography. In particular the films of Robert Siodmak have been widely neglected. The exilic dimension of Billy Wilder's cinema is discussed extensively in my *A Foreign Affair: Billy Wilder's American Films* (New York: Berghahn, 2008).
38. Thomas Elsaesser, *Weimar Cinema and After: Germany's Historical Imaginary* (London: Routledge, 2000), 380.
39. Joel Fineman, "The Structure of Allegorical Desire," in *Allegory and Representation*, ed. Stephen Greenblatt (Baltimore: Johns Hopkins University Press, 1981), 28.
40. Schüfftan made a lasting mark by devising a special effect for Lang's *Metropolis* (1926) that allowed for the insertion of actors into miniatures of skyscrapers and other sets through the help of special mirrors and that came to be known as the Schüfftan process. His many uncredited films include, among others, Douglas

Sirk's *Hitler's Madman*, *Summer Storm*, and *A Scandal in Paris*; and Edgar G. Ulmer's *Bluebeard*, *Strange Illusion*, *Club Havana*, and *The Wife of Monte Cristo*.
41. For a definition of the term *parallel modernities* see Edward Dimendberg, "Down These Seen Streets a Man Must Go: Siegfried Kracauer, 'Hollywood's Terror Films,' and the Spatiality of Film Noir," *New German Critique* 89 (2003): 113–43.
42. Hans Kafka, *Hollywood Calling: Die Aufbau-Kolumne zum Film-Exil*, ed. Roland Jaeger (Hamburg: ConferencePoint, 2002), 56.

1. A HISTORY OF HORROR

1. Edward Said, "Reflections on Exile," in *Out There: Marginalization and Contemporary Cultures*, edited by Russell Ferguson et al. (Cambridge, MA: MIT Press, 1990), 357–66.
2. Arianné Ulmer Cipes, quoted in Tag Gallagher, "All Lost in Wonder: Edgar G. Ulmer," *Screening the Past* (March 2001): http://tlweb.latrobe.edu.au/humanities/screeningthepast/firstrelease/fr0301/tgafr12a.htm.
3. Of all the professionals listed here, only G. W. Pabst would return to Nazi Germany.
4. A few years later her study *Refugees: Anarchy or Organization?* would provide the first sustained analysis of the "refugee problem."
5. In the summer of 1934 the *Weissbuch über die Erschiessungen am 30. Juni 1934*, an anonymous account of the so-called Roehm Putsch published in Paris, reached Hollywood, giving the émigrés a detailed picture of the Nazis' assassination of Roehm and hundreds of his SA minions. In its last chapter the *Weissbuch* warns its readers that the burning of the Reichstag and the events surrounding the killings of members of the SA are only precursors to a much greater horror, a new war. See *Weissbuch über die Erschiessungen am 30. Juni 1934: Authentische Darstellung der deutschen Bartholomäusnacht* (Paris: Carrefour, 1934), 145.
6. On Warner Bros.' relationship to Nazi Germany see Michael E. Birdwell, *Celluloid Soldiers: Warner Bros.'s Campaign Against Nazism* (New York: New York University Press, 1999).
7. Jan-Christoph Horak, "Pabst in Hollywood: A Modern Hero," in *The Films of G. W. Pabst: An Extraterritorial Cinema*, ed. Eric Rentschler (New Brunswick, NJ: Rutgers University Press, 1990), 155–66, here 166. Pabst himself reflected on his difficulties in Hollywood in a short essay, "Servitude et grandeur de Hollywood," written after his return to Paris in May 1936 (published in *Le rôle intellectuel du cinéma* [Paris: SDN-Institute international de coopération intellectuelle, 1937], 251–55).
8. After many years of neglect there has been a recent profusion of Ulmer scholarship. Publications include a collection of essays edited by Charles Tatum, *Edgar G. Ulmer: Le bandit démasqué* (Paris: Yellow Now, 2002); a 2008 BFI monograph on *Detour* by Noah Isenberg; an anthology edited by Gary D. Rhodes, *Edgar G. Ulmer: Detour on Poverty Row* (Lanham, MD: Lexington Books, 2008); and two edited volumes by Bernd Herzogenrath, *Edgar G. Ulmer: Essays on the King of the B's* (Jefferson, NC: McFarland, 2009) and *The Films of Edgar G. Ulmer* (Lanham,

MD: Scarecrow, 2009). See also the critical biography by Isenberg, *Edgar G. Ulmer: A Filmmaker at the Margins* (Berkeley: University of California Press, 2014). However welcome the deserved and much belated scholarly attention given to Ulmer, one has to lament the disparity in quality. The two anthologies by Herzogenrath are sloppily edited (as if to emulate Ulmer's B films) and include essays that vary significantly in substance and scope; many of them are dominated by fan-driven, hagiographic efforts that regurgitate well-known tropes of Ulmer the artiste and auteur.

9. "Edgar G. Ulmer," in Peter Bogdanovich, *Who the Devil Made It: Conversations with Legendary Film Directors* (New York: Ballantine, 1997), 566.
10. Quoted in Stefan Grissemann, *Mann im Schatten: Der Filmemacher Edgar G. Ulmer* (Vienna: Paul Zsolnay, 2003), 346.
11. Noah Isenberg, "Perennial Detour: The Cinema of Edgar G. Ulmer and the Experience of Exile," *Cinema Journal* 43, no. 2 (2004): 3–24, here 4. Pointing to the frequent use of exiles and émigrés in minor acting roles, as cameramen (notably Eugen Schüfftan and Franz Planer), and as composers, Stefan Grissemann has claimed that nearly all of Ulmer's films are "Emigrantenkino" (*Mann im Schatten*, 234).
12. Like the vast majority of émigrés and exiles, Ulmer was a strong supporter of Roosevelt and at the behest of Eleanor Roosevelt even directed a series of educational shorts commissioned by the National Tuberculosis Association. One also notices the prominent portrait of FDR in the final shot of Ulmer's *Girls in Chains* (1943).
13. For budget figures see the files in Box 277/8314 at the Cinema-Television Archives at the University of Southern California. See also Michael Brunas, John Brunas, and Tom Weaver, *Universal Horrors: The Studio's Classic Films, 1931–1949* (Jefferson, NC: McFarland, 1990); Gregory William Mank, *Karloff and Lugosi: The Story of a Haunting Collaboration* (Jefferson, NC: McFarland, 1990); and Paul Mandell, "Edgar Ulmer and *The Black Cat*," *American Cinematographer*, Oct. 1984, 34–47.
14. Ulmer, quoted in Bogdanovich, *Who the Devil Made It*, 592.
15. Andrew Sarris, *The American Cinema: Directors and Directions, 1929–1968* (New York: Dutton, 1968), 143.
16. John Belton, "Edgar G. Ulmer: A Reassessment," in Belton, *Cinema Stylists* (Metuchen, NJ: Scarecrow, 1983), 146–56, here 147.
17. See, e.g., Dana Polan, "*Detour's* History/History's *Detour*," in Herzogenrath, *Edgar G. Ulmer*, 137–49, esp. 138–42.
18. Bernd Herzogenrath, "Ulmer and Cult/ure," in Herzogenrath, *Edgar G. Ulmer*, 28.
19. Quoted in Bogdanovich, *Who the Devil Made It*, 575 and 576, respectively.
20. To be sure, associating oneself with the movements that made Germany famous in the early 1920s was a common survival strategy for émigrés; indeed, this often garnered one a contract at Hollywood's studios. But Ulmer pushed the limits of credulity. Elsewhere in the same interview he makes the completely unsubstantiated claim to have designed the sets for *Caligari*, and the long list of films in which he says he was involved include virtually everything done by Murnau, as well as Lang's *The Nibelungen* and *Metropolis*. Statements like these prompted Lotte Eisner to call Ulmer "the greatest liar in the history of cinema" (quoted in Deborah Lazaroff Alpi, *Robert Siodmak* [Jefferson, NC: McFarland, 1998], 20).

21. On Poelzig's contribution to film architecture see Claudia Dillmann, "Die Wirkung der Architektur ist eine magische: Hans Poelzig und der Film," in *Hans Poelzig: Bauten für den Film (Kinematograph* 12) (Frankfurt: Deutsches Filmmuseum, 1997), 20–75.
22. American observers concurred. See, for example, the widely discussed essay "Must America Go Fascist?" by J. B. Matthews and R. E. Shallcross in *Harper's Magazine*, June 1934, 1–15; and a symposium titled "Will Fascism Come to America?" in *Modern Monthly*, Sept. 1934. One year later, Sinclair Lewis's best-selling novel *It Can't Happen Here* was published, which imagines how America might become fascist.
23. Grissemann, *Mann im Schatten*, 139.
24. Edgar G. Ulmer, "Beyond the Boundary," unpublished and unpaginated manuscript. The quote is found at the beginning of chapter 3. Ulmer's misspellings have been amended. See the Edgar G. Ulmer Collection, Margaret Herrick Library, Academy of Motion Picture Arts and Sciences, Los Angeles (hereafter AMPAS).
25. Anton Kaes, *Shell Shock Cinema: Weimar Culture and the Wounds of War* (Princeton, NJ: Princeton University Press, 2009), 54.
26. See Lotte Eisner, *The Haunted Screen: Expressionism in the German Cinema and the Influence of Max Reinhardt*, trans. Roger Greaves (1952; Berkeley: University of California Press, 1973); and Siegfried Kracauer, *From Caligari to Hitler: A Psychological History of the German Film*, ed. Leonardo Quaresima (1947; Princeton, NJ: Princeton University Press, 2004).
27. Bernard Eisenschitz and Jean-Claude Romer, "Entretien avec Edgar G. Ulmer," *Midi-minuit fantastique* 13 (1965): 1–14, here 4.
28. On Lugosi's career see Arthur Lenning, *The Count: The Life and Films of Bela "Dracula" Lugosi* (New York: G. P. Putnam's Sons, 1974).
29. William K. Everson writes that "even some of Universal's 'B' Westerns of these years [the second half of the 1920s] had a Germanic look to them" (*Classics of the Horror Film* [Secaucus, NJ: Citadel Press, 1974], 26.) Other prominent exiles and émigrés who worked on horror films include Peter Lorre, Robert and Curt Siodmak, Karl Freund, and Joe May; even William Dieterle tried his hand at the genre and scored a major success with *The Hunchback of Notre Dame* (1939).
30. Grissemann, *Mann im Schatten*, 70; Mank, *Karloff and Lugosi*, 59.
31. Edgar Allan Poe, *Selected Writings* (Baltimore: Penguin, 1967), 150.
32. Donald Albrecht, *Designing Dreams: Modern Architecture in the Movies* (New York: Harper and Row, 1986), 101.
33. Everson, *Classics of the Horror Film*, 122. On Universal's overall production in the period see Clive Hirschborn, *The Universal Story* (New York: Crown, 1983).
34. William H. Rosar, "Music for the Monsters: Universal Pictures' Horror Film Scores of the Thirties," *Quarterly Journal of the Library of Congress* 40, no. 4 (1983): 391–421. The following remarks are indebted to Rosar's insightful analysis.
35. Grissemann, *Mann im Schatten*, 285.
36. Rosar, "Music for the Monsters," 404.

37. Tom Weaver, "An Interview with Shirley Ulmer," in Bernd Herzogenrath, ed., *The Films of Edgar G. Ulmer*, 265–87, here 269.
38. Gary D. Rhodes, "'Tremonstrous' Hopes and 'Oke' Results: The 1934 Reception of *The Black Cat*," in Rhodes, *Edgar G. Ulmer*, 301–22, here 319.
39. Censorship files, AMPAS. The *New York Herald Tribune*, in turn, reported that the film was banned in Austria because it included "a scene in which some of the actors appeared in the uniforms of Austrian army officers" (August 22, 1935).
40. Eisenschitz and Romer, "Entretien avec Edgar G. Ulmer," 4.
41. Originally, E. A. Dupont was slated to direct *The Black Cat*, based on a different story outline, which, however, was never turned into a full script. It remains doubtful whether Ruric and Ulmer actually read Poe's story; on the script housed in the Margaret Herrick Library, the American author's name is misspelled as "Edgar Allen Poe."
42. The spelling of locations mentioned in the film follows the script housed at AMPAS. It should be noted that the script contains some inconsistencies—we find, for example, alternate spellings of "Vishegrad" (scene A3) and "Vizhegrad" (scene A33)—which can be attributed to the great haste under which Ulmer and Ruric worked.
43. Interestingly, the script does not refer to this shot.
44. Quoted in Bogdanovich, *Who the Devil Made It*, 576.
45. David F. Burg and L. Edward Purcell, *Almanac of World War I* (Lexington: University Press of Kentucky, 1998), 112.
46. It is also possible that Ulmer further drew on Heinz Paul's 1931 film *Douaumont*, a curious restaging of the fight surrounding the fortress, which Ulmer may have seen in Berlin.
47. After filming was completed, the studio brass considered the film too vile for the public and ordered alterations to the script and reshooting. Originally, the script had Werdegast appear to be almost as menacing as Poelzig, but after objections from the studio executives several scenes were cut and new ones added to make Lugosi's role less ambiguous and far more sympathetic. Other changes included the cutting of Poelzig's rape of Joan Alison and the depicting of Karen as a benign and innocent beauty rather than as the cat-woman she was originally meant to be. Also toned down were the script's graphic depictions of Poelzig's skinning. For a detailed account of the production history, including alterations to the script, see Mank, *Karloff and Lugosi*, 45–83; and Mandell, "Edgar Ulmer and *The Black Cat*."
48. Herzogenrath, "Ulmer and Cult/ure," 30.
49. The most extensive discussion of these changes is found in Mank, *Karloff and Lugosi*, 45–83. Mank does not, however, mention many of the changes listed below.
50. For a discussion of the production and reception of this film see Rainer Rother, "Germany's *Douaumont* (1931): Verdun and the Depiction of World War I," *Historical Journal of Film, Radio and Television* 19, no. 2 (1999): 217–38; for an incisive discussion of German wartime films see Philip Stiansy, *Das Kino und der Krieg: Deutschland, 1914–1929* (Munich: Text + Kritik, 2009).

51. In his interview with Bogdanovich Ulmer not only cites Milestone's film with approval but quotes it as an example of the "intellectual picture making" (575) that paved the way for *The Black Cat*, thereby also ascribing to his own film a component of "high art" not usually associated with Universal's horror cycle.

2. TALES OF URGENCY AND AUTHENTICITY

1. "Wer Biograph wird, verpflichtet sich zur Lüge, zur Verheimlichung, Heuchelei, Schönfärberei und selbst zur Verhehlung seines Unverständnisses, denn die biographische Wahrheit ist nicht zu haben, und wenn man sie hätte, wäre sie nicht zu brauchen." See *Sigmund Freud und Arnold Zweig: Briefwechsel*, ed. W. Freud (Zurich: Ex Libris, 1980), 137 (unless otherwise indicated, all translations are my own). Freud wrote this letter to Zweig after learning that Zweig was intending to make him the subject of a biography.
2. Siegfried Kracauer, "The Biography as an Art Form of the New Bourgeoisie," in *The Mass Ornament*, trans. Thomas Y. Levin (Cambridge, MA: Harvard University Press, 1995), 101–5, here 105.
3. Exemplary of this trend was Emil Ludwig, whose numerous biographical subjects during the Weimar period included Napoleon, Bismarck, Stalin, Mussolini, and Lincoln, to which he later also added Roosevelt and Hindenburg. His celebratory pamphlet on David Frankfurter, the assassin of the National Socialist Wilhelm Gustloff, drew the ire of Joseph Goebbels, who commented in his diaries that he considered Ludwig's writings particularly dangerous.
4. Siegfried Kracauer, *Jacques Offenbach und das Paris seiner Zeit*, ed. Ingrid Belke (Frankfurt am Main: Suhrkamp, 2005), 103–4. The book was simultaneously published in German, English, and French editions in 1937.
5. Kracauer, "Biography as an Art Form," 104.
6. Kracauer, *Offenbach*, 12.
7. The long list of biographies written by exiled writers includes Stefan Zweig's *Erasmus von Rotterdam* (1934); Heinrich Mann's two novels on the French king Henry IV (1935 and 1938); Bruno Frank's *Cervantes* (1934); E. A. Rheinhardt's *Der große Herbst Heinrichs IV* (1935); Paul Frischauer's biographies on Prinz Eugen (1933), Garibaldi (1934), and Beaumarchais (1935); Ludwig Marcuse's *Ignatius von Loyola* (1935); Hermann Kesten's *Ferdinand und Isabella* (1936); Lion Feuchtwanger's Josephus trilogy (1932–41); Emil Ludwig's *Roosevelt* (1938); and, of course, Bertolt Brecht's play *Galileo*, which premiered in Los Angeles in 1947 and starred Charles Laughton.
8. Already in 1938, Kracauer thought of selling his "treatment" to a Hollywood studio, but Dieterle does not receive mention until March 1945, in a letter to the cinematographer Eugen Schüfftan (who had come to the United States in April 1941, traveling on the same boat for refugees as Kracauer). See *Nachrichten aus Hollywood, New York und anderswo: Der Briefwechsel Eugen und Marlise Schüfftans mit Siegfried und Lili Kracauer*, ed. Helmut G. Asper (Trier: Wissenschaftlicher Verlag, 2003), 60.

9. Henry Blanke was a friend of Dieterle's from their theater days in Berlin and first came to the United States in 1922 as part of Ernst Lubitsch's entourage.
10. Leo Löwenthal, "Biographies in Popular Magazines," in *Radio Research, 1942–1943*, ed. Paul F. Lazarsfeld and Frank N. Stanton (New York: Duell, Sloan and Pearce, 1944), 516.
11. See Günter Agde, "Schulden für Winnetou: Wilhelm Dieterle und die Ufa," in *Das Ufa-Buch*, ed. Hans-Michael Bock and Michael Töteberg (Frankfurt am Main: Zweitausendeins, 1992), 306–9. As Salka Viertel writes in her Hollywood memoir, Dieterle soon belonged to the inner circle of literati who congregated around Thomas Mann, Lion Feuchtwanger, and Franz and Alma Werfel. See Salka Viertel, *The Kindness of Strangers* (New York: Holt, Rinehart and Winston, 1969), 259. Dieterle proved also instrumental in bringing the likes of Lion Feuchtwanger and Bertolt Brecht to a safe haven in the United States. Between 1931 and 1957 Dieterle would direct more than fifty films in Hollywood, an impressive number by any standard.
12. Despite a long-lasting and varied career, Dieterle's status as stage and film actor, director, and producer has garnered little critical attention. Notable exceptions are Hervé Dumont, *William Dieterle: Un humaniste au pays du cinéma* (Paris: Cinémathèque française, 2002); Horst O. Hermanni, *William Dieterle: Vom Arbeitersohn zum Hollywood-Regisseur* (London: World of Books, 1992); and Marta Mierendorff, *William Dieterle: Der Plutarch von Hollywood* (Berlin: Henschel, 1993).
13. On Warner Bros.' anti-Nazi resolve see Michael E. Birdwell, *Celluloid Soldiers: Warner Bros.'s Campaign Against Nazism* (New York: New York University Press, 1991); and Thomas Doherty, *Projections of War: Hollywood, American Culture, and World War II* (New York: Columbia University Press, 1993). On the history of the studio in the 1930s see Nick Roddick, *A New Deal in Entertainment: Warner Brothers in the 1930s* (London: BFI, 1983); William R. Meyer, *Warner Brothers Directors: The Hard-Boiled, the Comic, and the Weepers* (New York: Arlington House, 1978); Rudy Behlmer, ed., *Inside Warner Bros. (1935–1951)* (New York: Viking, 1985); and Colin Shindler, *Hollywood in Crisis: Cinema and American Society, 1929–1939* (London: Routledge, 1996).
14. According to Hal Wallis, Zola's life offered strong parallels to the experience of the Depression and was one of the main reasons for the film's success. See Hal Wallis and Charles Higham, *Starmaker: The Autobiography of Hal Wallis* (New York: Macmillan, 1980), 58.
15. Brecht would later compare Dieterle's screen biographies to his own interest in the figure of Galileo. See Bertolt Brecht, "Wilhelm Dieterles Galerie großer bürgerlicher Figuren," in *Von Deutschland nach Hollywood: Retrospektive 23. Internationale Filmfestspiele Berlin*, ed. Walter Kaul (Berlin: Felgentreff und Goebel, 1973), 5–7, here 5.
16. Mann admonished his audiences that "democracy should answer . . . fascist strategy with a rediscovery of itself." See Thomas Mann, *The Coming Victory of Democracy* (New York: Knopf, 1938), 13. A close friend of Mann, Dieterle presided over Mann's inaugural lecture at the Shrine Auditorium on April 1, 1938.

17. In the *New York Times* Frank S. Nugent wrote: "Rich, dignified, honest, [the film] is at once the finest historical drama ever made and the greatest screen biography" (August 12, 1937), while the *Hollywood Reporter* applauded the film as "one of the outstanding productions of the year.... It definitely advances the art of the screen" (June 29, 1937).
18. The film also won the New York Critics Award that year, and a Jewish student organization placed Muni among the 120 most important living Jews, a list that also included Freud, Einstein, Max Reinhardt, Emil Ludwig, and Stefan Zweig. The film was banned in France, however, and boycotted in Italy, Spain, and Canada, significantly reducing Warner's overseas markets.
19. Like Blanke, Dieterle knew Herald from his Berlin days, when Herald was dramaturge at the Deutsches Theater in Berlin, where Dieterle performed under Max Reinhardt's direction. Other exiles and émigrés involved in the film include actor Vladimir Sokoloff (as Cézanne), composer Max Steiner, costume designer Ali Hubert, and in uncredited roles Iphigenie Castiglioni, Frank Reicher, Walter O. Stahl, and Wilhelm von Brincken.
20. Graham Greene took offense at the film's liberties with Zola's life, commenting that the script had Zola die on the eve of Dreyfus's rehabilitation, when in reality Zola died two years after Dreyfus's presidential pardon (but four years before his reinstatement in the army): "It's more than un-studio, it's un-American to live another two years." See Graham Greene's review of the film in *Night and Day*, Oct. 28, 1937. Frank Nugent, in an otherwise exuberant review, admonishes the film for the fact "that it skips recklessly over the political, racial background of the plot." See Frank Nugent, *New York Times*, August 12, 1937.
21. Among the few exceptions are Thomas Elsaesser, "Film History as Social History: The Dieterle/Warner Brothers Bio-pic," *Wide Angle* 8, no. 2 (1986): 15–32; Saverio Giovacchini, *Hollywood Modernism: Film and Politics in the Age of the New Deal* (Philadelphia: Temple University Press, 2001); and, more recently, Chris Robé, *Left of Hollywood: Cinema, Modernism, and the Emergence of Radical U.S. Film Culture* (Austin: University of Texas Press, 2010).
22. George F. Custen, *Bio/Pics: How Hollywood Constructed Public History* (New Brunswick, NJ: Rutgers University Press, 1992), 3.
23. Ibid., 35.
24. The files at the Warner Bros. Archives at the University of Southern California on *Zola* contain a ten-page single-spaced bibliography of sources, which includes books in several languages, plays, newspaper articles, and encyclopedia entries, as well as detailed summaries how the script produced by the screenwriters builds on and expands existing sources.
25. Jean-Louis Comolli, "Historical Fiction: A Body Too Much," *Screen* 19, no. 2 (1978): 41–53.
26. As Muni explained, "A biographer invents incidents, if necessary, to bring out hidden traits which explain a character more fully. The actor cannot invent incidents. But by concentration, voice and gesture, he re-creates a man." See Paul Muni, "The Actor Plays His Part," in *We Make the Movies*, ed. Nancy Naumburg (New York: Norton, 1937), 131–42, here 133.

27. In particular, Dieterle objected to Muni rehearsing his lines with the help of a tape recorder, because it fostered an unnatural and emphatic delivery. Yet Dieterle also paid Muni the highest compliment when he compared his acting style to that of Albert Bassermann, one of the greats at Reinhardt's Deutsches Theater, who would later star in both the Dr. Ehrlich and the Reuter film.
28. Undated memo, Lubitsch file, Margaret Herrick Library, Academy of Motion Picture Arts and Sciences, Los Angeles (hereafter AMPAS).
29. Wallis to makeup artist Perc Westmore, memorandum, March 2, 1937, Warner Bros. Archives, USC.
30. Muni would explain this achievement in quite different terms, stating that "it was no effort for me to think as he [Zola] did, to react to things as he did [because] we must have quite a bit in common" (Muni file, AMPAS).
31. Leo Braudy, "Zola on Film: The Ambiguities of Naturalism," *Yale French Studies* 42 (1969): 68–88. See also *Zola and Film: Essays in the Art of Adaptation*, ed. Anna Gural-Migdal and Robert Singer (Jefferson, NC: McFarland, 2005).
32. In 1919 Max Reinhardt hired Dieterle to join him at the Deutsches Theater in Berlin, and during the five years under Reinhardt's direction, Dieterle celebrated his major successes on the German stage.
33. How far Warner Bros. was in the 1930s from a modernist aesthetics can be seen quite clearly if one compares *The Maltese Falcon* adaptation *Satan Met a Lady* (1936), which Dieterle was forced to direct, with John Huston's 1941 version.
34. Dieterle's only bio-picture not made at Warner Bros., the 1942 *Tennessee Johnson*, revolves almost entirely around the aftermath of Lincoln's assassination; its numerous references to American racial politics caused constant friction between the director and MGM.
35. Wolfgang Reinhardt, "Phantom Crown," Feb. 15, 1938, Warner Bros. Archives, USC. The note was written in German, a language that apart from Blanke and Dieterle few executives could read.
36. Carol Clover, "Judging Audiences: The Case of the Trial Movie," in *Reinventing Film Studies*, ed. Christine Gledhill and Linda Williams (London: Arnold, 2000), 244–64, here 246.
37. For a discussion of the significance of the trial film of this period in U.S. film history see Norman Rosenberg, "Hollywood on Trials: Courts and Films, 1930–1960," *Law and History Review* 12, no. 2 (1994): 341–67.
38. Elsaesser, "Film History as Social History," 26.
39. The film's interventionist bent becomes all the more conspicuous if we bear in mind that *Zola* burst onto the scene only two months prior to Roosevelt's Neutrality Act Quarantine Speech of October 1937. This speech was largely understood as an anti-isolationism speech and was met with a firestorm of criticism in the American press, indicating the strong isolationist sentiments held by the majority of the American public, and it was followed up by a series of neutrality acts passed by Congress.
40. Describing his difficulties in convincing Warner Bros. to let him make the film, Dieterle stresses the virtues of obstinacy, stubbornness, and belief in one's work that are also found in the heroes of his films: "I held the story and production outline of

Zola on my desk for two years before it was finally approved; my faith in the subject eventually wore down the resistance of the studio." See William Dieterle, "Europeans in Hollywood," *Sight and Sound* 22, no. 1 (1952): 39–40, here 40. Reprinted in *Hollywood Directors, 1946–1971*, ed. Richard Koszarski (New York: Oxford University Press, 1977), 187–91.

41. Brecht, "Wilhelm Dieterles Galerie," 5.
42. Giovacchini, *Hollywood Modernism*, 88.
43. Elsaesser, "Film History as Social History," 25.
44. Lester Friedman, *Hollywood's Image of the Jew* (New York: Ungar, 1982), 78.
45. Shindler, *Hollywood in Crisis*, 204.
46. Patricia Erens, *The Jew in American Cinema* (Bloomington: Indiana University Press, 1984), 162–64. Along the same lines, Peter Hoffmann and Jim Purdy state that the film "makes but one fleeting reference to the anti-Semitism behind the Dreyfus affair." See *The Hollywood Social Problem Film: Madness, Despair, and Politics from the Depression to the Fifties* (Bloomington: Indiana University Press, 1981), 236.
47. Willi Breuning, ed., *Der Kampf um die Story: Die Hollywood- und Lebenserinnerungen des Schauspielers und Regisseurs William Dieterle* (Ludwigshafen: Stadtarchiv Ludwigshafen, 2000), 149.
48. Ibid., 156.
49. Dieterle's *Dr. Ehrlich's Magic Bullet* from 1940 is more overt in its critique of anti-Semitism, repeatedly showing the racist attitudes of the German scientific community under Bismarck. According to producers, Paul Ehrlich was chosen as the subject for a biopic precisely because he was "a good German" and a Jew (*ehrlich*, of course, meaning "honest" in German). As Robinson's character ages in the course of the film, he is made to look more and more like Sigmund Freud. *A Dispatch from Reuter's*, made later that year, never mentions the fact that Paul Julius Reuter was also Jewish, though much is made of his being a foreigner in England.
50. Klaus Mann, "What's Wrong with Anti-Nazi Films," originally published in *Decision*, August 1941; repr. in *New German Critique* 89 (2003): 173–82, here 178.
51. The U.S. press explicitly referred to the Dreyfus trial as an anticipation of the trial following the burning of the Reichstag in 1933, which the Nazis used as an opportunity to crack down on their political opponents.
52. Felicia Herman, "Hollywood, Nazism, and the Jews, 1933–1941," *American Jewish History* 89, no. 1 (2001): 61–89, here 81.
53. In Hollywood Muni's roles included an Italian American gangster in *Scarface* (1932), a Mexican in *Juarez*, the Frenchmen Pasteur and Zola, a Chinese in *The Good Earth* (1937), and Polish composer Frédéric Chopin in *A Song to Remember* (1945). As Neal Gabler commented, "His career became a paradigm for the tortured identity of the actor Jew in Hollywood—always dressed in someone else's ethnicity." See Neal Gabler, *An Empire of Their Own: How the Jews Invented Hollywood* (New York: Crown, 1988), 302.
54. See Andreas Ungerböck, "Zwischen zwei Welten: Josph Schildkraut—Porträt des Künstlers als schöner Mann," in vol. 1 of *Aufbruch ins Ungewisse*, ed. Chris-

tian Cargnelli and Michael Omasta (Vienna: Wespennest, 1993), as well as the entry "Joseph Schildkraut" in ibid., 2:124.
55. Matthew Josephson, *Zola and His Time* (New York: Macaulay, 1928), 399. Josephson forced Warner Bros. into giving him credit on the film for allegedly having used some lines from the book.
56. "Kennen Sie, meine Herren, nicht einen rechtskräftigen Justizmord, der seit bald zweitausend Jahren als die Schande der Menschheit gilt?" Hans Rehfisch and Wilhelm Herzog, *Die Affäre Dreyfus* (Munich: Desch, 1951), 78.
57. That same year Paramount approached Sergei Eisenstein about making a film based on the Zola trial, but the Russian director chose to move on to Mexico.
58. Like Rehfisch, Herzog, and Oswald, Weil had to flee Germany after Hitler came to power, escaping to France, where he was later interned in Le Vernet. In his book *Baracke 37-Stillgestanden!* (first published in 1941 by Estrellas in Buenos Aires), he chronicled his camp experience in France.
59. "Ihr jungen Menschen, kommt doch endlich zur Besinnung!"
60. Hans Rehfisch and Richard Oswald were well aware of Dieterle's appropriations. Both were hard up for money in their respective exiles in London and Los Angeles. Rehfisch sued Warner Bros. and after several years won a modest settlement, while Oswald declined to do so, apparently because he hoped his display of goodwill toward the studio would gain him employment there (which it did not).
61. Zola's significance for a leftist cause was first articulated by Heinrich Mann's influential 1915 essay "Zola," which was also consulted by Herald and Herzceg.
62. Collaborating with Max Reinhardt on the film *A Midsummer Night's Dream*, Dieterle had already revisited a very different Weimar stage tradition in 1935.
63. Joseph Breen to Jack Warner, Feb. 2, 1937, *The Life of Emile Zola* file, AMPAS.
64. Jack Warner, *My First Hundred Years in Hollywood* (New York: Random House, 1964), 264. Warner's autobiography is a less than reliable source. Given Warner's sympathy for Mussolini, it is well possible that the Italian dictator approached him, not Dieterle.
65. Eric Rentschler, *The Ministry of Illusion: Nazi Cinema and Its Afterlife* (Cambridge, MA: Harvard University Press, 1996), 182.
66. The film passed the censorship board in August of 1939; by the time it premiered, on September 26, the war against Poland had been raging for more than three weeks. In his recent book on Emil Jannings, Frank Noack also underscores the aesthetic similarities between Steinhoff's and Dieterle's films but vindicates the political dimensions of the German film: "As far as the politics of women and the family are concerned, Dieterle's film is closer to National Socialist ideology than Steinhoff's. Steinhoff takes the concerns of women seriously; his female characters always hover close to the precipice whereas Dieterle's actresses—not because of the director's fault, but because of Hollywood's mandates—make beautiful, radiant faces without any plot motivation" (Frank Noack, *Emil Jannings: Der erste deutsche Weltstar* [Munich: Heyne, 2012], 388). This vindication is in line with Noack's dubious project of reassessing Jannings's career during the Third Reich in primarily artistic rather than political terms.

67. When traveling to the Soviet Union in 1937 to study film production methods, he was warned by friends to forgo his plans to visit Germany, even though he had by then become an American citizen.
68. See Dieterle, "Europeans in Hollywood."
69. On Dieterle's role within the larger exile community see Marta Mierendorff, "William Dieterle: Vergessene Schlüsselfigur der Emigration. Seine Beziehungen zu exilierten Autoren," in *Das Exilerlebnis*, ed. Donald G. Daviau and Ludwig M. Fischer (Columbia, SC: Camden House, 1982), 81–100.
70. Mierendorff, *William Dieterle*, 195–98. In 1973 the Berlin Film Festival showcased several Dieterle films in a retrospective devoted to the director, thereby at last acknowledging his significance for (German) film history.
71. Benjamin wrote: "He has composed a text which only a few years ago would not have found a harsher critic than himself." See *Adorno-Benjamin: Briefwechsel, 1928–1940*, ed. Henri Lonitz (Frankfurt am Main: Suhrkamp, 1994), 241. Ernst Bloch, another of Kracauer's close friends, chided Kracauer for having written on a composer without actually addressing his compositions: "It's a unique book in its genre—as if someone were to write about Michelangelo without mentioning that he was a painter and sculptor. And yet that is what Kracauer did." See Ernst Bloch, "Der eigentümliche Glücksfall: Über *Jacques Offenbach* von Siegfried Kracauer," *Text und Kritik* 68 (1980): 73–75, here 75. The piece is based on a 1976 conversation between Karsten Witte and Ernst and Karola Bloch.
72. Simon Richter has shown that Dieterle consulted with Max Horkheimer on the making of his film *The Devil and Daniel Webster* (1941). See Simon Richter, "Practicing Critical Theory in Hollywood: William Dieterle, Max Horkheimer and Goethe's *Faust* in *The Devil and Daniel Webster*" (unpublished essay).

3. PERFORMING RESISTANCE, RESISTING PERFORMANCE

1. Rudolf Arnheim, "Chaplin as Teacher" [1932], in *Film Essays and Criticism*, trans. Brenda Benthien (Madison: University of Wisconsin Press, 1997), 222–23, here 222.
2. On the relationship between New York intellectuals, the émigré community, and established Hollywood film professionals see Saverio Giovacchini, *Hollywood Modernism: Film and Politics in the Age of the New Deal* (Philadelphia: Temple University Press, 2001).
3. Katz would later become the model for the resistance fighter in Lillian Hellman's play *The Watch on the Rhine*. On Katz see Marcus G. Patka, "'Columbus Discovered America, and I Discovered Hollywood': Otto Katz und die Hollywood Anti-Nazi League," *FilmExil* 17 (2003): 44–65.
4. For a concise summary of the history of the Anti-Nazi League see Larry Ceplair and Steven Englund, *The Hollywood Inquisition: Politics in the Film Community, 1930–1960* (Urbana: University of Illinois Press, 2003), 104–12. See also Johanna W. Roden, "Die Hollywood Anti-Nazi League, 1936–1940: Eine 'Volksfront' in Amerika," in *Deutsche Exilliteratur seit 1933, Band 3: USA*, ed. John M. Spalek, Konrad Feilchenfeldt, and Sandra H. Hawrylchak (Zurich: Saur, 2003), 514–31; and

Klaus Täubert, "Im Dienst der Volksfront: Hollywood Now," in *Wenn wir von gestern reden, sprechen wir über heute und morgen*, ed. Helmut G. Asper (Berlin: Sigma, 1991): 159–68.

5. The most detailed account of the cultural productions associated with the Popular Front remains Michael Denning's *The Cultural Front: The Laboring of American Culture in the Twentieth Century* (New York: Verso, 1996). Yet apart from the work of Orson Welles, the contributions of the American film industry are not considered by Denning.
6. E. Bond Johnson, "Der European Film Fund und die Exilschriftsteller in Hollywood," trans. Brigitta Strelka, in *Deutsche Exilliteratur seit 1933, Band 1: Kalifornien, Teil 1*, ed. John M. Spalek and Joseph Strelka (Berne: Francke, 1976), 135–46.
7. "The Production Code," in *Movies and Mass Culture*, ed. John Belton (New Brunswick, NJ: Rutgers University Press, 1996), 135–49, here 141.
8. The 2008 TCM documentary *Warner at War* states that Hitler personally protested against the film and that the Bund unsuccessfully tried to sue Warner Bros.
9. Thomas Doherty, *Projections of War: Hollywood, American Culture, and World War II* (New York: Columbia University Press, 1993), 126.
10. Scott Eyman, *Ernst Lubitsch: Laughter in Paradise* (New York: Simon and Schuster, 1993), 15.
11. Ali Hubert, Lubitsch's costume designer in Berlin and Hollywood, relates that Lubitsch rejected suggestions that he pretend to be Polish or Russian when he first came to Hollywood. See Hubert, *Hollywood: Legende und Wirklichkeit* (Leipzig: Seemann, 1930), 46. When *Madame Dubarry* premiered in the United States (as *Passion*), it was billed a "European film," and the name of the director was not mentioned in the reviews. For a detailed account of its U.S. release see David B. Pratt, "'O Lubitsch, Where Wert Thou?' *Passion*, the German Invasion and the Emergence of the Name 'Lubitsch,'" *Wide Angle* 13, no. 1 (1991): 34–70.
12. In this respect Lubitsch differs significantly from many other exile directors proper, especially Fritz Lang. Throughout his U.S. career Lang cultivated a certain Teutonic image that was not only part of his public persona but also his directorial style.
13. Graham Petrie, *Hollywood Destinies: European Directors in America, 1922–1931* (London: Routledge and Kegan Paul, 1985), 65.
14. See Thomas Elsaesser, "Ethnicity, Authenticity, and Exile: A Counterfeit Trade? German Filmmakers in Hollywood," in *Home, Exile, Homeland: Film, Media, and the Politics of Place*, ed. Hamid Naficy (New York: Routledge, 1999), 97–123.
15. François Truffaut, *The Films in My Life*, trans. Leonard Mayhew (New York: Simon and Schuster, 1978), 52.
16. Cf. Hassan Melehy, "Lubitsch's *To Be or Not to Be* and the Question of Simulation in Cinema," *Film Criticism* 26, no. 2 (2001/2): 19–40.
17. Eric Rentschler, *The Ministry of Illusion: Nazi Cinema and Its Afterlife* (Cambridge, MA: Harvard University Press, 1996), 1.
18. The Museum of Modern Art acquired a print of *Triumph of the Will* in the 1930s, where it became the object of much study, including by Siegfried Kracauer.

19. See Claudia Schmölders, *Hitler's Face: The Biography of an Image*, trans. Adrian Daub (Philadelphia: University of Pennsylvania Press, 2006).
20. Chaplin makes this claim in *My Autobiography* (New York: Simon and Schuster, 1964), 319.
21. See Robert Joseph, "The Research Experts Take a Back Seat," *New York Times*, March 1, 1942.
22. See Lester D. Friedman, *Hollywood's Image of the Jew* (New York: Ungar, 1982); Lester Friedman, ed., *Unspeakable Images: Ethnicity and the American Cinema* (Urbana: University of Illinois Press, 1991); Patricia Erens, *The Jew in American Cinema* (Bloomington: Indiana University Press, 1984); and Steven Carr, *Hollywood and Anti-Semitism: A Cultural History up to World War II* (Cambridge: Cambridge University Press, 2001).
23. "The Production Code," in *Movies and Mass Culture*, ed. John Belton (New Brunswick, NJ: Rutgers University Press, 1996), 141.
24. See Neal Gabler, *An Empire of Their Own: How the Jews Invented Hollywood* (New York: Crown, 1988). Warner Bros. is to a degree an exception to this ethnic camouflage, because it discontinued business relationships with Nazi Germany by 1934, and, among Hollywood studios, it led the fight against Hitler's Germany. See Michael E. Birdwell, *Celluloid Soldiers: Warner Bros.'s Campaign Against Nazism* (New York: New York University Press, 1999).
25. Lutz Koepnick, *The Dark Mirror: German Cinema Between Hitler and Hollywood* (Berkeley: University of California Press, 2002), 138.
26. The shooting script of the film includes additional dialogue (which was either cut or never shot) that underscores Greenberg's Jewishness even more. Thus Greenberg says in response to Dobosh's criticism that Bronski's Hitler is real: "I can smell [Hitler in him]. If I were to bring him home right now looking like that [in Hitler costume] my people would think I was tactless." The script for *To Be or Not to Be* is available at the Academy of Motion Picture Arts and Sciences archives (AMPAS) in Los Angeles.
27. Joel Rosenberg "Shylock's Revenge: The Doubly Vanished Jew in Ernst Lubitsch's *To Be or Not to Be*," *Prooftexts* 16 (1996): 209–44, here 219. The following remarks are indebted to Rosenberg's insightful essay.
28. In that respect Tura/Benny becomes exemplary for the many Jewish film stars passing as gentiles.
29. Bressart starred in two other features by Lubitsch—as Pirovitch in *The Shop Around the Corner* and as Buljanoff in *Ninotchka*, where he speaks the sentence that essentializes his status as a Hollywood exile: "They can't censor our memories." As Hans Helmut Prinzler has commented, Bressart "was an actor whose Jewish dark humor remains yet to be discovered." Hans Helmut Prinzler, "Berlin, 29.1.1892–Hollywood, 30.11.1947: Bausteine zu einer Lubitsch-Biografie," *Lubitsch*, ed. Hans Helmut Prinzler and Enno Patalas (Munich: Bucher, 1984), 8–59, here 55.
30. William Shakespeare, *The Merchant of Venice*, in *The Oxford Shakespeare*, ed. Jay L. Halio (Oxford: Oxford University Press, 1998), 161.
31. It is striking that while many critics have noted Greenberg's identification with Shylock, none have commented on these alterations to the Rialto speech. See Gra-

ham Petrie, "Theater, Film, Life," *Film Comment* 10, no. 3 (May 1974): 38–43; Friedman, *Hollywood's Image of the Jew*; William Paul, *Ernst Lubitsch's American Comedy* (New York: Columbia University Press, 1983); Doherty, *Projections of War*; and Annette Insdorf, *Indelible Shadows: Film and the Holocaust* (Cambridge: Cambridge University Press, 1989). Even Rosenberg, whose article presents the most detailed discussion of the Shylock figure, fails to note this instance of self-censorship.

32. For a more detailed account of the complex production history see Scott Eyman and Tino Balio, *United Artists: The Company Built by the Stars* (Madison: University of Wisconsin Press, 1976), 172–74. Even though Alexander Korda coproduced the film, Karol Kulik claims, "there is no evidence, either within the film or on its credits, to conclude that Korda played any creative role in the production." See Karol Kulik, *Alexander Korda* (New Rochelle: Arlington, 1975), 271. The strong presence of England in the film does suggest, however, that Korda's contribution was substantial. To a certain degree, Jack Benny—who literally puts the ham in Hamlet—can also be seen as a stand-in for Lubitsch. Like Joseph Tura, the actor Lubitsch dreamt of playing Hamlet (a wish that remained unfulfilled), and early reviews from Lubitsch's acting career often suggest that Lubitsch was himself a ham. As a reviewer for the *Berliner Tageblatt* wrote, "Ernst Lubitsch, als Lanzelot, gab etwas zuviel des Guten" (Ernst Lubitsch gave a bit more Lancelot than was called for). Quoted in Michael Hanisch, *Auf den Spuren der Filmgeschichte: Berliner Schauplätze* (Berlin: Henschel, 1991), 299.

33. On Lubitsch's various Sally figures see Jürgen Kasten, "Der Stolz der deutschen Filmkomödie: Die frühen Filme von Ernst Lubitsch, 1914–1918," *Mediengeschichte des deutschen Films*, ed. Corinna Müller and Harro Segeberg (Munich: Fink, 1996), 301–32; and Ofer Ashkenazi, *Weimar Film and Modern Jewish Identity* (New York: Palgrave, 2012). A richly illustrated account of Lubitsch's youth is found in Hanisch, *Auf den Spuren der Filmgeschichte: Berliner Schauplätze*, 256–331. See also Herta-Elisabeth Renk, *Ernst Lubitsch* (Reinbek: Rowohlt, 1992).

34. Many other films can be interpreted as more generally informed by Lubitsch's émigré sensibility. See, e.g., Leo Braudy, "The Double Detachment of Ernst Lubitsch," *MLN* 98, no. 5 (1983): 1071–84.

35. Joel Rosenberg speaks of "implicit Jews," that is, characters (such as the hunchback in *Sumurun* [1920], played by Lubitsch himself, the tutor Dr. Jüttner in *The Student Prince in Old Heidelberg* [1927], or Pirovitch in *The Shop Around the Corner* [1940]) who are present only "as faces, as guides or messengers between social realms, as marginalized or subversive presences in the plot, even as the Yiddishizing lilt in a turn of phrase uttered by an otherwise impeccably gentile character" (212). Frieda Grafe has similarly asserted that the performances of Maurice Chevalier are distant cousins to Lubitsch's embodiments of Sally Pinkus. See Frieda Grafe, "Was Lubitsch berührt," in *Lubitsch*, ed. Hans Helmut Prinzler and Enno Patalas (Munich: Bucher, 1984), 81–87, here 86.

36. See also Ruth Karpf, "Are Jewish Themes 'Verboten'?" *Aufbau*, August 27, 1943; repr. in *New German Critique* 89 (2003): 183–84. Commenting on Lubitsch's early films, Sabine Hake has argued that the many closed doors and objects of exclusion

"may very well be founded on [Lubitsch's] personal experience [and] the awareness of one's otherness in view of the social and cultural norms." See Sabine Hake, *Passions and Deceptions: The Early Films of Ernst Lubitsch* (Princeton, NJ: Princeton University Press, 1992), 50.
37. Jan-Christopher Horak counts 180 anti-Nazi films between 1939 and 1945 and claims that German exiles were involved in about one-third of these productions. See Horak, *Anti-Nazi-Filme der deutschsprachigen Emigration von Hollywood, 1939–1945* (Münster: Maks, 1985).
38. Doherty, *Projections of War*, 17.
39. J. S. H., review of *To Be or Not to Be*, *National Board of Review Magazine*, March 1942, 5.
40. D. A. Lejeune, review of *To Be or Not to Be*, *Observer*, March 5, 1942.
41. Bosley Crowther, "In *To Be or Not to Be* Ernst Lubitsch Has Opposed Real Tragedy with an Incongruous Comedy Plot," *New York Times*, March 22, 1942.
42. Ibid.
43. Paul, *Ernst Lubitsch's American Comedies*, 230.
44. Stephen Tifft, "Miming the Führer: *To Be or Not to Be* and the Mechanisms of Outrage," *Yale Journal of Criticism* 5, no. 1 (1991): 1–40, here 7.
45. Ernst Lubitsch, "Mr. Lubitsch Takes the Floor for Rebuttal," *New York Times*, March 29, 1942.
46. As William Paul observes, the outbreak of war during production occasioned only one change to the script, the addition of the voice-over lines, "Hate, hate, and more hate was the answer [of the Polish underground] to the Nazi terror" (Paul, *Ernst Lubitsch's American Comedies*, 226). As I have noted, Greenberg's final monologue was also altered.
47. As an actor in Max Reinhardt's ensemble, Lubitsch had roles in many Shakespeare productions, including Peto in *Henry V*, part 1 and David in part 2 (1912), Schnauz in *A Midsummer Night's Dream* (1913), Schreiber in *Much Ado About Nothing* (1913), Simson in *Romeo and Juliet* (1914), Fabian in *As You Like It* (1914), Autolycus in *Wintermärchen* (1916), a grave digger in *Hamlet* (1913), and Lanzelot in *Merchant of Venice* (1915). His own films continue this fascination with Shakespeare; they include an adaptation of *The Taming of the Shrew* transposed into the Bavarian mountains—*Kohlhiessels Töchter* (1920)—and *Romeo und Julia im Schnee* (1920) (Romeo and Juliet in the Snow), a not too tragic tragedy that takes place in the Black Forest. Gary Cooper, in *Bluebeard's Eighth Wife*, reads *The Taming of the Shrew* to learn how to domesticate his free-spirited wife.
48. Quoted in Tifft, "Miming the Führer," 1. As Tifft suggests, "Lubitsch might well have taken an expatriate's and a Jew's interest" in *Mein Kampf* (5).
49. For an extensive discussion of the problem of anti-Semitism in the play see Jay L. Halio's "General Introduction" to *The Merchant of Venice*, in *The Oxford Shakespeare*, 1–84. See also James Shapiro, *Shakespeare and the Jews* (New York: Columbia University Press, 1996); Martin Yaffe, *Shylock and the Jewish Question* (Baltimore: Johns Hopkins University Press, 1997); and Thomas H. Luxon, "A Second Daniel: The Jew and the 'True' Jew in *The Merchant of Venice*," *Early Modern Literary Studies* 4, no. 3 (1999): 31–37.

50. "When Chaplin at last put the finishing touches on his film, he must have realized by how much he had fallen short of his main purpose. And so, after nearly two hours of exposition, the puppet-master found it necessary to put his own head on the stage and say directly what he had failed to convey artistically." See Rudolf Arnheim, "Anti-Fascist Satire," in *Film Essays and Criticism*, 211–15, here 214.
51. Chaplin, quoted in David Robinson, *Chaplin: His Life and Art* (New York: McGraw-Hill, 1985), 485.
52. Theodor W. Adorno, "Commitment," in *Notes on Literature*, vol. 2, trans. Shierry Weber Nicholsen (New York: Columbia University Press, 1992), 76–94, here 84.
53. Thomas Elsaesser, *Das Weimarer Kinoaufgeklärt und doppelbödig*, trans. Michael Wedel (Berlin: Vorwerk 8, 1999), 272. This sentence does not appear in the English version, *Weimar Cinema and After: Germany's Historical Imaginary* (London: Routledge, 2000).

4. HISTORY AS PROPAGANDA AND PARABLE

1. Bertolt Brecht, *Reisen im Exil, 1933–1949* (Frankfurt am Main: Suhrkamp, 1996), 107.
2. Fritz Lang, in a 1969 interview with Charles Higham and Joel Greenberg; repr. in Barry Keith Grant, ed., *Fritz Lang Interviews* (Jackson: University Press of Mississippi, 2003), 105.
3. Thomas Mann, *Deutsche Hörer! Fünfundzwanzig Radiosendungen nach Deutschland*, in: *Politische Schriften und Reden*, vol. 3 (Frankfurt am Main: Fischer, 1968), 229.
4. Bertolt Brecht, *Arbeitsjournal*, 2 vols. (Frankfurt am Main: Suhrkamp, 1993), 1:306. The dating of the entry raises a number of questions: Did Brecht and Lang believe that Heydrich had died right away (when in fact he lived for more than a week)? And was the taking of hostages an invention of Brecht and Lang, or did they already know that this was one of the first measures taken by the Nazis to blackmail the population into betraying the assassins? (Brecht's idiosyncratic spelling in his journals has been reproduced here, which includes the refusal to capitalize many names.)
5. The details surrounding Heydrich's death are recounted in Miroslav Ivanov, *The Assassination of Heydrich*, trans. Patrick O'Brian (London: Hart-Davis, 1973); Callum MacDonald, *The Killing of Obergruppenführer Reinhard Heydrich* (New York: Free Press, 1989); and Robert Gerwarth, *Hitler's Hangman: The Life of Heydrich* (New Haven, CT: Yale University Press, 2011).
6. Stefan Heym, *Hostages* (New York: G. P. Putnam's Sons, 1942), 362. In the German version, translated by Heym himself and first published in the GDR in 1958 under the title *Der Fall Glasenapp*, the prediction of Heydrich's death is toned down, presumably because Heydrich's assassination was no longer a significant context for the novel.
7. See Uwe Naumann, *Faschismus als Groteske: Heinrich Manns Roman "Lidice"* (Worms: Heintz, 1980); and Elke Emrich, "Heinrich Manns Roman *Lidice*: Eine Legende von der menschlichen Verwandlung," in *Heinrich Mann: Das Werk im Exil*, ed. Rudolf Wolff (Bonn: Bouvier, 1985), 13–69.

8. Sirk, quoted in Jon Halliday, *Sirk on Sirk: Conversations with Jon Halliday* (London: Faber and Faber, 1997), 71–72.
9. See Reinhold Grimm and Henry Schmidt, "Bertolt Brecht and *Hangmen Also Die*," *Monatshefte* 61, no. 3 (1969): 232–49; James K. Lyon, "Bertolt Brecht's Hollywood Years: The Dramatist as Film Writer," *Oxford German Studies* 6 (1971): 145–74; Ben Brewster, "Brecht and the Film Industry," *Screen* 16, no. 4 (1975): 16–33; Wolfgang Gersch, *Film bei Brecht: Bertolt Brechts praktische und theoretische Auseinandersetzung mit dem Film* (Berlin: Henschel, 1975); Jürgen Schebera, "*Henker sterben auch*: Vom Versuch eines 'Brechtfilms' in Hollywoods Anti-Nazi-Produktion," in *Henker sterben auch: Drehbuch und Materialien zum Film*, ed. Jürgen Schebera (Berlin: Henschel, 1985), 210–33; Thomas Strack, "Fritz Lang und das Exil: Rekonstruktionen einer Erfahrung mit dem amerikanischen Film," *Exilforschung* 13 (1995): 184–203; James K. Lyon, "'Das hätte nur Brecht schreiben können': Zur Entstehung und Verfilmung von *Hangmen Also Die*," in *Brecht plus minus Film: Filme, Bilder, Bildbetrachtungen*, ed. Thomas Martin and Erdmut Wizisla (Berlin: Theater der Zeit, 2003), 26–37; and, more recently, Ehrhard Bahr, *Weimar on the Pacific: German Exile Culture in Los Angeles and the Crisis of Modernism* (Berkeley: University of California Press, 2007).
10. Anton Kaes, "A Stranger in the House: Fritz Lang's *Fury* and the Cinema of Exile," *New German Critique* 89 (2003): 33–58, here 34.
11. Lang, quoted in Marcus G. Patka, "'Columbus Discovered America, and I Discovered Hollywood': Otto Katz und die Hollywood Anti-Nazi League," *Filmexil* 17 (2003): 44–65, here 58.
12. Quoted in Patrick McGilligan, *Fritz Lang: The Nature of the Beast* (New York: St. Martin's, 1997), 271.
13. Brecht, *Arbeitsjournal*, 361.
14. Gersch, *Film bei Brecht*, 355–56.
15. See Bertolt Brecht, *Texte für Filme*, 2 vols., ed. Wolfgang Gersch and Werner Hecht (Frankfurt: Suhrkamp, 1969).
16. See Gerd Gemünden, "Re-fusing Brecht: The Cultural Politics of Rainer Werner Fassbinder's German Hollywood," *New German Critique* 63 (1994): 55–77.
17. See Klaus Kreimeier, *The Ufa Story: A History of Germany's Greatest Film Company, 1918–1945*, trans. Robert and Rita Kimber (New York: Hill and Wang, 1996).
18. Salka Viertel, *The Kindness of Strangers: A Theatrical Life. Vienna, Berlin, Hollywood* (New York: Holt, Rinehart and Winston 1969), 283–84.
19. On the origins of these documents see James K. Lyon, "The Original Story Version of *Hangmen Also Die*: A Recently Discovered Document," *Brecht Yearbook* 28 (2003): 1–8; and "*Hangmen Also Die* Once Again: Dispelling Last Doubts about Brecht's Role as Author," *Brecht Yearbook* 30 (2005): 1–16; see also Irène Bonnaud, "Widerstand in Widersprüchen: Bertolt Brecht und Fritz Lang im Streit um *Hangmen Also Die*," in Martin and Wizisla, *Brecht plus minus Film*, 38–46.
20. Screenwriter Maurice Rapf, who presided over the Guild's arbitration hearings, explained to me that Wexley had a reputation in the industry as a credit stealer, but since only written documents were admissible as evidence, there was nothing that

the Guild could do to discredit Wexley (interview by the author, Hanover, NH, March 2001).
21. Brecht, quoted in Gersch, *Film bei Brecht*, 193.
22. Brecht reports that he was particularly incensed that a scene of mourners at a mass grave (which would have constituted the first onscreen depiction of Jewish victims of the Nazi terror) was not included in the final cut. See McGilligan, *Fritz Lang*, 296.
23. Lang to James K. Lyon, August 23, 1971; quoted in *Fritz Lang, Leben und Werk, Bilder und Dokumente*, ed. Rolf Aurich, Wolfgang Jacobsen, and Cornelius Schnauber (Berlin: Jovis, 2001), 355.
24. The seven questions that the OWI asked filmmakers to consider are quoted in Clayton R. Koppes and Gregory D. Black, *Hollywood Goes to War: How Politics, Profits, and Propaganda Shaped World War II Movies* (London: Free Press, 1987), 66.
25. Jan-Christopher Horak, *Anti-Nazi-Filme der deutschsprachigen Emigration von Hollywood, 1939–1945* (Münster: Maks, 1985), 91. See also Horak, "Wunderliche Schicksalsfügung: Emigranten in Hollywoods Anti-Nazi-Film," *Exilforschung* 2 (1984): 257–70. A more critical summary of anti-Nazi films is found in Charles Higham and Joel Greenberg, *Hollywood in the Forties* (New York: A. S. Barnes, 1968). For a comprehensive list of titles see the website www.cine-holocaust.de/.
26. Given its proximity to crime fiction, film noir also was made to serve anti-Nazi narratives. See Michael Omasta, "*Background to Danger*: Notizen zum Film noir gegen die Nazis," in *Schatten. Exil: Europäische Emigranten im Film noir*, ed. Christian Cargnelli and Michael Omasta (Vienna: PVS, 1997), 105–26.
27. Sabine Hake, *Screen Nazis: Cinema, History, and Democracy* (Madison: University of Wisconsin Press, 2012), 32.
28. The anti-Nazi films have also been given little room within studies of Lang's films. Tom Gunning's authoritative *The Films of Fritz Lang: Allegories of Vision and Modernity* (London: BFI, 2000) all but bypasses Lang's anti-Nazi trilogy.
29. Lowell Mellet, "Wartime Motion Pictures," quoted in Horak, *Anti-Nazi-Filme der deutschsprachigen Emigration von Hollywood, 1939–1945*, 65.
30. Klaus Mann, "What's Wrong with Anti-Nazi Films," *Decision*, August 1941, 27–35, here 34.
31. On the relative merits of giving these roles to exile actors see Joseph Garncarz, "The Ultimate Irony," in *Journeys of Desire: European Actors in Hollywood*, ed. Alastair Phillips and Ginette Vincendeau (London: BFI, 2006), 103–13.
32. Sally Bick, "A Double Life in Hollywood: Hanns Eisler's Score for the Film *Hangmen Also Die* and the Covert Expressions of a Marxist Composer," *Musical Quarterly* 93, no. 1 (2010): 90–143, here 91.
33. Interestingly, Lang noted in 1948, "I ended the picture with the anti-fascist professor going to his death along with the other Czechoslovakian hostages." See Fritz Lang, "Happily Ever After," *Penguin Film Review* 5 (1948): 22–29, here 27.
34. Brecht, *Arbeitsjournal*, 2:348.
35. Theodor W. Adorno and Hanns Eisler, *Composing for the Films* (1947; London: Athlone Press, 1994), 25.

36. Eisler must have felt proud about his success at political camouflage, as his sparingly used score won him an Academy Award nomination.
37. Brecht, *Arbeitsjournal*, 2:348.
38. Jean-Louis Comolli and François Géré, "Two Fictions Concerning Hate," trans. Tom Milne, in *Fritz Lang: The Image and the Look*, ed. Stephen Jenkins (London: BFI, 1981), 125–46, here 129.
39. Ibid., 130.
40. Peter Bogdanovich, *Fritz Lang in America* (London: Movie Magazine, 1967), 62.
41. It is telling that many exiles, including Fritz Kortner and Alexander Granach, do not mention these roles in their respective memoirs.
42. Note Hartmut Bitomsky's critical observations on the conversion of the people: "At the end, when Czaka is to be delivered, the people [of Prague] are completely transformed. In the face of so much unity one wonders why Svoboda had such a hard time to hide. What made the people change? The answer remains in the off." See "Die Erklärung des Krieges," *Filmkritik* 19, no. 7 (1975): 290–97, here 294.
43. As Lang related to Bogdanovich, "I had a big fight with Joe Breen of the Hays Office on this picture. . . . He said 'How can I give my approval on a picture that glorifies a lie—the Quisling in the film is delivered to the Nazis through a lie of the Underground.' I had a day-long struggle until he finally said, 'It is against all my principles, it is a glorification of a lie, but I know I cannot forbid it'" (Bogdanovich, *Who the Devil Made It*, 62). Reflecting on the extraordinary impact of *Watch on the Rhine*, Hans Kafka reported in September 1943 in his column, "Hollywood Calling," that the film "is the first Hollywood picture dubbed in German language to be shown to German prisoners in this country." See Kafka, *Hollywood Calling: Die 'Aufbau'-Kolumne zum Film-Exil*, ed. Roland Jaefer (Hamburg: Conference-Point, 2002), 74.
44. Giles Deleuze, *Cinema 2: The Time-Image*, trans. Hugh Tomlinson and Robert Galeta (Minneapolis: University of Minnesota Press, 1989), 138.
45. Thomas Elsaesser, "From Anti-illusionism to Hyper-realism: Bertolt Brecht and Contemporary Film," in *Re-interpreting Brecht: His Influence on Contemporary Drama and Film*, ed. Pia Kleber and Colin Visser (Cambridge: Cambridge University Press, 1990), 170–85, here 184–85.
46. Joy Davidman, *New Masses* (May 4, 1943): 28–29. For a comprehensive list of reviews see the entry for *Hangmen Also* Die on the website www.cine-holocaust.de/. See also Sheri Chinen Biesen, *Blackout: World War II and the Origins of Film Noir* (Baltimore: Johns Hopkins University Press, 2005), 225n22.
47. Quoted in McGilligan, *Fritz Lang*, 304.
48. The anecdote exists in many versions; one of the more detailed ones is found in Lang's so-called "Autobiography," included in Lotte Eisner's *Fritz Lang*, trans. Gertrud Mander (London: Secker and Warburg, 1976), 14–15. The first to debunk this myth was Gösta Werner, "Fritz Lang and Goebbels: Myth and Facts," *Film Quarterly* 43, no. 3 (1990): 24–27. See also McGilligan, *Fritz Lang*, 174–82.
49. Quoted in Siegfried Kracauer, *From Caligari to Hitler: A Psychological History of the German Film*, ed. Leonardo Quaresima (1947; Princeton, NJ: Princeton Uni-

versity Press, 2004), 248. In her memoir Lotte Eisner endorses Lang's self-interpretation of *The Testament of Dr. Mabuse*: "I believe Lang when he says that . . . in the last film he made in Germany he consciously used Nazi slogans and Nazi mentality, without considering whether it might have endangered him." See Lotte Eisner, *Ich hatte einst ein schönes Vaterland* (Munich: DTV, 1988), 177. The list of scholars who followed Kracauer's and Eisner's lead is impressive and includes Peter Bogdanovich, Luc Moullet, and John Russell Taylor.

50. This gesture toward overassimilation repeats Lang's assuming German citizenship in 1924, when with his *Nibelungen* saga he created a celebration of German myth and origin that made him appear 110 percent German.
51. Joseph Kanon, *Stardust* (New York: Washington Square Press, 2009), 244.
52. Lang, "Happily Ever After," 25.
53. See Alexander Stephan, *"Communazis": FBI Surveillance of German Émigré Writers*, trans. Jan van Heuck (New Haven, CT: Yale University Press, 2000).
54. Similarly, Lion Feuchtwanger's play *Wahn oder der Teufel von Boston* (1948; English translation *The Devil in Boston*, 1953) uses the Salem witch hunts to draw parallels to contemporary events.
55. See the chapter "Im Visier des FBI," in Marta Mierendorff, *William Dieterle: Der Plutarch von Hollywood* (Berlin: Henschel, 1993).
56. Michael Henry Wilson, unpublished interview with Shirley Ulmer, May 6, 1996. I thank Noah Isenberg for bringing this source to my attention. For a more detailed account see the chapter "Back in Black" in Isenberg's critical biography of Ulmer, *Edgar G. Ulmer: A Filmmaker at the Margins* (Berkeley: University of California Press, 2014). See also Stefan Grissemann, *Mann im Schatten: Der Filmemacher Edgar G. Ulmer* (Vienna: Zsolnay, 2003), 253.

5. OUT OF THE PAST

1. Siegfried Kracauer, "Those Movies with a Message," in *Siegfried Kracauer's American Writings*, ed. Johannes von Moltke and Kristy Rawson (Berkeley: University of California Press, 2012), 72–81, here 73. Kracauer's essay was originally published in *Harper's Magazine*, June 1948, 567–72.
2. Theodor W. Adorno, *Minima Moralia: Reflections from Damaged Life*, trans. E. F. N. Jephcott (New York: Verso, 1974), 39. The German original reads, "Das Haus ist vergangen," which also implies that the house is gone.
3. MGM promotional materials from the Fred Zinnemann file, housed in the Margaret Herrick Library, Academy of Motion Picture Arts and Sciences, Los Angeles (hereafter AMPAS).
4. Quoted in David Reid and Jayne L. Walker, "Strange Pursuits: Cornell Woolrich and the Abandoned Cities of the Forties," in *Shades of Noir*, ed. Joan Copjec (New York: Verso, 1993), 56–96, here 61.
5. Paul Schrader, "Notes on Film Noir," in *The Film Noir Reader*, ed. Alain Silver and James Ursini (New York: Limelight, 1996), 53–63. See also Raymond Borde and Etienne Chaumeton, *A Panorama of American Film Noir, 1941–1953*, trans. Paul

Hammond (San Francisco: City Lights, 2002); Dana Polan, *Power and Paranoia: History, Narrative, and the American Cinema, 1940–1950* (New York: Columbia University Press, 1986); Sylvia Harvey, "Women's Place: The Absent Family of Film Noir," in *Women in Film Noir*, ed. E. Ann Kaplan (London: BFI, 1978), 22–34; Frank Krutnik, *In a Lonely Street: Film Noir, Genre, Masculinity* (London: Routledge, 1991); and Paul Young, "(Not) the Last Noir Essay: Film Noir and the Crisis of Postwar Interpretation," *Minnesota Review* 55–57 (2002): 203–21.

6. My own argument on the relationship between noir and exile is developed in my *A Foreign Affair: Billy Wilder's American Films* (New York: Berghahn, 2008), 32–36.
7. See Marc Vernet, "Film Noir on the Edge of Doom," in Copjec, *Shades of Noir*, 1–31; and Thomas Elsaesser, *Weimar Cinema and After: Germany's Historical Imaginary* (New York: Routledge, 2000).
8. Knowledgeable contemporary viewers will have recognized this weapon as a Colt model 1911, a .45 caliber semiautomatic, the standard sidearm in World Wars I and II.
9. Neil Sinyard, *Fred Zinnemann: Films of Character and Conscience* (Jefferson, NC: McFarland, 2003), 39.
10. Fred Zinnemann, *An Autobiography* (London: Bloomsbury, 1992), 16. Zinnemann's modesty here stands in contrast to Billy Wilder, Edgar G. Ulmer, and Curt and Robert Siodmak, all of whom in their respective memoirs and interviews sought to underscore their individual contributions to the film. It is nevertheless remarkable that Wilder, Robert Siodmak, Ulmer, and Zinnemann all went on to distinguish themselves as directors of noir, while Curt Siodmak would write a number of important horror films, and cinematographer Eugen Schüfftan would work on numerous noirs, often uncredited.
11. In a 1992 interview Zinnemann explained that when the second wave of immigrants arrived in the United States in 1933, he felt a sense of belonging to the refugees, but he also realized how in contrast to them he had already fully adopted an American lifestyle. See Verena Lücken, "Kämpfen in aussichtslosen Situationen: Interview mit Fred Zinnemann," *epd Film* 9 (1992): 12–19, here 14.
12. As Zinnemann wrote in his autobiography, "[*Act of Violence*] was the last movie I directed for MGM, and the first time I felt confident that I knew what I was doing and why I was doing it. Personally, I like this picture very much" (*An Autobiography*, 74).
13. In his autobiography Schary claims to have first spotted Zinnemann's talent while he made shorts at MGM. See Dore Schary, *Heyday: An Autobiography* (Boston: Little, Brown, 1970), 123.
14. The studio used a similar strategy of misdirection for Van Heflin by drawing on his role as the courageous star of *The Three Musketeers* (George Sidney, 1948).
15. Andrew Sarris, *The American Cinema: Directors and Directions, 1929–1968* (New York: Dutton, 1968), 169. As Sinyard points out, throughout his career Zinnemann never overcame Sarris's snubbing, even though he could have felt comforted by the company he kept in Sarris's rubric, which included the likes of Billy Wilder, Wil-

liam Wyler, Elia Kazan, Joseph Mankiewicz, David Lean, and John Huston (Sinyard, *Fred Zinnemann*, 162).

16. Zinnemann won Academy Awards for Best Short Subject for "That Mothers Might Live" (1938); for Best Documentary Short for "Benjy" (1951); and for Best Director for *From Here to Eternity* (1953) and *A Man for All Seasons* (1966); and he was nominated for *The Search* (1948), *High Noon* (1952), *The Nun's Story* (1959), and *Julia* (1977). He was voted Best Director four times by the New York Film Critics, and he was awarded the Lifetime Achievement Award from the Berlin Film Festival in 1994.

17. Gabriel Miller, ed. *Fred Zinnemann: Interviews* (Jackson: University Press of Mississippi, 2005), 139.

18. Antje Goldau, Hans Helmut Prinzler, and Neil Sinyard, *Zinnemann* (Munich: Filmland Presse, 1986), 15.

19. As a "Book of the Month Club" selection in October 1942, *The Seventh Cross* became an American best seller that according to Jan-Christopher Horak attracted "over 600,000 readers (many of them GIs who received a special Armed Forces edition in 1944)," making it probable that soldiers like Parkson and Enley had this novel on them for their tour in Germany. See Jan-Christopher Horak, "The Other Germany in Zinnemann's *The Seventh Cross* (1944)," in *German Film and Literature: Adaptations and Transformations*, ed. Eric Rentschler (New York: Methuen, 1986), 117–31, here 117; see also Alexander Stephan, "Anna Seghers' *The Seventh Cross*: Ein Exilroman über Nazideutschland als Hollywood-Film," *Exilforschung* 6 (1988): 214–29.

20. Like Wilder, Zinnemann must have suffered from the fact that he did not succeed in getting his parents out of Austria in time, though if survivor guilt informs his films, it does so through an intense probing of individual character rather than through a Wilderesque irreverent ridiculing of Nazi terror.

21. In his interview with Lücken, Zinnemann concedes that the film is "too mild," which he ascribes to the fact that at the time he did not know enough about the political situation in Germany. *The Search*, in contrast, was made with Zinnemann's awareness of the full extent of the Holocaust. See Lücken, "Kämpfen in aussichtslosen Situationen," 16. The fact, for example, that the sign "Konzentrazionslager" adorns the entry of the camp in *The Seventh Cross* must be read as proof that Zinnemann also commanded little control over the film. Not only is the word misspelled, but the Nazis used far more macabre slogans to mark such locations, such as the notorious "Arbeit macht frei" (Work will set you free) of Auschwitz.

22. Even in the seemingly apolitical *The Nun's Story* (1959), the war intrudes when Sister Luke's father dies at the hand of the Wehrmacht's machine guns; and in *The Member of the Wedding*, Frankie's brother, who is about to be married, is first shown in uniform.

23. As Zinnemann explained in a 1948 essay, the "concern was not to attempt an artistic achievement, but to dramatize contemporary history for the large American audience and to make them understand in emotional terms what the world outside

looks like today. We felt that if we could contribute even a small amount to such an understanding, all our efforts would not be in vain." Fred Zinnemann, "Different Perspective," originally published in *Sight and Sound* (Fall 1948); repr. in Richard Koszarski, *Hollywood Directors, 1941–1976* (New York: Oxford University Press, 1977), 144–47, here 144.

24. Zinnemann, *An Autobiography*, 24–26.
25. The critical success of *The Search*, particularly its Academy Award for Best Story, was used prominently in promoting *Act of Violence*.
26. Siegfried Kracauer, "The Mirror up to Nature," in von Moltke and Rawson, *Siegfried Kracauer's American Writings*, 105–8, here 108.
27. Enley's suicide attempt signals an acknowledgment of the profundity of his guilt and the futility of further repressing it that will be repeated for the very same reasons by Dr. Rothe in *Der Verlorene*, the only difference being that after a first aborted attempt Rothe goes through with the deed the next day.
28. Jonathan Auerbach, *Dark Borders: Film Noir and American Citizenship* (Durham, NC: Duke University Press, 2011), 6.
29. Zinnemann, quoted in Sinyard, *Fred Zinnemann*, 61.
30. The screenplay is part of the AMPAS collection. A somewhat different version is available online through the American Film Script database: http://solomon.afso.alexanderstreet.com/. Both versions differ from the final film, which has significantly less expository dialogue. The drafts also entail the following key changes: the theme of patriotism and the veteran is played up more, with a group of veterans standing at attention during the housing dedication ceremony, and an insert shot of a flag pole inscription that reads, "And Then Shall Ye Lay Down Your Arms And Dwell Together In Peace As Brothers," which also serves as the closing shot, the inscription now illuminated at night by the flames of the nearby car crash that killed Enley; after Enley's confession to her, Edith runs to an LA police station and tells the police about his death threat, but they don't take her seriously and make her leave; the scene between Ann and Edith is longer, with Ann stating, "War happened. . . . It smashes some of them one way, it smashes others another. Kill or be killed, for three or four years. . . . We don't know—we'll never really know. We're just the widows. Even after they've come back to us"; there is a scene downtown where Enley comes across a flashing neon sign, "Jesus Saves," and then enters a church where he sees frescoes of Judas kissing his master, followed by a voice-over, "And Judas cast down the pieces of silver . . . and went and hanged himself," which drives Enley from the church. Overall, the cuts make for a more sober, realist, and less symbol-laden film, which can be ascribed to both Schary's and Zinnemann's influence.
31. See Zinnemann materials in AMPAS collection.
32. Sinyard, *Fred Zinnemann*, 57.
33. Noirs that feature Bunker Hill include *Night Has a Thousand Eyes* (John Farrow, 1948), Robert Siodmak's *Criss Cross* (1949), Joseph Losey's remake of *M* (1951), and *Kiss Me Deadly* (Robert Aldrich, 1955). One of the most memorable representations of the area and its inhabitants is *The Exiles* (Kent MacKenzie, 1961), about displaced Native Americans.

34. Making Enley a contractor was another late addition to the script.
35. Norman M. Klein, "The Sunshine Strategy: Buying and Selling the Fantasy of Los Angeles," in *Twentieth Century Los Angeles: Power, Promotion, and Social Conflict*, ed. Norman M. Klein and Martin J. Schiesl (Claremont, CA: Regina Books, 1990), 1–38, here 24.
36. Edward Dimendberg, *Film Noir and the Spaces of Modernity* (Cambridge, MA: Harvard University Press, 2004), 151–52.
37. They loudly assert their faith in the postwar recovery to the tune of "Happy Days Are Here Again," which is played by the hotel orchestra.
38. Dimendberg, *Film Noir and the Spaces of Modernity*, 161.
39. Raymond Chandler, *The High Window* (1943; Harmondsworth: Penguin, 1967), 60.
40. The confusing geography has also led some critics to misread the actual locations. While Wheeler Winston Dixon mistakes the Hill Street tunnel for a "railroad tunnel," Sinyard claims it is a "subway tunnel." See Wheeler Winston Dixon, "*Act of Violence* and the Early Films of Fred Zinnemann," in *The Films of Fred Zinnemann: Critical Perspectives*, ed. Arthur Nolletti (Albany: State University of New York Press, 1999), 37–53, here 50; and Sinyard, *Fred Zinnemann*, 43.
41. Robert Surtees, "The Story of Filming *Act of Violence*," *American Cinematographer*, August 1948, 268, 282–84. Surtees emphasizes that Zinnemann's training as cameraman made for a particularly productive collaboration.
42. Patrick Keating, *Hollywood Lighting from the Silent Era to Film Noir* (New York: Columbia University Press, 2010), 245.
43. American Film Scripts Online, http://solomon.afso.alexanderstreet.com/.
44. Adorno, *Minima Moralia*, 38.
45. Nico Israel, *Outlandish: Writing Between Exile and Diaspora* (Stanford: Stanford University Press, 2000), 83; Adorno, *Minima Moralia*, 39.
46. Fred Zinnemann, *An Autobiography*, 74.
47. *New Pictures*, Jan. 31, 1949.
48. *Variety*, Dec. 22, 1948; *New Yorker*, Feb. 5, 1949.
49. *New York Times*, Jan. 24, 1949.
50. *Monthly Film Bulletin*, March 31, 1949.
51. As James Naremore points out, it is no coincidence that the two terms entered Anglo-American critical discourse at the same time. See James Naremore, *More Than Night: Film Noir and Its Contexts* (Berkeley: University of California Press, 1998), 26.
52. Kracauer, "Those Movies with a Message," 73.
53. Ibid., 76–77.
54. Richard Maltby, "The Politics of the Maladjusted Text," in *The Movie Book of Film Noir*, ed. Ian Cameron (New York: Continuum, 1993), 39–48, here 47.
55. John Belton, *American Cinema, American Culture* (New York: McGraw Hill, 2009), 225.
56. In an earlier draft of the script Ann states, "We are all widows," indicating that even those soldiers who survived the war will be unfit to build permanent relationships.

Collier's draft of the story describes the important scene between Edith and Ann as an encounter of "two women who are figuratively and literally widows of the living dead." Collier Young to producer Jerry Wald, memorandum, Sept. 24, 1947, 1–6, here 5 (AMPAS).
57. See Sinyard, *Fred Zinnemann*, 45; and Dixon, "The Early Films," 52.
58. DeMille nastily pronounced Zinnemann's name to give it a highly foreign charge, as both Jewish and disloyal to America.
59. Kenneth L. Geist, *Pictures Will Talk: The Life and Films of Joseph L. Mankiewicz* (New York: Charles Scribner's Sons, 1978), 168.
60. Sinyard, *Fred Zinnemann*, 69.
61. Belton, *American Cinema, American Culture*, 313.
62. Sinyard, *Fred Zinnemann*, 141.
63. Miller, *Fred Zinnemann: Interviews*, 151.

6. THE FAILURE OF ATONEMENT

1. Siegfried Kracauer, *From Caligari to Hitler: A Psychological History of the German Cinema*, ed. Leonardo Quaresima, (1947; Princeton, NJ: Princeton University Press, 2004), li.
2. Lorre's penciled comments appear in the margins of the *Der Verlorene* script housed in the Stiftung Deutsche Kinemathek, Berlin. According to *Der Spiegel* there exist at least six different versions of the script (see *Der Spiegel*, July 4, 1951, 32).
3. Quoted in Ed Sikov, *On Sunset Boulevard: The Life and Times of Billy Wilder* (New York: Hyperion, 1998), 236.
4. The date is based on Stephen D. Youngkin's meticulously researched biography, *The Lost One: A Life of Peter Lorre* (Lexington: University Press of Kentucky, 2005).
5. On Lorre's typecasting in American films see my essay, "From 'Mr. M' to 'Mr. Murder': Peter Lorre and the Actor in Exile," in *Light Motives: German Popular Film in Perspective*, ed. Randall Halle and Margaret McCarthy (Detroit: Wayne State University Press, 2003), 85–107. On Lorre's entire career see Sarah Thomas, *Peter Lorre: Face Maker: Stardom and Performance Between Hollywood and Europe* (New York: Berghahn, 2012).
6. "M kehrt zurück mit *Der Verlorene*: Peter Lorre im Interview mit Tom Granich" [1951], in *Peter Lorre: Ein Fremder im Paradies*, ed. Michael Omasta, Brigitte Mayr, and Elisabeth Streit (Vienna: Zsolnay, 2004), 181–83, here 181.
7. Thomas Brandlmeier, "Von Hitler zu Adenauer: Deutsche Trümmerfilme," in *Zwischen Gestern und Morgen: Westdeutscher Nachkriegsfilm, 1946–1962*, ed. Hilmar Hoffmann and Walter Schobert (Frankfurt am Main: Deutsches Filmmuseum, 1989), 32–59, here 47.
8. "Kaum ein Film hat den Faschismus so genau vorgezeichnet wie *M*, und kaum ein Film hat den Faschismus so genau nachgezeichnet wie *Der Verlorene*." From the voice-over in Harun Farocki's film *Das doppelte Gesicht: Peter Lorre* (1984).

9. In an ironic twist Nebenzal financed *Der Verlorene* through the postwar compensation (*Wiedergutmachung*) he received for the dispossession of his company, Cine-Allianz, by the Nazis. On the history of Pressburger's production company, Cine-Allianz, see Christoph Fuchs, "Im Labyrinth der Allianzen: Die Metamorphose des Firmenlabels 'Cine-Allianz,'" in *Alliierte für den Film: Arnold Pressburger, Gregor Rabinowitsch und die Cine-Allianz*, ed. Jan Distelmeyer (Munich: Text + Kritik, 2004), 34–45.
10. Maureen Turim, *Flashbacks in Film: Memory and History* (New York: Routledge, 1989), 172.
11. The novel was written by Lorre and Egon Jacobson and published in serial form in the *Münchner Illustrierte* to coincide with the film's release in Germany.
12. Peter Lorre, *Der Verlorene* (Munich: Belleville, 1996), 85. Apart from Inge's murder scene, the most significant alterations in the novel include a replacement of the voice-over flashback narration with the investigations of a journalist whose curiosity is piqued by a short newspaper report of Rothe's suicide; a lengthy episode in which Rothe, as if to redeem himself, saves several people from burning buildings after bombing raids, until finally killing a woman he had saved after being aroused by her; and a scene in which the prostitute, who barely escaped being strangled by Rothe, testifies to the police that this man was certainly *not* the murderer, allowing him to escape. It remains unclear why she would not betray the culprit; it is also significant in that the police make no appearance in the film except briefly during the first scene of murder, where they are quickly dismissed by Winkler, who explains that his unit is in charge.
13. The film was originally called "Das Untier" (The Beast), as the script in the Stiftung Deutsche Kinemathek indicates, a title that was kept until shortly before the film's release. "The Horla" was a favorite story of Lorre's. He performed a radio play version of it on the NBC radio show *Mystery in the Air* on August 21, 1947, one of his many radio shows in which he got to embellish his trademark voice.
14. On the significance of hands in *Mad Love* see Lutz Koepnick, "*Mad Love*: Remembering Berlin in Hollywood," in *Caught by Politics: Hitler Exiles and American Visual Culture*, ed. Sabine Eckmann and Lutz Koepnick (New York: Palgrave, 2007), 195–222.
15. The score was composed by Willy Schmidt-Gentner, a prolific German composer who moved to Vienna in 1933. After a brief membership in the Nazi Party, Schmidt-Gentner scored mostly Vienna-based films, often for Willi Forst or Gustav Ucicky, making him one of several holdovers from the Nazi screen who participated in *Der Verlorene*.
16. Jennifer M. Kapczynski, *The German Patient: Crisis and Recovery in Postwar Culture* (Ann Arbor: University of Michigan Press, 2008), 180.
17. Ibid., 177.
18. Enno Patalas, "Schatten der Vergangenheit," *Süddeutsche Zeitung*, Nov. 3, 1972.
19. Schriftgutsammlung of the Stiftung Kinemathek, Berlin.
20. Tony Williams, "Peter Lorre's *Der Verlorene*: Trauma and Recent Historical Memory," in *Caligari's Heirs: The German Cinema of Fear After 1945*, ed. Steffen Hantke (Lanham, MD: Scarecrow, 2007), 17–35, here 25.

21. Anton Kaes questions to what degree Lang can be seen as the sole director of the film: "In the final analysis, is not *M* as much a Peter Lorre film as it is a Fritz Lang film?" See Kaes, *M* (London: BFI, 2000), 26.
22. Kurt Joachim Fischer, "Der Fall Peter Lorre," *Filmforum* (May 1952): 10.
23. See Anton Kaes, "The Cold Gaze: Notes on Mobilization and Modernity," *New German Critique* 59 (1993): 105–17.
24. Tim Bergfelder, "German Cinema and Film Noir," in *European Film Noir*, ed. Andrew Spicer (Manchester: Manchester University Press, 2007), 138–63, here 152–53.
25. According to the script Rothe's first words in *Der Verlorene* were to have been, "Fear, fear . . ."
26. Ulrich Gregor and Enno Patalas, *Geschichte des Films*, vol. 2 (Reinbeck: Rowohlt, 1976), 420. Although Gregor and Patalas do not mention Robert Siodmak's *Abschied* (1930) and *Voruntersuchung* (1931), these films certainly come to mind here.
27. *Mad Love*, too, contains a lengthy scene in which Dr. Gogol examines himself in the mirror while an "other" Gogol suddenly appears in the reflection, another clear indication of the duplicity of the protagonist.
28. Trowe here plays off of her role in *Straßenbekanntschaft* (Peter Pewas, 1948), in which she portrays a young woman in postwar Germany who leaves her mother's home and almost slips into prostitution. Lorre's casting choice reflects his familiarity with the artistically ambitious German films of the postwar period.
29. Romuald Karmakar in the documentary *Displaced Person: Peter Lorre und sein Film "Der Verlorene"* (Robert Fischer, 2007). Karmakar also acknowledges that his own film, *Der Totmacher* (1995), a portrait of the serial killer Fritz Haarmann, one of two historical models for Lorre's role in *M*, was inspired by *Der Verlorene*.
30. Anton Kaes, *Shell Shock Cinema: Weimar Culture and the Wounds of War* (Princeton, NJ: Princeton University Press, 2009).
31. Apart from producer Pressburger and cinematographer Vích, the film starred Johanna Hofer as Inge's mother. The wife of famous actor and director Fritz Kortner, Hofer, like Lorre, was a reemigrant whose career straddled both the German and the American screen and stage. She costarred opposite Ufa veterans Karl John and Josef Dahmen, who had a small part in *M*. Lorre shared screenplay credit with Benno Vigny and Axel Eggebrecht, who after several months in a concentration camp worked in the German film industry of the 1930s and 1940s under an alias. Lorre's cowriter of the novelization was his longtime friend Egon Jacobson (who changed his name in exile to Jameson); according to Ulrich Döge it was Jacobson who provided the basic idea for Lang's *M*. See Ulrich Döge, "Deutschland—Psychopathenland: *Berlin-Alexanderplatz* und *Der Verlorene* als Roman und Film," in Distelmeyer, *Alliierte für den Film*, 130–40, here 137.
32. As *Der Spiegel* reported, the representative of German film producers, Ernst Purger, intervened on behalf of von Baky's film because he had a personal stake in its success: he and his counterpart in Italy "knew each other well from the better days of the Third Reich." See *Der Spiegel*, Sept. 5, 1951, 30.
33. Staudte, like Lorre, wanted to end his film in an act of self-justice; his protagonist was to shoot the Nazi-turned-industrialist rather than hand him over to the au-

thorities. The Soviet censors did not allow this scene because they did not want to endorse vigilante justice.

34. Thomas Brandlmeier, for instance, calls Lorre's film "einen Schlußstein," a keystone of the rubble film cycle ("Von Hitler zu Adenauer: Deutsche Trümmerfilme," 57). On the rubble film see also Robert Shandley, *Rubble Films: German Cinema in the Shadow of the Third Reich* (Philadelphia: Temple University Press, 2001); and Eric Rentschler, "The Place of Rubble in the *Trümmerfilm*," *New German Critique* 37, no. 2 (2010): 9–30.
35. Wolfgang Schivelbusch, *In a Cold Crater: Cultural and Intellectual Life in Berlin, 1945–1948*, trans. Kelly Barry (Berkeley: University of California Press, 1998), 137.
36. Hans Schmid, "Unternehmen Babylon oder Das Haus der Oberst Winkler," in *Der Verlorene*, 311–32, here 320.
37. Lutz Koepnick, *The Dark Mirror: German Cinema Between Hitler and Hollywood* (Berkeley: University of California Press, 2002), 194.
38. See, in particular, Bergfelder, "German Cinema and Film Noir"; and Jennifer Fay and Justus Nieland, *Film Noir: Hard-Boiled Modernity and the Cultures of Globalization* (New York: Routledge, 2010). For a different discussion of German cinema within a larger European context that is not confined to noir, see *Schatten des Krieges: Innovation und Tradition im europäischen Kino, 1940–1950*, ed. Olaf Brill and Johannes Roschlau (Munich: Text + Kritik, 2010).
39. An early champion of *Der Verlorene* was fellow émigré film historian Lotte Eisner, who defended the film's uniqueness: "To portray the reign of the Third Reich, many lesser directors deem it necessary to present a profusion of resistance fighters, people declaiming 'Heil Hitler,' and torture scenes. Here there is nothing of the kind: the Nazi who plays an important part throughout the film is completely defined by his manner, his laugh, and his language, and only once do we see him in the extreme situation of the killer. And that's all." See Lotte H. Eisner, *The Haunted Screen: Expressionism in the German Cinema and the Influence of Max Reinhardt*, trans. Roger Greaves (1952; Berkeley: University of California Press, 1965), 339.
40. Lorre, quoted in Jerry Talmer, "Reel Finds: The Lost Film by Peter Lorre," *New York Post*, July 26, 1984.
41. Marita Krauss, *Heimkehr in ein fremdes Land: Geschichte der Remigration nach 1945* (Munich: Beck, 2001), 9. The following remarks are indebted to Krauss's study.
42. See Herbert Lehnert, "Bert Brecht und Thomas Mann im Streit über Deutschland," in *Deutsche Exilliteratur seit 1933: Band 1. Kalifornien*, ed. John M. Spalek and Joseph Strelka (Bern: Francke, 1976), 62–88.
43. The original reads, "einen furchtbaren Irrtum, der halb schuldhaft und halb Verhängnis war." See Thomas Mann, *Deutsche Hörer! 55 Radiosendungen nach Deutschland von Thomas Mann* (Stockholm: Bermann-Fischer, 1945), 119.
44. The original reads, "dem sein Bestes durch Teufelslist zum Bösen ausschlug." See Thomas Mann, "Deutschland und die Deutschen," in *Deutschland und die Deutschen: Essays, 1938–1945* (Frankfurt am Main: Fischer, 1996), 260–81, here 279.

45. Walter von Molo, "Offener Brief an Thomas Mann," *Münchner Zeitung*, August 13, 1945; repr. in *Thomas Mann im Urteil seiner Zeit*, ed. Klaus Schröter (Frankfurt am Main: Klostermann, 2000), 334–36, here 335.
46. Thomas Mann, "Warum ich nicht nach Deutschland zurückkehre," in *Essays VI: 1945–1950*, ed. Herbert Lehnert (Frankfurt am Main: Fischer, 2009), 72–82, here 76.
47. Frank Thieß, "Die innere Emigration," *Münchner Zeitung*, August 18, 1945; repr. in Schröter, *Thomas Mann im Urteil seiner Zeit*, 336–38.
48. On Lorre's return to Germany, *Der Spiegel*, which provided ample reporting of his German plans, asked if he was aware that reemigrant actors were often met with resentment, to which Lorre replied, "I find that completely understandable." Yet it quickly became obvious to Lorre that he severely underestimated the apprehension and resistance he would encounter and that merely "being tactful" would not suffice to deal with it. See *Der Spiegel*, Sept. 27, 1950, 38.
49. Krauss, *Heimkehr in ein fremdes Land*, 58.
50. "Höre, wir rufen dich zurück. Verjagter / Jetzt sollst du wiederkommen." Bertolt Brecht, *Poems, 1913–1956*, ed. John Willett and Ralph Mannheim (New York: Methuen, 1976), 418.
51. Hans-Peter Kochenrath, "Kontinuität im deutschen Film," in *Film und Gesellschaft: Dokumente und Materialien*, ed. Wilfried von Bredow and Rolf Zurek (Hamburg: Hoffmann und Campe, 1975), 286–92.
52. Curt Siodmak, *Wolf Man's Maker*, 347.
53. Pommer, quoted in Brandlmeier, "Von Hitler zu Adenauer: Deutsche Trümmerfilme," 35. Six years later, Billy Wilder found that little had changed, stating that contemporary German films were "so pedestrian" ("So schön ist Europa," *Der Spiegel*, June, 18, 1952, 28).
54. This development stands in stark contrast to the successful reemigration to East Germany of Konrad Wolf and Gustav von Wangenheim from the Soviet Union, and Slatan Dudow from Switzerland, who would all find success at Deutsche Film-Aktiengesellschaft (DEFA).
55. Robert Siodmak, quoted in Joe Hembus, *Der deutsche Film kann gar nicht besser sein: Ein Pamphlet von gestern, eine Abrechung von heute* (Munich: Rogner und Bernhard, 1981), 137. In his autobiography Siodmak stated, "I am not proud of the films I made after my return from America," exempting only *Die Ratten / The Rats* (incidentally also a film that uses flashback voice-over narration) and *Nachts, wenn der Teufel kam*. See Robert Siodmak, *Zwischen Berlin und Hollywood: Erinnerungen eines großen Filmregisseurs*, ed. Hans C. Blumenberg (Munich: Goldman, 1980), 232.
56. Sirk's experiences in Germany, while shooting *A Time to Love and a Time to Die* (1957), match those of other reemigrants: "In Germany then, in the late fifties, everyone was full of self-pity. . . . I meet someone I knew from way back and he keeps telling me how bad things were for them, how they suffered, how they endured, how many examples he could give of courage, and so on, and how splendid, comfortable, and serene the life of an émigré must have been. This is one of the reasons I

couldn't live there any more." See *Sirk on Sirk: Conversations with Jon Halliday*, ed. Jon Halliday (Boston: Faber and Faber, 1997), 145.
57. On Wilder's work in postwar Germany see my *A Foreign Affair: Billy Wilder's American Films* (New York: Berghahn, 2008), esp. 54–75.
58. On Brauner's role for the reemigrants see Claudia Dillmann-Kühn, *Artur Brauner und die CCC: Filmgeschäft, Produktionsalltag, Studiogeschichte, 1946–1990* (Frankfurt: Deutsches Filmmuseum, 1990). Beyond the film professionals listed above, Dillmann-Kühn also mentions Leon Askin, Walter Bluhm, Blandine Ebinger, Camilla Spira, and Christa Winsloe. See also Helmut G. Asper, "Remigration und Remigranten im deutschen Film nach 1945," in *Zwischen den Stühlen: Remigranten und Remigration in der deutschen Medienöffentlichkeit der Nachkriegszeit*, ed. Claus-Dieter Krohn and Axel Schildt (Hamburg: Christians, 2002), 161–79; and Tim Bergfelder, *International Adventures: German Popular Cinema and European Co-productions in the 1960s* (New York: Berghahn, 2005). Yet Bergfelder's claim that the reemigrants brought back by Brauner were largely the filmmakers who "helped reshape the popular genres of the 1950s and 1960s" (108) is only correct in terms of commercial success. Artistically, Lang, Dieterle, and Siodmak, who all made films for Brauner at one point, were never able to rise to the level of their best work in Hollywood nor to that of their prewar German careers.
59. Spalek and Strelka, *Deutsche Exilliteratur seit 1933*, 778.
60. On Dietrich's troubled relationship with Germany see Mary Desjardins and Gerd Gemünden, "Marlene Dietrich's Appropriations," in *Dietrich Icon*, ed. Gemünden and Desjardins (Durham, NC: Duke University Press, 2007), 1–24, esp. 1–7.
61. Perhaps the most concrete way to fathom the permanent loss that German culture suffered is to look at the long list of all those artists and filmmakers who are buried in or near Los Angeles. They include Vicki Baum, Curtis Bernhardt, Henry Blanke, John Brahm, Felix Bressart, Curt Courant, Michael Curtiz, Helmut Dantine, E. A. Dupont, Rudi Fehr, Lion and Marta Feuchtwanger, Oskar Fischinger, Paul Frank, Karl Freund, Paul Henreid, Ali Hubert, Gina Kaus, Paul Kohner, Erich Wolfgang Korngold, Martin Kosleck, Henry Koster, Fritz Lang, Francis Lederer, Peter Lorre, Ernst Lubitsch, Fritzi Massary, Joe May, Joe Pasternak, Franz Planer, Erich Pommer, Gottfried Reinhardt, Arnold Schoenberg, Curt Siodmak, Vladimir Sokoloff, William Thiele, Ernst Toch, Conrad Veidt, Franz Waxman, Franz Werfel, and Billy Wilder. And in New York we find Albert Bassermann, Ludwig Donath, Alexander Granach, Dolly Haas, Siegfried Kracauer, Otto Preminger, Max Reinhardt, Walter Slezak, Victor Trivas, Hans Heinrich von Twardowski, and Kurt Weill.

EPILOGUE

1. The few but important exceptions are noted in my introduction and reflected in the bibliography. Karen Thomas's PBS documentary *Cinema's Exiles* (2009) and Peter Rosen's *Shadows in Paradise: Hitler's Exiles in Hollywood* (2008) are also notable.
2. Wim Wenders, "Death Is No Solution," in *Emotion Pictures: Reflections on the Cinema*, trans. Sean Whiteside (Boston: Faber and Faber, 1986), 107.

3. Rainer Werner Fassbinder, "Imitation of Life: On the Films of Douglas Sirk" [1971], in *The Anarchy of the Imagination*, trans. Krishna Winston, ed. Michael Töteberg and Leo A. Lansing (Baltimore: Johns Hopkins University Press, 1992), 77–89.
4. The 2013 Berlin Film Festival continued this tradition with the retrospective "The Weimar Touch: The International Influence of Weimar Cinema after 1933," which focused extensively on exile cinema in the United States and elsewhere.
5. Arjun Appadurai, *Modernity at Large: Cultural Dimensions of Globalization* (Minneapolis: University of Minnesota Press, 1996).
6. Theodor W. Adorno, *Minima Moralia: Reflections from Damaged Life*, trans. E. F. N. Jephcott (New York: Verso, 1978), 39.
7. Edward Said, "Reflections on Exile," in *Reflections on Exile and Other Essays* (Cambridge, MA: Harvard University Press, 2000), 173–86, here 185.

SELECTED BIBLIOGRAPHY

GENERAL BIBLIOGRAPHY ON EUROPEAN AND U.S. FILM HISTORY AND INTELLECTUAL HISTORY

Adelson, Leslie A. "Against Between: A Manifesto." In *Zafer Şenocak*, edited by Tom Cheesman and Karin E. Yeşilada, 130–43. Cardiff: University of Wales Press, 2003.

Adorno, Theodor W. "Auferstehung der Kultur in Deutschland." *Frankfurter Hefte* 5, no. 5 (1950): 469–76.

———. *Minima Moralia: Reflections from Damaged Life*. Translated by E. F. N. Jephcott. New York: Verso, 1978.

———. "Scientific Experiences of a European Scholar in America." Translated by Donald Fleming. In *The Intellectual Migration: Europe and America, 1930–1960*, edited by Donald Fleming and Bernard Bailyn, 338–70. Cambridge, MA: Harvard University Press, 1969.

Alton, John. *Painting with Light*. Berkeley: University of California Press, 1995.

Anderson, Benedict. "Exodus." *Critical Inquiry* 20, no. 2 (1994): 314–27.

———. *Imagined Communities: Reflections on the Origin and Spread of Nationalism*. London: Verso, 1991.

Appadurai, Arjun. "Disjuncture and Difference in the Global Economy." In Featherstone, *Global Culture*, 295–310.

———. *Modernity at Large: Cultural Dimensions of Globalization.* Minneapolis: University of Minnesota Press, 1996.
Ashkenazi, Ofer. *Weimar Film and Modern Jewish Identity.* New York: Palgrave, 2012.
Asper, Helmut G., ed. *"Etwas Besseres als den Tod . . .": Filmexil in Hollywood.* Marburg: Schüren, 2002.
———. *Filmexilanten im Universal Studio, 1933–1960.* Berlin: Bertz und Fischer, 2005.
———. "Hollywood—Hölle oder Paradies." *Exilforschung* 10 (1992): 187–200.
———. "'. . . um Himmels willen vergessen Sie Ihre Vergangenheit': Integrationsbemühungen und- probleme der Filmemigranten." *Exilforschung* 14 (1996): 186–99.
———, ed. *Wenn wir von gestern reden, sprechen wir über heute und morgen.* Berlin: Sigma, 1991.
Auerbach, Jonathan. *Dark Borders: Film Noir and American Citizenship.* Durham, NC: Duke University Press, 2011.
Bahr, Ehrhard. *Weimar on the Pacific: German Exile Culture in Los Angeles and the Crisis of Modernism.* Berkeley: University of California Press, 2007.
Balio, Tino. *United Artists: The Company Built by the Stars.* Madison: University of Wisconsin Press, 1976.
Bammer, Angelika, ed. *Displacements: Cultural Identities in Question.* Bloomington: Indiana University Press, 1994.
Barron, Stephanie, ed. *Exiles and Émigrés: The Flight of European Artists from Hitler.* Los Angeles: LACMA, 1997.
Bartov, Omer. *The "Jew" in Cinema: From "The Golem" to "Don't Touch My Holocaust."* Bloomington: Indiana University Press, 2005.
Bauman, Zygmunt. "From Pilgrim to Tourist—or a Short History of Identity." In *Questions of Cultural Identity*, edited by Stuart Hall and Paul du Gay, 18–36. London: Sage, 1996.
———. "Modernity and Ambivalence." In Featherstone, *Global Culture*, 143–69.
Baxter, John. *The Hollywood Exiles.* New York: Taplinger, 1976.
Belton, John. *American Cinema, American Culture.* New York: McGraw Hill, 2009.
Benz, Wolfgang, and Marion Neiss, eds. *Deutsch-jüdisches Exil—das Ende der Assimilation? Identitätsprobleme deutscher Juden in der Emigration.* Berlin: Metropol, 1994.
Bergfelder, Tim. "German Cinema and Film Noir." In *European Film Noir*, ed. Andrew Spicer, 138–63. Manchester: Manchester University Press, 2007.
Bergfelder, Tim, and Christian Cargnelli, eds. *Destination London: German-Speaking Émigrés and British Cinema, 1925–1950.* New York: Berghahn, 2008.
Bergfelder, Tim, Erica Carter, and Deniz Göktürk, eds. *The German Cinema Book.* London: BFI, 2002.
Bernstein, Matthew. *Controlling Hollywood: Censorship and Regulation in the Studio Era.* New Brunswick, NJ: Rutgers University Press, 1999.
Bhabha, Homi. *The Location of Culture.* New York: Routledge, 1994.
Bhabha, Homi, and Jonathan Rutherford. "The Third Space: Interview with Homi Bhabha." In *Identity: Community, Culture, Difference*, edited by Jonathan Rutherford, 207–21. London: Lawrence and Wishart, 1990.
Blubacher, Thomas. *Paradies in schwerer Zeit: Denker im Exil in Pacific Palisades und Umgebung.* Munich: Elisabeth Sandman, 2011.

Bogdanovich, Peter. *Who the Devil Made It: Conversations with Legendary Film Directors*. New York: Ballantine, 1997.
Borchmeyer, Dieter, and Till Heimeran, eds. *Weimar am Pazifik: Literarische Wege zwischen den Kontinenten*. Tübingen: Niemayer, 1985.
Borde, Raymond, and Etienne Chaumetonism. *A Panorama of American Film Noir, 1941–1953*. Translated by Paul Hammond. San Francisco: City Lights, 2002.
Bordwell, David, Janet Staiger, and Kristin Thompson. *The Classical Hollywood Cinema: Film Style and Mode of Production to 1960*. New York: Columbia University Press, 1985.
Boyers, Robert, ed. *The Legacy of the German Refugee Intellectuals*. New York: Schocken, 1972.
Brill, Olaf, and Johannes Roschlau, eds. *Schatten des Krieges: Innovation und Tradition im europäischen Kino, 1940–1950*. Munich: Text + Kritik, 2010.
Brook, Vincent. *Driven to Darkness: The Jewish Émigré Directors and the Rise of Film Noir*. New Brunswick, NJ: Rutgers University Press, 2009.
Burgoyne, Robert. *Film Nation: Hollywood Looks at U.S. History*. Minneapolis: University of Minnesota Press, 1997.
Cameron, Ian, ed. *The Movie Book of Film Noir*. New York: Continuum, 1993.
Cargnelli, Christian and Michael Omasta, eds. *Aufbruch ins Ungewisse: Österreichische Filmschaffende in der Emigration vor 1945*. 2 vols. Vienna: Wespennest, 1993.
———. *Schatten. Exil: Europäische Emigranten im Film noir*. Vienna: PVS, 1997.
Carr, Steven. *Hollywood and Anti-Semitism: A Cultural History up to World War II*. Cambridge: Cambridge University Press, 2001.
Carroll, John. "National Identity." In *Intruders in the Bush*, edited by John Carroll, 209–25. Melbourne: Oxford University Press, 1982.
Ceplair, Larry, and Steven Englund. *The Inquisition in Hollywood: Politics in the Film Community, 1930–1960*. New York: Anchor/Doubleday, 1980.
Chambers, Iain. "Citizenship, Language, and Modernity." *PMLA* 117, no. 1 (2002): 24–31.
———. *Migrancy, Culture, Identity*. London: Routledge, 1994.
Forsyth, Scott, Florence Jacobowitz, Richard Lippe, Susan Morrison, and Robin Wood, eds. Special issue on Exiles and Émigrés. *Cineaction* 52 (2000).
Clifford, James. "Diasporas." *Cultural Anthropology* 9, no. 3 (1994): 302–38.
Copjec, Joan, ed. *Shades of Noir*. New York: Verso, 1993.
Crawford, Dorothy Lamb. *A Windfall of Musicians: Hitler's Émigrés and Exiles in Southern California*. New Haven, CT: Yale University Press, 2010.
Crofts, Stephen. "Concepts of National Cinema." In *The Oxford Guide to Film Studies*, edited by John Hill and Pamela Church Gibson, 385–94. Oxford: Oxford University Press, 1998.
———. "Reconceptualizing National Cinema/s." *Quarterly Review of Film and Video* 14, no. 3 (1993): 49–67.
Davidson, John, and Sabine Hake, eds. *Framing the Fifties: Cinema in a Divided Germany*. New York: Berghahn, 2007.
Davis, Mike. *City of Quartz*. New York: Vintage, 1992.
De Grazia, Victoria. "Mass Culture and Sovereignty: The American Challenge to European Cinema, 1920–1960." *Journal of Modern History* 61 (1989): 53–87.

Deleuze, Gilles, and Félix Guattari. *Kafka: Toward a Minor Literature*. Translated by Dana Polan. Minneapolis: University of Minnesota Press, 1986.

———. *Nomadology: The War Machine*. Translated by Brian Massumi. New York: Semiotexte, 1986.

Denning, Michael. *The Cultural Front: The Laboring of American Culture in the Twentieth Century*. London: Verso, 1997.

Dickstein, Morris. *Dancing in the Dark: A Cultural History of the Great Depression*. New York: Norton, 2009.

Dimendberg, Edward. "Down These Seen Streets a Man Must Go: Siegfried Kracauer, 'Hollywood's Terror Films,' and the Spatiality of Film Noir." *New German Critique* 89 (2003): 113–43.

———. *Film Noir and the Spaces of Modernity*. Cambridge, MA: Harvard University Press, 2004.

Distelmeyer, Jan, ed. *Alliierte für den Film: Arnold Pressburger, Gregor Rabinowitsch und die Cine-Allianz*. Munich: Text + Kritik, 2004.

Doblhofer, Ernst. "Exil—eine Grundbefindlichkeit des Individuums seit der Antike." In *Innen-Leben: Ansichten aus dem Exil*, edited by Hermann Haarmann, 13–40. Berlin: Fannei and Walz, 1995.

Doherty, Thomas. *Cold War, Cool Medium: Television, McCarthyism, and American Culture*. New York: Columbia University Press, 2003.

———. *Hollywood and Hitler, 1933–1939*. New York: Columbia University Press, 2013.

———. *Hollywood's Censor: Joseph I. Breen and the Production Code Administration*. New York: Columbia University Press, 2007.

———. *Projections of War: Hollywood, American Culture, and World War II*. New York: Columbia University Press, 1993.

Eckmann, Sabine, and Lutz Koepnick, eds. *Caught by Politics: Hitler Exiles and American Visual Culture*. New York: Palgrave, 2007.

Eisner, Lotte. *The Haunted Screen: Expressionism in the German Cinema and the Influence of Max Reinhardt*. Translated by Roger Greaves. 1952. Reprint, Berkeley: University of California Press, 1973.

Eley, Geoff, and Ronald Gregor Suny, eds. *Becoming National: A Reader*. New York: Oxford University Press, 1996.

Elsaesser, Thomas. "Ethnicity, Authenticity, and Exile: A Counterfeit Trade? German Filmmakers and Hollywood." In *Home, Exile, Homeland: Film, Media, and the Politics of Place*, edited by Hamid Naficy, 97–123. New York: Routledge, 1999.

———. "A German Ancestry to Film Noir?" *Iris* 12 (1996): 129–44.

———. "Heavy Traffic: Perspektive Hollywood—Emigranten oder Vagabunden." In Schöning, *London Calling*, 21–41.

———. "Hollywood Berlin." *Sight and Sound* 7, no. 11 (1997): 14–17.

———. "Moderne und Modernisierung: Der deutsche Film der dreißiger Jahre." *Montage/av* 3, no. 2 (1994): 23–40.

———. "Two Decades in Another Country: Hollywood and the Cinéphiles." In *Superculture: American Popular Culture and Europe*, edited by C. W. E. Bigsby, 199–225. Bowling Green: Bowling Green University Press, 1975.

———. *Weimar Cinema and After: Germany's Historical Imaginary*. London: Routledge, 2000.

Everson, William K. *Classics of the Horror Film*. Secaucus, NJ: Citadel Press, 1974.

Exil: Sechs Schauspieler aus Deutschland. Berlin: Stiftung Deutsche Kinemathek, 1983.

Fay, Jennifer. *Theaters of Occupation: Hollywood and the Reeducation of Postwar Germany*. Minneapolis: University of Minnesota Press, 2008.

Fay, Jennifer, and Justus Nieland. *Film Noir: Hard-Boiled Modernity and the Cultures of Globalization*. New York: Routledge, 2010.

Featherstone, Mike, ed. *Global Culture: Nationalism, Globalization and Modernity*. London: Sage, 1990.

FilmExil. Volumes 1–22. Munich: Text + Kritik, 2011.

Fleming, Donald, and Bernard Bailyn, eds. *The Intellectual Migration: Europe and America, 1930–1960*. Cambridge, MA: Harvard University Press, 1969.

Flügge, Manfred. *Das flüchtige Paradies: Künstler an der Côte d'Azur*. Berlin: Aufbau, 2008.

Freyermuth, Gundolf. *Reise in die Verlorengegangenheit*. Hamburg: Rasch und Röhring, 1990.

Friedrich, Otto. *City of Nets: A Portrait of Hollywood in the 1940s*. Berkeley: University of California Press, 1997.

Gabler, Neal. *An Empire of Their Own: How the Jews Invented Hollywood*. New York: Doubleday, 1989.

Garncarz, Joseph. "Hollywood in Germany: Die Rolle des amerikanischen Films in Deutschland." In Jung, *Der deutsche Film*, 167–213.

———. "The Ultimate Irony." In *Journeys of Desire: European Actors in Hollywood*, edited by Alastair Phillips and Ginette Vincendeau, 103–13. London: BFI, 2006.

Gemünden, Gerd. *A Foreign Affair: Billy Wilder's American Films*. New York: Berghahn, 2008.

Gemünden, Gerd, and Anton Kaes, eds. "Film and Exile." Special issue, *New German Critique* 89 (2003).

Ghosh, Bishnupriya, and Bhaskar Sarkar. "The Cinema of Displacement: Towards a Politically Motivated Poetics." *Film Criticism* 20, no. 1–2 (1995–96): 102–13.

Giovacchini, Saverio. *Hollywood Modernism: Film and Politics in the Age of the New Deal*. Philadelphia: Temple University Press, 2001.

Goebel, Eckart, and Sigrid Weigel, eds. *"Escape to Life": German Intellectuals in New York—A Compendium on Exile After 1933*. Boston: de Gruyter, 2012.

Graebner, William. *The Age of Doubt: American Thought and Culture in the 1940s*. Boston: Twayne, 1990.

Gumprecht, Holger. *"New Weimar" unter Palmen: Deutsche Schriftsteller im Exil in Los Angeles*. Berlin: Aufbau, 1998.

Hake, Sabine. *Screen Nazis: Cinema, History, and Democracy*. Madison: University of Wisconsin Press, 2012.

Hall, Stuart. "Cultural Identity and Diaspora." In *Colonial Discourse and Post-colonial Theory*, edited by Patrick Williams and Laura Chrisman, 392–403.. New York: Columbia University Press, 1994.

Hall, Stuart, and Paul du Gay, eds. *Questions of Cultural Identity*. London: Sage, 1996.
Hantke, Steffen, ed. *Caligari's Heirs: The German Cinema of Fear After 1945*. Lanham, MD: Scarecrow, 2007.
Heilbut, Anthony. *Exiled in Paradise: German Refugee Artists and Intellectuals in America, from the 1930s to the Present*. Boston: Beacon, 1983.
Higham, Charles, and Joel Greenberg. *Hollywood in the Forties*. New York: A. S. Barnes, 1968.
———. *The Celluloid Muse: Hollywood Directors Speak*. Chicago: Henry Regnery, 1969.
Higson, Andrew, and Richard Maltby, eds. *"Film Europe" and "Film America": Cinema, Commerce and Cultural Exchange, 1920–1939*. Exeter: University of Exeter Press, 1999.
Higson, Andrew. "The Concept of National Cinema." *Screen* 30, no. 4 (1989): 36–44.
Hilchenbach, Maria. *Kino im Exil: Die Emigration deutscher Filmkünstler, 1933–1945*. Munich: Saur, 1982.
Hirsch, Foster. *The Dark Side of the Screen: Film Noir*. New York: Da Capo, 1981.
Hjort, Mette, and Scott Mackenzie. *Cinema and Nation*. London: Routledge, 2000.
Hoberman, James, and Jeffrey Shandler. *Entertaining America: Jews, Movies, and Broadcasting*. Princeton, NJ: Princeton University Press, 2003.
Hochscherf, Tobias. *The Continental Connection: German-Speaking Émigrés and British Cinema, 1927–45*. Manchester: Manchester University Press, 2011.
Hoffman, Hilmar, and Walter Schobert. *Von Babelsberg nach Hollywood: Filmemigranten aus Nazideutschland*. Frankfurt am Main: Deutsches Filmmuseum, 1987.
———, eds. *Zwischen Gestern und Morgen: Westdeutscher Nachkriegsfilm, 1946–1962*. Frankfurt am Main: Deutsches Filmmuseum, 1989.
Hondo, Abid Med. "The Cinema of Exile." In *Film and Politics in the Third World*, edited by John D. H. Downing, 69–76. New York: Praeger, 1987.
Horak, Jan-Christopher. *Anti-Nazi-Filme der deutschsprachigen Emigration von Hollywood, 1939–1945*. Münster: Maks, 1985.
———. "Exilfilm, 1933–1945." In *Geschichte des deutschen Films*, edited by Wolfgang Jacobsen, Anton Kaes, and Hans Helmut Prinzler, 101–18. Stuttgart: Metzler, 1993.
———. "Filmkünstler im Exil: Ein Weg nach Hollywood." In *Die Künste und Wissenschaften im Exil, 1933–1945*, edited by Edith Böhme and Wolfgang Motzkau-Valeton, 231–54. Gerlingen: Lambert und Schneider, 1992.
———. *Fluchtpunkt Hollywood*. Münster: Maks, 1984.
———. "German Exile Cinema, 1933–1950." *Film History* 8 (1996): 373–89.
———. *Middle European Émigrés in Hollywood (1933–1945): An American Film Institute Oral History Under the Sponsorship of the Louis B. Mayer Foundation*. Beverly Hills: AFI, 1977.
———. "Wunderliche Schicksalsfügung: Emigranten in Hollywoods Anti-Nazi-Film." *Exilforschung* 2 (1984): 257–70.
Hufen, Fritz, and Thomas Jäschke, eds. *Ausgestoßen: Schicksale in der Emigration*. Munich: Goldmann, 1982.
Hughes, H. Stuart. *The Sea Change: The Migration of Social Thought, 1930–1965*. New York: Harper and Row, 1975.

Humphries, Reynold. *Hollywood's Blacklists: A Political and Cultural History*. Edinburgh: Edinburgh University Press, 2010.
Isenberg, Noah. *Weimar Cinema: An Essential Guide to Classic Films of the Era*. New York: Columbia University Press, 2009.
Israel, Nico. *Outlandish: Writing Between Exile and Diaspora*. Stanford: Stanford University Press, 2000.
Jackman, Jarrell C. "German Émigrés in Southern California." In *The Muses Flee Hitler: Cultural Transfer and Adaptation, 1930–1945*, edited by Jarrell C. Jackman and Carla M. Borden, 95–110. Washington: Smithsonian, 1983.
Jackman, Jarrell C., and Carla M. Borden, eds. *The Muses Flee Hitler: Cultural Transfer and Adaptation, 1930–1945*. Washington: Smithsonian, 1983.
Jacobsen, Wolfgang, Hans Helmut Prinzler, and Werner Sudendorf, eds. *Filmmuseum Berlin*. Berlin: Nicolaische Verlagsbuchhandlung, 2000.
Jay, Martin. "The German Migration: Is There a Figure in the Carpet." In Barron, *Exiles and Émigrés*, 326–37.
———. *Permanent Exiles*. New York: Columbia University Press, 1985.
Johnson, E. Bond. "Der European Film Fund und die Exilschriftsteller in Hollywood." In Spalek and Strelka, *Deutsche Exilliteratur seit 1933*, 135–46.
Jones, Ken D., and Arthur F. McClure. *Hollywood at War: The American Motion Picture and World War II*. New York: Castle, 1973.
Jung, Uli, ed. *Der deutsche Film: Aspekte seiner Geschichte von den Anfängen bis zur Gegenwart*. Trier: Wissenschaftlicher, 1993.
Jusdanis, Gregory. "The Importance of Being Minor." *Journal of Modern Greek Studies* 8 (1990): 5–33.
Kaes, Anton. "The Cold Gaze: Notes on Mobilization and Modernity." *New German Critique* 59 (1993): 105–17.
———. "Leaving Home: Film, Migration, and the Urban Experience." *New German Critique* 74 (1998): 179–92.
———. *Shell Shock Cinema: Weimar Culture and the Wounds of War*. Princeton, NJ: Princeton University Press, 2009.
Kafka, Hans. *Hollywood Calling: Die Aufbau-Kolumne zum Film-Exil*. Edited by Roland Jaeger. Hamburg: ConferencePoint, 2002.
———. "What Our Immigration Did for Hollywood—and Vice Versa." *Aufbau* 10, no. 51 (Dec. 22, 1944): 40.
Kaplan, E. Ann, ed. *Women in Film Noir*. London: BFI, 1978.
Kapczynski, Jennifer M. *The German Patient: Crisis and Recovery in Postwar Culture*. Ann Arbor: University of Michigan Press, 2008.
Karpf, Ruth. "Are Jewish Themes Verboten?" *Aufbau* 9, no. 35 (August 27, 1943): 11.
Keating, Patrick. *Hollywood Lighting: From the Silent Era to Film Noir*. New York: Columbia University Press, 2010.
Kemper, Tom. *Hidden Talent: The Emergence of Hollywood Agents*. Berkeley: University of California Press, 2010.
Kerr, Paul. "Out of What Past? Notes on the B Film Noir." In *The Hollywood Film Industry*, edited by Paul Kerr, 220–44. London: Routledge, 1986.

Klapdor, Heike. "Ein Exil soll das Land sein / Not a home, but an exile..." In Jacobsen, Prinzler, and Sudendorf, *Filmmuseum Berlin*, 221–62.

———. "Erforschung des Filmexils." In *Recherche: Film*, edited by Hans-Michael Bock and Wolfgang Jacobsen, 37–46.. Munich: Text + Kritik, 1997.

Knop, Matthias. "Am Leben bleiben und warten: Die deutschsprachige Filmemigration 1933–1945 und das Filmthema Exil." In Jung, *Der deutsche Film*, 111–138.

Koebner, Thomas. "Caligaris Wiederkehr in Hollywood? Stummfilm-Expressionismus, 'Filmemigranten' und Film Noir." In *Innen-Leben: Ansichten aus dem Exil*, edited by Hermann Haarmann, 107–19. Berlin: Fannei und Walz, 1995.

Koepnick, Lutz. *The Dark Mirror: German Cinema Between Hitler and Hollywood*. Berkeley: University of California Press, 2002.

Koppes, Clayton R., and Gregory D. Black. *Hollywood Goes to War: How Politics, Profits, and Propaganda Shaped World War II Movies*. New York: Free Press, 1987.

Koszarski, Richard. *Hollywood Directors, 1941–1976*. New York: Oxford University Press, 1977.

Kracauer, Siegfried. *From Caligari to Hitler: A Psychological History of the German Film*. Edited by Leonardo Quaresima. 1947. Reprint, Princeton, NJ: Princeton University Press, 2004

Kreimeier, Klaus. *The Ufa Story: A History of Germany's Greatest Film Company, 1918–1945*. Translated by Rita and Robert Kimber. New York: Hill and Wang, 1996.

Krohn, Claus-Dieter. *Intellectuals in Exile: Refugee Scholars and the New School for Social Research*. Translated by Rita and Robert Kimber. Amherst: University of Massachusetts Press, 1993.

Krohn, Claus-Dieter, Patrick zur Mühlen, Gerhard Paul, and Lutz Winckler, eds. *Handbuch der deutschsprachigen Emigration, 1933–1945*. Darmstadt: Primus, 1998.

Krutnik, Frank. *In a Lonely Street: Film Noir, Genre, Masculinity*. London: Routledge, 1991.

Lamberti, Marjorie. "German Antifascist Refugees in America and the Public Debate on 'What Should Be Done with Germany After Hitler.'" *Central European History* 40 (2007): 279–305.

Leff, Leonard, and Jerrold L. Simmons. *The Dame in the Kimono: Hollywood Censorship and the Production Code from the 1920s to the 1960s*. New York: Anchor, 1990.

Lenning, Arthur. *The Count: The Life and Films of Bela "Dracula" Lugosi*. New York: G. P. Putnam's Sons, 1974.

Lingeman, Richard R. *The Noir Forties: The American People from Victory to Cold War*. New York: Perseus, 2012.

Loacker, Armin, and Martin Prucha, eds. *Unerwünschtes Kino: Der deutschsprachige Emigrantenfilm, 1934–1937*. Vienna: Filmarchiv Austria, 2000.

Lowey, Ronny. "Konstrukte des Bösen in den Filmstudios von Los Angeles: Hitler als Figur in Hollywood." In *Hitler darstellen: Zur Entwicklung und Bedeutung einer filmischen Figur*, ed. Rainer Rother and Karin Herbst-Meßlinger, 34–41. Munich: Text + Kritik, 2008.

———. "Lachen über den Atlantik hinweg." *Jüdischer Almanach des Leo Baeck Instituts* (2004): 101–12.

Lustig, Frank. "Exil in Hollywood." *epd Film* 5 (1996): 16–18.
Mann, Klaus. "What's Wrong with Anti-Nazi-Films?" *Decision*, August 1941, 27–35.
Mayr, Brigitte, and Michael Omasta. "Film Im Exil: Das unerwünschte Kino der dreißiger Jahre." *epd Film* 6 (2000): 9–11.
Meyer, William R. *Warner Brothers Directors: The Hard-Boiled, the Comic, and the Weepers*. New Rochelle, NY: Arlington House, 1978.
Middell, Eike, et al. *Exil in den USA*. Frankfurt am Main: Rödersberg, 1980.
Moeller, Hans-Bernhard. "Exilautoren als Drehbuchautoren." In Spalek and Strelka, *Deutsche Exilliteratur seit 1933*, 676–714.
Moeller, Robert G. *War Stories: The Search for a Usable Past in the Federal Republic of Germany*. Berkeley: University of California Press, 2001.
Morley, David. *Home Territories: Media, Mobility and Identity*. London: Routledge, 2000.
Morley, David, and Kevin Robins. *Spaces of Identity: Global Media, Electronic Landscapes and Cultural Boundaries*. New York: Routledge, 1995.
Morrison, James. *Passport to Hollywood: Hollywood Films, European Directors*. Albany: State University of New York Press, 1998.
Munby, Jonathan. "The 'Un-American' Film Art: Robert Siodmak, Fritz Lang, and the Political Significance of Film Noir's German Connection." In *Public Enemies, Public Heroes: Screening the Gangster Film from "Little Cesar" to "Touch of Evil,"* 186–220. Chicago: University of Chicago Press, 1999.
Muscio, Guiliana. *Hollywood's New Deal*. Philadelphia: Temple University Press, 1996.
Naficy, Hamid. *Accented Cinema: Exilic and Diasporic Filmmaking*. Princeton, NJ: Princeton University Press, 2001.
———, ed. *Home, Exile, Homeland: Film, Media, and the Politics of Place*. New York: Routledge, 1999.
———. *The Making of Exile Cultures: Iranian Television in Los Angeles*. Minneapolis: University of Minnesota Press, 1993.
Naremore, James. *More Than Night: Film Noir and Its Context*. Berkeley: University of California Press, 1998.
Neve, Brian. *Film and Politics in America: A Social Tradition*. London: Routledge, 1992.
Noack, Frank. *Jannings: Der erste deutsche Weltstar*. Munich: Heyne, 2012.
Nowell-Smith, Geoffrey, and Steven Ricci. *Hollywood and Europe: Economics, Culture, National Identity, 1945–96*. London: BFI, 1998.
O'Brien, Geoffrey. *Hard-Boiled America*. New York: Van Nostrand Reinhold, 1981.
Palmer, R. Barton. *Hollywood's Dark Cinema: The American Film Noir*. New York: Twayne, 1994.
Palmier, Jean-Michel. *Weimar in Exile: The Antifascist Emigration in Europe and America*. Translated by David Fernbach. London: Verso, 2006.
Petrie, Graham. *Hollywood Destinies: European Directors in America, 1922–1931*. New York: Routledge, 1985.
Phillips, Alastair. *City of Darkness, City of Lights: Émigré Filmmakers in Paris, 1929–1939*. Amsterdam: Amsterdam University Press, 2004.

Phillips, Alastair, and Ginette Vincendeau, eds. *Journeys of Desire: European Actors in Hollywood*. London: BFI, 2006.

Polan, Dana. *Power and Paranoia: History, Narrative, and the American Cinema, 1940–1950*. New York: Columbia University Press, 1986.

———. "Réflexions méthodologiques sur l'étude de l'acteur émigré." Translated by Karla Grierson. In *Les Européens dans le cinéma américain : Émigration et exil*, ed. Irène Bessière and Roger Odin, 65–73. Paris: Presses Sorbonne nouvelle, 2004.

Prawer, Siegbert S. *Between Two Worlds: The Jewish Presence in German and Austrian Film, 1910–1933*. New York: Berghahn, 2005.

Radkau, Joachim. *Die deutsche Emigration in den USA: Ihr Einfluss auf die amerikanische Europapolitik, 1933–1945*. Düsseldorf: Bertelsmann, 1971.

Rentschler, Eric. *The Ministry of Illusion: Nazi Cinema and Its Afterlife*. Cambridge, MA: Harvard University Press, 1996.

———. "The Place of Rubble in the *Trümmerfilm*." *New German Critique* 37, no. 2 (2010): 9–30.

Robé, Chris. *Left of Hollywood: Cinema, Modernism, and the Emergence of U.S. Radical Film Culture*. Austin: University of Texas Press, 2010.

Rogowski, Christian, ed. *The Many Faces of Weimar Cinema*. Rochester, NY: Camden House, 2010.

Rosen, Philip. "History, Textuality, Nation: Kracauer, Burch, and Some Problems in the Study of National Cinemas." *Iris* 2 (1984): 69–83.

Rosten, Leo C. *Hollywood: The Movie Colony, the Movie Makers*. New York: Harcourt, Brace, 1941.

Rother, Rainer, ed. *Mythen der Nationen: Völker im Film*. Munich: Koehler und Amelang, 1998.

Roud, Richard, ed. *Cinema: A Critical Dictionary*. London: Secker and Warburg, 1980.

Sabalius, Romey. "Exile Studies as Interdisciplinary and Transnational German Studies." In *Germanics Under Construction: Intercultural and Interdisciplinary Prospects*, edited by Jörg Roche and Thomas Salumets, 77–90. Munich: Iudicum, 1996.

Said, Edward. "The Mind of Winter: Reflections on Life in Exile." *Harper's*, Sept. 1984, 49–55.

———. "Reflections on Exile." In *Out There: Marginalization and Contemporary Cultures*, edited by Russell Ferguson et al., 357–66. Cambridge, MA: MIT Press, 1990.

———. *Representations of the Intellectual*. London: Vintage, 1994.

Saunders, Thomas. *Hollywood in Berlin: American Cinema and Weimar Germany*. Berkeley: University of California Press, 1994.

Schaber, Will, ed. *Aufbau/Reconstruction: Dokumente einer Kultur im Exil*. New York: Overlook, 1972.

Schatz, Thomas. *Boom and Bust: The American Cinema in the 1940s*. New York: Scribner's, 1997.

———. *The Genius of the System: Hollywood Filmmaking in the Studio Era*. New York: Pantheon, 1989.

———. *Hollywood Genres: Formulas, Filmmaking, and the Studio System*. New York: McGraw-Hill, 1981.

———. "World War II and the Hollywood 'War Film.'" In *Refiguring American Film Genres: Theory and History*, edited by Nick Browne, 89–128. Berkeley: University of California Press, 1998.

Schnauber, Cornelius. *Spaziergänge durch das Hollywood der Emigranten.* Zurich: Arche, 1992.

Schöning, Jörg, ed. *London Calling: Deutsche im britischen Film der dreißiger Jahre.* Munich: Text + Kritik, 1993.

Schreiber, Rebecca M. *Cold War Exiles in Mexico: U.S. Dissidents and the Culture of Critical Resistance.* Minneapolis: University of Minnesota Press, 2008.

Segebrecht, Harro, ed. *Mediale Mobilmachung II: Hollywood, Exil und Nachkrieg.* Munich: Wilhelm Fink, 2006.

Shandley, Robert R. *Rubble Films: German Cinema in the Shadow of the Third Reich.* Philadelphia: Temple University Press, 2001.

———. *Runaway Romances: Hollywood's Postwar Tour of Europe.* Philadelphia: Temple University Press, 2009.

Silberman, Marc. "What Is German in the German Cinema?" *Film History* 8, no. 3 (1996): 297–315.

Silver, Alain, and James Ursini. *Film Noir Reader.* New York: Limelight, 1996.

———. *The Noir Style.* New York: Overlook, 1999.

Silver, Alain, and Elizabeth Ward, eds. *Film Noir: An Encyclopedia of the American Mind.* Woodstock: Overland, 1992.

Simmel, Georg. "The Stranger" [1908]. In *On Individuality and Social Forms.* Edited by Donald N. Levine, 143–49. Chicago: University of Chicago Press, 1971.

Smedley, Nick. *A Divided World: Hollywood Cinema and Émigré Directors in the Era of Hitler and Roosevelt, 1933–1948.* Bristol: Intellect, 2011.

Spalek, John M., Konrad Feilchenfeldt, and Sandra H. Hawrylchak, eds. *Deutschsprachige Exilliteratur seit 1933: Band 3: USA.* Zurich: Saur, 2003.

Spalek, John M., and Joseph Strelka, eds. *Deutsche Exilliteratur seit 1933: Band 1: Kalifornien.* Bern: Francke, 1976.

Spicer, Andrew, ed. *European Film Noir.* Manchester: Manchester University Press, 2007.

Staiger, Janet. *The Studio System.* New Brunswick, NJ: Rutgers University Press, 1995.

Steinbauer-Grötsch, Barbara. *Die lange Nacht der Schatten: Film noir und Filmexil.* Berlin: Bertz, 1997.

Stephan, Alexander. *Communazis: FBI Surveilannce of German Émigré Writers.* Translated by Jan van Heurck. New Haven, CT: Yale University Press, 2000.

———, ed. *Exile and Otherness: New Approaches to the Experience of Nazi Refugees.* Oxford: Peter Lang, 2005.

Suleiman, Susan Rubin. *Exile and Creativity: Signposts, Travelers, Outsiders, Backward Glances.* Durham, NC: Duke University Press, 1998.

Täubert, Klaus. "Im Dienste der Volksfront: Hollywood Now." In Asper, *Wenn wir von gestern reden*, 159–68.

Taylor, John Russell. *Strangers in Paradise: The Hollywood Émigrés, 1933–1950.* London: Faber and Faber, 1983.

Telotte, J. P. *The Narrative Patterns of Film Noir*. Urbana: University of Illinois Press, 1985.
Thompson, Kristin. "Early Alternatives to the Hollywood Mode of Production: Implications for Europe's Avant Gardes." *Film History* 5, no. 4 (1993): 386–404.
———, ed. "Émigré Filmmakers and Filmmaking." Special issue, *Film History* 11, no. 2 (1999).
———. "Nation, National Identity and the International Cinema." *Film History* 8, no. 3 (1996): 259–60.
———. "National or International Films? The European Debate During the 1920s." *Film History* 8, no. 3 (1996): 281–96.
Tudor, Andrew. "The Famous Case of 'German Expressionism': Film Movements." In *Passport to Hollywood Film Immigrants*, edited by Don Whitemore and Philip Alan Cecchettini, 169–86. New York: McGraw-Hill, 1976.
Turim, Maureen. *Flashbacks in Film: Memory and History*. New York: Routledge, 1989.
Tuska, John. *Dark Cinema: American Film Noir in Cultural Perspective*. Westport, CT: Greenwood Press, 1984.
Urwand, Ben. *The Collaboration: Hollywood's Pact with Hitler*. Cambridge: Harvard University Press, 2013.
Von Moltke, Johannes, and Kristy Rawson, eds. *Siegfried Kracauer's American Writings*. Berkeley: University of California Press, 2012.
Walsh, Michael. "National Cinema, National Imaginary." *Film History* 8, no. 1 (1996): 5–17.
Wanger, Walter. "The Role of Movies in Morale." *American Journal of Sociology* 47, no. 3 (1941): 378–83.
Weitz, Eric D. *Weimar Germany: Promise and Tragedy*. Princeton, NJ: Princeton University Press, 2007.
Welky, David. *The Moguls and the Dictators: Hollywood and the Coming of World War II*. Baltimore: Johns Hopkins University Press, 2008.
Weschler, Lawrence. "Paradise: The Southern California Idyll of Hitler's Cultural Exiles." In Barron, *Exiles and Émigrés*, 341–57.
Wheatland, Thomas. *The Frankfurt School in Exile*. Minneapolis: University of Minnesota Press, 2009.
Whittemore, Don, and Philip Alan Cecchettini. *Passport to Hollywood Film Immigrants*. New York: McGraw-Hill, 1976.
Willemen, Paul. "The National." In *Looks and Frictions: Essays in Cultural Studies and Film Theory*, 206–19. London: BFI, 1994.
Wilms, Wilfried, and William Rasch, eds. *German Postwar Films: Life and Love in the Ruins*. New York: Palgrave, 2008.

MEMOIRS, AUTOBIOGRAPHIES, NOVELIZATIONS

Alberts, Jürgen. *Hitler in Hollywood oder: Die Suche nach dem Idealscript*. Göttingen: Steidl, 1997.
Baum, Vicki. *I Know What I'm Worth*. London: Michael Joseph, 1964.

Bergner, Elisabeth. *Bewundert viel und viel gescholten: Unordentliche Erinnerungen.* Munich: Bertlesmann, 1978.
Bernhardt, Curtis, and Mary Kiersch. *Curtis Bernhardt: A Directors Guild of America Oral History.* Metuchen, NJ: Scarecrow, 1986.
Bois, Curt. *So schlecht war mir noch nie.* Königstein: Athenäum, 1984.
———. *Zu wahr, um schön zu sein.* Berlin: Henschel, 1980.
Colpet, Max. *Im Sandmeer der Zeit: 60 Jahre Filmschaffen—eine moderne Odysee.* Saarbrücken: Logos, 1975.
De Toth, André. *Fragments: Portrait from the Inside.* Boston: Faber and Faber, 1994.
Dietrich, Marlene. *Ich bin, Gott sei Dank, Berlinerin.* Translated by Nicola Volland. Frankfurt am Main: Ullstein, 1998.
Eisner, Lotte. *Ich hatte einst ein schönes Vaterland.* Munich: DTV, 1988.
Epstein, Leslie. *Pandaemonium.* New York: St Martin's Griffin, 1997.
Feuchtwanger, Marta. *Nur eine Frau.* Munich: LangenMüller, 1983.
Forster, Rudolf. *Das Spiel, mein Leben.* Berlin: Propyläen, 1967.
Frank, Leonard. *Links, wo das Herz ist.* Munich: Nymphenburger Verlagshandlung, 1963.
Fry, Varian. *Surrender on Demand.* New York: Random House, 1945.
Henreid, Paul. *Ladies Man.* New York: St. Martin's, 1984.
Hollaender, Friedrich. *Those Torn from Earth.* New York: Liveright, 1941. German translation: *Menschliches Treibgut.* Translated by Stefan Weidle. Bonn: Weidle, 1995.
———. *Von Kopf bis Fuß: Mein Leben mit Text und Musik.* Edited by Volker Kühn. Bonn: Weidle, 1996.
Hubert, Ali. *Hollywood: Legende und Wirklichkeit.* Leipzig: Seemann, 1930.
Isherwood, Christopher. *Prater Violet.* New York: Random House, 1945.
Jacobsen, Wolfgang, and Heike Klapdor, eds. *In der Ferne das Glück: Geschichten für Hollywood von Vicki Baum, Ralph Benatzky, Fritz Kortner, Joseph Roth sowie Heinrich und Klaus Mann u.a.* Translated by Gesine Schröder. Berlin: Aufbau, 2013.
Jannings, Emil. *Theater, Film, das Leben und ich.* Edited by C. C. Bergius. Berchtesgaden: Zimmer und Herzog, 1951.
Kanon, Joseph. *Stardust.* New York: Washington Square Press, 2009.
Kaus, Gina. *Und was für ein Leben.* Hamburg: Albrecht Knaus, 1979.
———. *Von Wien nach Hollywood.* Edited by Sybille Mulot. Frankfurt: Suhrkamp, 1990.
Klapdor, Heike, ed. *Ich bin ein unheilbarer Europäer: Briefe aus dem Exil.* Berlin: Aufbau, 2007.
Koestler, Arthur. *Als Zeuge der Zeit: Das Abenteuer meines Lebens.* Frankfurt: Fischer-Taschenbuch, 1986.
Kohner, Frederick. *The Magician of Sunset Boulevard: The Improbable Life of Paul Kohner, Hollywood Agent.* Palos Verdes, CA: Morgan, 1977.
Kortner, Fritz. *Aller Tage Abend.* Munich: Knaur, 1996.
Koster, Henry. *Interviewed by Irene Kahn Atkins.* A Directors Guild of America Oral History. Metuchen, NJ: Scarecrow, 1987.
Lamarr, Hedy. *Ecstasy and Me: My Life as a Woman.* New York: Bartholomew House, 1966.

Lewinsky, Charles. *Gerron*. Zurich: Nagel und Kimche, 2011.
Leyens, Erich, and Lotte Andor. *Die fremden Jahre: Erinnerungen an Deutschland*. Frankfurt am Main: Fischer, 1991.
Löwenstein, Hubertus Prinz zu. *Botschafter ohne Auftrag*. Düsseldorf: Droste, 1972.
Marcuse, Ludwig. *Mein zwanzigstes Jahrhundert: Auf dem Weg zu einer Autobiographie*. Zurich: Diogenes, 1960.
Modick, Klaus. *Sunset*. Frankfurt: Eichborn, 2011.
Negri, Pola. *Memoirs of a Star*. Garden City, NY: Doubleday, 1970.
Ophüls, Max. *Spiel im Dasein: Eine Rückblende*. Stuttgart: Henry Goverts, 1959.
Palmer, Lilli. *Dicke Lilli–Gutes Kind*. Darmstadt: Droemer, 1974.
Pasternak, Joe. *Easy the Hard Way*. New York: Putnam, 1956.
Preminger, Otto. *An Autobiography*. New York: Doubleday, 1977.
Reinhardt, Gottfried. *Der Liebhaber: Erinnerungen seines Sohnes Gottfried Reinhardt an Max Reinhardt*. Munich: Droemer Knaur, 1973. English translation: *The Genius: A Memoir of Max Reinhardt by His Son Gottfried Reinhardt*. New York: Knopf, 1979.
———. *Hollywood, Hollywood*. Göttingen: Lamuv, 1992.
Reinhardt-Thimig, Helene. *Wie Max Reinhardt lebte*. Percha: Schulz, 1973.
Rodman, Howard A. *Destiny Express*. New York: Atheneum, 1990.
Sahl, Hans. *Das Exil im Exil: Memoiren eines Moralisten II*. Munich: DTV, 1994.
———. *Memoiren eines Moralisten*. Munich: DTV, 1995.
Viertel, Salka. *The Kindness of Strangers: A Theatrical Life. Vienna, Berlin, Hollywood*. New York: Holt, Rinehart and Winston, 1969.
Siodmak, Curt. *Wolf Man's Maker*. Boston: Scarecrow, 2001.
Siodmak, Robert. *Zwischen Berlin und Hollywood*. Edited by Hans C. Blumenberg. Munich: Goldmann, 1980.
Slezak, Walter. *What Time's the Next Swan*. New York: Doubleday, 1962.
Völker, Klaus, and Elisabeth Bergner. *Elisabeth Bergner: Das Leben einer Schauspielerin*. Berlin: Hentrich, 1990.
Weill, Kurt, and Lotte Lenya. *Speak Low (When You Speak Love): The Letters of Kurt Weill and Lotte Lenya*. Translated by Lys Symonette and Kim Kowalke. Berkeley: University of California Press, 1996.
Wicclair, Walter. *Von Kreuzberg bis Hollywood*. Berlin: Henschel, 1975.
Zinnemann, Fred. *A Life in the Movies: An Autobiography*. New York: Macmillan, 1992.
Zweig, Stefan. *The World of Yesterday*. New York: Viking, 1943.

INDIVIDUAL FILM PROFESSIONALS

Bergner, Elisabeth

Bolbecher, Siglinde, Konstantin Kaiser, and Jüdisches Museum der Stadt Wien. *Unsere schwarze Rose Elisabeth Bergner*. Wien: Historisches Museum, 1993.
Eloesser, Arthur. *Elisabeth Bergner*. Charlottenburg: Williams, 1927.

Heymann, Margret. *Elisabeth Bergner, mehr als eine Schauspielerin.* Berlin: Vorwerk 8, 2008.
Hochholdinger-Reiterer, Beate. *Vom Erschaffen der Kindfrau: Elisabeth Bergner—ein Image.* Wien: Braumüller, 1999.
Jackson, Russell. "Remembering Bergner's Rosalind: *As You Like It* on Film in 1936." *Shakespeare, Memory and Performance,* edited by Peter Holland, 237–55. Cambridge: Cambridge University Press, 2006.
Orbanz, Eva. *Elisabeth Bergner.* Berlin: Stiftung Deutsche Kinemathek, 1983.
Reiterer, Beate. "'Herr Direktor Heine, sehen Sie sich Frl. Bergner an.' Die Rezeption der Schauspielerin Elisabeth Bergner in den Wiener Printmedien—eine Marginalie?" *Maske und Kothurn: Internationale Beiträge zur Theaterwissenschaft* 43, no. 1–3 (1997): 45–71.
Roth, Wilhelm. "Nachruf." *epd Film* 6 (1986): 6.

Bernhardt, Curtis

Belach, Helga, Gero Gandert, Hans Helmut Prinzler, ed. *Aufruhr der Gefühle: Die Kinowelt des Curtis Bernhardt.* Munich: Bucher, 1982.
"Curtis Bernhardt." In Higham and Greenburg, *The Celluloid Muse,* 41–54.
Jochum, Norbert. "Die allerverführerischsten Blicke: Curtis Bernhardt." *Die Zeit,* Feb. 12, 1982.
Koepnick, Lutz. "Screening Fascism's Underground: Kurt Bernhardt's *The Tunnel.*" *New German Critique* 74 (1998): 151–78.
Porfirio, Robert, Alain Silver, and James Ursini. *Film Noir 3: Interviews with Filmmakers of the Classic Noir Period.* New York: Limelight, 2001. 229–232

Brecht, Bertolt

Bitomski, Hartmut, Harun Farocki, and Wolfgang Gersch, eds. "Fritz Lang and Bertolt Brecht." Special issue, *Filmkritik* 223 (1975).
Brewster, Ben. "Brecht and the Film Industry." *Screen* 16, no. 4 (1975): 16–33.
Cook, Bruce. *Brecht in Exile.* New York: Holt, Rinehart, and Winston, 1982.
Elsaesser, Thomas. "From Anti-illusionism to Hyper-realism: Bertolt Brecht and Contemporary Film." In *Re-interpreting Brecht: His Influence on Contemporary Drama and Film,* edited by Pia Kleber and Colin Visser, 170–85. Cambridge: Cambridge University Press, 1990.
Fetscher, Iring. "Bertolt Brecht in America." In *The Legacy of the German Refugee Intellectuals,* edited by Robert Boyers, 246–72. New York: Schocken, 1972.
Gemünden, Gerd. "Brecht in Hollywood: *Hangmen Also Die* and the Anti-Nazi Film." *The Drama Review* 164 (1999): 65–76.
Gersch, Wolfgang. *Film bei Brecht: Bertolt Brechts praktische und theoretische Auseinandersetzung mit dem Film.* Berlin: Henschel, 1975.

Grimm Reinhold, and Henry Schmidt. "Bertolt Brecht and *Hangmen Also Die*." *Monatshefte* 61, no. 3 (1969): 232–49.

Lyon, James K. *Bertolt Brecht in America*. Princeton, NJ: Princeton University Press, 1980.

———. "Bertolt Brecht's Hollywood Years: The Dramatist as Film Writer." *Oxford German Studies* 6 (1971): 145–74.

Lyon, James K., and John B. Fuegi. "Bertolt Brecht." In Spalek and Strelka, *Deutsche Exilliteratur seit 1933*, 268–98.

Polan, Dana. "Daffy Duck and Bertolt Brecht: Toward a Politics of Self-Reflexive Cinema." In *American Media and Mass Culture: Left Perspectives*, edited by Donald Lazere, 345–56. Berkeley: University of California Press, 1987.

Curtiz, Michael

Francisco, Charles. *You Must Remember This: The Filming of Casablanca*. Englewood Cliffs, NJ: Prentice-Hall, 1980.

Harmetz, Aljean. *Round Up the Usual Suspects: The Making of "Casablanca"—Bogart, Bergman, and World War II*. New York: Hyperion, 1992.

Missler-Morell, Andreas. *"Ich seh' dir in die Augen, Kleines": Casablanca—der Kultfilm*. Munich: Heyne, 1992.

Ray, Robert. "The Culmination of Classic Hollywood: *Casablanca*." In *A Certain Tendency of the Hollywood Cinema, 1930–1980*, 89–112. Princeton, NJ: Princeton University Press, 1985.

Robertson, James C. *The Casablanca Man: The Cinema of Michael Curtiz*. New York: Routledge, 1993.

Rosenzweig, Sidney. *Casablanca and Other Major Films of Michael Curtiz*. Ann Arbor: UMI Press, 1982.

Dieterle, William

Agde, Günter. "William Dieterles Filmregie-Vorlesungen am Max Reinhardt Workshop 1938." In Asper, *Wenn wir von gestern reden*, 181–90.

Dieterle, William. "Der Film und die öffentliche Moral." Lecture to the Teachers Association of California, 1940.

———. "Europeans in Hollywood." *Sight and Sound* 22, no. 1 (1952): 39–40.

———. "Hollywood and the European Crisis." *Studies in Philosophy and Social Science* 9 (1941): 96–103.

———. "P.S. to Movie Symposium." *Decision*, April 1940, 85.

———. "Über Regie im Spielfilm." Three Lectures Held at the Max Reinhardt Workshop, Hollywood, July 6, 14, 28, 1938.

———. "Und der deutsche Film?" *Freies Deutschland* 3, no. 12 (1944): 21–22.

———. "What the Public Thinks it Wants." *California Arts and Architecture* 57, no. 6 (1940): 21.
Elsaesser, Thomas. "Film History as Social History: The Dieterle/Warner Brothers Biopic." *Wide Angle* 8, no. 2 (1986): 15–32.
Hermanni, Horst O. *William Dieterle: Vom Arbeiterbauernsohn zum Hollywood-Regisseur*. London: World of Books, 1992.
Kaul, Walter. *William Dieterle: Von Deutschland nach Hollywood*. Berlin: Filmfestspiele Berlin, 1973.
Mierendorff, Marta. *William Dieterle: Der Plutarch von Hollywood*. Berlin: Henschel, 1993.
Robé, Chris. "Taking Hollywood Back: The Historical Costume Drama, the Biopic, and Popular Front U.S. Film Criticism." *Cinema Journal* 48, no. 2 (2009): 70–87.
Vanderwood, Paul J., ed. *Juárez*. Madison: University of Wisconsin Press, 1983.

Dietrich, Marlene

Bach, Steven. *Marlene Dietrich: Life and Legend*. New York: Morrow, 1992.
Bronfen, Elisabeth. "Leni Riefenstahl und Marlene Dietrich: Zwei deutsche Stars / Leni Riefenstahl and Marlene Dietrich: Two German Stars." In Jacobsen, Prinzler, and Sudendorf, *Filmmuseum Berlin*, 169–90.
Clarens, Carlos. "Marlene Dietrich." In Roud, *Cinema*, 275.
Dickens, Homer. *The Complete Films of Marlene Dietrich*. Revised and updated by Jerry Vermilye. New York: Citadel, 1992.
Drosz, René. *Marlene Dietrich und die Psychologie des Vamps*. Zurich: Sansouci, 1961.
Jacobsen, Wolfgang, and Heike Klapdor. Special issue on Marlene Dietrich. *Film-Exil* 8 (1996).
Film und Fernsehen 8, no. 12 (1980). Special issue on Marlene Dietrich.
Garber, Marjorie. "From Dietrich to Madonna: Cross-Gender Icons." In *Women and Film: A Sight and Sound Reader*, edited by Pam Cook and Philip Dodd, 16–20. Philadelphia: Temple University Press, 1993.
Gemünden, Gerd, and Mary Desjardins, eds. *Dietrich Icon*. Durham, NC: Duke University Press, 2007.
Higham, Charles. *Marlene: The Life of Marlene Dietrich*. New York: Norton, 1977.
Hoffmann, Barbara. *Marlene Dietrich: Die Privatsammlung*. Frankfurt am Main: Deutsches Filmmuseum Frankfurt, 1993.
Jacob, Lars, ed. *Apropos Marlene Dietrich*. Frankfurt: Neue Kritik, 2000.
Knight, Arthur. "Marlene Dietrich." *Films in Review* 5, no. 10 (1954): 497–514.
Koch, Gertrud. "Exorcised: Marlene Dietrich and German Nationalism." In *Women and Film: A Sight and Sound Reader*, edited by Pam Cook and Philip Dodd, 10–15. Philadelphia: Temple University Press, 1993.
Kosta, Barbara. *Willing Seduction: The Blue Angel, Marlene Dietrich and Mass Culture*. New York: Berghahn, 2009.

Loewenstein, Joseph, and Lynne Tatlock. "The Marshall Plan at the Movies: Marlene Dietrich and Her Incarnations." *German Quarterly* 65, no. 3–4 (1992): 429–42.

Marschall, Susanne. "Vis-à-vis: Marilyn und Marlene." In *Schauspielkunst im Film*, edited by Thomas Koebner, 97–106. St. Augustin: Gardez!, 1998.

Morley, Sheridan. *Marlene Dietrich*. London: Elm Tree, 1976.

Reichmann, Hans-Peter. "Der Marlene Dietrich Nachlass in Berlin." *epd Film* 5 (1995): 6–8.

Reichmann, Hans-Peter, and Werner Sudendorf. *Marlene Dietrich*. Frankfurt am Main: Deutsches Filmmuseum, 1998.

Riva, Maria. *Marlene Dietrich*. New York: Knopf, 1993.

Sanders-Brahms, Helma. *Marlene und Jo: Recherche einer Leidenschaft*. Berlin: Argon, 2000.

Seydel, Renate. *Marlene Dietrich: Eine Chronik ihres Lebens in Bildern und Dokumenten*. Berlin: Henschel, 1984.

Spoto, Donald. *Blue Angel: The Life of Marlene Dietrich*. New York: Doubleday, 1992.

Studlar, Gaylyn. *In the Realm of Pleasure: Von Sternberg, Dietrich, and the Masochistic Aesthetic*. New York: Columbia University Press, 1988.

Sudendorf, Werner. "Dear Marlene: Der Nachlass von Marlene Dietrich." *FilmExil* 4 (1994): 32–34.

———, ed. *Marlene Dietrich*. 2 vols. Munich: Hanser, 1977.

———. "Marlene Dietrich: Von Kopf bis Fuss / Marlene Dietrich: From Head to Toe." In Jacobsen, Prinzler, and Sudendorf, *Filmmuseum Berlin*, 131–68.

Witte, Karsten. "Die klassische Nostalgie: Marlene Dietrich zum 90. Geburtstag." *epd Film* 12 (1991): 18–21.

Dupont, Ewald André

Brandlmeier, Thomas. "Porträt: Ewald André Dupont." *epd Film* 2 (1992): 5–7.

Bretschneider, Jürgen, ed. *Ewald André Dupont: Autor und Regisseur*. Munich: Text + Kritik, 1992.

Koszarski, Richard. "E. A. Dupont." In Roud, *Cinema*, 310.

Freund, Karl

Brandlmeier, Thomas. "Deutsche Kamerapioniere der zwanziger Jahre." *epd Film* 12 (1994): 20–26.

Deschner, Donald. "Karl Freund." *Cinema* 5, no. 4 (1979): 24–27.

Telotte, J. P. "Doing Science in Machine Age Horror: The Mummy's Case." *Science Fiction Studies* 30, no. 2 (2003): 217–30.

Hollaender, Friedrich

Akademie der Künste. *"Bei uns um die Gedächtniskirche rum . . .": Friedrich Hollaender und das Kabarett der Zwanziger Jahre.* Berlin: Akademie der Künste, 1996.
Delabar, Walter, and Carsten Würmann. *Literatur zum Gebrauch. Hollaender und andere: Beiträge zu einer Kulturgeschichte der Weimarer Republik.* Berlin: Weidler, 2002.
Kühn, Volker. *Spötterdämmerung: Vom langen Sterben des grossen kleinen Friedrich Hollaender.* Berlin: Parthas, 1996.
Newberry, Ilse. "Nicht länger mehr 'draußen vor der Tür'—oder doch? Friedrich Hollaenders Rückkehr." *German Quarterly* 63, no. 2 (1990): 245–59.
Rotthaler, Viktor. "Im Ohr: Berlin und Wien." *FilmExil* 9 (1997): 5–18.

Jackson, Felix

Asper, Helmut G. "Happy Birthday, Felix Jackson." *epd Film* 7 (1992): 8–9.
Asper, Helmut G., and Jan-Christopher Horak. "Three Smart Guys: How a Few Penniless German Émigrés Saved Universal Studios." *Film History* 11, no. 2 (1999): 134–53.
Kraus, Joseph. "Felix Jackson." In Spalek and Strelka, *Deutsche Exilliteratur seit 1933*, 731–37.

Kohner, Frederick

Mack, Gerhard G. "Frederick Kohner." In Spalek and Strelka, *Deutsche Exilliteratur seit 1933*, 762–70.

Kohner, Paul

Kemper, Tom. *Hidden Talent: The Emergence of Hollywood Agents.* Berkeley: University of California Press, 2010.
Klapdor, Heike, ed. *Ich bin ein unheilbarer Europäer: Briefe aus dem Exil.* Berlin: Aufbau, 2007.
———, ed. Special issue on Paul Kohner. *FilmExil* 1 (1992).
Sudendorf, Werner, and Lothar Schwab. *Sammlung Paul Kohner Agency: Inventarverzeichnis.* Berlin: Stiftung Deutsche Kinemathek, 1995.

Korda, Alexander

Kulik, Karol. *Alexander Korda: The Man Who Could Work Miracles.* New Rochelle: Arlington House, 1975.
Tabori, Paul. *Alexander Korda.* London: Oldbourne, 1959.

Korngold, Erich Wolfgang

Behlmer, Rudy. "Erich Wolfgang Korngold." *Films in Review* 18, no. 2 (1967): 86–100.

Kortner, Fritz

Asper, Helmut G. "Fritz Kortners Rückkehr und sein Film *Der Ruf*." In Asper, *Wenn wir von gestern reden*, 287–300.
Völker, Klaus. "'Aufklärung ist wichtiger als Verurteilung': Zu Fritz Kortners Film *Der Ruf*." *FilmExil* 3 (1993): 5–12.

Koster, Henry

Asper, Helmut G. "'I'm the Only Jew Who Goes Regularly to Church': Die religiösen Filme von Hermann/Henry Koster(litz)." In *Deutsch-jüdisches Exil—das Ende der Assimilation? Identitätsprobleme deutscher Juden in der Emigration*, edited by Wolfgang Benz and Marion Neiss, 115–24. Berlin: Metropol, 1994.
Asper, Helmut G., and Jan-Christopher Horak. "Three Smart Guys: How a Few Penniless German Émigrés Saved Universal Studios." *Film History* 11, no. 2 (1999): 134–53.
Henry Koster: Interviewed by Irene Kahn Atkins. A Directors Guild of America Oral History. Metuchen, N.J.: Scarecrow, 1987.
Mierendorff, Marta. "Henry Koster." In Spalek and Strelka, *Deutsche Exilliteratur seit 1933*, 771–79.

Kracauer, Siegfried

Belke, Ingrid. "Identitätsprobleme Siegfried Kracausers." In *Deutsch-jüdisches Exil: Das Ende der Assimilation?* ed. Wolfgang Benz and Marion Neiss, 45–66. Berlin: Metropol, 1994.
Gemünden, Gerd, and Johannes von Moltke, eds. *Culture in the Anteroom: The Legacies of Siegfried Kracauer*. Ann Arbor: University of Michigan Press, 2012.
Koch, Gertrud. *Siegfried Kracauer: An Introduction*. Translated by Jeremy Gaines. Princeton, NJ: Princeton University Press, 2000.
Schlüpmann, Heide. *Ein Detektiv des Kinos: Studien zu Siegfried Kracauers Filmtheorie*. Basel: Stroemfeld, 1998.
Von Moltke, Johannes, and Kristy Rawson, eds. *Siegfried Kracauer's American Writings: Essays on Film and Popular Culture*. Berkeley: University of California Press, 2012.
Witte, Karsten. "Siegfried Kracauer im Exil." *Exilforschung* 5 (1987): 135–49.

Laemmle, Carl

Bayer, Udo. *Carl Laemmle und die Universal: Eine transatlantische Biographie*. Würzburg: Königshausen, 2013.

Stanca-Mustea, Cristina. *Carl Laemmle: Der Mann, der Hollywood erfand*. Hamburg: Osburg, 2013.

Lamarr, Hedy

Barton, Ruth. *Hedy Lamarr: The Most Beautiful Woman in Film*. Lexington: University Press of Kentucky, 2010.

Brem, Richard, and Theo Ligthart, eds. *Hommage à Hedy Lamarr*. Vienna: Selene, 1999.

Körte, Peter. *Hedy Lamarr: Die stumme Sirene*. Munich: Belleville, 2000.

Kranzpiller, Peter. *Hedy Lamarr*. Bergatreute: Eppe, 1997.

Schönfelder, Bodo. "Nachruf." *epd Film* 3 (2000): 8–9.

Shearer, Michael Stephen. *Beautiful: The Life of Hedy Lamarr*. New York: St. Martin's, 2010.

Lang, Fritz

Appel, Alfred. "Fritz Lang's American Nightmare." *Film Comment* 10, no. 6 (1974): 12–17.

Armour, Robert. *Fritz Lang*. Boston: Twayne, 1977.

Bellour, Raymond. "Le regard de Haghi." *Iris* 7 (1986): 5–13.

Benson, Edward. "Décor and Decorum from *La chienne* to *Scarlet Street*: Franco-U.S. Trade in Film During the Thirties." *Film and History* 12, no. 3 (1982): 57–64.

Bergstrom, Janet. "The Mystery of *Blue Gardenia*." In *Shades of Noir*, edited by Joan Copjec, 97–120. London: Verso, 1993.

Bernstein, Matthew. "Fritz Lang, Incorporated." *Velvet Light Trap* 22 (1986): 33–52.

———. "A Tale of Three Cities: The Banning of *Scarlet Street*." *Cinema Journal* 35, no. 1 (1995): 27–52.

Bitomski, Hartmut, Harun Farocki, and Wolfgang Gersch, eds. "Fritz Lang and Bertolt Brecht." Special issue, *Filmkritik* 223 (1975).

Bogdanovich, Peter. *Fritz Lang in America*. London: Studio Vista, 1967.

Brandlmeier, Thomas. "Lang-Renoir, Renoir-Lang." *epd Film* 10 (1984): 19–22.

Bronfen, Elisabeth. "Liebe als Rückkehr zum heimlichen Leid: *Secret Beyond the Door*." In *Heimweh: Illusionsspiele in Hollywood*. Berlin: Volk und Welt, 1999. 409–464.

Burch, Noel. "Fritz Lang: German Period." Translated by Tom Milne. In Roud, *Cinema*, 583–99.

Conley, Tom. "The Law of the Letter: *Scarlet Street*." In *Film Hieroglyphs: Ruptures in Classical Cinema*. Minneapolis: University of Minnesota Press, 1991. 20–45.

Carroll, Noël. "Lang, Pabst, and Sound." *Ciné-Tracts* 2, no. 1 (1978): 15–23.
Dadoun, Roger. "*Metropolis*: Mother—City—Mittler—Hitler." *Camera Obscura* 15 (1986): 137–174.
Dimendberg, Edward. "From Berlin to Bunker Hill: Urban Space, Late Modernity, and Film Noir in Fritz Lang's and Joseph Losey's M." *Wide Angle* 19 (1997): 62–93.
Eibel, Alfred, ed. *Fritz Lang: Trois Lumières*. Paris: Flammarion, 1988.
Eisenschitz, Bernard et al. *M—le maudit un film de Fritz Lang*. Paris: Cinémathèque française, 1990.
Eisenschitz, Bernard. *Manhunt de Fritz Lang*. Paris: Editions Yellow Now, 1992.
Eisner, Lotte. *Fritz Lang*. London: Secker and Warburg, 1976.
"Fritz Lang." In Bogdanovich, *Who the Devil Made It*, 170–234.
"Fritz Lang." In Higham and Greenburg, *The Celluloid Muse*, 104–27.
Grafe, Frieda, et al. *Fritz Lang*. Munich: Hanser, 1976.
Grant, Barry Keith, ed. *Fritz Lang Interviews*. Jackson: University Press of Mississippi, 2003.
Gunning, Tom. *The Films of Fritz Lang: Allegories of Vision and Modernity*. London: BFI, 2000.
Hall, J. "'A Little Trouble with Perspective': Art and Authorship in Fritz Lang's *Scarlet Street*." *Film Criticism* 21, no. 1 (1996): 34–47.
Heinzlmeier, Adolf. *Fritz Lang*. Rastatt: Pabel, 1990.
Humphries, Reynold. *Fritz Lang: Genre and Representation in His American Films*. Baltimore: Johns Hopkins University Press, 1989.
Jacobowitz, Florence. "The Man's Melodrama: *Woman in the Window* and *Scarlet Street*." *Cineaction* 12–13 (1988): 64–73.
Jenkins, Stephen. *Fritz Lang: The Image and the Look*. London: BFI, 1971.
Jensen, Paul. *The Cinema of Fritz Lang*. New York: Barnes, 1969.
Kaes, Anton. *M*. London: BFI, 2000.
Kaplan, E. Ann. *Fritz Lang: A Research and Reference Guide*. Boston: G. K. Hall, 1980.
———. "Ideology and Cinematic Practice in Lang's *Scarlet Street* and Renoir's *La chienne*." *Wide Angle* 5, no. 3 (1983): 32–43.
———. "The Place of Women in Fritz Lang's *The Blue Gardenia*." In *Women in Film Noir*, edited by E. Ann Kaplan, 83–90. London: BFI, 1980.
Knops, Tilo. "Kino des Übergangs: Fritz Langs auktorialer Stil." *Merkur* 9–10 (1991): 838–53.
Kurman, George. "*Scarlet Street*: A 'Remake' with a Key." *Literature/Film Quarterly* 18, no. 2 (1990): 111–15.
Leblanc, Gérard, and Brigitte Devismes. *Le double scénario chez Fritz Lang*. Paris: Arman Colin, 1991.
Lehman, Peter. "Another Nothing Man: Edward G. Robinson and *Scarlet Street*." In *Running Scared: Masculinity and the Representation of the Male Body*, 85–104. Philadelphia: Temple University Press, 1993.
Levin, David. *Richard Wagner, Fritz Lang and "Die Nibelungen": The Dramaturgy of Disavowal*. Princeton, NJ: Princeton University Press, 1998.
McArthur, Colin. *The Big Heat*. London: BFI, 1992.
McGilligan, Patrick. *Fritz Lang: The Nature of the Beast*. New York: St. Martin's, 1997.
McGivern, William. *The Big Heat*. London: Simon and Schuster, 1988.

Michel, Marie. *M, le maudit, Fritz Lang Etude Critique*. Paris: Nathan, 1993.
Morrison, James. "Masscult Modernism, Modernism Masscult: Cultural Hierarchy in *Scarlet Street*." In *Passport to Hollywood: Hollywood Films, European Directors*, 109–42. Albany: State University of New York Press, 1998.
Ott, Frederick W. *The Films of Fritz Lang*. Secaucus, NJ: Citadel Press, 1979.
Pye, Douglas. "Running Out of Places: Fritz Lang's *Clash by Night*." *Cineaction* 52 (2000): 12–17.
Schnauber, Cornelius. *Fritz Lang in Hollywood*. Vienna: Europa, 1986.
Schönemann, Heide. *Fritz Lang: Filmbilder/Vorbilder*. Berlin: Hentrich, 1992.
Schütze, Larissa. *Fritz Lang im Exil: Filmkunst im Schatten der Politik*. Munich: Meidenbauer, 2006.
Smedley, Nick. "Fritz Lang Out-Foxed: The German Genius as Contract Employee." *Film History* 4, no. 4 (1990): 289–304.
———. "Fritz Lang's Trilogy: The Rise and Fall of a European Social Commentator." *Film History* 5, no. 1 (1993): 1–21.
Strack, Thomas. "Fritz Lang und das Exil: Rekonstruktionen einer Erfahrung mit dem amerikanischen Film." *Exilforschung* 13 (1995): 184–203.
Sturm, Georges. *Fritz Lang: Films/Textes/References*. Nancy: Presses universitaires de Nancy, 1990.
Tatar, Maria. *Lustmord: Sexual Murder in Weimar Germany*. Princeton, NJ: Princeton University Press, 1995.
Töteberg, Michael. *Fritz Lang*. Reinbek: Rowohlt, 1985.
Waldman, Diane. "The Childish, the Insane, and the Ugly: The Representation of Modern Art in Popular Films and Fiction of the Forties." *Wide Angle* 5, no. 2 (1982): 52–65.
Welsche, Tricia. "Sound Strategies: Lang's Rearticulation of Renoir." *Cinema Journal* 39, no. 3 (2000): 51–65.
Werner, Gösta. "Fritz Lang and Goebbels: Myths and Facts." *Film Quarterly* 43, no. 3 (1990): 24–27.
Wood, Robin. "Fritz Lang: 1936–1960." In Roud, *Cinema*, 599–609.
———. "Lang and Brecht." *Cineaction* 52 (2000): 4–11.

Lederer, Francis

Omasta, Michael. "Nachruf." *epd Film* 7 (2000): 8–9.

Lorre, Peter

Beyer, Friedemann. *Peter Lorre: Seine Filme, sein Leben*. Munich: Heyne, 1988.
Döge, Ulrich. "Deutschland—Psychopathenland: *Berlin-Alexanderplatz* und *Der Verlorene* als Roman und Film." In *Alliierte für den Film: Arnold Pressburger, Gregor Rabinowitsch und die Cine-Allianz*, edited by Jan Distelmeyer, 130–40. Munich: Text + Kritik, 2004.
Dyer, Peter John. "Fugitive from Murder." *Sight and Sound* 33 (1964): 125–27.

Farin, Michael, and Hans Schmid, eds. *Peter Lorre: Der Verlorene*. Munich: Belleville, 1996.

Gemünden, Gerd. "From 'Mr. M' to 'Mr. Murder': Peter Lorre and the Actor in Exile." In *Light Motives: German Popular Film in Perspective*, edited by Randall Halle and Margaret McCarthy, 85–107. Detroit: Wayne State University Press, 2003.

Hoffmann, Felix, and Stephen D. Youngkin. *Peter Lorre: Portrait des Schauspielers auf der Flucht*. Munich: Belleville, 1998.

Koepnick, Lutz. "*Mad Love*: Re-membering Berlin in Hollywood Exile." In *Caught by Politics: Hitler Exiles and American Visual Culture*, edited by Sabine Eckmann and Lutz Koepnick, 195–222. New York: Palgrave, 2007.

Omasta, Michael, Brigitte Mayr, and Elisabeth Streit, eds. *Peter Lorre: Ein Fremder im Paradies*. Vienna: Zsolnay, 2004.

Sennett, Ted. *Masters of Menace: Greenstreet and Lorre*. New York: Dutton, 1979.

Svehla, Gary J., and Susan Svehla. *Peter Lorre*. Baltimore: Midnight Marquee, 1999.

Thomas, Sarah. *Peter Lorre: Face Maker: Stardom and Performance Between Hollywood and Europe*. New York: Berghahn, 2012.

Youngkin, Stephen D. *The Lost One: A Life of Peter Lorre*. Lexington: University Press of Kentucky, 2005.

Youngkin, Stephen D., James Bigwood, and Raymond G. Cabana Jr. *The Films of Peter Lorre*. Secaucus, NJ: Citadel Press, 1982.

Lubitsch, Ernst

Binh, N. T., and Christian Viviani. *Lubitsch*. Paris: Rivages, 1991.

Bowman, Barbara. *Master Space: Film Images of Capra, Lubitsch, Sternberg, and Wyler*. New York: Greenwood, 1992.

Braudy, Leo. "The Double Detachment of Ernst Lubitsch." *MLN* 98, no. 5 (1983): 1071–84.

Carringer, Robert, and Barry Sabath. *Ernst Lubitsch: A Guide to References and Resources*. Boston: G. K. Hall, 1978.

Eisenschitz, Bernard. *Lubitsch*. Paris: Anthologie du cinéma, 1968.

Eisenschitz, Bernard, and Jean Narboni. *Ernst Lubitsch*. Paris: Cinémathèque française, 2006.

Eyman, Scott. *Ernst Lubitsch: Laughter in Paradise*. New York: Simon and Schuster, 1993.

Fink, Guido. "Essere e non essere: La parola e i suoi codici." In *Il doppiaggio: Trasposizioni linguistiche e culturali*, edited by Raffaella Baccolini et al., 29–39. Bologna: Cooperativa Lib. Univ., edited by Bologna, 1994.

———. *Lubitsch*. Firenze: La nuova Italia, 1977.

Hake, Sabine. *Passions and Deceptions: The Early Films of Ernst Lubitsch*. Princeton, NJ: Princeton University Press, 1992.

Hall, Kenneth E. "Von Sternberg, Lubitsch, and Lang in the Work of Manuel Puig." *Literature/Film Quarterly* 22, no. 3 (1994): 181–86.

Hanisch, Michael. *Ein Junge aus der Schönhauser. Auf den Spuren der Filmgeschichte: Berliner Schauplätze*, 256–331. Berlin: Henschel, 1991.

Henry, Nora. *Ethics and Social Criticism in the Hollywood Films of Erich von Stroheim, Ernst Lubitsch and Billy Wilder*. Westport, CT: Praeger, 2001.

Horak, Jan-Christopher. *Ernst Lubitsch and the Rise of Ufa, 1917–1922*. Master's thesis, Boston University, 1975.

———. "The Pre-Hollywood Lubitsch." *Image* 18, no. 4 (1975): 19–29.

Kasten, Jürgen. "Der Stolz der deutschen Filmkomödie: Die frühen Filme von Ernst Lubitsch, 1914–1918." In *Mediengeschichte des Films*, Vol. 2, edited by Corinna Müller and Harro Segeberg, 301–32. Munich: Fink, 1998.

Macksey, Richard. "Four Émigré Directors: Shadows of Careers." *MLN* 98, no. 5 (1983): 1187–96.

Mills, Robert Wilson. *The American Films of Ernst Lubitsch: A Critical History*. PhD diss., University of Michigan, Ann Arbor, 1976.

Nacache, Jacqueline. *Lubitsch*. Paris: Edilig, 1987.

Patalas, Enno. "Ernst Lubitsch." In Roud, *Cinema*, 639–43.

Paul, William. *Ernst Lubitsch's American Comedy*. New York: Columbia University Press, 1983.

Poague, Leland. *The Cinema of Ernst Lubitsch*. New York: Bobbs-Merrill, 1978.

Pratt, David B. "'O Lubitsch, Where Wert Thou?': *Passion*, the German Invasion and the Emergence of the Name 'Lubitsch.'" *Wide Angle* 13, no. 1 (1991): 34–70.

Prinzler, Hans Helmut, and Enno Patalas, eds. *Lubitsch*. Munich: Bucher, 1984.

Raphaelson, Samson. "Freundschaft." *New Yorker*, May 11, 1981, 38–66.

Renk, Herta-Elisabeth. *Ernst Lubitsch*. Reinbek: Rowohlt, 1992.

Rosenberg, Joel. "Shylock's Revenge: The Doubly Vanished Jew in Ernst Lubitsch's *To Be or Not to Be*." *Prooftexts: A Journal of Jewish Literary History* 16, no. 3 (1996): 209–44.

Sarris, Andrew. "Ernst Lubitsch." In Roud, *Cinema*, 643–50.

Schmidt, Christoph. "'Gejagte Vorgänge voll Pracht und Nacktheit': Eine unbekannte kinematographische Quelle zu Thomas Manns Roman *Der Zauberberg*." *Wirkendes Wort* 38, no. 1 (1988): 1–5.

Sipiere, Dominique. "Ernst Lubitsch et la crise du sérieux." *La licorne* 36 (1996): 127–38.

———. "Quel usage Lubitsch fait-il de l'illisibilité des sentiments?" *La licorne* 37 (1996): 93–103.

Spaich, Herbert. *Ernst Lubitsch und seine Filme*. Munich: Heyne, 1992.

Thompson, Kristin. *Herr Lubitsch Goes to Hollywood: German and American Film After World War I*. Amsterdam: Amsterdam University Press, 2005.

Tifft, Stephen. "Miming the Führer: *To Be or Not to Be* and the Mechanisms of Outrage." *Yale Journal of Criticism* 5, no. 1 (1991): 1–40.

Warner, Marina. "Women against Women in the Old Wives' Tale." In *Cinema and the Realms of Enchantment: Lectures, Seminars and Essays by Marina Warner and Others*, edited by Duncan Petrie, 63–84. London: BFI, 1993.

Weinberg, Herman. *The Lubitsch Touch*. New York: Doubleday, 1964.

Wood, Stephen Holmes. *Ernst Lubitsch: A Continental Dreamer Out of His Time*. PhD diss., University of Southern California, 1977.

Ophüls, Max

Annenkov, Georges. *Max Ophüls*. Paris: Le terrain vague, 1962.
Archer, Eugene. "Ophuls and the Romantic Tradition." *Yale French Studies* 17 (1956): 3–5.
Asper, Helmut G. "Max Ophüls gegen Hitler." *Exilforschung* 3 (1985): 173–82.
———. *Max Ophüls: Eine Biographie*. Berlin: Bertz, 1998.
Bacher, Lutz. "Max Ophuls: Hollywood Screenwriter." In Asper, *Wenn wir von gestern reden*, 207–15.
———. *Max Ophuls in the Hollywood Studios*. New Brunswick, NJ: Rutgers University Press, 1996.
Beylie, Claude. *Max Ophüls*. Paris: Seghers, 1963.
Durgnat, Raymond. "Midnight Sun." *Films and Filming* 8, no. 8 (1962): 21–23.
Eichsfelder, Ben. "Kosmopolit der Leinwand." *Filmforum* 3, no. 3 (1953): 5–6.
Jacobsen, Wolfgang, and Heike Klapdor, eds. Special issue on Max Ophüls. *FilmExil* 2 (1993).
Koch, Gertrud. "Die masochistische Lust am Verkennen: Zur Rolle der Hörwelt in *Letter from an Unknown Woman*." In *Was ich erbeute sind Bilder: Zum Diskurs der Geschlechter im Film*, 77–82. Basel: Stroemfeld, 1989.
Loewy, Ronny, ed. "Max Ophüls." Special issue, *Filmkonzepte* 24. Munich: Text + Kritik, 2011.
Müller, Martina. "Vom Souffleurkasten über das Mikro auf die Leinwand: Max Ophüls." *Frauen und Film* 42 (1987): 60–71.
Perkins, V. F. "'Same Tune Again!': Repetition and Framing in *Letter from an Unknown Woman*." *Cineaction* 52 (2000): 40–48.
White, Susan. *The Cinema of Max Ophuls: Magisterial Vision and the Figure of Woman*. New York: Columbia University Press, 1995.
Willemen, Paul, ed. *Ophuls*. London: BFI, 1978.

Oswald, Richard

Belach, Helga, and Wolfgang Jacobsen, eds. *Richard Oswald: Regisseur und Produzent*. Munich: Text + Kritik, 1990.
Jäger, Klaus. "Marginalien zur Person und zum Werk Richard Oswalds." *Kirche und Film* 9 (1983): 51–56.
Kaul, Walter, and Robert G. Scheuer. *Richard Oswald*. Berlin: Stiftung Deutsche Kinemathek, 1970.

Pabst, G. W.

Amengual, Bathélemy. *Georg Wilhelm Pabst*. Paris: Seghers, 1966.
Atwell, Lee. *G. W. Pabst*. Boston: Twayne, 1977.
Carroll, Noël. "Lang, Pabst, and Sound." *Ciné-Tracts* 2, no. 1 (1978): 15–23.
Cozarinsky, Edgardo. "G. W. Pabst." In Roud, *Cinema*, 752–61.
Jacobsen, Wolfgang, ed. *G. W. Pabst*. Berlin: Argon, 1997.
Joseph, Rudolph. "Filmarbeit mit G. W. Pabst in Paris." In Asper, *Wenn wir von gestern reden*, 105–17.
Kappelhoff, Hermann. *Der möblierte Mensch: Georg Wilhelm Pabst und die Utopie der Sachlichkeit*. Berlin: Vorwerk 8, 1994.
Rentschler, Eric, ed. *The Films of G. W. Pabst: An Extraterritorial Cinema*. New Brunswick, NJ: Rutgers University Press, 1990.

Pasternak, Joe

Asper, Helmut G. "Nachruf." *epd Film* 1 (1992): 2–3.
Asper, Helmut G., and Jan-Christopher Horak. "Three Smart Guys: How a Few Penniless German Émigrés Saved Universal Studios." *Film History* 11, no. 2 (1999): 134–153.

Pommer, Erich

Hardt, Ursula. *From Caligari to California: Erich Pommer's Life in the International Film Wars*. Oxford: Berghahn, 1996.
Jacobsen, Wolfgang. *Erich Pommer*. Berlin: Argon, 1989.

Preminger, Otto

Archer, Eugene. "Why Preminger?" *Movie* 2 (1962): 11–30.
Brandlmeier, Thomas. "Otto Preminger: Annäherungen an einen Verkannten." *epd Film* 2 (1999): 16–23.
Frischauer, Willi. *Behind the Scenes of Otto Preminger*. New York: William Morrow, 1974.
Fujiwara, Chris. *The World and Its Double: The Life and Work of Otto Preminger*. New York: Faber and Faber, 2008.
Grob, Norbert. "Nachruf." *epd Film* 6 (1986): 4–5.
Grob, Norbert, Rolf Aurich, and Wolfgang Jacobsen, eds. *Otto Preminger*. Berlin: Jovis, 1999.
Hirsch, Foster. *Otto Preminger: The Man Who Would Be King*. New York: Knopf, 2007.
"Otto Preminger." In Bogdanovich, *Who the Devil Made It*, 605–39.
Pratley, Gerald. *The Cinema of Otto Preminger*. New York: Castle, 1971.

Preminger, Otto. *An Autobiography*. New York: Doubleday, 1977.
Rosenbaum, Jonathan. "Otto Preminger." In Roud, *Cinema*, 794–99.

Rainer, Luise

Bronner, Edwin. "Luise Rainer." *Films in Review* 6, no. 8 (1955): 390–93.
Kernan, Michael, "The Return of Luise Rainer." *International Herald Tribune*, April 21, 1982, 12.

Reinhardt, Gottfried

Roth, Wilhelm. "Nachruf." *epd Film* 9 (194): 11.
Sudendorf, Werner. "'Ich wollte nach Europa, nicht Deutschland': Zu Gottfried Reinhardts Film *Stadt ohne Mitleid*." *FilmExil* 3 (1993): 39–42.

Reinhardt, Max

Dieterle, William. "Max Reinhardt in Hollywood." In *Max Reinhardt, 1873–1973: A Centennial*. Binghamton, NY: Max Reinhardt Archive, 1973.
Führich-Leisler, Edda, and Gisela Prossnitz. *Max Reinhardt in Amerika*. Salzburg: Otto Müller, 1976.
Harris, Edward. "Max Reinhardt." In Spalek and Strelka, *Deutsche Exilliteratur seit 1933*, 789–800.
Jahnke, Eckart. "Max Reinhardt und der Film." *Prisma, Kino- und Fernsehalmanach* 4 (1973): 255–65.
Max Reinhardt, 1873–1973: A Centennial. Binghamton, NY: Max Reinhardt Archive, 1973.

Richter, Hans

Benson, Timothy O. *Hans Richter: Encounters*. Los Angeles: DelMonico, 2013.

Schünzel, Reinhold

Omasta, Michael. "Nachruf." *epd Film* 9 (1994): 11–12.
Schöning, Jörg. *Reinhold Schünzel: Schauspieler und Regisseur*. Munich: Text + Kritik, 1989.

Siodmak, Curt

Miles, David. "Curt Siodmak." In Spalek and Strelka, *Deutsche Exilliteratur seit 1933*, 811–19.
Siodmak, Curt. "Epistles to the Germans." *Story Magazine* 32, no. 128 (1948): 94–116.
Jacobsen, Wolfgang, and Hans Helmut Prinzler, eds. *Siodmak Bros.: Berlin-Paris-London-Hollywood*. Berlin: Argon, 1998.

Siodmak, Robert

Alpi, Deborah Lazaroff. *Robert Siodmak: A Biography*. Jefferson, NC: McFarland, 1998.
Dumont, Hervé. *Robert Siodmak: Le maître du film noir*. Lausanne: L'Age d'homme, 1981.
Heins, Laura. "Criss-Crossings of Robert Siodmak: The Time and Space of Cinematic Exile." In *Exiles Traveling Exploring Displacement: Crossing Boundaries in German Exile Arts and Writings, 1933–1945*, edited by Johannes F. Evelein, 201–22. Amsterdam: Rodopi, 2009.
Jacobsen, Wolfgang, and Hans Helmut Prinzler, eds. *Siodmak Bros.: Berlin-Paris-London-Hollywood*. Berlin: Argon, 1998.
Masson, Alain. "Des genres creux, du clinquant, du simili." *Positif* 259 (1982): 32–37.
Sannwald, Daniela. "Von Schatten und Ratten: Robert Siodmaks Neuanfänge in Hollywood und in der Bundesrepublik." *FilmExil* 3 (1993): 33–38.
Taylor, John Russell. "Robert Siodmak." In Roud, *Cinema*, 924.

Sirk, Douglas

Ascheid, Antje. "A Sierckian Double Image: The Narration of Zarah Leander as a National Socialist Star." *Film Criticism* 23, no. 2–3 (1999): 46–73.
Babington, Bruce. "Written by the Wind: Sierck/Sirk's *La Habanera* (1937)." *Forum for Modern Language Studies* 31, no. 1 (1995): 24–36.
Basinger, Jeanine, ed. *Douglas Sirk: The Complete American Period*. Mansfield: University of Connecticut Film Society, 1974.
Bourget, Jean-Loup. *Douglas Sirk*. Paris: Edilig, 1984.
Bronfen, Elisabeth. "Zwischen Heimat und Fremde: *Las Habanera* (Detlef Sierck) und *Imitation of Life* (Douglas Sirk)." In *Heimweh: Illusionsspiele in Hollywood*. Berlin: Volk und Welt, 1999. 245–326.
Butler, Judith. "Lana's 'Imitation': Melodramatic Repetition and the Gender Performative." *Genders* 9 (1990): 1–18.
Elsaesser, Thomas. "Tales of Sound and Fury: Observations on the Family Melodrama." *Monogram* 4 (1972): 2–15.

Fassbinder, Rainer Werner. "Imitation of Life: On the Films of Douglas Sirk." Translated by Krishna Winston. In *The Anarchy of the Imagination*, edited by Michael Töteberg and Leo A. Lensing, 77–89. Baltimore: Johns Hopkins University Press, 1992.

Feil, Ken. "Ambiguous Sirk-Camp-Stance: Gay Camp and the 1950s Melodramas of Douglas Sirk." *Spectator* 15, no. 1 (1994): 31–49.

Fischer, Lucy, ed. *Imitation of Life*. New Brunswick, NJ: Rutgers University Press, 1991.

———. "Lifestyles of the Rich and Famous: *Imitation of Life*." *Post Script* 10, no. 2 (1991): 5–13.

———. "Sirk and the Figure of the Actress: *All I Desire*." *Film Criticism* 23, no. 2–3 (1999): 136–49.

Flitterman-Lewis, Sandy. "Imitation(s) of Life: The Black Woman's Double Determination as Troubling 'Other.'" *Literature and Psychology* 34, no. 4 (1988): 44–57.

Gallagher, Tag. "Douglas Sirk: White Melodrama." *Film Comment* 34 (1998): 16–27.

Gemünden, Gerd, ed. Special issue on Detlef Sierck / Douglas Sirk. *Film Criticism* 23, no. 2–3 (1999).

Godard, Jean-Luc. "Des larmes et de la vitesse." *Cahiers du cinéma* 94 (1959): 51–54. Repr. as "Tears and Speed." Trans. Susan Bennett. *Screen* 12, no. 2 (1971): 95–98.

Grosz, Dave. "*The First Legion*: Vision and Perception in Sirk." *Screen* 12, no. 2 (1971): 99–117.

Hake, Sabine. "The Melodramatic Imagination of Detlef Sierck: *Final Chord* and Its Resonances." *Screen* 38, no. 2 (1997): 129–48.

Halliday, Jon. "Notes on Sirk's German Films." *Screen* 12, no. 2 (1971): 8–13.

———. *Sirk on Sirk: Conversations with Jon Halliday*. New and rev. ed. Boston: Faber and Faber, 1997.

Haralovich, Mary Beth. "*All that Heaven Allows*: Color, Narrative Space, and Melodrama." In *Close Viewings: An Anthology of New Film Criticism*, edited by Peter Lehman, 57–72. Tallahassee: Florida State University Press, 1990.

Horak, Jan-Christopher. "Sirk's Early Exile Films: *Boefje* and *Hitler's Madman*." *Film Criticism* 23, no. 2–3 (1999): 122–35.

Klinger, Barbara. *Melodrama and Meaning: History, Culture, and the Films of Douglas Sirk*. Bloomington: Indiana University Press, 1994.

Koch, Gertrud. "From Detlef Sierck to Douglas Sirk." Translated by Gerd Gemünden. *Film Criticism* 23, no. 2–3 (1999): 14–32.

Koepnick, Lutz. "En-gendering Mass Culture: The Case of Zarah Leander." *Gender and Germanness: Cultural Productions of Nation*, edited by Patricia Herminghouse and Magda Mueller, 161–75. Providence, RI: Berghahn, 1997.

———. "Sirk and the Culture Industry: *Zu neuen Ufern* and *The First Legion*." *Film Criticism* 23, no. 2–3 (1999): 94–121.

Kuzniar, Alice. "Zarah Leander and Transgender Specularity." *Film Criticism* 23, no. 2–3 (1999): 74–93.

Läufer, Elisabeth. *Skeptiker des Lichts: Douglas Sirk und seine Filme*. Frankfurt am Main: Fischer, 1987.

Lawrence, Amy. "Trapped in a Tomb of Their Own Making: Max Ophul's *The Reckless Moment* and Douglas Sirk's *There's Always Tomorrow*." *Film Criticism* 23, no. 2–3 (1999): 150–66.

Mayr, Brigitte. "Glaube, Liebe, Hoffnung: *Shookproof* von Douglas Sirk (1949)." In *Schatten. Exil: Europäische Emigranten im Film noir*, edited by Christian Cargnelli and Michael Omasta, 289–95. Vienna: PVS, 1997.

Mulvey, Laura. "Fassbinder and Sirk." In *Visual and Other Pleasures*, 45–48. Bloomington: Indiana University Press, 1989.

———. "Notes on Sirk and Melodrama." *Movie* 25 (1977–78): 53–56.

———. "Social Hieroglyphics: Reflections on Two Films by Douglas Sirk." In *Fetishism and Curiosity*, 29–39. London: BFI, 1996.

Mulvey, Laura, and Jon Halliday, eds. *Douglas Sirk*. Edinburgh: Edinburgh Film Festival, 1972.

Rentschler, Eric. *The Ministry of Illusion: Nazi Cinema and Its Afterlife*. Cambridge, MA: Harvard University Press, 1996.

Rosenbaum, Jonathan. "Sirk's Works." *Soho Weekly News*, August 27, 1980, 40.

Stern, Michael. *Douglas Sirk*. Boston: Twayne, 1979.

Trumpener, Katie. "The René Clair Moment and the Overlap Films of the 1930s: Detlef Sierck's *April, April*." *Film Criticism* 23, no. 2–3 (1999): 33–45.

Willemen, Paul. "Distanciation and Douglas Sirk." *Screen* 12, no. 2 (1971): 63–67.

———. "Towards an Analysis of the Sirkian System." *Screen* 13, no. 4 (1972–73): 128–34.

Ulmer, Edgar G.

Belton, John. "Edgar G. Ulmer: A Reassessment." In *Cinema Stylists*, 146–56. Metuchen, NJ: Scarecrow, 1983.

"Edgar G. Ulmer." In Bogdanovich, *Who the Devil Made It*, 558–604.

Eisenschitz, Bernard, and Jean-Claude Romer, "Entretien avec Edgar G. Ulmer." *Midi-minuit fantastique* 13 (1965): 1–14.

Gallagher, Tag. "All Lost in Wonder: Edgar G. Ulmer." *Screening the Past* (March 2001): http://tlweb.latrobe.edu.au/humanities/screeningthepast/firstrelease/fr0301/tgafr12a.htm.

Grissemann, Stefan. *Mann im Schatten: Der Filmemacher Edgar G. Ulmer*. Vienna: Paul Zsolnay, 2003.

Herzogenrath, Bernd, ed. *Edgar G. Ulmer: Essays on the King of the B's*. Jefferson, NC: McFarland, 2009.

———, ed. *The Films of Edgar G. Ulmer*. Lanham, MD: Scarecrow, 2009.

Isenberg, Noah. *Detour*. London: BFI, 2008.

———. *Edgar G. Ulmer: A Filmmaker at the Margins*. Berkeley: University of California Press, 2014.

———. "Perennial *Detour*: The Cinema of Edgar G. Ulmer and the Experience of Exile." *Cinema Journal* 43, no. 2 (2004): 3–24.

Mandell, Paul. "Edgar Ulmer and *The Black Cat.*" *American Cinematographer*, Oct. 1984, 34–47.
Mank, Gregory William. *Karloff and Lugosi: The Story of a Haunting Collaboration.* Jefferson, NC: McFarland, 1990.
Rhodes, Gary D. *Edgar G. Ulmer: Detour on Poverty Row.* Lanham, MD: Lexington Books, 2008.
Tatum, Charles, ed. *Edgar G. Ulmer: Le bandit démasqué.* Paris: Yellow Now, 2002.

Veit, Conrad

Allen, Jerry C. *Conrad Veidt: From "Caligari" to "Casablanca."* Pacific Grove, CA: Boxwood, 1993.
Gemünden, Gerd. "Allegories of Displacement." In *Destination London: German-Speaking Émigrés and British Cinema, 1925–1950*, edited by Tim Bergfelder and Christian Cargnelli, 142–54. London: Berghahn, 2008.
Freund, Rudolf. "Ein diesseitiger Dämon: Der Schauspieler Conrad Veidt." *Prisma: Kino- und Fernsehalmanach* 4 (1973): 266–277.
Jacobsen, Wolfgang, ed. *Conrad Veidt: Lebensbilder.* Berlin: Argon, 1993.
Sannwald, Daniela. "Continental Stranger: Conrad Veidt und seine britischen Filme." In Schöning, *London Calling*, 89–97.

Viertel, Salka

Bilski, Emily D., and Emily Brown. "The Salon in Exile." In *Jewish Women and Their Salons*, edited by Emily D. Bilski and Emily Brown, 138–47. New Haven, CT: Yale University Press, 2005.
Lentz, Michael. "Nachwort." In Salka Viertel, *Das unbelehrbare Herz: Erinnerungen an ein Leben mit Künstlern des 20. Jahrhunderts.* Translated by Helmut Degner. Frankfurt am Main: Die andere Bibliothek, 2011.
Prager, Katharina. *"Ich bin nicht gone Hollywood!": Salka Viertel, ein Leben in Theater und Film.* Vienna: Braumüller, 2007.
Steiner, Marion. *Schauspielerinnen im Exil (1930): Vier exemplarische Lebensläufe. Therese Giehse, Lilli Palmer, Salka Viertel, Helene Weigel.* Saarbrücken: VDM, 2008.

Waxman, Franz

Cook, Page. "Franz Waxmann [sic]." *Films in Review* 19, no. 7 (1968): 415–30.

Wilder, Billy

Aurich, Rolf, Andreas Hutter, Wolfgang Jacobsen, and Günter Krenn, eds. *"Billie": Billy Wilders Wiener jounalistische Arbeiten*. Vienna: Filmarchiv Austria, 2006.
"Billy Wilder." In Higham and Greenburg, *The Celluloid Muse*, 244–53.
Crowe, Cameron. *Conversations with Wilder*. New York: Alfred Knopf, 1999.
Dick, Bernhard F. *Billy Wilder*. Boston: Twayne, 1980.
Gemünden, Gerd. *A Foreign Affair: Billy Wilder's American Films*. New York: Berghahn, 2008.
Hutter, Andreas, and Klaus Kamolz. *Billie Wilder: Eine europäische Karriere*. Vienna: Böhlau, 1998.
Karasek, Hellmuth. *Billy Wilder*. Hamburg: Hoffmann und Campe, 1992.
Kraus, Joseph. "Billy Wilder." In Spalek and Strelka, *Deutsche Exilliteratur seit 1933*, 820–26.
Lally, Kevin. *Wilder Times*. New York: Henry Holt, 1996.
Madsen, Axel. *Billy Wilder*. Bloomington: Indiana University Press, 1969.
Millar, Gavin. "Billy Wilder." In Roud, *Cinema*, 1081–87.
Naumann, Michaela. *Billy Wilder, hinter der Maske der Komödie: Der kritische Umgang mit dem kulturellen Selbstverständnis amerikanischer Identität*. Marburg: Schüren, 2011.
Phillips, Gene. *Some Like It Wilder: The Life and Controversial Films of Billy Wilder*. Lexington: University Press of Kentucky, 2010.
Schickel, Richard. *Double Indemnity*. London: BFI, 1992.
Seidman, Steve. *The Film Career of Billy Wilder*. Boston: G. K. Hall, 1977.
Sikov, Ed. *On Sunset Boulevard: The Life and Times of Billy Wilder*. New York: Hyperion, 1998.
Sinyard, Neil, and Adrian Turner. *Billy Wilders Filme*. Berlin: Volker Spiess, 1980.
Wilder, Billy. *Der Prinz von Wales geht auf Urlaub: Berliner Reportagen, Feuilletons und Kritiken der zwanziger Jahre*, edited by Klaus Siebenhaar. Berlin: Fannei & Walz, 1996.
———. *Double Indemnity*. Berkeley: University of California Press, 2000.
———. *The Lost Weekend*. Berkeley: University of California Press, 2000.
———. *Stalag 17*. Berkeley: University of California Press, 1999.
———. *Sunset Boulevard*. Berkeley: University of California Press, 1999.
Wilder, Billy, and I. A. L. Diamond. *The Apartment*. Boston: Faber and Faber, 1998.
Wood, Tom. *The Bright Side of Billy Wilder, Primarily*. Garden City, NY: Doubleday, 1970.
Zolotow, Maurice. *Billy Wilder in Hollywood*. New York: Limelight, 1977.

Zinnemann, Fred

Goldau, Antje, Hans Helmut Prinzler, and Neil Sinyard. *Zinnemann*. Munich: Filmland Presse, 1986.

Hart, Henry. "Zinnemann on the Verge." *Films in Review* 4, no. 2 (1953): 80–81.

Horak, Jan-Christopher. "The Other Germany in Fred Zinnemann's *The Seventh Cross*." In *German Film and Literature: Adaptations and Transformations*, edited by Eric Rentschler, 117–31. New York: Methuen, 1986.

Knight, Arthur. "Fred Zinnemann." *Films in Review* 2, no. 1 (1951): 21–24.

Luecken, Verena. "Kämpfen in aussichtslosen Situationen: Interview mit Fred Zinnemann." *epd Film* 9 (1992): 12–19.

Miller, Gabriel, ed. *Fred Zinnemann: Interviews*. Jackson: University Press of Mississippi, 2005.

Nolletti, Arthur, ed. *The Films of Fred Zinnemann: Critical Perspectives*. Albany: State University of New York Press, 1999.

Sinyard, Neil. *Fred Zinnemann: Films of Character and Conscience*. Jefferson, NC: McFarland, 2003.

Smyth, J. E. "Fred Zinnemann's *Search* (1945–48): Reconstructing the Voices of Europe's Children." *Film History* 23, no. 1 (2011): 75–92.

Stephan, Alexander. "Anna Seghers' *The Seventh Cross*: Ein Exilroman über Nazideutschland als Hollywood-Film." *Exilforschung* 6 (1988): 214–29.

INDEX

"abnormal" sexuality, 121
Act of Clemency, 180
Act of Violence (film): about, 18, 160–61, 220*n*25; Bunker Hill sequence in, 148, 178–79; cast and characters in, 134, 134*f*, 138, 143, 144–53, 157–58, 160, 178–79, 220*n*27; cinematography in, 149; noir features in, 135–36, 157; plot of, 136–37, 143–44; reviews of, 144, 153–54; score in, 136, 145; sequences in, 133–38, 145–53; subject matter of, 142, 144–45, 159; use of train tracks in, 172
Adelson, Leslie, 197*n*29
Adenauer, Konrad, 180
Adorno, Theodor W.: *Composing for the Films,* 119; on exile, 192; on *The Great Dictator,* 101; on his "damaged life," 8; on Kracauer, 72–73; *Minima Moralia,* 152–53, 192
Die Affäre Dreyfus (play), 69
Albrecht, Donald, 33–34
Alison, Joan, 2–3, 34, 201*n*47
All Quiet on the Western Front (film), 47, 139–40
All Through the Night (film), 115, 123
The American Cinema (Sarris), 140
American Film Script database, 220*n*30
American isolationism, 79, 80
amnesia, used in postwar noir, 156, 158
Die andere Seite (film), 46–48
Anders, Rudolf, 121
Anna Boleyn (film), 53
Anschluss of Austria, 78
anti-illusionism, 124

anti-Nazi films, 17, 114–16, 125–28, 212n37
Anti-Nazi League, 77–78, 208–209n4
anti-Semitism, 79–80, 112, 212n49
Appadurai, Arjun, 192
Arbeitsjournal (Brecht), 109, 113
Arise, My Love (film), 116
Arliss, George, 66
Arnheim, Rudolf, 77
Arsenic and Old Lace (film), 181
"Ärztefilm" (doctor film), 181
Asper, Helmut G., 11, 194n7, 196n27
Astor, Mary, 149
Auerbach, Jonathan, 144
auteurism, 26–27, 140
authenticity, 57–58, 81

Bach, Johann Sebastian, 37
Bahr, Ehrhard, 4, 13
Bassermann, Albert, 70
The Battle of Russia (film), 115
Baum, Vicki, 7–8, 116, 173
Beethoven, Ludwig van, 37
Behold a Pale Horse (film), 142
Beim nächsten Kuss knall ich ihn nieder (film), 190–91
Belton, John, 26, 156, 159
Bendix, William, 155
Benjamin, Walter, 72–73, 208n71
Benny, Jack, 91
Berger, Ludwig, 6
Bergfelder, Tim, 176
Bergman, Ingrid, 2
Berlin Air Lift, 159
Berlin Film Festival, 228n4
Bernhardt, Curtis, 188
Bessie, Alvah, 174
The Best Years of Our Lives (film), 154–55, 156
Beyond the Boundary (Ulmer), 29
Bick, Sally, 117
The Big Parade (film), 47
Billy, How Did You Do It? (TV documentary), 190

"Biographies in Popular Magazines" (Löwenthal), 50
"The Biography as an Art Form of the New Bourgeoisie" (Kracauer), 48
biopics: comparing fiction and historical truth in, 55; of Dieterle, 61–62, 64; as a genre, 49, 52–62; growing popularity of, 71–72; historical research in, 53–54; narratives of, 65; use of actors/actresses in, 60; Warner Bros. on, 49–50
bio-picture. *See* biopics
Bitomsky, Hartmut, 216n42
The Black Cat (film): about, 17, 24; as auteurist work, 27; Black Mass, 44f; budget for, 26; cast and characters in, 25–26, 32–43, 33f, 35f, 40f, 44f, 45–46, 201n47; conflict in, 45; Hollywood view of, 38–39; horror in, 171; modernism in, 35–36; plot in, 25; presenting a fictional history of World War I, 42; production quality in, 25–26; score in, 36–37; sequences in, 39–41; set design in, 32, 34; settings in, 43, 45
"The Black Cat" (Poe), 32
Black Fury (film), 51
blacklisting, 126, 127, 186, 187
Blanke, Henry, 49, 62, 203n9
Bloch, Ernst, 208n71
Blockade (film), 77, 127–28
Bluebeard (film), 37
The Blue Dahlia (film), 155, 156
Blumenberg, Hans-Christopher, 190–91
Bogart, Humphrey, 1–2, 115, 123, 155, 156
Bogdanovich, Peter, 24, 26–28, 41–42, 121, 191, 202n51, 216n43
Bois, Curt, 21, 185
Boomerang (film), 154–55
Borde, Raymond, 132
Brahms, Johannes, 36
Brandlmeier, Thomas, 225n34
Brando, Marlon, 141, 142
Braudy, Leo, 61

Braun, Harald, 186
Brauner, Artur, 187, 227n58
Brecht, Bertolt: *Arbeitsjournal,* 109, 113; aversion to Hollywood of, 110–111; background of, 110–112; belief in two Germanies of, 184; collaboration with Lang, 112–14; collaboration with Viertel, 111; on Dieterle, 65, 203n15; on Heydrich's death, 103, 213n4; during HUAC hearings, 127; *Kuhle Wampe,* 111; left United States for Paris, 127; tension between Lang and, 109; "To the Actor P.L. in Exile," 185. *See also Hangmen Also Die* (film)
Breen, Joseph, 66–67, 71
Brennan, Walter, 108
Bressart, Felix, 90, 210n29
Broken Lullaby (film), 47, 95
Browning, Tod, 31
Bundesfilmpreis Awards, 180
Bunker Hill, 148–49, 150f, 178–79, 220n33
Burnett, Murray, 2–3

The Cabinet of Dr. Caligari (film), 27–28, 30, 34, 47, 199n20
Cain, James M., 139–40, 148
California Community Redevelopment Act (1945), 148
Cantor, Eddie, 78
Capra, Frank, 115
Carradine, John, 37, 107
Casablanca (film), 1–4, 57, 123, 132, 181
Castle, Shirley, 26
The Castle of Otranto (film), 32
The Cat and the Canary (film), 30
censorship, 31, 96–98
Chandler, Raymond, 148–49
Chaney, Lon, 30–31
Chaplin, Charlie, 80, 86f, 88, 90, 100, 116, 213n50
Charell, Erik, 188
Charha-Gesellschaft, 50–51

Chaumeton, Etienne, 132
Chopin, Frédéric, 37
Clift, Montgomery, 142
Cloak and Dagger (film), 115
Cold War, 144, 158, 159, 185
Cole, Lester, 107–108
Comolli, Jean-Louis, 58, 119–21
Composing for the Films (Adorno and Eisler), 119
confessional flashback, 168–69
Confessions of a Nazi Spy (film), 79, 90
Cook, Alton, 125
Cooper, Gary, 159
Corman, Roger, 182
Cornered (film), 127, 156
The Court-Martial of Billy Mitchell (film), 53
CRA (California Redevelopment Agency), 148
crime melodrama. *See* film noir
Criss Cross (film), 151f
The Crooked Way (film), 156
Crossfire (film), 140, 154–55, 157
The Cross of Lorraine (film), 116, 122
Crowther, Bosley, 98, 153
Curtiz, Michael, 2, 193n5
Custen, George F., 53, 57–58

Dahmen, Josef, 224n31
Dantine, Helmut, 193n5
Danton (film), 53
Davidman, Joy, 125
Dead Reckoning (film), 156, 157
Deleuze, Gilles, 123–24
DeMille, Cecil B., 158
Denning, Michael, 209n5
Desire Me (film), 156
Detour (film), 25
The Devil and Daniel Webster (film), 208n72
Devotion (film), 53
"diasporados," 13
Dies, Martin, 127
Dieterle, Charlotte, 78

Dieterle, William: aesthetic similarities with Steinhoff's films, 207n66; Americanization of, 72; biopics of, 47, 61–62, 64; blacklisting of, 186, 187; Brecht on, 203n15; citizenship of, 110; collaboration with Horkheimer, 208n72; collaboration with Reinhardt, 205n32, 207n62; as a director, 51; emigration of, 5; *Fog over Frisco*, 23; gray-listing of, 72, 186; hired by Warner Bros., 6, 50–51; during HUAC hearings, 127–28; relationship with Muni, 51, 205n27; resistance on returning to Germany, 6–7, 183; returned to Germany, 186, 187; as screen biography pioneer, 49, 50, 53, 71; *Tennessee Johnson*, 205n34; on virtues of obstinacy and stubborness, 205–206n40. *See also The Life of Emile Zola* (film)
Dietrich, Marlene, 5–8, 183, 188
Dimendberg, Ed, 148
A Dispatch from Reuter's (film), 49, 62
Displaced Persons Camp, 143, 163, 172
Disraeli (film), 66
Dixon, Wheeler Winston, 221n40
Dmytryk, Edward, 156
Döblin, Alfred, 111–12, 127
Doherty, Thomas, 98
Dollfuss, Engelbert, 22
Donlevy, Brian, 108
Douaumont (film), 46–47
Double Indemnity (film), 140, 149–50, 157, 168, 172
Douglas, Kirk, 156
Dr. Ehrlich's Magic Bullet (film), 49, 55, 71–72, 206n49
Dr. Holl (film), 181
Dr. Jekyll and Mr. Hyde (film), 31
Dr. Socrates (film), 51
Dracula (film), 26, 31
Drei/Three (film), 191
Dreyfus (film), 53, 70

Dreyfus, Alfred, 54–55, 66–70, 67f, 204n20
Dreyfus trial, U.S. press on, 206n51
Dudow, Slatan, 111

Edgar G. Ulmer: The Man Off Screen (film), 190
Eggebrecht, Axel, 224n31
Ehrlich, Paul, 206n49
Eichberg, Richard, 188
Eisenstein, Sergei, 207n57
Eisler, Gerhart, 127
Eisler, Hanns, 103, 117, 119, 127
Eisner, Lotte, 30, 95, 190, 199n20, 225n39
Elsaesser, Thomas, 2–3, 64–65, 101, 123–24
émigrés, 133, 199n11. *See also* exiles
Ennis House, 32
Erens, Patricia, 66
Der ewige Jude/The Eternal Jew (film), 81, 162–64
Escape (film), 116
European Film Fund, 13, 78
Everson, William K., 35
exile cinema, 4–5, 10–15, 192
exiles: Adorno on, 192; considering permanent returns to Germany, 128; defined, 5; existential restlessness of, 25; German culture of, 227n61; in minor acting roles, 199n11; obstacles encountered by, 186; performativity and, 80–81; prevalence of in Hollywood, 194n7; reading for, 15–16
Eylau, Hans Ulrich, 182

"The Fall of the House of Usher" (Poe), 32
Farocki, Harun, 164
fascism, 17, 77, 113, 125–28, 141
Fassbinder, Rainer Werner, 190, 191
Faust (film), 50
female filmmakers, 7–8

Feuchtwanger, Lion, 127
film noir, 131–33, 135–36, 215n26. See also *Act of Violence* (film)
Film Weekly, 37
Five Graves to Cairo (film), 116
Flaherty, Robert, 142
flashbacks, 168–69, 170–71
Florey, Robert, 2
Fly-by-Night (film), 116
Fog over Frisco (film), 23
Foreman, Carl, 158–59
Franco, Francisco, 78
Frank, Leonard, 111–12
Frank, Lisl, 78
Frankenstein (film), 26, 31
Frankfurter, David, 202n3
Freud, Sigmund, 48
Freund, Karl, 31
Friedman, Lester, 66
From Here to Eternity (film), 142
Fury (film), 109, 112–13

Galileo (play), 127
Garnett, Tay, 168
Gaudio, Tony, 49
Geist, Kenneth L., 158
genres, 14, 49, 52–62, 97–101, 114–15
Gentleman's Agreement (film), 154–55
George, Heinrich, 6, 53
Géré, François, 119–21
German American Bund, 66
German exile cinema, 10, 192
German expressionist cinema, 30, 132
German noir, 180
Germans and Germany: culture of exiles, 227n61; defined, 4–5; early 1930s cinema, 6; emigration to Hollywood of, 7, 21, 193n5
Germany Year Zero (film), 172–73
Giovacchini, Saverio, 65
Gliese, Rochus, 30
Gmeyner, Anna, 7–8
Godard, Jean-Luc, 72

Goebbels, Joseph, 22, 23, 71, 85–86, 202n3
The Golem: How He Came into the World (film), 28, 30, 41–42
Granach, Alexander, 103, 108, 122
Grant, Cary, 101
gray-listing, 126, 186
Great War. See World War I
The Great Dictator (film), 80, 86f, 88, 90, 100, 101, 116
Greene, Graham, 204n20
Greenstreet, Sydney, 2
Gregor, Ulrich, 176
Grissemann, Stefan, 29, 37
Gropius, Walter, 28
Grün ist die Heide (film), 181
Gustloff, Wilhelm, 202n3

Haarmann, Fritz, 191
Haas, Hugo, 186
Hake, Sabine, 115
Hamlet (play), 92, 100
"the Hangman." See Heydrich, Reinhard
Hangmen Also Die (film): backdrop in, 165; cast and characters in, 108, 113, 117–18, 119, 121, 122, 123, 188; channeling viewer identification in, 117, 165; expressionism of, 132; as hostage film, 103; masses and the mob in, 119–20; misleading viewers in, 124; mobilizing public opinion with, 106, 107, 108; modernism in, 17–18 on performativity, 124–25; release of, 114; reviews of, 108–109, 125–26; use of family in, 117
Harlan, Veit, 186
Harvey, Lilian, 6
Harvey, Sylvia, 132
A Hatful of Rain (film), 142, 158–59
Heflin, Van, 135–38, 156
Heilbut, Anthony, 8–9
Heinrich, George, 70
Hellman, Lillian, 142, 159, 208n3

Henreid, Paul, 2
Herald, Heinz, 52, 60, 204n19
Herman, Felicia, 68
Herzceg, Geza, 52, 60
Herzog, Werner, 190
Herzog, Wilhelm, 69
Herzogenrath, Bernd, 27
Heydrich, Reinhard, 89, 102–103, 213n4, 213n5, 213n6. *See also Hangmen Also Die* (film)
Heym, Stefan, 105, 116
High Noon (film), 140, 158–59
High Wall (film), 156
The High Window (Chandler), 148–49
Hindenburg, Paul von, 22
Hintertreppe/Backstairs (film), 50
Hippler, Fritz, 81
Hitchcock, Alfred, 132
Hitler, Adolf: on Lubitsch, 81; Mann on, 67–68; *Mein Kamp*, 100; rise to power of, 22, 81, 87–88; in Warsaw, 82–89
Hitler's Hangman. See *Hitler's Madman* (film)
Hitler's Madman (film), 103, 106, 107
Hitler-Stalin pact (1939), 78
Hofer, Johanna, 106, 224n31
Hoffmeister, Adolf, 105
Hollywood: censorship laws in, 97–98; exile and émigré community, 77; as Lorre's strongest competitor, 181; output in 1920s, '30s, and '40s, 189–90; Zinnemann resisting purges in, 158
Hollywood Anti-Nazi League, 77–78
Hollywood cinema, compared with exile cinema, 10–15
Holm, Gustav, 104–105
Holocaust, 174, 176, 183
Homolka, Oskar, 108, 113
Horak, Jan-Christopher: on anti-Nazi films, 114, 116, 212n37; on exile cinema, 11; on hybrid films, 180; on link between human sexuality and money, 23; on number of film exiles, 194n7
Horkheimer, Max, 73, 208n72

Horla motif, 176
horror films. See *Dracula* (film); *Frankenstein* (film); *The Black Cat* (film)
Hostages (film), 103, 105, 106, 107–108, 116
Hotel Berlin (film), 116, 173–75
Hotel Berlin (Baum), 173
House Un-American Activities Committee (HUAC), 126, 127, 159
The House of Rothschild (film), 66
Hubert, Ali, 209n11
Hubertus zu Loewenstein (Prince), 77
Hugenberg, Alfred, 111
Human Desire (film), 172
Hunde, wollt ihr ewig leben (Stalingrad: Dogs, Do You Want to Live Forever?) (film), 188
Hungarian Rhapsody (Liszt), 36

I Am a Fugitive from a Chain Gang (film), 51
I Saw Hitler (Thompson), 22–23
Ich küsse ihre Hand, Madame (film), 139
Im weissen Rössel (film), 188
In a Lonely Place (film), 155
Das indische Grabmahl (film), 186
Isenberg, Noah, 24–25
isolationism, 79, 80
Israel, Nico, 153
It's a Wonderful Life (film), 154–55

Jacobson, Egon, 224n31
Jannings, Emil, 6, 53, 207n66
Januskopf (film), 31
Jelinek, Elfriede, 191
Jews: absence of in *To Be or Not to Be*, 89–97; first- or second-generation immigrants, 12; Holocaust, 174, 176, 183; Reichskristallnacht, 79; representation of in 1930s and 1940s by Hollywood, 66; role in Hollywood, 68; Rosenberg on "implicit Jews," 211n35; victimhood of downplayed, 79
John, Karl, 180, 224n31

Joseph, Albrecht, 106
Josephson, Matthew, 68
Juarez (film), 49, 62
Jud Süss (film), 186
Julia (film), 142, 159

Kaes, Anton, 9, 29–30, 47, 109, 224*n*21
Kafka, Hans, 17
Kaiserhof speech (Goebbels), 22
Kampf um Rom/Battle for Rome (film), 187
Kanon, Joseph, 126
Kapczynski, Jennifer, 170, 171
Kaper, Bronislaw, 134, 136, 145
Karloff, Boris, 25, 26, 31, 32, 38
Karmakar, Romuald, 179, 191
Katz, Otto, 77, 109, 208*n*3
Kaus, Gina, 7–8
Kertész, Mihály. *See* Curtiz, Michael
The Kindness of Strangers (Viertel), 111
Kiss Me Deadly (film), 151*f*
Kluge, Alexander, 190
Koepnick, Lutz, 12–13, 90, 181–82
Kohner, Paul, 5, 78, 194*n*11
Kolberg (film), 87
Kollektivschuld, 174
Kominternlied, 117
Der Kongress tanzt/Congress Dances (film), 188
Korda, Alexander, 211*n*32
Korean War, 159
Korngold, Erich Wolfgang, 21
Kortner, Fritz, 70, 161, 224*n*31
Kosleck, Martin, 122
Koster, Henry, 7, 8, 188
Kracauer, Siegfried: Adorno and Benjamin on, 72–73; on biographies, 48–52; "The Biography as an Art Form of the New Bourgeoisie," 48; Bloch on, 208*n*71; *From Caligari to Hitler*, 179; "Hollywood's Terror Films," 132; on parallels between experience of veterans and immigrants, 138–39; on *The Search*, 143; selling his "treatment" to Hollywood, 202*n*8; "Those Movies with a Message," 154
Krauss, Marita, 183, 185
Krutnik, Frank, 132
Kubelski, Benny. *See* Benny, Jack
Kuhle Wampe (film), 111
Kulik, Karol, 211*n*32

Ladd, Alan, 155
Laemmle, Carl, 30, 78, 128
Laemmle, Carl, Jr., 47
Laemmle, Carl, Sr., 37
Lamarr, Hedy, 7–8
Land, Robert, 139
Lang, Fritz: adapting to new language and culture, 7; anti-Nazi films of, 115; background of, 109–110; black- and gray-listing of, 186; citizenship of, 5, 110; *Cloak and Dagger* (film), 115; collaboration with Bogdanovich, 216*n*43; collaboration with Brecht, 112–14; *Der Tiger von Eschnapur*, 186, 190; emigration to Hollywood of, 7, 21, 189; exilic dimension of his oeuvre, 196*n*24; on Heydrich's death, 213*n*4; Horkheimer's film proposal to, 73; during HUAC hearings, 126–27; influence on noir of, 133; interview with Bogdanovich, 121, 191, 216*n*43; in *Le mépris*, 72; *Man Hunt* (film), 115, 116; *Metropolis* (film), 28, 47, 112–13; *Ministry of Fear* (film), 115; mise-en-scène, 123–24; photograph of, 6*f*; postwar German films by, 186; quote by, 102; returned to Germany, 186; signed petitions against DeMille, 158; tension between Brecht and, 109; *The Testament of Dr. Mabuse*, 125; Teutonic image of, 209*n*12. *See also* *Hangmen Also Die* (film); *M* (film)
Laughton, Charles, 110, 127
Lazlo, Victor (*Casablanca* character), 3
Lee, Anna, 108, 113
Leigh, Janet, 135–38

Lengyel, Melchior, 83
Leni, Paul, 30–31
Levy, Dani, 191
Lidice, 102, 104
Lidice (Mann), 104, 106
Lidice Lives Forever, 104
Liebeneiner, Wolfgang, 186
The Life of Emile Zola (film): about, 17, 49; cast and characters in, 54, 68; claim to realism of, 61; files in archives for, 204n24; influences of, 69; monologue in, 64; plot elements and editing devices in, 70; portrayal of anti-Semitism in, 66; references to Nazi Germany in, 62, 63f; representation of Jews in, 90; sequences in, 55–57; Warner Bros. success of, 51–52
Lincoln, Abraham, 62
Liszt, Franz, 36
Litvak, Anatole, 79, 115
Lombard, Carole, 84
Lorre, Peter: Brecht's screenplay for, 110; in *Casablanca*, 1–2; as character in *Der Verlorene*, 164; comments on *Der Verlorene*, 222n2; in *The Cross of Lorraine*, 122; death of, 182; emigration to Hollywood of, 4, 7, 21; end of career, 182; Hollywood as strongest competitor of, 181; during HUAC hearings, 127; on *M*, 179; performances of mentally disturbed killers, 191; reemigration of, 162–64; return to Germany, 185–87, 226n48; role in *Hotel Berlin*, 173–74. *See also Der Verlorene/The Lost One* (film)
"Lorrealismus," 172
Los Angeles California Redevelopment Agency (CRA), 148
Lost Weekend (film), 132
Löwenthal, Leo, 50
Lubitsch, Ernst: acting career of, 99; alterations to Shakespeare's play by, 93; as an exile, 5; citizenship of, 110; comedy of, 88; costume designer for, 209n11; death of, 127; in European Film Fund, 78; Hitler on, 81; left Germany, 80–81, 101; left the Anti-Nazi League, 78; *Madame Dubarry*, 52–53; politically daring aesthetic strategies of, 100; reception history of his films, 101; replies to his critics, 98–99; resistance to returning to Germany, 6, 188; roles in Shakespeare productions, 212n47; Tykwer and Levy on, 191; version of teatrum mundi, 89. *See also To Be or Not to Be* (film)
Ludwig, Emil, 106, 184, 202n3
Lugosi, Bela, 25, 26, 31, 32, 38
Lustig, Hans, 78

M (film): Lorre on, 179; lynch mobs in, 112–13; murders in, 175–79; parallel modernities of *Der Verlorene* and, 176, 178; popularity of, 162; surveillance systems in, 176
Mad Love (film), 171, 181
Madame Curie (film), 53
Madame Dubarry (film), 52–53
Maltby, Richard, 155
The Maltese Falcon (film), 181, 205n33
Mamoulian, Rouben, 31
Man Hunt (film), 115, 116
A Man for All Seasons (film), 53, 73
Mankiewicz, Joseph, 158
Mann, Heinrich, 104, 106, 111–12, 127, 207n61
Mann, Klaus, 67–68, 116
Mann, Thomas: "The Coming Victory of Democracy" lecture, 52; controversy surrounding, 183–85; on democracy, 203n16; on Heydrich's death, 103; during HUAC hearings, 127
Mannhart, Renate, 162–63
The Man I Killed (a.k.a. *Broken Lullaby*), 47, 95
The Man Who Laughs (film), 30

Margin for Error (film), 116
Martin, Paul, 6
The Mask of Dimitrios (film), 181
Maté, Rudolph, 84
May, Joe, 7, 21, 23, 186
May, Karl, 187
Mayer, Edwin Justus, 83–84
Mayer, Louis B., 9, 78, 140
McCarey, Leo, 100
McGilligan, Patrick, 126
Mehring, Walter, 111–12
Mein Führer-Die wirklich wahrste Wahrheit über Adolf Hitler/My Führer (film), 191
Mein Kamp (Hitler), 100
Mellet, Lowell, 115–16
Menschen am Sonntag/People on Sunday (film), 24, 28, 139
Menschen im Hotel (Grand Hotel) (Baum), 173
The Men (film), 142–44, 158–59
Le mépris (film), 72
The Merchant of Venice (play), 97, 100
Mescall, John, 35
Metropolis (film), 28, 47, 112–13
Meyrinck, Gustav, 41–42
MGM, 139–40
A Midsummer Night's Dream (film), 51, 207n62
migration, patterns of, 4–8
Millay, Edna St. Vincent, 104
Minima Moralia (Adorno), 152–53, 192
Ministry of Fear (film), 115
Ministry of Propaganda and Enlightenment, 85–86
The Miracle (musical), 24
A Modern Hero (film), 23
More, Thomas, 73
The Mortal Storm (film), 116, 123
The Mummy (film), 31
Muni, Paul: acting style of, 60; banned from German screen, 68; on biographers, 204n26; on Dieterle, 205n27;

in *The Life of Emile Zola*, 49, 54f, 64, 205n30; range of, 58–59; relationship with Dieterle, 51, 205n27; roles of, 206n53
Münzenberg, Willi, 77
The Murderers Are Among Us (film), 181
Murders in the Rue Morgue (film), 31
"The Murder of Lidice" (St. Vincent Millay), 104
Murnau, F. W., 5, 24, 30–31, 190
Music in the Air (film), 23
Mussolini, Benito, 78
My First Hundred Years in Hollywood (Warner), 207n64

Nacht fiel über Gotenhafen (Darkness Fell on Gotenhafen) (film), 188
Nachts, wenn der Teufel kam (The Devil Strikes at Midnight) (film), 187
Naficy, Hamid, 12–13
Namenlose Helden (film), 46–47
Nana (Zola), 54, 55
Napoleon Bonaparte, 62
National Socialist German Workers Party (NSDAP), 22
Nazi Agent (film), 116
Nazis: erasure of Lidice, 104; forms of self-representation by, 85; penchant for pomp and spectacle of, 88; reaction to assassination of Heydrich, 102; view of Shakespeare, 100
Nazism: fighting before Pearl Harbor, 77–80; link with "abnormal" sexuality, 121; signs of in *Der Verlorene*, 163–64. See also *Casablanca* (film)
Nazty Nuisance (film), 114–15
Nebenzal, Seymour, 106, 223n9
Neumann, Kurt, 186
Neutrality Act Quarantine Speech, 205n39
New German Cinema, 191
New Objectivity, 28
New York Critics Award, 204n18

New York Yiddish Theater, 68
Die Nibelungen (film), 47
Niemandsland (film), 46–47
Nightingale, Florence, 62
Ninotchka (film), 210n29
Noack, Frank, 207n66
noirs: aesthetics of, 171; featuring Bunker Hill, 220n33. *See also Der Verlorene/ The Lost One* (film)
None Shall Escape (film), 116
Nosferatu (film), 30, 31–32, 47
Nosferatu, the Vampyre (film), 190
Nosseck, Max, 186
"Notes on Noir" (Schrader), 132
The Nun's Story (film), 219n22

Offenbach, Jacques, 49, 72–73
Office of Military Government, United Stated (OMGUS), 161
Office of War Information (OWI), 114, 116, 131
Once upon a Honeymoon (film), 100–101, 114
Die 1000 Augen des Dr. Mabuse (film), 186
Oswald, Richard, 70, 207n60

Pabst, G. W., 5, 6f, 23, 111
Page, Joy, 2
Paisan (film), 143
Palm, Michael, 190
Pasteur (film), 62
Patalas, Enno, 171, 176
Paul, William, 212n46
PCA (Production Code Administration), 66, 67
Pearl Harbor, 77–80
Pen, John, 105
performativity, 80–81, 124–25
Peter der Grosse (film), 53
Petzold, Christian, 191
Poe, Edgar Allan, 32
Poelzig, Hans, 28

Polan, Dana, 132
Polgar, Alfred, 111–12
Pommer, Erich, 5, 21, 23, 186
Popular Front, 8, 77–78, 209n5
The Postman Always Rings Twice (film), 139–40, 168
postwar noir, 154–56, 158
Preminger, Otto, 7, 8, 133, 188, 189
Pressburger, Arnold, 103, 180
Pressburger, Fred, 180
Price, Vincent, 182
Prinzler, Hans Helmut, 210n29
Production Code, 31, 79, 90
Production Code Administration (PCA), 66, 67
Der Prozess des Hauptmanns Dreyfus (Weil), 70
Purger, Ernst, 224n32

Queen Christina (film), 53

Rabenalt, Arthur Maria, 186
Rainer, Luise, 7–8, 108
Rains, Claude, 2
Rapf, Maurice, 214–15n20
Ray, Nicholas, 155
Red Scare, 128, 144, 158
Redes/The Wave (film), 142
reemigration of filmmakers, history of, 161–64, 188
Rehfisch, Hans José, 69, 207n60
Reichskristallnacht, 79
Reichsprotector, 102. *See also Hangmen Also Die* (film)
Reinhardt, Max: collaboration with Dieterle, 205n32, 207n62; influence of, 61; *A Midsummer Night's Dream,* 51; *The Miracle,* 24; Shakespeare productions of, 99; theater of, 94, 96
Reinhardt, Wolfgang, 62
Reisch, Walter, 21, 158
Remarque, Erich Maria, 116
Rentschler, Eric, 71, 87

Rhodes, Gary D., 38
Rialto speech, 92, 93, 94f, 210–11n31
Richard, Robert L., 136–37
Richter, Simon, 208n72
Ridges, Stanley, 83–84
Riefenstahl, Leni, 78–79, 87
Robert Koch, der Bekämpfer des Todes (film), 71–72
Robinson, Edward G., 49, 60, 79–80
Roehm, Ernst, 22
Roehm Putsch, 198n5
Roemheld, Heinz, 36
Rogers, Ginger, 101
Romeo and Juliet (Tchaikovsky), 36
Roosevelt, Franklin Delano, 79, 173–74, 199n12, 205n39
Rosar, William, 36–37
Rosenberg, Joel, 90–91, 211n35
Rudolph, Helmut, 163
Der Ruf (The Last Illusion) (film), 161
Ruman, Sig, 84, 121–22
Rushdie, Salman, 9
Ruthless (film), 128
Ryan, Robert, 134–38, 134f, 140, 157

Sachsenhausen concentration camp, 89
Said, Edward, 9–10, 21
Sakall, S. Z., 2
Sapphic Ode (Brahms), 36
Sarris, Andrew, 26, 140
Satan Met a Lady (film), 205n33
Scarlet Street (film), 157
Schary, Dore, 78, 140, 218n13
Schildkraut, Joseph, 6f, 52, 68
Schivelbusch, Wolfgang, 181
Schlöndorff, Volker, 190
Schmidt-Gentner, Willy, 223n15
Schrader, Paul, 132
Schüfftan, Eugen, 16, 24, 139, 197–98n40, 202n8
Schünzel, Reinhold, 7, 103, 121, 188
screen biographies. *See* biopics
Screen Directors Guild, 158

The Search (film), 141–44, 172, 219n21, 220n25
Second Piano Prelude (Chopin), 37
Seghers, Anna, 116, 141
Selwart, Tonio, 103, 121
Seventh Symphony (Beethoven), 37
The Seventh Cross (film), 116, 141, 143, 146
The Seventh Cross (Horak), 219n19, 219n21
Shadow of a Doubt (film), 132
Shakespeare, William, 99
Shindler, Colin, 66
The Shop Around the Corner (film), 210n29
Der Schut (Yellow Devil) (film), 187
Sinyard, Neil: on *Act of Violence*, 138; on Hill Street tunnel, 221n40; on Zinnemann, 146–47, 158, 218–19n15
Siodmak, Curt, 13, 24, 186, 218n10
Siodmak, Robert: emigration to Hollywood of, 7; influence on noir of, 133; *Menschen am Sonntag/People on Sunday*, 24; as noir director, 218n10; return to Germany, 186; *The Spiral Staircase*, 132, 181–82; success as reemigrant, 187
Sirk, Douglas: adapting to new language and culture, 7; experiences in Germany, 226–27n56; extended U.S. careers, 189; Fassbinder on, 190, 191; *Hitler's Madman*, 103, 106, 107, 107f; not returning to Germany, 188; returning from Germany, 187
Slepcova píšetalka aneb Lidice (The blind man's whistle) (play), 105
So Ends Our Night (film), 116
Die Söhne des Herrn Gaspary (film), 161–62
Sokoloff, Vladimir, 52, 68
Somewhere in the Night (film), 156
Sonata in B Minor (Liszt), 36
Sondergaard, Gale, 58, 60, 78

The Song of Scheherazade (film), 53
Spellbound (film), 156
The Spiral Staircase (film), 132, 181–82
The Spirit of St. Louis (film), 53
Stack, Robert, 84, 99
Stanwyck, Barbara, 156
Stardust (film), 126
The State of Things (film), 190
Staudte, Wolfgang, 224–25n33
Steiner, Max, 2
Steinhoff, Hans: aesthetic similarities with Dieterle's films, 207n66; *Robert Koch, der Bekämpfer des Todes*, 71–72
Stemmle, Robert A., 186
Stern Park Gardens, 104
Stevens, George, 155
Stevenson, Robert Louis, 144
Stewart, James, 123
Stiftung Deutsche Kinemathek, Berlin, 191
Stoessel, Ludwig, 106
The Story of Louis Pasteur (film), 49
The Story of Two People, 104
Strand, Paul, 142
Stranger on the Third Floor (film), 2, 181
Strangers in Paradise (Taylor), 8–9
The Strange Death of Adolf Hitler (film), 116
The Strange Love of Martha Ivers (film), 156
Straßenbekanntschaft (film), 224n28
Streep, Meryl, 141
Stromboli (film), 172
Struss, Karl, 31
Sunrise (film), 24, 30–31
Sunset Blvd. (film), 9
Surtees, Robert, 136, 149
Székely, Hans. *See* Pen, John

Tarzan Triumphs (film), 115
Tasso theme (Liszt), 36
Tavernier, Bertrand, 26
Taylor, John Russell, 8–9
Tchaikovsky, Pyotr Ilyich, 36

Tennessee Johnson (film), 205n34
Teresa (film), 142–44, 146
The Testament of Dr. Mabuse (film), 125
Die Teufelsanbeter (film), 31
Thiele, William, 115
Third Reich, 66, 176, 185, 186
This Was Lidice (Holm), 104–105
Thompson, Dorothy, 22–23
"Those Movies with a Message" (Kracauer), 154
Threepenny Opera (Brecht), 111
Thunder over Texas (film), 26
Tifft, Stephen, 98
Der Tiger von Eschnapur (film), 186, 190
title cards, 55–56
To Be or Not to Be (film): absence of Jews in, 89–97; cast and characters in, 83–85, 87, 88, 90–97, 91f, 92f, 97, 99, 100; comedy of, 17, 80; performance of *Hamlet* in, 92; performativity in, 124–25; plot of, 83–84; as prime example of exile cinema, 81; release of, 114; reviews of, 97–98, 125; sequences in, 82–83; stills from, 83f, 91f, 92f; use of family in, 117; viewer identification with occupied citizens in, 117
"To the Actor P.L. in Exile" (Brecht), 185
Toccata, Adagio and Fugue in C (Bach), 37
Tonight We Raid Calais (film), 116
totalitarianism, 17
Der Totmacher/The Deathmaker (film), 191
Tracy, Spencer, 141
Triumph of the Will (film), 87
Trouble in Paradise (film), 191
Trowe, Gisela, 178–179, 224n28
Truffaut, François, 26, 83
"Trümmerfilm" (rubble film), 181
"The Truth Is on the March." *See The Life of Emile Zola* (film)
Turim, Maureen, 168–69
Turrou, Leon G., 79
Tuttle, Frank, 103

Tykwer, Tom, 191
typecasting, 121–22

Ucicky, Gustav, 186
Ufa, 111, 181
Ugarte (*Casablanca* character), 1–2
Ulmer, Edward G.: *Beyond the Boundary*, 29; black- and gray-listing of, 186; on *Caligari*, 199n20; compared with Zinnemann, 218n10; "cult" status of, 10; *Detour*, 25; during HUAC hearings, 128; importance of topicality of World War I to, 45–46; inability to return to Germany, 6; influence on noir of, 133; interview with Bogdanovich, 24, 27–28, 41–42, 202n51; modernism of, 24–27; political concerns of, 27; returned to Germany, 186; *Thunder over Texas*, 26. See also *The Black Cat* (film)
Ulmer, Shirley, 128
Ulmer Cipes, Arianné, 21, 24
Underground (film), 116
The Unfaithful (film), 156
United Artists, 94

Valetti, Lisa, 106
van der Rohe, Mies, 28
Veidt, Conrad, 2, 6–7, 121
Venice Film Festival, 180
Der Verlorene/The Lost One (film): cast and characters in, 162–73, 174–79; conventions of film noir in, 165, 167–68; Eisner on, 225n39; Farocki on, 164; financing of, 223n9; historical truth in, 172; horror in, 171; Lorre's comments on script of, 222n2; murders in, 163, 175–79; novelization of, 169–70; parallel modernities of *M* and, 176, 178; plot in, 223n12; plot of, 162–63; production and release of, 174–75, 179–80; on reemigration, 18, 161, 164–65; reviews of, 162, 171, 181–82; sequences in, 165–73; setting in, 143; signs of Nazism in, 163–64; stills from, 167*f*, 177*f*, 178*f*; use of flashbacks in, 170–71; visual and narrative repertoire in, 164, 167, 167*f*, 176
Vích, Václav, 172
Viertel, Berthold, 6, 127
Viertel, Hans, 112
Viertel, Salka: absence of literature on, 195n15; collaboration with Brecht, 110, 111; on Dieterle, 203n11; during HUAC hearings, 127; instrumental in raising political awareness, 8; *The Kindness of Strangers*, 111; popularity of, 7–8
Vigny, Benno, 224n31
Vom Gehen im Eis/On Walking on Ice (Herzog), 190
von Baky, Josef, 161, 180–81, 186
von Fritsch, Günter, 6
von Harbou, Thea, 125, 186
von Molo, Walter, 184
von Stroheim, Erich, 6*f*, 121
von Twardowski, Hans, 103, 106, 121

Das Wachsfigurenkabinet/Waxworks (film), 50
Wallis, Hal, 49, 60–61, 203n14
Walpole, Horace, 32
Wanger, Walter, 127
Wannsee Conference, 103
Warner, Harry, 78
Warner, Jack, 51, 66, 71, 207n64
Warner Bros.: anti-Nazi resolve of, 47, 203n13; archives, 204n24; biopics from, 49–50; downplaying Jewish aspect, 68; Erens on, 66; hiring of Germans, 6; modernist aesthetics of, 205n33; shut down operations in Germany, 23, 210n24; shut down operations in Vienna, 78; success of *The Life of Emile Zola*, 51–52
Watch on the Rhine (play), 208n3
Watch the Rhine (film), 116
Waxman, Franz, 21, 23

Wegener, Paul, 28, 30, 41–42
Weigel, Helene, 113
Weil, Bruno, 70
Weimar Bauhaus, 28
Weimar cinema, 46–47, 52–53
Weimar Germany, 105
Weimar modernism, 29
Weimar on the Pacific (Bahr), 4
Weimar Straßenfilm (street film), 132
Wenders, Wim, 190
Werfel, Alfred, 127
Westfront (film), 46–47
Wexley, John, 79–80, 112, 127
The White Angel (film), 49, 62
Why We Fight (series), 115
Wiene, Robert, 28
Wilder, Billy: arrived in Hollywood, 5, 9, 21; citizenship of, 110; compared with Zinnemann, 219n20; exilic dimension of his oeuvre, 196n24; extended U.S. career of, 189; influence on noir of, 133; *Lost Weekend,* 132; *Menschen am Sonntag/People on Sunday,* 24; re-emigration of, 187; resisted returning to Germany, 8, 188; returned to Germany, 161; Schlöndorff's documentary on, 190; script for *Music in the Air,* 23; signed petitions against DeMille, 158
Wilson, Dooley, 2
Wilson, Michael Henry, 128
Wings of Desire (film), 185
World War I, 38–47, 41f
World War II, 79
Wright, Frank Lloyd, 32
Wysbar, Frank, 7, 187–88

You Can't Do That to Svoboda (Pen), 105
Young, Collier, 136–37

Zilzer, Wolfgang, 106
Zinnemann, Fred: Academy Awards of, 141, 219n16; arrived in Hollywood, 5; on auteurism, 140; in autobiography, 218n12; background of, 139; *Cineaste* interview of, 159; communist witch hunts, 158; compared with Wilder, 219n20; exilic dimension of his cinema, 141; interviews of, 218n11, 219n21; *A Man for All Seasons,* 73; *Menschen am Sonntag/People on Sunday,* 24; modesty of, 218n10; number of films produced by, 140–41; postwar experience of, 141; realism in films, 141–43; representation of fascism by, 141; resisted returning to Germany, 6, 8, 158, 188; returned to Germany, 161; returning from Germany, 187; Schary on, 218n13; scholarly attention to, 141; Sinyard on, 146–47, 218–19n15; style of, 140; thematic concerns for, 140, 142; training of, 139–40; use of locations as realistic and symbolic sites, 172; war tetralogy of, 142. See also *Act of Violence* (film)
Zola, Emile, 54, 55, 203n14. See also *The Life of Emile Zola* (film)
Zola and His Time (Josephson), 68
Zukor, Adolf, 12
Zwischen gestern und morgen (film), 161–62

FILM AND CULTURE

A series of Columbia University Press
Edited by John Belton

What Made Pistachio Nuts? Early Sound Comedy and the Vaudeville Aesthetic, Henry Jenkins

Showstoppers: Busby Berkeley and the Tradition of Spectacle, Martin Rubin

Projections of War: Hollywood, American Culture, and World War II, Thomas Doherty

Laughing Screaming: Modern Hollywood Horror and Comedy, William Paul

Laughing Hysterically: American Screen Comedy of the 1950s, Ed Sikov

Primitive Passions: Visuality, Sexuality, Ethnography, and Contemporary Chinese Cinema, Rey Chow

The Cinema of Max Ophuls: Magisterial Vision and the Figure of Woman, Susan M. White

Black Women as Cultural Readers, Jacqueline Bobo

Picturing Japaneseness: Monumental Style, National Identity, Japanese Film, Darrell William Davis

Attack of the Leading Ladies: Gender, Sexuality, and Spectatorship in Classic Horror Cinema, Rhona J. Berenstein

This Mad Masquerade: Stardom and Masculinity in the Jazz Age, Gaylyn Studlar

Sexual Politics and Narrative Film: Hollywood and Beyond, Robin Wood

The Sounds of Commerce: Marketing Popular Film Music, Jeff Smith

Orson Welles, Shakespeare, and Popular Culture, Michael Anderegg

Pre-Code Hollywood: Sex, Immorality, and Insurrection in American Cinema, 1930–1934, Thomas Doherty

Sound Technology and the American Cinema: Perception, Representation, Modernity, James Lastra

Melodrama and Modernity: Early Sensational Cinema and Its Contexts. Ben Singer

Wondrous Difference: Cinema, Anthropology, and Turn-of-the-Century Visual Culture, Alison Griffiths

Hearst over Hollywood: Power, Passion, and Propaganda in the Movies, Louis Pizzitola

Masculine Interests: Homoerotics in Hollywood Film, Robert Lang

Special Effects: Still in Search of Wonder, Michele Pierson

Designing Women: Cinema, Art Deco, and the Female Form, Lucy Fischer

Cold War, Cool Medium: Television, McCarthyism, and American Culture, Thomas Doherty

Katharine Hepburn: Star as Feminist, Andrew Britton

Silent Film Sound, Rick Altman

Home in Hollywood: The Imaginary Geography of Hollywood, Elisabeth Bronfen

Hollywood and the Culture Elite: How the Movies Became American, Peter Decherney

Taiwan Film Directors: A Treasure Island,
    Emilie Yueh-yu Yeh and Darrell William Davis

*Shocking Representation: Historical Trauma, National Cinema,
    and the Modern Horror Film,* Adam Lowenstein

China on Screen: Cinema and Nation, Chris Berry and Mary Farquhar

The New European Cinema: Redrawing the Map, Rosalind Galt

George Gallup in Hollywood, Susan Ohmer

Electric Sounds: Technological Change and the Rise of Corporate Mass Media,
    Steve J. Wurtzler

The Impossible David Lynch, Todd McGowan

*Sentimental Fabulations, Contemporary Chinese Films: Attachment in
    the Age of Global Visibility,* Rey Chow

Hitchcock's Romantic Irony, Richard Allen

Intelligence Work: The Politics of American Documentary, Jonathan Kahana

Eye of the Century: Film, Experience, Modernity, Francesco Casetti

Shivers Down Your Spine: Cinema, Museums, and the Immersive View, Alison Griffiths

Weimar Cinema: An Essential Guide to Classic Films of the Era,
    Edited by Noah Isenberg

African Film and Literature: Adapting Violence to the Screen, Lindiwe Dovey

Film, A Sound Art, Michel Chion

Film Studies: An Introduction, Ed Sikov

Hollywood Lighting from the Silent Era to Film Noir, Patrick Keating

Levinas and the Cinema of Redemption: Time, Ethics, and the Feminine, Sam B. Girgus

Counter-Archive: Film, the Everyday, and Albert Kahn's Archives de la Planète,
    Paula Amad

Indie: An American Film Culture, Michael Z. Newman

Pretty: Film and the Decorative Image, Rosalind Galt

Film and Stereotype: A Challenge for Cinema and Theory, Jörg Schweinitz

Chinese Women's Cinema: Transnational Contexts, Edited by Lingzhen Wang

Hideous Progeny: Disability, Eugenics, and Classic Horror Cinema, Angela M. Smith

Hollywood's Copyright Wars: From Edison to the Internet, Peter Decherney

Electric Dreamland: Amusement Parks, Movies, and American Modernity,
    Lauren Rabinovitz

*Where Film Meets Philosophy: Godard, Resnais, and Experiments
    in Cinematic Thinking,* Hunter Vaughan

The Utopia of Film: Cinema and Its Futures in Godard, Kluge, and Tahimik,
    Christopher Pavsek

Hollywood and Hitler, 1933–1939, Thomas Doherty

Cinematic Appeals: The Experience of New Movie Technologies, Ariel Rogers

GPSR Authorized Representative: Easy Access System Europe, Mustamäe tee 50, 10621 Tallinn, Estonia, gpsr.requests@easproject.com

www.ingramcontent.com/pod-product-compliance
Lightning Source LLC
Chambersburg PA
CBHW030300010526
44108CB00038B/878